American Architects and the Mechanics of Fame

American Architects and the Mechanics of Fame

ROXANNE KUTER WILLIAMSON

University of Texas Press, Austin

First Edition, 1991

Requests for permission to reproduce material from this work
should be sent to Permissions, University of Texas Press, Box
7819, Austin, Texas 78713-7819.

The publication of this book was assisted by a grant from the
Andrew W. Mellon Foundation.

Library of Congress Cataloging-in-Publication Data

Williamson, Roxanne, 1928–
   American architects and the mechanics of fame / by
Roxanne Kuter Williamson.—1st ed.
      p.   cm.
   Includes bibliographical references.
ISBN 0-292-75121-4 (cloth : alk. paper)
1. Architects—United States—Selection and appointment.
2. Architects and patrons—United States.   3. Architectural
services marketing—United States.   I. Title.
NA1996W48   1990
720'.973—dc20   90-35729
                                                               CIP

Contents

Plates

Charts

Tables

Acknowledgments

Because I believe that there are similar patterns in other creative fields and that the analysis of these patterns may explain something about creativity, it is my hope that this book can be read by people who have only a moderate interest in the lives of specific architects.

However, for architectural historians, there are extensive notes on the career connections of somewhat less well known designers who had some relationship to those who were more famous and an index that includes the names of over 800 American architects.

Several architects were courteous in granting me interviews, among them, Robert A. M. Stern, Michael Graves, Charles Moore, and Leslie Gallery. However, this study is obviously heavily dependent upon facts gathered by hundreds of other architectural historians and their patient research on individual architects' lives. People in the profession have been aware of the intersection of various major architects. However, no one has looked at the pattern formed by these linkages of architects to one another. The bulk of my research was completed before the *Macmillan Encyclopedia of Architects* was published in 1982. I have referred to it many times in my notes as the latest and probably most accurate source for biographical material.

I especially wish to thank Wayne Attoe, Juan Pablo Bonta, Hal Box, Roger Conover, Marian Davis, James Marston Fitch, and Carol Herselle Krinsky for their active and personal support for this project. A vigorous effort was made to avoid inaccuracies, but it is inconceivable that perfection was achieved. These errors are my sole responsibility. However, even if there are minor flaws, too much evidence has come to light to leave any question of the fact that there is frequently a direct connection between fame and certain career patterns.

American Architects and the Mechanics of Fame

ONE

A Network of Connections

The first part of this study provides evidence not only that most of the famous American architects in history connect to each other through an experience like apprenticeship,[1] but that the timing of these connections may significantly affect their ability and drive to produce the kind of designs that are featured in architectural history textbooks. Certain patterns occur again and again during the apprenticeship years of America's best-known architects. Although at first glance this may appear to be a documentation of an establishment network, the subject is more specifically the factors that trigger creativity, genius, and architectural design strength.

These patterns are more than a string of coincidences: they invite us to a close examination of their probable impact on each individual's design power and eventual fame. It appears that the same patterns may exist in other creative disciplines as diverse as composing music or writing television comedy, where early career connections seem parallel to this study of the mechanics of fame in architectural design.

Usually the connections described were of short duration, a matter of a few years of employment (five at most). Quite a few ultimately famous architects experienced a double connection—first during their own apprenticeship and then, later, in their own office with an employee who would also become celebrated. But just the fact that they were employed by some famous architect is not especially significant—in all probability many people worked for that designer. The timing of the connections is crucial.

Six of the following chapters are arranged so that they focus on the careers of representative architects, beginning with the most famous, Louis Sullivan, Frank Lloyd Wright, and H. H. Richardson. My previous attempts to trace the apprenticeship connections chronologically led to confusion because, as in the family tree that chart 1 so closely resembles, there are lateral branches that go off in many different directions. (This sort of problem is still evident in the chapter on McKim, Mead & White and also in the material on the descendants of James Renwick, Jr.) Readers with only a moderate interest in the explicit training of architects may refer to the index to find the material on architects of interest to them. But architects and architectural historians will find overwhelming evidence that what was true for Wright, Sullivan, Walter Gropius, Ludwig Mies van der Rohe, and Charles McKim was also true for architects like Harvey Corbett or Cass Gilbert and still appears to hold true in the cases of numerous designers who are currently attracting attention.

When the career connections of famous American architects are mapped, they form a network so interwoven as to be nearly unreadable by the time of Louis Sullivan, Daniel Burnham, and Charles McKim. We tend to think that architects on the West Coast became famous in isolation from the Chicago and Boston and New York establishments. Some architectural historians are surprised to see that the California designers Greene & Greene, Bernard Maybeck, and Irving Gill—or Florida's Addison Mizner—all have East Coast or Chicago roots. The major skyscraper architects of the 1920s, who are now receiving the attention of serious historians for the first time, are all part of the web: men like Corbett, or Shreve, Lamb & Harmon (Empire State Building), and William Van Alen (Chrysler Building). Two points must be repeated. First, even though there seem to be a great number of names on the chart, they represent only a very small fraction of all architects practicing in the United States at a given time. Second, there is rarely much stylistic continuity between connecting architects once they have found their own gift.

In addition, without stopping to think, people make the assumption that the main reason that most of the famous architects in American history worked for each other was simply that there were not many other architects around. For the first few decades after the revolution this assumption holds true to some extent. However, oddly enough, it is during these same years that the highest percentage of famous "loners" are recorded. By the middle of the nineteenth century there were a great many firms and individuals designing and building. Ten thousand people claimed to be architects by 1900, and the United States Census of 1970 listed over fifty thousand in the profession. How many of these are or will ever be famous?

Because a number of architects served their apprenticeships in Europe, the scope of the connections can probably be extended to include similar dynasties in England, France, Germany, and Austria.

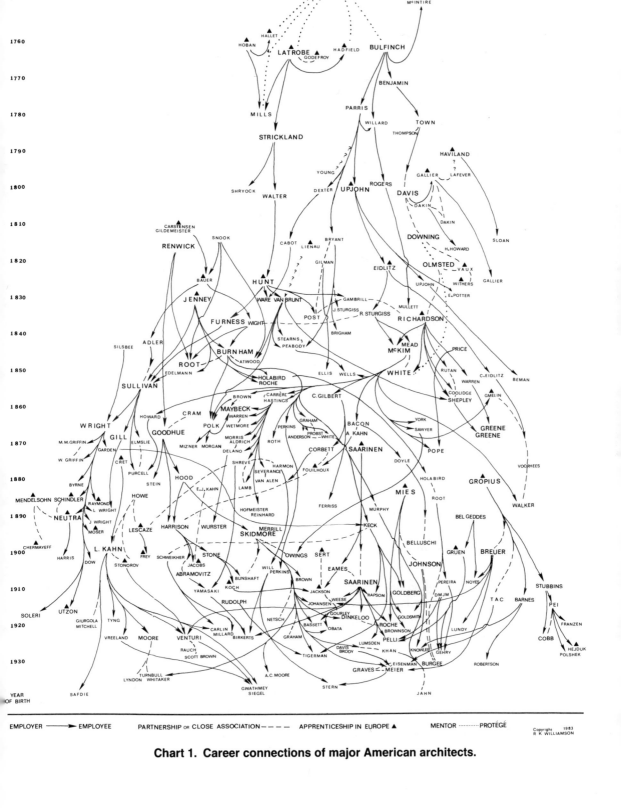

Chart 1. Career connections of major American architects.

These architects, whether Benjamin Latrobe, H. H. Richardson, Walter Gropius, or William Le Baron Jenney, may connect not only to their American lines of descent, but to European designers as well. Though sometimes quite significant, an apprenticeship in Europe is represented on the chart only by a broad arrow. Finally, chart 1 also includes names of "connectors," architects whose names are not in the Index of Fame—like Jacques André Fouilhoux or Augustus Bauer—but who connect in several directions with those who do appear in the upper ranks of fame. Upon occasion, a close association of contemporaries or a new partnership may produce the same kind of interaction that more often happens during an apprenticeship. These formal and informal partnerships are represented on the chart by a dashed line.

To some extent, the many lines that diverge from a famous architect's name can be explained because the students or employers of the architect became important when they were noticed by architectural historians. Interest in one architect led to interest in others with whom the first was in contact. For a long time this was true of the attention given to Sullivan's employer, Frank Furness. He was frequently mentioned during the many years when historians judged his designs as perfectly dreadful primarily because of his connections to Sullivan and Richard Morris Hunt. It was only in the 1960s that his architecture began to receive favor from major historians.

The second part of this book is concerned with elements that are not essential to my thesis but that, nevertheless, are important in any discussion of fame. In the course of examining biographical material in the literature of architecture, I found factors that surfaced with surprising regularity. Family advantage, schools, and social connections—although not unique to architecture—are also important. In fact, it would be naive to overlook the fact that, in most careers, an avid contender for fame or financial success often gains considerable advantage from a social background providing natural contact with power brokers. For architects this means contact with wealthy potential clients and with decision makers, whether they are politically or socially based. A number of famous architects did gain access to clients because of their families' social contacts and because they attended Ivy League schools where their classmates included potential future clients. Others, like Wright, who did not attend those schools, found other ways to reach clients. Wright, for example, not only benefited from his relationship with his uncle and his uncle's congregation, but actively courted his early clients by joining their organizations and activities. These advantages are not specific to fame in the sense that it is used in this book. Many not-so-famous people also profited from the same circumstances.

The results of some of my investigations surprised me. Scholarships, for example, would appear to be an early measure of true talent and a direct indicator of future success. But, by exploring two examples in detail, I found that they were no real measure of future fame. My findings would have been disappointing except for the confirmation that in every single case those of the scholarship winners who did achieve fame worked for a famous architect at the time when he or she was making a *dynamic shift*. Though there was no further mention of the great majority of Rotch or American Academy winners as outstanding designers, it is possible that a number of them had locally successful practices. Nevertheless, the die may have been cast when the obviously able young architects missed the opportunity to work for the right emergent architect before they began their own practice. I have no statistics on the success of scholarship winners in general—that is, in all professions—but the fact that there were no exceptions to the apprenticeship rule in architecture surely is telling.

One would expect a close connection between fame and celebration by the American Institute of Architects (AIA), the major professional organization of architects in this country. In the nineteenth century several of the people who had been the leaders of the profession (as judged by historians) also were the leaders of the AIA. But by about 1910, with an occasional exception, this no longer proved to be true. Even the Gold Medal, the highest AIA honor, usually came years after the architect had actually become famous. (Three of the winners are virtually unknown today: Milton Medary, Howard Van Doren Shaw, and Charles Maginnis.) All in all, the AIA has been less influential than the international organization CIAM (Congrès internationaux d'architecture moderne) and the Arts and Crafts societies, which were effective promotional institutions because they attracted writers who took up their causes and solidified the fame of certain members. Of course, the AIA acts largely as a trade organization concerned with administering standards and protecting the profession, whereas these other groups were idealistic and program-oriented. They dreamed dreams, which made them more interesting to writers, the public, and change-oriented architects.

Part II also reveals that a great number of America's famous architects have been very active in promoting themselves by writing, lecturing, presenting exhibitions of their work, and forming organizations. Again, there are parallels in other professions, but for many years architects were not permitted by their code to hire agents or advertising firms to do this type of promotional activity. I can think of no other profession outside of literature and journalism where the members do so much writing about themselves and their colleagues. It has proven to be effective; several architects had made their reputations before they saw any of their buildings constructed. But self-promotional activity is often as characteristic of the financially successful but unexciting architect as it is of those we classify as famous. It is not the key to fame.

In a sense this is an open-ended study because it is difficult to stop with this sort of research. There is always another book to read, another article—and new names to consider. However, enough material has been collected to show that the important constant in the professional lives of famous architects is the apprenticeship connection; other factors, although important, are secondary. First, the promising young architect, who would later produce works featured in architectural history texts, was an employee at the time the senior designer was in the process of creating his or her first really important work, generally a few years after establishing a practice. Second, other employees who may have had similar potential continued to work under the wing of the employer and did not become independently famous unless the senior architect died and they not only inherited the practice but also changed its name (as happened in the offices of Richardson and Eero Saarinen, for example). Third, the senior designer frequently had some public recognition immediately before producing the significant design in question. Fourth, the younger architect destined for fame was likely to repeat this pattern with employees when working on his or her own most important early design. While evidence proves that these relationships existed for the great majority of famous architects, any explanation of how and why they were significant to design ability must remain tentative. My conclusion, however, is not that genius seeks genius, but that under certain circumstances genius *creates* genius.

TWO

The Time as Well as the Place

The most famous architects in American history have acquired reputations for being loners, solitary geniuses of legend. However, a closer look shows that they were not isolated and independent. Their successful careers grew out of a network of connections that can be traced back to the time of Jefferson and now embraces many of our most exciting contemporary architects. Most of the best-known architects in American history, including those in the limelight today, either trained or were trained by another celebrated architect. The similarity in career patterns is not coincidental: there has to be a causal relationship beyond the platitude that genius seeks genius.

A study of the careers of more than 600 architects in American history dispels the myth of the genius who creates masterpieces in isolation from contact with other creative designers. The overwhelming majority of the architects who are important enough to be mentioned in architectural history texts served an apprenticeship of sorts with another famous architect; their careers intersected. But the relationship is even more sensitive than this. I found that these career connections occurred *early* in the practices of the employers, the senior architects, and just at that point when they were producing not their first designs, but the first designs that would make them famous. In a very few instances, the older architect was experiencing a burst of fresh creativity after a fallow period.

The timing of these moments of contact forms a pattern that may explain a great deal about the difference between architectural genius and architectural competency. Those younger architects, who later became famous themselves, were present at the time of their employers' sudden surges of inventiveness and strong design that led to fame. They were witnesses when a practicing architect came forth with the daring new solution or dramatically creative turn that histo-

rians seek out and record—the kind of design that ultimately distin-
guishes the famous from the rest. Several years after this event, when
the older architect had become fully established, equally able employees who entered the firm were not likely to become famous themselves (unless they moved on to still another office where inspiration
could be passed).

Many architectural historians and biographers have mused over
the meaning of the apprenticeship relationship for particular individuals. Some have discovered that timing was an interesting element
in a master-protégé relationship; some have even suggested that the
relationship provided the younger designer with the courage eventually to develop his or her own designs in a more powerful way. No
one, however, has realized that the value of a particular moment in
certain apprenticeships might be *essential* to the generation of genius,
not only in architecture but possibly in other creative disciplines. In
architecture most people who know anything at all about Frank Lloyd
Wright's career know that he was employed by Louis Sullivan before
setting up practice for himself. Architecture students learn that Walter Gropius and Ludwig Mies van der Rohe each served as an employee or junior designer in the office of Peter Behrens in Berlin: Gropius for twenty months between 1907 and 1909, Mies from 1908 to
about 1912. Histories of architecture that mention the firm of McKim,
Mead & White nearly always comment that Charles McKim and Stanford White both were employed by Henry Hobson Richardson on the
design of Trinity Church. However, no one has analyzed the apparent
coincidence that in each instance, though the senior architect had
been designing for several years, at that time Sullivan, Behrens, and
Richardson were working on the *first* major buildings that would ultimately be featured in textbooks.

By the time that Wright was employed by Adler & Sullivan in
1888, the firm had already produced some thirty buildings. Although
some of these early commissions are still of interest, most of them
would have been forgotten if Sullivan had not revealed a new surge of
design strength during the development of the Chicago Auditorium
Building commission (1886–1890), which was already in process
when Wright arrived. It was the Auditorium Building that solidified
Sullivan's fame.

Behrens' AEG Turbine Factory in Berlin (1908–1909) is usually
illustrated in books dealing with the development of twentieth-century architecture. Behrens' first building designed eight years before
this commission has recently been described as "honorable if not exceptional";[1] thus, like Sullivan, Behrens had been in design practice

Adler & Sullivan: Au-
ditorium Building, Chi-
cago, 1886–1890

Behrens: AEG Turbine
Factory, Berlin, 1908–
1909

Perret: 25 bis rue Frank-
lin, Paris, 1903–1904

for almost a decade before he began to work on the precedent-setting factory when Gropius and Mies were in his office.

Though Le Corbusier arrived late for actual design process, he was also in contact with Behrens, briefly, when the building was being completed, from November 1910 to April of the following year. Le Corbusier had a similar experience in Paris three years earlier when he joined the atelier of Auguste Perret. Perret's first highly publicized works, the apartment building at 25 bis rue Franklin (1903–1904) and his Garage Ponthieu (1906), were radically innovative, recently completed designs that were receiving a good deal of attention. Jacques Barzun remembered the stir of excitement Perret's apartment building created when he was a child: "Almost my earliest memories are of architectural discussions among my elders, at the house of one of the founders of modern architecture, Auguste Perret. That house, which he built for himself at 25 bis rue Franklin, was the first modern apartment house in Paris. Going in to it with my parents, I would often see, to my continued surprise, little knots of sightseers outside, snickering and pontificating and occasionally struck dumb by its height, its multiple exposure to light and air, its concrete and ceramic facade."[2] These buildings by Behrens and Perret were frequently the only ones selected by historians to illustrate the fame of their designers in general surveys. There is no question that Le Corbusier was actively seeking these experiences; he saw and reacted to architects who were suddenly finding powerful talents.

This is the key moment to which all of the facts of the first part of this book are addressed—the association of an architect who will become famous with another celebrated architect at a peak event in his or her own early career. Even famous contemporary architects who have been there are unclear about exactly what happens, but it must be a combination of things: a change in tone and an awareness of excitement in an office, the firsthand experience of seeing insight and confidence grow as the senior architect extends or simplifies and strengthens the concept, and, in some cases, a chance to witness the thinking process that led to the new idea. More than anything else, it is the ability of the learner to equate his or her own potential with that of the role model.

McKim and White had a similar experience when they worked on Trinity Church in Boston (1872–1877), the building that gave H. H. Richardson his first national publicity. Charles McKim worked on the preliminary designs and Stanford White on the more developed solutions. Again, it must be pointed out that even the celebrated Richardson's earlier work is considered to be relatively undistinguished.

Richardson: Trinity
Church, Boston,
1872–1877

As with Sullivan and Behrens, it was a moment of transition and emergence for Richardson.

Architects like Le Corbusier may actively seek out those who are working on exciting new designs, but they do not always credit their employers with having had a great deal of influence on their careers. When asked to name a mentor, well-known architects are less likely to talk about early employers than about design professors—men like Jean Labatut at Princeton University are hallowed in the memories of alumni. Unlike most academic disciplines, architecture fosters a one-to-one relationship between the teacher and the student and strong bonds are sometimes established. The office situation is quite different. The entire staff must work together under a leader to produce a satisfactory product, and individual effort is just a means to that end, with dissension over authorship more than bonds as the result. Without question, school experiences are of major importance in nurturing talent and creativity, but the first few years of the apprenticeship period appear to be more significant in terms of separating the few really creative architects from the great majority of their colleagues. The connection made during the apprenticeship period is not necessarily that of mentor and protégé; the employer and employee may not even like each other. It is not a matter of one architect helping another—nor is it a matter of one architect's personal style being handed on to a successor.

It must be stressed at the outset that the connection of one famous architect to another is not one of stylistic similarity. It happens that the opposite is more often true. If there are hints of Louis Kahn in the work of Robert Venturi, or Earl Carlin, or Moshe Safdie, they are subtle indeed. Frank Furness' buildings bear little resemblance to those of his teacher and employer, Richard Morris Hunt. Louis Sullivan's mature designs are different in styling from those of either of his former employers, Frank Furness and William Le Baron Jenney. Yet, if he had not worked for those particular designers at the time that they were first demonstrating vigorous control, his own work might have turned out differently.

What is passed from one architect to another is design power, an ability that requires courage and an unshakable belief in one's own talent. Courage and conviction are necessary to produce the sort of designs that attract the attention of fame makers—in the case of architecture, the historians. According to one early historian, Thomas Tallmadge, "the pivotal buildings alone are described in detail, and only those few greatest personalities who, like mountain peaks, elevate themselves above the foot hills." "These men," he says, "are the 'heroes' of architecture, and their names will live long after their earthly works have perished."[3] The word "pivotal" in his statement is important in that it implies a shift in direction. It is rare, indeed, that the kind of design that makes an architect famous is absolutely un-heralded and without predecessors. Instead, the pivotal building re-sults from a bolder, more powerful statement of design trends already in existence. The architect dares to make the wall still thinner, or thicker, to chop off half the roof or to flatten out one that was low, to have an arch spring right from the floor, or to make the columns short and squat.

No famous architect was predestined to fame at birth. Not even the incredible Frank Lloyd Wright was an instant genius (the rosy mists of his memory in *An Autobiography* notwithstanding). There is much to be learned. For every ambitious, able, and talented individual who achieves greatness there are a number of others of equal merit who will never acquire the courage and self-confidence necessary to follow through with their convictions about architectural design, to develop those ideas that are teasing at the brains of a number of other bright people. (The converse is, unfortunately, also true. There are courageous designers who lack innate talent.)

If for "schooling" we read "apprenticeship," what George Kubler observed to be true in art history is true of the architectural profession as well.

> ... the great differences between artists are not so much those of talent as of entrance and position in a sequence. Talent is a pre-disposition: a talented pupil begins younger; he masters the tradi-tion more quickly; his inventions come more fluently than those of his untalented fellows. But undiscovered talents abound as well among people whose schooling failed to gear with their abilities, as among people whose abilities were unrequited in spite of their talent. Predispositions are probably much more numerous than ac-tual vocations allow us to suppose. The quality talented people share is a matter of kind more than degree, because the gradations of talent signify less than its presence.
>
> It is meaningless to debate whether Leonardo was more tal-ented than Raphael. Both were talented. But the followers had bad luck. They came late when the feast was over through no fault of their own. The mechanics of fame are such that their predeces-sors' talent is magnified, and their own diminished, when talent itself is only a relatively common predisposition for visual order, without a wide range of differentiation. Times and opportunities differ more than degree of talent.[4]

There are few forerunners, men and women of genius whose thinking is so far ahead of its time that any appreciative contemporary audience is impossible. (For one thing, architecture usually requires

an audience of one, a client.) If the work of such a genius is ever celebrated, it will be either as a historical curiosity or as a precursor of a
direction finally taken by society. It is my contention that nearly all the
great architects were created by a social process rather than born to
greatness. If the process is understood, perhaps it can be opened up
for wider participation.

THREE

A Consensus of Who Is Famous and Who Is Not: The Index of Fame

The need for a good working definition of "fame" became apparent sometime after I first began this research in 1976. In the beginning, it seemed that there would be no problem in making a distinction between famous designers like Wright, Sullivan, Gropius, or even contemporaries like Robert Venturi and Charles W. Moore, and the great majority of architects who have been in practice. However, fame varies widely from one region of the country to another. Names are celebrated in California that, as an architectural historian in Texas, I knew nothing about. In Texas, O'Neil Ford is the most honored twentieth-century architect and Nicholas Clayton the most famous from the nineteenth century—but neither is nationally celebrated. Historians and architects in Washington, D.C., are more aware of John Russell Pope than is the profession at large. An impartial and acceptable consensus was needed.

Another problem in definition arises from the fact that in architecture, more than in many fields, there are quite different kinds of success. Financial success is seldom equatable with the kind of success that makes an architect famous. Many of the large firms and prosperous designers who produce the bulk of America's architecture are concerned primarily with the client's satisfaction, and it is not clients who make architects famous. The biggest and wealthiest firms with the greatest volume of business are only rarely known beyond the generation they are serving at the time. Another kind of success is the establishment of a place in history. That is the focus of my study. "Fame," as used here, means the sort of reputation that arises out of truly innovative designs, the kind of work deemed important enough to be included in the history textbooks. Writers and photographers who produce the texts for architectural students are the arbiters of fame, the "fame makers" if you will. The good, competent designs generated by the most financially successful firms are not sufficient to attract the attention of these fame makers. Neither are designs that are concerned primarily with function or economy or energy efficiency. The designs destined for the textbooks most often are those that result from bold aesthetic decisions, those that signal the winds of change. Though this is currently true, it is possible that fame in the twenty-first century may be based on other criteria.

In order to establish an impartial and usable consensus regarding fame, I began counting and listing the names entered in the indexes of some sixty books on American architecture and on world architecture that included the United States. Many of these were regional studies. Some were limited to a particular style such as the Greek Revival, the Shingle Style, Art Deco, or Postmodernism. Three or four concentrated on drawings or unbuilt projects. The formats of many volumes were similar to museum catalogs, they simply provided a showcase for contemporary architects. In several cases, these books—as well as the books and catalogs of the Museum of Modern Art—were important sources for survey writers and other fame makers. I tried to devise a way to include feature articles in professional periodicals but soon found that this sort of fame was ephemeral.

As my lists began to grow to extraordinary lengths, I discovered that the names of many architects I personally thought were famous were not included in more than one or two of the general surveys of American architecture. It was surprising to find that Edward Larabee Barnes and Julia Morgan were mentioned so rarely in surveys, and I expect many knowledgeable readers will experience disbelief over names missing from the Index of Fame (table 1 at the conclusion of this chapter), the ultimate result of my effort.

There has been a growing interest in regional architecture and in designs that were not on the cutting edge of architectural history. Nevertheless, the darlings of the authors of surveys covering the past two centuries of American architecture remain those whose names are most familiar at a national level. These authors became the potent fame makers, and their works were used as textbooks in architectural education, where students first seek heroes and role models. The power of writers like Henry-Russell Hitchcock, Lewis Mumford, Vincent Scully, and others must be underscored. If publicity and fame are almost the same thing, publicity alone does not guarantee that interest will be sustained. A literal "place in history" is closer to the real meaning of the word "fame" as I am using it, or, more accurately, "a place in the history books."

The more we understand about the mechanics of fame, the more we realize that it is quite impossible to immortalize one's contemporaries. We are always nearsighted in choosing which among us will be included in tomorrow's history books. Even great architectural critics and journal editors promoted and supported designers to whom the future showed indifference as well as those who have been championed by the writers of histories. Montgomery Schuyler sang the praises of his contemporaries Richardson and Sullivan, but he was equally interested in the work of Charles Coolidge Haight and Leopold Eidlitz. Even the powerful fame-making institution, the Museum of Modern Art, never scored more than about 75 percent in terms of the staying power of those it championed in exhibitions and accompanying catalogs.

Even though it is unwise to weigh the ultimate fame of one's contemporaries, in the study that follows I have taken the liberty to include some younger living architects whose work has generated attention. Though they may not be famous to future generations, they still demonstrate that the connections made during the apprenticeship period remain important today.

The Index of Fame was compiled from the indexes of twenty-four books: twenty histories and four encyclopedias. Even if it were to be revised annually, the shifts in degree of fame would occur primarily in the last entries. For example, a four-volume encyclopedia of architects was published by Macmillan late in 1982. This massive work included the names of hundreds of American architects, many with very brief fifty- or hundred-word biographies. Even so, as can be seen in that column of the Index of Fame, the amount of space the editors allocated to the most famous corresponds fairly closely to the upper rankings by other authors. The rationale for the selection of these books is given in a later chapter.

There can be little argument that this Index of Fame provides a working consensus on the degree of fame among the major American architects in history, at least through 1982. The bracketed letter and number after an architect's name in subsequent chapters indicate his or her position in the Index of Fame, representing the section letter and the number of books that cite the name.

If the Index of Fame had been extended to include every architect mentioned in one, *and only one,* survey, or to include those mentioned in two or three of the more than sixty books with which I began, the continued dominance of the names at the top of the lists would become overwhelmingly evident. With an extended index, these names would rise even higher in proportion to the others, because over the years these architects were always mentioned in histories, whereas there was much less agreement about the lesser-known candidates.

Ranking the famous is a difficult task. Nikolaus Pevsner named only twenty-three American architects in the "American Postscript" he added to his major survey *An Outline of European Architecture.* They included Walter Gropius, Mies van der Rohe, and Marcel Breuer, although he did not mention their buildings in the United States. Of these twenty-three, only three did not work for or employ someone on the Index of Fame (John McComb, Jr., Pierre Charles L'Enfant, and Joseph Jacques Ramée). The editors of the *Encyclopaedia Britannica* (1968) were only a bit more generous in giving thirty-three American architects major biographical entries in their two-hundredth anniversary edition—as prestigious a measure of fame as anyone could desire. Architects and historians would surely quibble over the selection of a few of these choices and favor others whom they consider to be more worthy candidates. To take a specific example, Ralph Adams Cram was included. He was important, particularly as an influential designer of Neo-Gothic churches, but the editors did not elect to give an entry to Bertram Grosvenor Goodhue, who was Cram's partner and, in fact, the designer at the time Cram & Goodhue won its first major commission, the chapel at the U.S. Military Academy at West Point. It could be convincingly argued that, by the time of his death in 1924, Goodhue had become more famous than Cram ever was.

There is no doubt that several people might complain that there was no reason to choose Harvey Wiley Corbett, one of several designers of Rockefeller Center in New York, over any number of other skyscraper designers of the 1920s and 1930s. Nevertheless, an examination of the attention given to individual architects in general surveys of American architectural history proved the *Britannica*'s restricted selections to be within reason. (Only two of the thirty-three, L'Enfant and Richard Upjohn, did not connect directly with at least one other of the thirty-three.)

The following books were used to tabulate the Index of Fame:
1924 Lewis Mumford, *Sticks and Stones: A Study of American Architecture and Civilization* (indexed by Roxanne Williamson)
1926 Talbot F. Hamlin, *The American Spirit in Architecture*
1927 Thomas E. Tallmadge, *The Story of Architecture in America*
1928 Fiske Kimball, *American Architecture*
1929 Henry-Russell Hitchcock, *Modern Architecture: Romanticism and Reintegration*
1941 Sigfried Giedion, *Space, Time and Architecture: The Growth of a New Tradition* (a + or − sign indicates revisions in the 1967 edition)

1947 Wayne Andrews, *Architecture, Ambition and Americans: A Social History of American Architecture*

1948 Nikolaus Pevsner, *An Outline of European Architecture* (the first edition with an American postscript; a + or − indicates revisions in the 1960 edition)

1953 Talbot Hamlin, *Architecture through the Ages* (contains plates that feature architects not necessarily mentioned in the text; only the index was used)

1958 Henry-Russell Hitchcock, *Architecture: Nineteenth and Twentieth Centuries*

1959 Henry-Russell Hitchcock, "Art of the United States: Architecture—Americas: Art since Columbus," *Encyclopedia of World Art*, v. 1, pp. 246–278

1961 Banister Fletcher, *A History of Architecture on the Comparative Method* (revised by R. A. Cordingley)

1961 John Ely Burchard and Albert Bush-Brown, *The Architecture of America: A Social and Cultural History*

1964 Alan Gowans, *Images of American Living: Four Centuries of Architecture and Furniture as Cultural Expression*

1966 James Marston Fitch, *American Building: The Historical Forces That Shaped It*

1966 Leonardo Benevolo, *History of Modern Architecture* (translated by H. J. Landry from 1961 edition)

1968 *Encyclopaedia Britannica* (200th anniversary edition)

1969 Vincent Scully, *American Architecture and Urbanism*

1977 J. M. Richards, with Adolph Placzek (editors), *Who's Who in Architecture from 1400 to the Present*

1979 Leland M. Roth, *A Concise History of American Architecture*

1981 Marcus Whiffen and Frederick Koeper, *American Architecture 1607–1976*

1982 Adolph Placzek (editor-in-chief), *Macmillan Encyclopedia of Architects* (approximate number of columns, number of illustrations)

1985 Spiro Kostof, *A History of Architecture: Settings and Rituals*

1987 John Musgrove (editor), *Sir Banister Fletcher's A History of Architecture*

Readers might wonder why the popular surveys of world art and/or architecture by Helen Gardner, *Gardner's Art through the Ages* (revised by Horst de la Croix and Richard G. Tansey), H. W. Janson, *History of Art,* and Henry A. Millon (editor), *Key Monuments of History of Architecture,* were not used. Gardner cites only sixteen American architects; Millon only twenty-two; and Janson only ten.

The Index of Fame is divided into three sections: architects in practice after 1776 and born before 1875 and, thus, of an age to have been mentioned in every survey; architects born between 1875 and 1905; and architects born after 1905 and before 1926 who would be unlikely to be mentioned in the earlier surveys. Within each of these sections names are listed in order of the number of times they appeared in an index of a survey. Within each rank—for example, when a number of architects were mentioned in only eight surveys—the names are generally entered by priority of publication date of the book since an alphabetical listing would imply that a name beginning with "A" was more famous than one beginning with "B." The actual amount of attention architects received within each book tends to be in direct proportion to their ranking in the Index of Fame. Thus, Richardson, Sullivan, and Wright are the subjects of pages of commentary, whereas architects mentioned in the last ranks may not even merit a full sentence.

Entries were recorded for individuals and by the lead name of a firm; for example, Charles McKim was counted both as an individual and as the first name in references that cited only the firm of McKim, Mead & White. Thus, he ranks higher than either of his partners in the Index of Fame and Mead and White were counted only when they were given individual entries in an index. Firm names shift over the years upon occasion and pose a problem. For example, there was one entry for Murphy & Dana and two for Richard Henry Dana. In order to be consistent, this was not counted as three entries for Dana and he was not included in the Index of Fame.

European architects who practiced in America—Gropius, Mies, Marcel Breuer, and Eric Mendelsohn—were mentioned by authors before they emigrated to this country. These entries are marked by a # in table 1. When their American work began to receive comment, the # is removed.

Buckminster Fuller, Norman Bel Geddes, Frederick Olmsted, and a few others were not technically architects. However, they are mentioned frequently in architectural history and were thus included.

The asterisks in tables 1 and 2 indicate "loners," designers who did not have an employer, employee, or close colleague in the Index of Fame.

Table 1
The Index of Fame

Number of Citations		Mumford 1924	Hamlin 1926	Tallmadge 1927	Kimball 1928	Hitchcock 1929	Giedion 1941 +/− = 1967	Andrews 1947	Pevsner 1948 +/− = 1960	Hamlin 1953	Hitchcock 1958	Encyclopedia of World Art 1959	Fletcher 1961 +/− = 1987	Burchard & Bush-Brown 1961	Gowans 1964	Fitch 1966	Benevolo 1966	Britannica 1968	Scully 1969	Richards 1977	Roth 1979	Whiffen & Koeper 1981	Macmillan Encyclopedia of Architects 1982 # of columns (# of illustrations)	Kostof 1985	Fletcher 1987
A—Architects Born before 1875 and in Practice after 1776																									
24	Wright, Frank Lloyd	X	X	X	X	X	X	X	X	X	X	X	X	X	X	X	X	X	X	X	X	X	21 (14)	X	X
24	Richardson, H. H.	X	X	X	X	X	X	X	X	X	X	X	X	X	X	X	X	X	X	X	X	X	22 (14)	X	X
24	Sullivan, Louis	X	X	X	X	X	X	X	X	X	X	X	X	X	X	X	X	X	X	X	X	X	16 (11)	X	X
24	McKim, Mead & White	X	X	X	X	X	−	X	X	X	X	X	X	X	X	X	X	X	X	X	X	X	13 (10)	X	X
23	Burnham, Daniel (& Root)	X	X	X	X	X	X	X		X	X	X	X	X	X	X	X	X	X	X	X	X	5 + (4)	X	X
23	Jefferson, Thomas	X	X	X	X	X		X	+	X	X	X	X	X	X	X	X	X	X	X	X	X	14 (3)	X	X
23	Latrobe, Benjamin	X	X	X	X	X		X	+	X	X	X	X	X	X	X	X	X	X	X	X	X	9 (6)	X	X
23	Renwick, James	X	X	X	X	X		X	+	X	X	X	X	X	X	X	X	X	X	X	X	X	13 (6)	X	X
22	Bulfinch, Charles	X	X	X	X	X		X	+	X	X	X	X	X	X	X	X	X	X	X	X	X	11 (8)	X	X
22	Hunt, Richard M.	X	X	X	X			X	+	X	X	X	X	X	X	X	X	X	X	X	X	X	11 (8)	X	X
22	Mills, Robert		X	X	X	X		X	+	X	X	X	X	X	X	X	X	X	X	X	X	X	12 (4)	X	X
22	Jenney, William L. B.			X	X	X	X	X	X	X	X	X	X	X	X	X	X	X	X	X	X	X	4 (3)	X	X
21	Upjohn, Richard	X	X	X	X	X		X	+	X	X	X	X	X	X	X		X	X	X	X	X	16 (9)	X	
20	Root, John Wellborn	X		X	X	X	X	X				X	X	X	X	X	X	X	X	X	X	X	3 + (1)	X	X
20	Saarinen, Eliel		X	X	X	X	X	X		X	X	X	X	X	X	X	X	X	X	X	X	X	see Eero		X
20	Strickland, William		X	X	X			X	+	X	X	X	X	X	X	X		X	X	X	X	X	6 (10)	X	X
19	Holabird & Roche		X	X	X	X	X	X	X		X	X	X	X	X		X		X	X	X	X	3 + (2)		X
19	Walter, Thomas U.		X	X	X		X			X	X	X	X	X	X	X		X	X	X	X	X	6 (10)	X	X
18	Goodhue, Bertram G.	X	X	X	X	X	X			X	X	X		X	X	X			X	X	X	X	3+		X
18	Cram, Ralph A.	X	X	X	X	X	X			X	X	X	X	X	X			X		X	X	X	4 (2)		X
18	L'Enfant, Pierre Charles*	X	X	X	X			X	+	X	X	X			X	X	X	X	X	X	X		6 (4)		
18	Thornton, William*		X	X	X			X		X	X	X	X	X	X	X		X	X	X	X	X	1+		X
18	Davis, Alexander J.	X			X		−	X	+	X	X			X	X	X		X	X	X	X	X	13 (10)	X	X
17	Gilbert, Cass	X	X		X	X	X			X	X	X	X					X	X	X	X	X	1 + (4)	X	X
17	White, Stanford	X		X	X	X	X			X	X	X	X	X	X			X	X	X	X		5 + (2)		X
17	Adler, Dankmar (& Sullivan)		X			X	X	X		X	X	X	X	X	X	X	X	X	X	X	X		1		X
16	McIntire, Samuel	X	X	X	X		−	X		X				X	X	X		X	X	X	X		4 + (2)	X	
15	Bacon, Henry	X	X	X	X					X	X	X	X	X	X			X	X	X			−1		X
15	Carrère & Hastings	X	X		X	X	X			X	X		X	X	X					X	X	X	1 + (2)		X
15	Pope, John Russell	X	X		X	X	X			X	X	X	X	X	X					X	X		−1		X
15	Kahn, Albert		X		X	X	X					X	X		X			X		X	X	X	2 + (1)	X	X
15	Maybeck, Bernard			X			X			X	X	X	X	X	X	X				X	X	X	2 + (3)	X	X
15	Greene & Greene						X			X	X	X	X	X	X	X			X	X	X	X	9 (8)	X	X
14	Olmsted, Frederick Law	X			X		X	X		X						X	X	X	X	X	X	X	7 (2)	X	
14	Benjamin, Asher		X	X	X		X			X	X	X						X	X	X	X	X	2+	X	
14	Town, Ithiel (& Davis)		X	X	X		X		+	X	X		X	X	X				X		X	X	4+		

Table 1 (*continued*)
The Index of Fame

Number of Citations		Mumford 1924	Hamlin 1926	Tallmadge 1927	Kimball 1928	Hitchcock 1929	Giedion 1941 +/- = 1967	Andrews 1947	Pevsner 1948 +/- = 1960	Hamlin 1953	Hitchcock 1958	Encyclopedia of World Art 1959	Fletcher 1961 +/- 1987	Burchard & Bush-Brown 1961	Gowans 1964	Fitch 1966	Benevolo 1966	Britannica 1968	Scully 1969	Richards 1977	Roth 1979	Whiffen & Koeper 1981	Macmillan Encyclopedia of Architects 1982 — # of columns (# of illustrations)	Kostof 1985	Fletcher 1987
14	Polk, Willis		X	X				X		X	X	X	X	X	X	X				X	X		1	X	
14	Post, George B.		X	X				X		X	X	X		X	X	X				X	X	X	4 + (1)	X	
14	Parris, Alexander		X		X		X	X		X	X	X		X	X	X				X	X		1 + (1)	X	
14	Furness, Frank				X	X		X			X	X	X	X	X				X	X	X	X	7 (2)		X
14	Haviland, John				X			X		X	X	X	X	X	X	X			X	X	X	X	3 + (6)		X
14	Bogardus, James*						X	X			X	X	X	X	X	X	X	X	X	X	X	X	2 + (1)		
13	McComb, John, Jr.*	X	X	X	X			X	+	X				X	X	X				X	X		−1		
13	Hoban, James	X	X	X				X		X	X	X	X		X		X			X	X		−1		
13	Price, Bruce		X			X		X			X	X		X	X				X	X	X		−1/2	X	X
13	Gill, Irving						−	X			X	X		X	X	X			X	X	X	X	1 + (1)		X
12	Rogers, James Gamble	X	X	X	X						X	X		X					X	X	X		−1		X
12	Rogers, Isaiah		X	X				X		X	X	X	X	X	X	X				X	X		2 + (3)		
12	Lafever, Minard		X					X		X	X			X	X	X				X	X	X	4 + (1)	X	
11	Corbett, Harvey W.	X	X		X						X			X				X	X	X	X		1+		X
11	Mangin, Joseph (& McComb)		X	X	X			X		X				X	X	X				X	X		−1/2		
11	Platt, Charles Adams*		X	X	X			X			X	X		X	X						X		−1		X
11	Delano, William (& Aldrich)		X	X	X			X			X	X		X		X			X		X		1 + (1)		
11	Howells, John Mead (& Stokes)(& Hood)		X		X			X		X	X	X		X		X				X	X		−1/2		
11	Vaux, Calvert		X								X			X	X	X			X	X	X		2+	X	X
11	Ramée, J. J.			X			X	X		X	X			X	X					X	X		1/2	X	
11	Downing, Andrew J.			X				X		X	X	X			X	X			X		X		5 (3)	X	
11	Hastings, Thomas			X				X		X	X			X	X	X	X				X		0		X
10	Eidlitz, Leopold	X									X	X		X	X					X	X	X	3 + (3)		
10	Warren & Wetmore		X			X				X	X	X	X							X	X		1 (1)		
10	Flagg, Ernest*		X					X			X	X		X				X	X	X	X		2 + (1)		
10	Sturgis, Russell			X			−	X			X			X	X					X	X		1/2		
10	Godefroy, Maximilian				X			X		X	X			X	X	X				X	X		1 + (2)		
10	McArthur, John, Jr.*					X					X		X	X	X	X			X	X	X		−1		
9	Hallet, Etienne S.		X	X	X			X		X				X	X				X				1/2		
9	Ware, William R. (& Van Brunt)		X	X				X		X				X				X	X	X	X		2 + (1)		
9	Emerson, William R.*		X					X			X	X		X	X				X		X		1 + (1)		
9	Van Brunt, Henry (& Howe)			X	X			X		X				X	X					X	X		2 (1)		
9	Young, Ammi B.			X				X		X	X				X				X	X	X		2 (1)		
9	Roche, Martin						X	X		X	X	X	X							X	X		0		X

Table 1 (continued)
The Index of Fame

Number of Citations	Name	Mumford 1924	Hamlin 1926	Tallmadge 1927	Kimball 1928	Hitchcock 1929	Giedion 1941 +/− = 1967	Andrews 1947	Pevsner 1948 +/− = 1960	Hamlin 1953	Hitchcock 1958	Encyclopedia of World Art 1959	Fletcher 1961 +/− 1987	Burchard & Bush-Brown 1961	Gowans 1964	Fitch 1966	Benevolo 1966	Britannica 1968	Scully 1969	Richards 1977	Roth 1979	Whiffen & Koeper 1981	Macmillan Encyclopedia of Architects 1982	# of columns (# of illustrations)	Kostof 1985	Fletcher 1987
9	Purcell, William (& Elmslie)							X			X	X			X	X	X		X		X			3 + (2)		
8	Buffington, Leroy	X					X	X			X				X						X	X		1+		
8	Hooker, Philip*		X	X				X			X			X							X	X		−1		
8	Ferriss, Hugh		X			X															X	X		1+		X
8	Howard, John Galen	X						X			X	X			X	X						X		1/2		
8	Shepley, Rutan & Coolidge	X						X			X			X	X							X		1 + (1)		X
8	Atwood, Charles		X	X				X			X				X	X						X		2 (1)		
8	Eyre, Wilson*				X	X		X			X								X		X	X		1 + (1)		
8	Bryant, Gridley J. F. (& Gilman)						X				X	X	X						X		X	X		1 (1)		
8	Willard, Solomon							X			X	X	X		X						X	X		−1		
8	Austin, Henry							X			X				X	X			X		X	X		2		
8	Notman, John*							X				X	X		X	X					X	X		2+		
8	Warren, Russell							X			X			X	X							X		1/2	X	X
8	Lienau, Detlef										X	X	X		X	X					X	X		3+		
7	Day, Frank Miles* (& Day)(& Klauder)		X	X	X										X	X						X		−1/2		
7	Bragdon, Claude		X	X	X										X	X	X							−1		
7	Stevens, John Calvin	X						X							X	X	X		X					−1		
7	Olmsted, F. L. Jr. (& Olmsted)		X	X											X	X	X			X				0		X
7	Mead, William R.			X				X		X					X						X	X		0		X
7	Maher, George						X	X				X	X		X	X	X							0		
7	Shyrock, Gideon							X				X	X		X	X								−1		X
7	Bucklin, James							X			X			X	X					X				−1		X
7	Elmslie, George							X							X	X	X				X	X		0		
7	Mizner, Addison							X								X	X				X	X		1+		X
7	Mullett, Alfred B.										X					X	X				X	X		4		X
6	Bennett, Edward	X	X					X										X				X		−1/2		
6	Lindeberg, Harrie		X	X	X	X										X		X						0		
6	Perkins, Dwight		X	X	X			X								X	X							0		
6	Cope, Walter (& Stewardson)		X	X	X											X				X				−1		
6	Cobb, Henry I. (& Frost)		X					X			X				X		X			X						
6	Schmidt, R. E. (& Garden)	X							–			X	X		X									1/2		
6	Little, Arthur	X									X				X						X	X		−1/2		
6	Upjohn, R. M.	X									X				X	X						X		1 + (1)		

Table 1 (*continued*)
The Index of Fame

Number of Citations	Mumford 1924	Hamlin 1926	Tallmadge 1927	Kimball 1928	Hitchcock 1929	Giedion 1941 +/− = 1967	Andrews 1947	Pevsner 1948 +/− = 1960	Hamlin 1953	Hitchcock 1958	*Encyclopedia of World Art* 1959	Fletcher 1961 +/− 1987	Burchard & Bush-Brown 1961	Gowans 1964	Fitch 1966	Benevolo 1966	Britannica 1968	Scully 1969	Richards 1977	Roth 1979	Whiffen & Koeper 1981	*Macmillan Encyclopedia of Architects* 1982	# of columns (# of illustrations)	Kostof 1985	Fletcher 1987
6 Graham, Ernest R. (Graham, Anderson, Probst & White)			X			−							X						X	X			1		
6 Potter, Edward		X					X		X	X												X	2 (2)		
6 Peabody, Robert (& Stearns)		X								X				X				X				X	2 + (1)		
6 Hadfield, George				X			X			X				X								X	−1 (1)		
6 Greene, John Holden							X			X		X		X								X	1/2		
6 Potter, William							X			X			X									X	−1		X
6 Sloan, Samuel							X						X	X					X	X			2 + (2)		
6 Tefft, Thomas										X	X		X						X	X			1 + (1)		
6 Gilman, Arthur										X			X	X					X	X			2 (1)		
6 York & Sawyer		X	X				X							X									1		X
5 Helmle, Frank (& Corbett)	X	X	X							X	X												0		
5 Hoadley, David*	X		X											X								X	1/2+		
5 Hunt, Myron*		X	X		X								X	X									0		
5 Magonigle, H. Van B.	X		X										X	X									1 + (1)		
5 Sturgis, John (& Brigham)	X									X			X									X	1+		
5 LeBrun, Napoleon	X									X	X		X										−1		
5 Bosworth, Welles	X									X	X		X										−1		
5 Maginnis, Charles (& Walsh)	X									X			X									X	−1		
5 Atterbury, Grosvenor	X												X			X		X					1+		
5 Ellis, Harvey		X					X		X													X	2		
5 Manigault, Gabriel*		X					X							X					X				−1/2		
5 Cummings, Charles (& Sears)		X									X		X						X				−1/2		
5 Jay, William*							X	X						X								X	1 + (1)		
5 Gallier, James, Sr.							X	X						X								X	2 + (2)		
5 Dakin, James							X	X						X								X	−1/2		
5 Mason, George DeWitt							X				X		X	X									−1/2		
5 Trumbauer, Horace*							X			X			X									X	1		
5 Griffin, Marion Mahony							X										X		X	X			1 + (1)		
5 Johnston, William L.*										X	X		X	X									1 + (1)		
5 Coolidge, Charles (Coolidge, Shepley, Bulfinch & Abbott)										X	X		X	X								X	0		

Table 1 (*continued*)
The Index of Fame

Number of Citations		Mumford 1924	Hamlin 1926	Tallmadge 1927	Kimball 1928	Hitchcock 1929	Giedion 1941 +/− = 1967	Andrews 1947	Pevsner 1948 +/− = 1960	Hamlin 1953	Hitchcock 1958	*Encyclopedia of World Art* 1959	Fletcher 1961 +/− 1987	Burchard & Bush-Brown 1961	Gowans 1964	Fitch 1966	Benevolo 1966	Britannica 1968	Scully 1969	Richards 1977	Roth 1979	Whiffen & Koeper 1981	*Macmillan Encyclopedia of Architects* 1982	# of columns (# of illustrations)	Kostof 1985	Fletcher 1987
5	Beman, Solon S.										X			X								X	X	2 (1)		
5	Van Osdel, John*										X			X		X						X		-1/2		
5	Silsbee, J. Lyman										X				X							X	X	-1 (1)		
4	Hoffman, F. Burrall													X	X	X						X		0		
4	Ackerman, Fred L.	X												X								X		4 + (4)		
4	Shaw, Howard Van Doren		X	X										X	X									0		
4	Mullgardt, Louis C.		X	X										X										5 (4)		
4	Ittner, William B.*		X	X										X										-1/2		
4	Lowell, Guy*		X		X									X										-1/2		
4	Mould, Jacob Wray	X											X								X			2		
4	Smith, George W.*			X	X									X										1/2		
4	Babb, George (Babb, Cook & Willard)					X				X				X										1/2		
4	Howard, Henry										X			X	X									-1/2		
4	Gaynor, John P.*										X			X							X			-1/2		
4	Brady, Josiah										X				X						X			-1/2		
4	Long, Robert Cary, Jr.								X					X							X			1 + (1)		
4	Kellum, John*										X			X	X									-1/2 (1)		
4	Carstensen & Gildemeister										X			X	X									-1/2		
4	Urban, Joseph										X			X								X		-1/2		
4	Gilbert, Bradford Lee										X			X								X		-1/2		
4	Newton, Dudley*										X											X	X	1/2		
4	Cady, Berg & See													X	X				X					1/2		
3	Morris, Benjamin W.	X												X						X				0		
3	Thompson, Martin								X					X							X			0		
3	Pond & Pond	X		X										X										0		
3	Carter, Elias	X											X		X									0		
3	de Pouilly, Jacques B.*		X											X	X									0		
3	Codman, Henry S.		X											X						X				0		
3	Aldrich, Chester H.				X					X	X													0		
3	Wells, Joseph M.				X					X											X			0		
3	Garden, Hugh						X			X					X									0		
3	Mueller, Paul							X		X					X									0		
3	Hatfield, R. G.*									X				X								X		0		
3	La Farge, C. Grant													X	X							X		0		

Table 1 (continued)
The Index of Fame

B—Architects Born after 1875 and before 1905

No. of Citations	Name	Mumford 1924	Hamlin 1926	Tallmadge 1927	Kimball 1928	Hitchcock 1929	Giedion 1941 +/− = 1967	Andrews 1947	Pevsner 1948 +/− = 1960	Hamlin 1953	Hitchcock 1958	Encyclopedia of World Art 1959	Fletcher 1961 +/− 1987	Burchard & Bush-Brown 1961	Gowans 1964	Fitch 1966	Benevolo 1966	Britannica 1968	Scully 1969	Richards 1977	Roth 1979	Whiffen & Koeper 1981	Macmillan Encyclopedia of Architects 1982 # of columns (# of illustrations)	Kostof 1985	Fletcher 1987
19	Hood, Raymond	X	X	X			X	X	+	X	X		X	X	X	X			X	X	X	X	2 + (2)	X	X
19	Gropius, Walter				#		X	X	X	X	X	X	X	X	X	X	X	X	X	X	X	X	19 (12)	X	X
19	Mies van der Rohe, Ludwig				#		X	X	+	X	X	X	X	X	X	X	X	X	X	X	X	X	19 (8)	X	X
19	Breuer, Marcel				#		X	X	+	X	X	X	X	X	X	X		X	X	X	X	X	1 + (1)	X	X
19	Neutra, Richard						X	X		X	X	X	X	X	X	X	X	X	X	X	X	X	3 (2)	X	X
16	Harrison, Wallace (& Abramovitz)						+	X	+	X	X	X	X	X	X	X	X	X	X	X	X	X	2 + (6)		
16	Howe, George (& Lescaze)							X	+	X	X	X	X	X	X	X			X	X	X	X	2	X	X
15	Skidmore, Owings & Merrill							X	+	X	X	X	X	X	X	X			X	X	X	X	2 + (4)		
14	Griffin, Walter B.				X		X	X		X	X			X	X	X			X	X	X	X	3+		X
13	Fuller, R. Buckminster*								+	X	X	X		X	X	X	X		X	X	X	X	2 + (1)		
13	Schindler, R. M.				X		X				X	X		X	X	X			X	X	X	X	3 + (3)	X	
13	Lescaze, William				X					X	X	X		X	X	X			X	X	X	X	−1	X	
13	Mendelsohn, Eric				#	#	#	X	+	X	X	X	X	X					X	X			2 + (2)	X	X
13	Kahn, Louis I.										X		X	X	X	X	X		X	X	X	X	11 (9)	X	X
11	Harris, Harwell H.										X	X		X	X	X			X	X	X		1/2		X
10	Belluschi, Pietro										X	X	X	X	X	X			X	X	X		1 + (1)		
10	Shreve, Lamb & Harmon										X	X	X	X	X	X			X				−1		X
10	Wurster, William W.										X	X	X		X		X		X	X	X		−1/2		X
10	Stone, Edward Durell									X	X	X	X					X	X	X	X		1+	X	
8	Mellor, Meigs & Howe	X						X							X		X			X	X		0		X
8	Kiesler, Frederick			X								X	X	X	X					X	X		−1		
8	Sert, Josep Lluis						X									X	X	X		X			1 + (1)		X
7	Walker, Ralph	X		X	X						X	X	X										−1		
7	Goodwin, Philip	X										X	X					X		X	X		1/2		
7	Cret, Paul Philippe	X														X	X			X	X		1+		
7	Goff, Bruce*															X	X		X	X			4 + (1)		X
7	Gruen, Victor															X	X	X	X	X			−1		
6	Bel Geddes, Norman	X														X	X	X	X				1		
6	Harmon, Arthur Loomis	X		X	X					X	X		X										0		
6	Reinhard & Hofmeister		X							X					X				X				−1/2		X
6	Byrne, Barry				X		X			X		X										X	1+		
6	Wright, Lloyd				X					X		X								X		X	1+		
5	Dailey, Gardner						X									X	X	X	X				0		
5	Kocher & Frey				X											X		X					1/2		X
5	Dow, Alden										X					X	X		X				−1/2		

Table 1 (*continued*)
The Index of Fame

Number of Citations		Mumford 1924	Hamlin 1926	Tallmadge 1927	Kimball 1928	Hitchcock 1929	Giedion 1941 +/− = 1967	Andrews 1947	Pevsner 1948 +/− = 1960	Hamlin 1953	Hitchcock 1958	Encyclopedia of World Art 1959	Fletcher 1961 +/− 1987	Burchard & Bush-Brown 1961	Gowans 1964	Fitch 1966	Benevolo 1966	Britannica 1968	Scully 1969	Richards 1977	Roth 1979	Whiffen & Koeper 1981	Macmillan Encyclopedia of Architects 1982	# of columns (# of illustrations)	Kostof 1985	Fletcher 1987
5	Stein, Clarence													X		X			X		X			1		
5	Stonorov, Oskar													X			X		X		X			1+		
4	Johnson, Reginald*	X	X											X							X			0		
4	Drummond, William						X							X	X							X			0		
4	Kahn, Ely Jacques				X	X								X										1		
4	Van Alen, William													X								X	X	−1 (1)		
3	Dinwiddie, James						X							X			X							0		
3	Murphy, C. F.																		X			X	X	0		
	C—Architects Born after 1905 and before 1926																									
18	Saarinen, Eero						X		+	X	X	X	X	X	X	X	X	X	X	X	X	X		10 + (9)	X	X
14	Rudolph, Paul									X	X	X		X	X	X	X		X	X	X	X		1 + (1)	X	X
13	Johnson, Philip										X	X	X	X	X	X			X	X	X	X		2 + (3)	X	X
11	Pei, I. M.										X	X		X	X	X			X	X	X	X		2 + (1)		X
9	Bunshaft, Gordon						X		+	X				X	X	X				X	X			1 + (1)		
9	Yamasaki, Minoru										X				X	X	X	X	X	X	X			−1		
8	Eames, Charles						X					X		X	X		X					X		3+		X
7	Esherick, Joseph						X			X				X						X	X			1	X	
7	The Architects' Collaborative						X			X				X			X	X		X				1 + (2)		
6	Nowicki, Matthew*									X				X	X					X	X			−1		
6	Soleri, Paolo													X	X							X		−1	X	X
6	Moore, Charles																		X	X	X			1 + (1)	X	X
6	Venturi, Robert																		X	X	X			3 + (3)	X	X
5	Yeon, John						X				X	X		X										−1/2		
5	Perkins & Will							X				X	X							X				−1/2		
5	Abramovitz, Max									X		X	X							X	X			0		
5	Stubbins, Hugh										X	X								X	X			1		
5	Mitchell-Giurgola																		X	X	X			1/2	X	
5	Roche & Dinkeloo																		X	X	X			−1		X
4	Graham, Bruce														X					X	X			−1		
4	Kallmann, McKinnell & Knowles																	X		X				1/2		
4	Goldberg, Bertrand																		X	X	X			−1/2		
3	De Mars, Vernon											X			X									0		
3	Soriano, Raphael						X					X			X									0		
3	Koch, Carl							X				X									X			0		
3	Brownson, Jacques																		X	X	X			0		

Not yet practicing in the United States.

* Loners; see chapter 12.

Table 2
Architects in the Index of Fame and Their Rank

Name	Rank	Name	Rank	Name	Rank
Abramovitz, Max	C5	Flagg, Ernest*	A10	Kocher & Frey	B5
Ackerman, Fred L.	A4	Fuller, R. Buckminster*	B13	La Farge, C. Grant	A3
Adler, Dankmar (& Sullivan)	A17	Furness, Frank	A14	Lafever, Minard	A12
Aldrich, Chester H.	A3	Gallier, James, Sr.	A5	Latrobe, Benjamin	A23
Atterbury, Grosvenor	A5	Garden, Hugh	A3	LeBrun, Napoleon	A5
Atwood, Charles	A8	Gaynor, John P.*	A4	L'Enfant, Pierre Charles*	A18
Austin, Henry	A8	Gilbert, Bradford Lee	A4	Lescaze, William	B13
Babb, George (Cook &		Gilbert, Cass	A17	Lienau, Detlef	A8
Willard)	A4	Gill, Irving	A13	Lindeberg, Harrie	A6
Bacon, Henry	A15	Gilman, Arthur	A6	Little, Arthur	A6
Bel Geddes, Norman	B6	Godefroy, Maximilian	A10	Long, Robert Cary, Jr.	A4
Belluschi, Pietro	B10	Goff, Bruce*	B7	Lowell, Guy*	A4
Beman, Solon S.	A5	Goldberg, Bertrand	C4	Maginnis, Charles (& Walsh)	A5
Benjamin, Asher	A14	Goodhue, Bertram G.	A18	Magonigle, H. Van B.	A5
Bennett, Edward	A6	Goodwin, Philip	B7	Maher, George	A7
Bogardus, James*	A14	Graham, Bruce	C4	Mangin, Joseph (& McComb)*	A11
Bosworth, Welles	A5	Graham, Ernest R.	A6	Manigault, Gabriel*	A5
Brady, Josiah	A4	Greene & Greene	A15	Mason, George DeWitt	A5
Bragdon, Claude	A7	Greene, John Holden*	A6	Maybeck, Bernard	A15
Breuer, Marcel	B19	Griffin, Marion Mahony	A5	McArthur, John Jr.*	A10
Brownson, Jacques	C3	Griffin, Walter B.	B14	McComb, John, Jr.*	A13
Bryant, Gridley J. F.		Gropius, Walter	B19	McIntire, Samuel	A16
(& Gilman)	A8	Gruen, Victor	B7	McKim, Mead & White	A24
Bucklin, James*	A7	Hadfield, George	A6	Mead, William R.	A7
Buffington, Leroy	A8	Hallet, Etienne S.	A9	Mellor, Meigs & Howe	B8
Bulfinch, Charles	A22	Harmon, Arthur Loomis	B6	Mendelsohn, Eric	B13
Bunshaft, Gordon	C9	Harris, Harwell H.	B11	Mies van der Rohe, Ludwig	B19
Burnham, Daniel (& Root)	A23	Harrison, Wallace		Mills, Robert	A22
Byrne, Barry	B6	(& Abramovitz)	B16	Mitchell-Giurgola	C5
Cady, Berg & See	A4	Hastings, Thomas	A11	Mizner, Addison	A7
Carrère & Hastings	A15	Hatfield, R. G.*	A3	Moore, Charles	C6
Carstensen & Gildemeister	A4	Haviland, John	A14	Morris, Benjamin W.	A3
Carter, Elias	A3	Helmle, Frank (& Corbett)	A5	Mould, Jacob Wray	A4
Cobb, Henry I. (& Frost)	A6	Hoadley, David*	A5	Mueller, Paul	A3
Codman, Henry S.	A3	Hoban, James	A13	Mullett, Alfred B.	A7
Coolidge, Charles	A5	Hoffman, F. Burrall	A4	Mullgardt, Louis C.	A4
Cope, Walter	A6	Holabird & Roche	A19	Murphy, C. F.	B3
Corbett, Harvey W.	A11	Hood, Raymond	B19	Neutra, Richard	B19
Cram, Ralph A.	A18	Hooker, Philip*	A8	Newton, Dudley*	A4
Cret, Paul Philippe	B7	Howard, Henry	A4	Notman, John*	A8
Cummings, Charles (& Sears)	A5	Howard, John Galen	A8	Nowicki, Matthew	C6
Dailey, Gardner	B5	Howe, George (& Lescaze)	B16	Olmsted, F. L., Jr. (& Olmsted)	A7
Dakin, James	A5	Howells, John Mead	A11	Olmsted, Frederick Law	A14
Davis, Alexander J.	A18	Hunt, Myron*	A5	Parris, Alexander	A14
Day, Frank Miles*	A7	Hunt, Richard M.	A22	Peabody, Robert (& Stearns)	A6
Delano, William (& Aldrich)	A11	Ittner, William B.*	A4	Pei, I. M.	C11
De Mars, Vernon	C3	Jay, William*	A5	Perkins & Will	C5
de Pouilly, Jacques B.*	A3	Jefferson, Thomas	A23	Perkins, Dwight	A6
Dinwiddie, James	B3	Jenney, William L. B.	A22	Platt, Charles Adams*	A11
Dow, Alden	B5	Johnson, Philip	C13	Polk, Willis	A14
Downing, Andrew J.	A11	Johnson, Reginald*	B4	Pond & Pond	A3
Drummond, William	B4	Johnston, William L.*	A5	Pope, John Russell	A15
Eames, Charles	C8	Kahn, Albert	A15	Post, George B.	A14
Eidlitz, Leopold	A10	Kahn, Ely Jacques	B4	Potter, Edward	A6
Ellis, Harvey	A5	Kahn, Louis I.	B13	Potter, William	A6
Elmslie, George	A7	Kallmann, McKinnell &		Price, Bruce	A13
Emerson, William R.*	A9	Knowles	C4	Purcell, William (& Elmslie)	A9
Esherick, Joseph	C7	Kellum, John*	A4	Ramée, J. J.*	A11
Eyre, Wilson*	A8	Kiesler, Frederick	B8	Reinhard & Hofmeister	B6
Ferriss, Hugh	A8	Koch, Carl	C3	Renwick, James	A23

Table 2 (*continued*)
Architects in the Index of Fame and Their Rank

Richardson, H. H.	A24	Soriano, Raphael	C3	Van Osdel, John*	A5
Roche & Dinkeloo	C5	Stein, Clarence	B5	Vaux, Calvert	A11
Roche, Martin	A9	Stevens, John Calvin	A7	Venturi, Robert	C6
Rogers, Isaiah	A12	Stone, Edward Durell	B10	Walker, Ralph	B7
Rogers, James Gamble	A12	Stonorov, Oskar	B5	Walter, Thomas U.	A19
Root, John Wellborn	A20	Strickland, William	A20	Ware, William R.	A9
Rudolph, Paul	C14	Stubbins, Hugh	C5	Warren & Wetmore	A10
Saarinen, Eero	C18	Sturgis, John (& Brigham)	A5	Warren, Russell*	A8
Saarinen, Eliel	A20	Sturgis, Russell	A10	Wells, Joseph M.	A3
Schindler, R. M.	B13	Sullivan, Louis	A24	White, Stanford	A17
Schmidt, R. E. (& Garden)	A6	Tefft, Thomas*	A6	Willard, Solomon	A8
Sert, Josep Lluis	B8	The Architect's Collaborative	C7	Wright, Frank Lloyd	A24
Shaw, Howard Van Doren	A4	Thompson, Martin	A3	Wright, Lloyd	B6
Shepley, Rutan & Coolidge	A8	Thornton, William*	A18	Wurster, William W.*	B10
Shreve, Lamb & Harmon	B10	Town, Ithiel (& Davis)	A14	Yamasaki, Minoru	C9
Shryock, Gideon	A7	Trumbauer, Horace*	A5	Yeon, John	C5
Silsbee, J. Lyman	A5	Upjohn, R. M.	A6	York & Sawyer	A6
Skidmore, Owings & Merrill	B15	Upjohn, Richard	A21	Young, Ammi B.	A9
Sloan, Samuel	A6	Urban, Joseph	A4		
Smith, George W.*	A4	Van Alen, William	B4		
Soleri, Paolo	C6	Van Brunt, Henry (& Howe)	A9		

*Loners; see chapter 12.

PART I

Case Studies: The Apprenticeship Connection

FOUR

Louis Sullivan

Frank Lloyd Wright, Sullivan's employee, is surely the most famous of all American architects. But it is the career of Wright's "Lieber Meister" Louis Henry Sullivan [A24] that is the perfect model of the mechanics of fame.

Sullivan grew up in Boston, where he spent much of his childhood on the farm of his indulgent grandparents—a period in his life when, according to his autobiography, Sullivan was deeply influenced by his passion for nature and growing plants. Pensive and fiercely independent, as a youth he had a history of truancy and little academic self-discipline. Nevertheless, in 1872 he managed to enroll in William Robert Ware's advanced classes in architecture at MIT soon after this first American professional program had opened. By today's standards the classes were extremely small, with only a handful of students. Ware [A9] was the principal professor and, forty years later, Sullivan remembered him as quiet and amiable but "not imaginative enough to be ardent."[1] He complained about his distaste for Ware's teaching mannerisms. It is probable that, as a student, Sullivan was aware of the fact that Ware, with his partner Henry Van Brunt [A9], was in the process of designing the bold High Victorian style Memorial Hall (1865–1878) for Harvard, a full-breasted polychrome mix of Gothic and nineteenth-century motifs and one of the more important designs of the 1870s in the Boston area (although Van Brunt later recanted the building). Sullivan's subsequent admiration of Furness' work indicates that he still accepted a Victorian aesthetic at this time.

Ware & Van Brunt: Memorial Hall, Harvard, Cambridge, 1865–1878

In terms of the connection of one major architect to another, it matters little if he did or did not admire Ware either as an architect or as a teacher. Also, Sullivan was a student, not an employee, and this type of contact seems less significant than contact that occurs in an office. However, though of minor importance compared to later

Year of Birth   **Chart 2. Sullivan and Wright and their connections.**

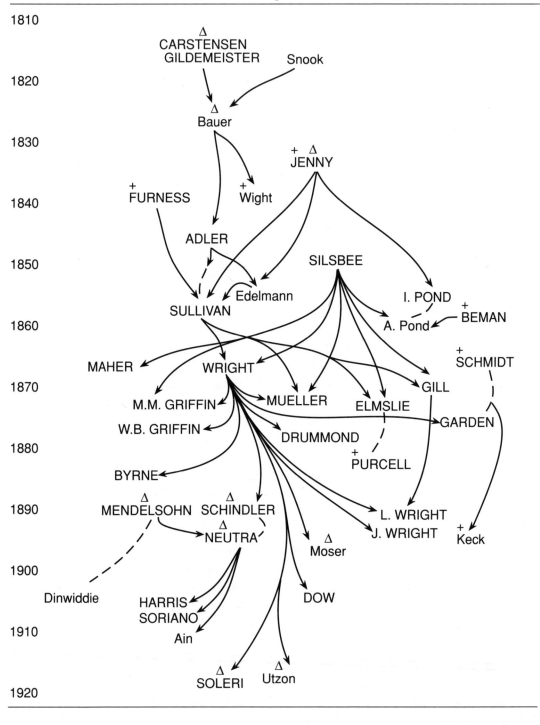

Employment	NAME ON THE INDEX OF FAME
Partnership	Name not on the Index of Fame
Mentorship	
European training Δ	Connects to others on another chart +

events, this contact was the first career "event" in a pattern that he would later experience. Sullivan was in a position to be in direct contact with an architect at the time when that man's first important building was going up—in Ware's case, the only important building to be associated with his name as a designer. Sullivan claimed to be disappointed with the course at MIT and, without completing the program, he headed off to live with his grandfather, who was in Philadelphia. He stopped in New York, apparently with a letter of introduction to Richard Morris Hunt, possibly written by Ware, Hunt's own ex-pupil. An employee in Hunt's office told Sullivan that, when he arrived in Philadelphia, he should "look up the firm of Furness & Hewitt."[2] Sullivan later stated that he looked about in Philadelphia, saw and liked some buildings that Furness had designed, and presented himself in Furness' office with the announcement that the firm would employ him. He was a very self-assured seventeen-year-old at the time. He was hired while the Pennsylvania Academy of the Fine Arts, an even more idiosyncratic and vigorous combination of English High Victorian and Romanesque details, was Furness' major project.

Furness' own career supports the hypothesis about fame and apprenticeship. Frank Furness [A14] had been a fellow student in the same Richard Morris Hunt atelier that Ware and Van Brunt had attended in New York. So were two other men whose careers are discussed later, George B. Post and Charles Gambrill. Hunt is celebrated in architectural history texts as the first native-born American to be trained at the Ecole des Beaux-Arts in Paris. Furness was the youngest of these five students and the last to arrive, but all of these young architects not only were able to observe their own master at the time he was first generating attention as a designer, but actually were working in the building that was establishing his reputation—the just completed and relatively suave Studio Building of 1857. Post and Gambrill left Hunt in 1860 and shared an office in a loose partnership for the next seven years, at which time they became active participants in H. H. Richardson's career. Ware and Van Brunt formed their partnership in 1863. But Furness was more than Hunt's student; he became an employee and was sent to Newport, Rhode Island, in 1861 when Hunt's Griswold House (1861–1863) was in the design stage.

Though it was not done in Hunt's normal métier and did not presage his future design direction, this angular, bristling house was a vigorously self-assured design and inventive, creative, and unusual for the early 1860s—an early essay in a style that was later labeled the "Stick Style" by Vincent Scully. Working for Hunt during its generation gave the young assistant the chance to see design conviction and daring on the part of a still young employer—his own important career connection. This was Furness' link to an existing chain. Furness served in the Union Army from 1861 to 1864 and then returned to Hunt's office. Then he moved to Philadelphia, where he worked for John Fraser, just as Fraser completed the Union League Club (1864–1865). In 1866 he established his own practice in Philadelphia.

But the focus of this chapter is Louis Sullivan. Sullivan joined Furness' staff seven years later, in 1873, at the time of Furness' greatest creativity. His masterworks in Philadelphia are the Pennsylvania Academy of the Fine Arts (1871–1876) and the Guarantee Trust Building (1873–1875). (At most only two others, the Provident Trust Company [1879] and the much later University of Pennsylvania Library [1890], are normally reproduced when Furness is included in architectural history surveys.) This was probably the best possible year for Sullivan to have been there, in spite of the fact that it was the year of a national financial panic, which meant that he stayed only a short time before the economic situation led to his dismissal. Furness fascinated the young Sullivan:

> Frank Furness "made buildings out of his head." . . . And Furness as a freehand draftsman was extraordinary. He had Louis hypnotized, especially when he drew and swore at the same time. . . . In looking back upon that time Louis Sullivan gives thanks that it was his great good fortune to have made his entry into the practical world in an office where standards were so high—where talent was so manifestly taken for granted, and the atmosphere the free and easy one of a true work shop, savoring of the guild where craftsmanship was paramount and personal.[3]

Sullivan left Philadelphia and Furness in November and went to Chicago, where his parents then were living. Chicago architects were only lightly touched by the panic of 1873 due to the city's intense need for new buildings after the fire of 1871. Most scholars agree that Sullivan's reminiscences cannot be completely trusted.[4] However, he said that he was attracted by the Portland Block of 1872—William Le Baron Jenney's first major commission for a commercial building. Sullivan was hired by Jenney: "The Major took Louis in immediately upon application, as he needed more help. And to the fact that Louis had been at 'Tech' he attached the highest importance—as alumni of any school are apt to do; so much for temperamental personality."[5]

As it happens, William Le Baron Jenney [A22] had not attended MIT. It did not yet exist when Jenney was educated. Jenney graduated from Phillips Academy in Andover, Massachusetts; since he and William Ware were exactly the same age, they were likely to have been classmates there. The fact that Sullivan's first, second, and third contacts in 1873 probably all knew each other was not mentioned in

Hunt: Griswold House, Newport, 1861–1863

Furness: Pennsylvania Academy of the Fine Arts, Philadelphia, 1871–1876

Jenney: Portland Block, Chicago, 1872

his autobiography. Indeed, it may have been a coincidence, but by the 1870s there were more than 2,000 other potential employers in practice. Sullivan seemed to be instinctively following a network.

Jenney, like Ware, had studied engineering for two years at Harvard's Lawrence Scientific School. But unlike Ware, he sailed for France, where he entered the Ecole Centrale des Arts et Manufactures in Paris in 1853. It was a rigorous program: "Of the class to which Jenney belonged only 66 of an original 176 were graduated."[6] The brilliant engineer Gustave Eiffel was in the class just one year ahead of Jenney. After graduation Jenney first returned to the United States and served as a railroad engineer for one year, 1857–1858, and then returned to Paris to work in unspecified offices in 1858 and 1859. Since Eiffel not only attended Jenney's school but in the late 1850s "held a series of positions with firms constructing railroad equipment or engaged in building railroads themselves,"[7] it is tempting to want to search for a connection between Jenney and Eiffel or to guess that perhaps both had been stimulated by a creative older engineer. But there is no one on record in Jenney's own career who played the role for him that he himself served as an inspiration to younger employees.

With the outbreak of the American Civil War, Jenney returned home again, this time to work as an engineer in the Union Army. After the war he established his practice in Chicago in 1868, three years before the great fire. Sanford Loring became his partner in 1869, and they worked in an ordinary and vernacular American version of the Victorian Gothic style that would never have made them famous. There is a residue of this approach to style in the façade of the Portland Block.

There is no question that the first architectural historians to trace the development of modern architecture overpraised Jenney and his contribution to the development of the skyscraper. Nevertheless, it is that sort of fame that is the key in this study of connections, and Jenney began to establish his fame with the Portland Building of 1872. A remarkable group of apprentices and employees in his office between 1868 and 1875 also would be favored by future architectural historians. In historical surveys the firms of Burnham & Root and Holabird & Roche shared the spotlight with those of Adler & Sullivan and Jenney himself.

The year Sullivan was hired "there was work enough in the office to keep five men busy and a boy, provided they took intervals of rest, which they did."[8] One of these employees was John Edelmann, who became Sullivan's personal mentor. Another was Martin Roche [A9]. Roche's future partner, William Holabird [A19], would be employed the following year, and Daniel Burnham [A23] had left Jenney's office in 1869. Other employees are given in the notes.[9] But, like the famous cluster of architects in Peter Behrens' office in Berlin later, a number of ultimately major architects were connected to Jenney in a short period of six years, at the time of Jenney's *first featured* design.

William Jordy commented on the Jenney office in *American Buildings and Their Architects* and proposed the idea that "intensive regional developments often disclose three elements. These are, first, a hospitable environment; then, an older man of vision whose impact is not to be measured in terms of specific influence alone, but as the embodiment of a diffuse point of view; finally, a cluster of venture-some young men, cooperating and competing with one another to force a development to a rapid climax."[10] This is a valid appraisal and close in substance to my thesis. However, these three elements—ready clients, an employer, and colleagues—should not specifically be linked to "regional developments." There is a more universal con-dition at work here. There may not have to be colleagues in the office (though there must always be a receptive client). Jordy even implied the significance of timing in one of his three qualifiers, "a hospitable environment." What he missed is that this environment is a specific creative moment, the first emergence into strength (and fame) of the "older man of vision."

Sullivan did not like Jenney: "The major was a free-and-easy cultured gentleman, but not an architect except by courtesy of terms. His true profession was that of engineer. . . . He spoke French with an accent so atrocious that it jarred Louis's teeth, while his English speech jerked about as though it had St. Vitus's dance. He was mon-strously pop-eyed, with hanging mobile features, sensuous lips . . . Louis soon found out that the Major was not, really, in his heart, an engineer at all, but by nature, and in toto, a bon vivant, a gourmet."[11]

As will become evident, it was not important for Sullivan to ad-mire his employer—nor is it for any employee who is able to believe that he himself can produce as strong a design as the one his master is producing or has just finished.

In July 1874 Sullivan left Chicago for France to try to enter the Ecole des Beaux-Arts in Paris. He was admitted into the atelier of Emile Vaudremer in September; though he seems to have begun with enthusiasm, Sullivan was not a disciplined scholar. He did learn to dress impressively and impeccably, matured in his choice of reading material, and spent two months in Italy; but he had returned to Amer-ica by the following May. That winter he was hired by John Edelmann, Jenney's foreman when Sullivan had worked briefly for Jenney. Edelmann had just set up his own office, and Sullivan was assigned the interior decoration for Johnston & Edelmann's Moody Tabernacle (1876). This caught the attention of a local newspaper critic when the congregation raised a commotion over Sullivan's designs. The critic argued persuasively in favor of the work (possibly with some coaching from its artist), and Sullivan had his first publicity as an architect, at the age of twenty. Then Edelmann left Chicago for four years. In spite of having Sullivan's autobiography, there are gaps in the record of Sullivan's employment from 1875 to 1881. Whether Edelmann brought Sullivan to Adler's attention or whether Sullivan was already working for Adler when Edelmann returned to the office is still unclear.[12] But either in 1879 or by 1882 Sullivan was an employee of Dankmar Adler.

At fifteen, Dankmar Adler [A17] had come to the United States with his German father. He was apprenticed to John Schaeffer and then to E. Willard Smith, local architects in Detroit, where Adler's father served a congregation as its liberal rabbi. The Adlers moved to Chicago, and, before and after serving in the Topographical Engineer's Office during the Civil War, he worked for Augustus Bauer, a man who certainly is not famous, but had his own connections with others in the Index of Fame.[13]

Adler had a series of brief partnerships, but was working alone for the first time when Sullivan was employed. Depending on the actual date, Adler was either just completing his first major commission or had actually built it. The Central Music Hall of 1879 proved Adler's genius for acoustical engineering. At this time "Adler began in a hesitant way to enter the mainstream of the Chicago movement. . . . Eighteen rather undistinguished years of engineering and architectural experience lay behind the design of the Central Music Hall."[14] It is obvious from old photographs that this building was not in the forefront of advanced façade design—above all Sullivan's concern. Nevertheless, Adler's reputation was established at the right moment for Sullivan. It is this person-to-person connection, and its timing, that is more significant than any thought of stylistic influence. This was Sullivan's *fourth* opportunity to watch an employer (or professor) in the first blush of success. He was still only in his early twenties. In the face of mounting evidence it seems quite possible that these connections were significant to Sullivan's own eventual power.

Adler: Central Music Hall, Chicago, 1879

Sullivan was Adler's partner by 1883. Sullivan was the designer, the partner who concentrated on the art of architecture, while Adler concerned himself more with functional and structural design. Their partnership, which lasted until 1896, produced nearly all of the buildings for which Sullivan would be internationally celebrated. Does it follow, therefore, that Sullivan had a significant hand in that first important building, the design of Adler's Music Hall? According to

Twombly, he could not have done so, though Paul Sprague relies more on the dates given in the Sullivan *Autobiography*. If his presence could be securely documented, it is probable that the presence of the employee did have an effect on the senior designer.

But, as will be seen, Sullivan's real fame began the year *before* Wright was employed. By this time, Sullivan had become "an insular person with relatively few friends, who devoted himself largely to his intellectual and spiritual quest for a new architecture."[15] He had given his first public speech (1885), published in 1886, and had started to convey an image of himself as the scorned mystic, oracle of modern architecture, the reshaper of society. At twenty-two, Wright may or may not already have envisioned himself as a prophet and messiah of great and enormous stylistic change, but, given his personality, he was ripe for conversion. He provided an enraptured audience for Sullivan's views and possibly incited him to greater heights of grandeur. Thus the benefits of the sort of connection I am tracing may go both ways upon occasion. Not only may the receptive and bright employee respond, but it is likely that his very presence stimulates the senior designer to take an idea further, and then again still further, than he would have dared before. Fundamentally, it is usually this daring that creates those monuments so often featured in architectural history. However, there are limits to assuming a two-way response. I doubt that Sullivan's presence in either Frank Furness' office or William Jenney's office had any effect whatsoever on their design ability. As in many cases, it was the employee who gained strength in watching the master gain his. Where there is a certain empathy, as there was between Sullivan and Wright and with Richardson, McKim, and White, sparks fly in both directions.

Wright is the subject of the following chapter, but one other architect praised by architectural historians was in Adler & Sullivan's office in the early years of their international fame and deserves discussion. Irving Gill [A13] worked for them from 1890 to 1892. Gill was the son of a Syracuse, New York, builder and had his first employment in that city. When he arrived in Chicago he entered the same office where Wright first worked, that of J. Lyman Silsbee [A5], an architect who had previously practiced in Syracuse. When Gill was hired by Sullivan, the Auditorium Building was just being completed. This was the time of the Wainwright Building (1891) in St. Louis, with preparations underway for the World's Columbian Exposition of 1893. Gill's assignment at Adler & Sullivan was the Transportation Building for the fair. "The liberating influence of Sullivan was vital to Gill's development, and the respect Sullivan instilled in his draftsmen for the sheer walls of indigenous African architecture proved important [to

Adler & Sullivan: Auditorium Building, Chicago, 1886–1890

Gill's future design power]."[16] Gill's relationship with Sullivan offers further support for my thesis.

Not only is it important that Wright and Gill were there in the first bloom of Sullivan's real power—a second key concept of my thesis is that, in order to reap the benefits of this sort of connection, a promising young designer should not stay too long with the master, five years at the maximum. Like Wright and Gill, George Elmslie [A7] moved from Silsbee's office into Adler & Sullivan's firm. Beginning in 1889, for twenty years, the Scottish Elmslie was Sullivan's shy and patient "Faithful George." And because Wright, and Sullivan as well, made Sullivan into such a hero, the importance of Elmslie's hand in Sullivan's designs has only recently been understood. Obviously talented, but not apparently personally ambitious, Elmslie remained with Sullivan well after his decline into untenable pomposity, alcoholism, and bitterness. Finally, in 1909, Elmslie went into partnership with William Purcell [A9], who had also worked for Sullivan, though for only five months, in the first decade of this century. Their firm was responsible for a number of excellent buildings in the Prairie style, although they are not nearly as well known nationally as Wright and Gill. William Drummond [B4] and Paul Mueller [A3] were also Sullivan employees, but their connection was to Wright. Nevertheless, the careers of even the greatest architects do wax and wane, and it appears that it makes a considerable difference whether a young architect is present in the emerging period or at a later time in the senior architect's career.

FIVE

Frank Lloyd Wright

There were certain decades in American architectural history that were luckier than most for young architects just beginning their careers. The 1880s were good years throughout the country, but especially in Chicago. The devastating 1871 fire and the city's continuing growth as a commercial center had created a huge demand for new office buildings. At least ten firms were working on large office blocks, and other offices concentrated on churches and houses. As it was, Frank Lloyd Wright [A24] chose to work for Joseph Lyman Silsbee [A5].

Silsbee had attended Harvard and was one of the first students at MIT. By 1872 he had opened an office in upstate New York and ten years later he moved to Chicago. Wright's uncle, the Reverend Jenkin Lloyd Jones, had hired Silsbee to design two buildings: a family chapel in Spring Green, Wisconsin, and a church in Chicago. The Shingle Style was then, briefly, the most fashionable architectural style with the wealthy old families of New England, and Silsbee's chapel was a small and severely simple example of that expansive but intrinsically residential style. All Souls' (Unitarian) Church in Chicago could easily have been seen as a large house. They were Silsbee's first essays in that mode and, when compared to his Syracuse Savings Bank of 1876, they show that he had progressed into a new design mastery. Nevertheless, though better than average, Silsbee would not become a famous architect. Indeed, but for the fact that the nineteen-year-old Wright moved to Chicago in 1887 and worked for him, Silsbee would not be mentioned in textbooks at all.

Nevertheless, Silsbee was an impressive role model and his office seems to have been quite a nursery for architects destined to be mentioned by architectural historians.[1] Wright remembered:

Silsbee: All Souls' Church, Chicago, 1885–1886

Silsbee: Syracuse Savings Bank, Syracuse, 1876

Silsbee could draw with amazing ease. He drew with soft, deep black lead pencil strokes and he would make remarkable freehand sketches of that type of dwelling peculiarly his own at the time. His superior talent in design had made him respected in Chicago. His work was a picturesque combination of gable, turret and hip, with broad porches quietly domestic and gracefully picturesque. A contrast to the awkward stupidities and brutalities of the period elsewhere. He would come out to the draughting room as though we, the draughtsmen, did not exist. . . . [He was] the picture of indifference or scorn. . . . He was grudging of words and shy of patience. All [were] awed by him.[2]

Not only did Wright learn to draw—Silsbee was an innovative residential designer (for Chicago) and Wright's early practice actually showed nearly as much design influence from Silsbee as it did from Sullivan. But Wright himself may have provided an explanation for the reason why his first employer would not pass on more than the tinder to light a torch of genius. He quoted his fellow worker, Cecil Corwin, on Silsbee: "'He's a kind of genius, but something is the matter with him. He doesn't seem to take any of it or take himself half seriously. The picture interests him. The rest bores him. You'll see, he is an architectural genius spoiled by way of the aristocrat. . . . [He is] too contemptuous of everything.' . . . And I did see. I saw that Silsbee was just making pictures."[3]

Wright felt that he was not being paid well enough by Silsbee and left to work for a few weeks for Beers, Clay & Dutton; but he had returned to Silsbee's office when he heard of an opening for a draftsman in the Adler & Sullivan office. The firm had a staff of about twenty when Wright was interviewed and hired in 1888. They had begun work on the Auditorium Building and Hotel (1886–1890), in its day a behemoth of a building. Adler had been in practice for many years and Sullivan had been working in Chicago for fourteen years. Thus the Auditorium was by no means Sullivan's first commission. It was, however, both the most spectacular building in Chicago up to that time and the first by Sullivan fated to be described as seminal in architectural history.

Adler & Sullivan: Auditorium Building, Chicago, 1886–1890

Wright had nothing whatsoever to do with the birth of power that Sullivan experienced at the outset of that commission. Wright was employed the year after the design for the exterior was settled. The client had been shown the presentation drawing in 1886 (plate 1) and immediately insisted that most of the pinnacles, towers, and fussy dormers be removed. He was still skeptical when the second drawings were finished and, since he was about to commit a great sum of money, called in an expert as consultant. This was the leading archi-

Plate 1. Presentation rendering of Adler & Sullivan's Auditorium Building, 1886. (Courtesy of The Museum of Modern Art, New York)

tectural educator in America, William Robert Ware of MIT and Columbia, Sullivan's former professor. For a fee of $1,000 Ware removed one more flourish, the pyramid on the main tower, and he and the client changed the number and grouping of stories and increased the height of the tower. Ware then endorsed the project and the commission was granted in 1887.[4] The Auditorium Building as completed (plate 2) demonstrates the change in Sullivan's design strength that year. Neither the client nor Ware had shown concern for the appearance of the interior of the building. They trusted Adler's genius as an acoustical engineer to make the Opera House work.

Sullivan's handling of the ornament of the interior also showed a sudden maturity. The coarseness of his style prior to 1887 disappeared, and the lovely fluid control that we think of as the essence of Sullivan's talent emerged. Frank Lloyd Wright was present just after Sullivan began to reach his full potential.

Wright respected Adler and adored Sullivan, though Sullivan's manner with his staff was arrogant, abrupt, even gruff. As Wright later said, "The Master's very walk at this time bore dangerous resemblance to a strut,"[5] and "he seemed to have no respect at all for anybody there except Adler and Paul Mueller," his office foreman.[6] It was Adler who played a fatherly role.

Wright was "unpopular from the first day with the others in the office" and was accused of being a "Sullivan toady."[7] It would be hard

Plate 2. The Auditorium Building, 1886–1890, as completed. (Courtesy of the Chicago Architectural Photographing Co.)

to argue that he was not Sullivan's sycophant. It has been said that "Sullivan's recreation was a monologue with one listener,"[8] and Wright served as the respectful audience for Sullivan's views. Even as a young and untried apprentice, however, Wright's ego was already vigorous enough that, while he could make a hero of his master, he was also able to envision himself in the same guise. He was already a posturer himself and must have been particularly attracted to Sullivan's conception of the architect as the misunderstood champion of mankind.

The theme of all of these chapters on the apprenticeship period of famous architects is the ability of one architect, seeing the dramatic maturation of a powerful designer while in the office, to equate his or her own potential to that of the employer. Wright, unlike most of his own future employees and apprentices, may have been somewhat in awe of Sullivan, but apparently was not overwhelmed by his employer.

From 1888 to 1893, the years of Wright's employment by Adler & Sullivan, Sullivan designed the façades and ornament of all of his most published buildings except two (for which Adler had already begun negotiations). Sullivan continued to grow stronger in terms of his design power at an astonishing rate. Wright saw the fruition of the Auditorium Building and the Walker Warehouse. He was there for the beginnings of the Getty Tomb, the Schiller Building, and the Transportation Building at the World's Columbian Exposition (all in Chicago) and saw the full mastery of a new approach to façade design in the Wainwright Building for St. Louis. In spite of the implications in Wright's self-important and often inaccurate autobiography, Wright was always an employee. Adler & Sullivan were the designers, as can be seen in Sullivan's continuing evolution in the Guarantee Building for Buffalo and the Carson, Pirie, Scott Building in Chicago after Wright left. But Wright's presence in a cheering section may have sustained Sullivan's momentum to some degree.

Wright's Office

After being dismissed for accepting unauthorized and secret commissions from clients of Adler & Sullivan, Wright set up his own practice in 1893 and felt his way for eight years, producing highly promising as well as moderately dull designs as he tried out various styles. Even Wright was not an instant genius. If he had died at the age of thirty-three, he would have been remembered only as the best of a group of interesting regional architects. He had not yet produced his great works. Then in 1900, 1901, and 1902 came such houses as the Warren Hickox House in Kankakee, the Bradley House in the same city, and the Ward Willits House in Highland Park, Illinois, where Wright dramatically pushed many of his ideas much further: low-pitched, oversailing roofs; strong and clear massing; clearer articulation of parts; the pinwheel plan that spread out in all four directions from a cluster of hearths. If any of his employees were to receive the spark of genius, that was the moment when they should have been standing behind Wright at his drawing board; one man, Walter Burley Griffin, was there who did become somewhat famous—though more so in Australia than in the United States.

The case of Wright includes a significant exception to the thesis, having to do with personality and personal style. Wright's career spanned sixty-six years, yet a mere eleven of his employees and students earned enough of a reputation to merit inclusion in the massive four-volume *Macmillan Encyclopedia of Architects* (1982). It is especially notable in the context of this study that four of them—Richard Neutra, R. M. Schindler, Werner Moser, and Jørn Utzon—each had influential relationships of the sort being traced with other well-known architects *before* they joined Wright and that all but one of the others were with Wright at specifically fertile times in Wright's many-phased career. The remaining man was somewhat unusual—Alden Dow had the advantage of personal wealth. He was present just before Wright came forth with a new burst of strength with Falling Water in the 1930s.

More star architects probably would have spun out of the galaxy that formed around Wright, except for the magnetic force of this autocrat. During his early years several of Wright's colleagues assisted him at times and were responsive to his emerging genius. Those of his employees who admired him may have been somewhat cowed by his personality even while he was in his thirties. In imitation of Sullivan, Wright was also donning a prophet's mantle. In his *Testament* he described the architect—and for architect we should read Frank Lloyd Wright: "A poet, artist, or architect, is likely—if not careful, to have the term 'genius' applied to him; in which case he will no longer be thought human, trustworthy or companionable. . . . I saw the architect as savior of the culture of modern American society; his services the mainspring of any future cultural life in America—savior now as for all civilizations here-to-fore. . . . A small clique formed about me, myself naturally the leader."[9]

Wright so dominated most of his employees and apprentices that they continued to remain in his shadow, even though many proved to be competent architects and received local prominence. It could not have been easy for an independent soul to work for Wright. He said, "I have never had an 'office' in the conventional manner. . . . My office is 'me.' And therein is one great difference between my own and current practice."[10] This could be received with resentment or with awed respect, like a novice in a quasi-religious institution. Only those who possessed an equally inflated faith in themselves dared to measure their own ambitions against Wright's. A glimpse of Wright among his employees and students comes from James Marston Fitch, who visited Wright's studio at Taliesin in the 1930s. By that time Fitch was a highly respected critic and writer for professional journals. Passing along the drafting tables he stopped to admire and praise an apprentice's design that was both imaginative and quite un-Wrightian. "Wright walked up and said 'It is fascist'—absolutely negative!" Fitch said, "Wright, you are not a teacher!" Wright replied, after a pause, "Yes, you are right—always wanted to be a root stem, an influence, an infusion." Wright wanted so badly to teach, not only his students but all of society.[11]

It is on record that he kept his formative ideas totally to himself.

No one, for example, saw Wright make any false starts on the design of Falling Water. He presented his drawings as a *fait accompli*, after months of expectant waiting on the part of his staff.[12]

During the first sixteen years of his practice, there was a great deal of turnover in Wright's office. Several of his employees not only worked for other architects upon occasion, but were also in business for themselves even while they did renderings or working drawings for Wright.[13] Walter Burley Griffin [B14] worked on and off for Wright from 1901 to 1905 but also designed his own buildings at the same time. Griffin had graduated from the University of Illinois in 1899. Like Wright, he was talented and, significantly, he had a firm sense of his own worth. To an unpracticed eye, Griffin's houses are indistinguishable from Wright's own work, though it is undeniable that Wright's very best designs surpassed the Prairie Style houses done by Griffin. But Griffin was in Wright's office when the seminal Ward Willits House was undertaken. "Wright found him most stimulating, and discussed with him, at length, work that he was designing. . . . Griffin, therefore, served as a useful critic, a lens through which Wright could re-examine his own ideas."[14]

Wright: Ward Willits
House, Highland Park,
1901–1902

Griffin's wife, Marion Mahony Griffin [A5], is remembered almost entirely because of the role she played in Wright's early career. She was the artist behind many of the exquisite fairy-drawn renderings of Wright's designs. An architect in her own right, she is one of the very few women in American architectural history to be mentioned in textbooks (though never as often as her husband). The second woman to graduate from MIT, Marion Mahony was first employed by her cousin Dwight Perkins [A6] on Steinway Hall in 1894, in the first year of his practice. Perkins had been a Burnham & Root employee during the important years of 1888 to 1893 when their most celebrated buildings were going up. He was in charge of the busy downtown office while the others were concentrating on the 1893 exhibition. Burnham gave Perkins the commission for Steinway Hall (1894–1896), the building that became headquarters for a number of Prairie School architects, including Wright.[15] Marion Mahony probably worked for Silsbee as well but was in Wright's office in 1898 and remained with him for eleven years, though she did drawings for other architects during that same period. In 1902 she designed an independent work of her own, the small All Souls' Unitarian Church in Evanston, Illinois. Although the building was quite modest, it is possible that she was responding to Wright's flash of power at that time. Nevertheless, in the early twentieth century, a woman architect was an oddity. Marion Mahony Griffin might have had the potential and did have the spunk to enter a man's training, but she was too far ahead of her time to practice out of the shadow of a man. Though they were both in Wright's office in 1901 and 1902, she negated her fame by marrying an architect—it was Walter Griffin who received the torch of fame.

By the final year of Wright's enormously creative Prairie School period, Wright's personal life required a retreat and he left the United States to supervise the production of a lavish portfolio of drawings of his work, the *Ausgeführte Bauten und Entwürfe von Frank Lloyd Wright,* published by Wasmuth in Berlin in 1910. Marion Mahony was still with Wright in 1909 when he abandoned his practice and disappeared to Europe with a client's wife, having collected his fees in advance. She bitterly resented not only being left with his incomplete work, but also his indifference to the payment of his employees' salaries. Needless to say, she retained no love at all for her former employer. She joined briefly in association with Hermann Von Holst,[16] but it was not an alliance that she willingly chose. Von Holst had purchased part of Wright's abandoned practice. In 1911 she married Griffin; in 1912, with the help of his wife's astonishing ability as a renderer, Griffin won the international competition for a plan for the city of Canberra and they left for Australia, where, in spite of problems evolving from World War I and the Depression, they established a very successful practice.

Barry Byrne [B6], like Griffin, was one of the eleven Wright employees given an entry in the Macmillan encyclopedia. Yet, outside of the circle of architectural historians, he is not well known except regionally. He had only an elementary school education and was employed by Wright in 1902, an auspicious time in Wright's development. Byrne was eighteen at the time and stayed with Wright until 1909—the final year of Wright's enormously creative Prairie School designs. Byrne commented on what he learned in his years with Wright: "as for teaching, in the ordinarily accepted sense of the word, there was none. It was a true atelier where one learned, if one had the capacity, by working on the buildings that Mr. Wright designed."[17] When Wright left, Byrne moved over to Griffin's office but soon left to spend three years in Seattle. He returned to Chicago and assumed Griffin's practice when Griffin left for Australia. By 1917 Byrne was in practice alone and later would gain recognition for his Modernistic churches built in the Midwest.

Two of Wright's sons were recognized in the Macmillan encyclopedia. Lloyd Wright [B6] and John Lloyd Wright were both trained by their father. But they missed what would prove to be their father's most significant creative moments in his early career; they were only twelve and nine years old in 1902. Lloyd Wright left the University of Wisconsin two years after he enrolled and went to Europe to join his

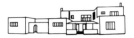

Gill: Dodge House, Holly-
wood, 1914–1916

father in the preparation of the Wasmuth volumes. Next he found employment as an apprentice landscape architect in the office of Olmsted & Olmsted in Boston while they were working on the Chicago Waterfront project. By the fall of 1911 Lloyd Wright was in San Diego, working in the Olmsted nursery there. The following year he joined Irving Gill's staff of about seven draftsmen, where he remained until 1915. (Gill, strange to say, never told Lloyd Wright that he had worked with his father in the Adler & Sullivan office.) [18]

Gill was not famous in his own lifetime; his fame waited for later historians. However, when Gill's work is represented in surveys of American architectural history, it is usually the Dodge House (1914–1916, razed) in Hollywood that is illustrated. This was not Gill's first mastery of simple cubical geometries and the medium of concrete, but it was his masterpiece. Nothing else during the remaining twenty years of Gill's life would be its equal. Even though Lloyd Wright's particular assignment was workers' housing for Torrance, California, and he did not work on the Dodge House, he was present in the office at the right time.

A young employee does not have to have had any specific part in the seminal design; he simply needs to be there. This event could possibly explain why Lloyd Wright became a more forceful designer than did his brother, John Lloyd Wright.

When Frank Lloyd Wright returned from Germany, he had lost a measure of the wonderful clarity that created the best of his work in the previous decade. He shifted to a different, nervously elaborate manner, and by 1914 had produced a fantastically ornamented structure in his Midway Gardens pavilion in Chicago (with John Lloyd Wright and Paul Mueller as assistants). This mood became even fussier by 1916 when he was working on a commission from the emperor of Japan for a Western-style hotel for businessmen visiting Tokyo. At that time, another architect went to work for Wright who, like Griffin, would make his reputation in the Far East instead of in America.

Antonin Raymond was born in Czechoslovakia and educated at the technical college at Prague. He came to the United States in 1910 at the age of twenty-two and almost immediately joined the staff of twenty-four men in Cass Gilbert's office [A17]. He stayed with Gilbert for six years, becoming "assistant superintendent" for the Woolworth Building—with time off for a trip to Europe in 1914.[19] This was Gilbert's most daring and most publicized design.

In 1916, because of a friendship between Raymond's wife and Wright's mistress, they were invited to Taliesin and lived in the heart of Wright's extended family until, with relief, they were permitted to occupy Wright's nearby but abandoned Hillside School (which had

Gilbert: Woolworth
Building, New York,
1911–1913

been subject to decay and vandalism). Work was "practically nonexistent,"[20] and they returned to New York, where Raymond began to work for H. Van Buren Magonigle [A5] before being drafted into the U.S. Army. Soon an officer in army intelligence, he served in Europe until 1919 when he was hired by Wright and went with him to Tokyo.

Raymond worked as Wright's assistant on the Imperial Hotel until 1921, when he set up his own office in Japan. Eventually they quarreled—as was often the case with Wright's stronger employees. One of Raymond's comments on his experience in Wright's office is telling:

Wright: Imperial Hotel, Tokyo, 1914–1922

It did not take long to acquire a certain amount of ability to simulate Wright's mannerisms, his vocabulary as he called it, and I would prepare things for him to work on. I am sure that nobody who ever worked with Wright was ever allowed to design anything by himself, and that all Wright's work—even to the smallest detail—is his, and nobody else's. His inventiveness and energy were simply fantastic. He gave of himself generously, inspiring us who lived in close daily proximity to him. . . . The experience we gained in those Taliesin days was of tremendous value, especially the example of courage which was Wright's and his unswerving fidelity to the vision he had in the face of a country filled with contempt and hatred for him.[21]

Those words "the example of courage" will be echoed in other cases where an employee picked up something remarkably useful from an employer—though not often with the implications in Raymond's use of the words. When Raymond set up practice in Japan he shook off the Wrightian mannerisms and became a leading designer in his own right. In the early 1930s, Raymond's houses were, upon occasion, as advanced as those of Schindler or Neutra. Later, as Hiroshi Yamaguchi says, "His prize winning work, the Reader's Digest Office in Tokyo (1950–1952), was far beyond the Japanese level and shocked Japanese fellow architects."[22] In fact, Raymond, as the employer of such architects as Kunio Maekawa and Junzo Yoshimura, introduced a new branch of connections, a Japanese architectural dynasty. Maekawa, however, had an even more dramatic connection. He had first been employed by Le Corbusier in the late 1920s. Maekawa's own employee, Kenzo Tange, continued the chain.

R. M. Schindler [B13] worked for Wright from 1918 to 1921. Richard Neutra [B19] was at Taliesin in 1924. Schindler and Neutra were both born and educated in Vienna, and both came under the spell of the elderly Otto Wagner, one of Sullivan's and Wright's most vocal admirers in Europe in the period around 1910. Those historians who were influential in promoting what we call "modern" architecture usually illustrated Otto Wagner's Postal Savings Bank in Vienna

Wagner: Postal Savings
Bank, Vienna, 1904–
1906, 1910–1912

Loos: Steiner House,
Vienna, 1910

(1904–1906 and 1910–1912) as a major early monument in the direction of ornament-free architecture that clearly revealed its underlying structure.[23] This bank was just being completed at the time Neutra entered architectural training in that city. Neutra did not actually study under Wagner, but the slightly older Schindler was Wagner's student at the time.[24]

Neutra and Schindler met in 1912 when both were active members of Adolf Loos' circle of friends and admirers. The one building that usually represents Loos' work had just been completed—the naked Steiner House in Vienna (1910), which demonstrated his conviction that ornament of any sort was actually degenerate. The two young men were in close contact with this architect just as he was startling the architectural profession with something extremely strong and quite unusual.

Schindler's early designs reflected the influence of Wagner.[25] But he was eager to see the work of Louis Sullivan in America and, after three years in the office of Hans Mayr and Theodor M. Mayer, he answered an advertisement placed in Austrian newspapers by the Chicago firm of Ottenheimer, Stern & Reichert (although he probably did not know that Harry A. Ottenheimer had worked for Sullivan). After his arrival in the United States, Schindler was able to meet his hero, though by that time Sullivan was alcoholic, bitter, and very difficult. He was almost totally without clients.

Schindler was unable to return home because of the war, so he continued to work for the same firm through 1917; he was hired by Wright early in 1918 because Wright was in need of Schindler's engineering background.[26] Two years later Schindler was in charge of Wright's practice during Wright's absences in Japan. Although at this time he admired Wright intensely,[27] given Wright's office habits, this physically distant "connection" was probably more valuable to Schindler's self-confidence than the close domination that was more common for Wright's employees.

Wright's Barnsdall House (1917–1921) in Hollywood signaled a brief new period of experimentation in Wright's many-staged career. Schindler supervised the construction, with the assistance of Lloyd Wright, and had to make small alterations and modifications in the process. Immediately thereafter, in 1921, Schindler opened his own office in the Los Angeles area. Schindler expressed the same sort of resentment about Wright's indifference to salaries that had angered Marion Mahony Griffin and he had also been puzzled as early as 1919 over the fact that "not one of Wright's men has yet found a word to say for himself" as a designer.[28] Although his break with Wright was gradual, eventually they quarreled heatedly over their respective roles in the firm while the Barnsdall House was being built.

When Schindler sailed for America in 1914, his friend Richard Neutra joined the German artillery, but was allowed to return to Vienna to complete his studies there in 1917 and 1918 with subsequent courses under Karl Moser in Zurich.[29] From 1921 to 1922 Neutra "worked for Mendelsohn,"[30] according to his statement, though it was apparently as a near equal because the two designers jointly won a competition for the Mediterranean Business Center in Haifa.

Wright: Barnsdall House, Hollywood, 1917–1921

Eric Mendelsohn [B13] had set up an exhibition of his extraordinarily prescient sketches in 1919 and received his first commission at that time. This, the Einstein Tower (1919–1924) in Potsdam, was under construction when he and Neutra were working in the same office. Even though Mendelsohn had a long and interesting career in many parts of the world, including the United States, if his fame were to be illustrated by just one design, it would be the Einstein Observatory, built while Neutra was either an employee or a close colleague.

After fruitlessly begging the seldom-paid Schindler for the price of the fare, Richard Neutra finally arrived in the United States in 1923 on his share of the prize money he and Mendelsohn had won. He first found employment in the large office of Holabird & Roche [A19] in Chicago and was able to put this experience to his advantage by writing *Wie Baut Amerika,* which described, for the interested German architects, the way a large American firm operated in the design of huge commercial buildings. Neutra met his hero, Sullivan, as he was dying, poor and neglected.

Mendelsohn: Einstein Tower, Potsdam, 1919–1924

It was at Sullivan's funeral that Neutra met Wright. Wright invited Neutra to Taliesin as a guest. He could not hire Neutra because the then fifty-eight-year-old Wright had no work. This situation was explained in part as a response by potential clients to a scandalous series of liaisons and incidents in Wright's personal life. Neutra's style and personality were nearly as flamboyant as those of Wright and he did not stay long before he left to join Schindler in Los Angeles, where he moved into Schindler's house and shared his studio from 1925 to 1928. Neutra's connection to Wright, therefore, can hardly count at all in terms of passing on design courage as one architect watches another gain power. However, the relationship between Schindler and Neutra in the twenties can best be described as a stimulating friendship. Neutra did not work for Schindler; he worked beside him. But Neutra was as much in conjunction with emerging strong designers, first with Wagner and Loos, then with Mendelsohn, and finally with Schindler, as Wright had been as an employee of Silsbee and of Adler &

Sullivan. A colleague connection can produce the same sparks as those that occur in the more formal employer-employee relationships.

Schindler had already had a number of commissions, three for one client, Dr. P. M. Lovell. He was experiencing a sudden surge of design strength when Neutra joined him. His one major design to be featured in architectural history was the Lovell Beach House (1922–1926) at Newport Beach, California, which was then being completed. Neutra's own most published building followed immediately, the Lovell "Health House" (1927–1929) in Los Angeles, for the same client—a design that influenced Wright in his own design for Falling Water five years later. Neutra's apprentice at that stage carried on the mechanics of fame. Harwell Hamilton Harris [B11] would become featured in the professional journals.[31]

Neutra: Lovell "Health House," Los Angeles, 1927–1929

At the time Neutra visited Wright in 1924, another European-trained employee was in Wright's office. This was the beginning of the bleakest period in Wright's long career, and thus, according to my theory, it was not the time for any employee to gain very much. Although Werner Moser is not a name familiar to most Americans interested in architecture, it is quite well known in Switzerland. The son, grandson, and, in time, father of a famous line of Swiss architects, Werner Moser had come to America because of Wright's great reputation in Europe. In May 1925 he reported back to Europe in an article, "Frank Lloyd Wright und amerikanische Architektur," published in *Das Werk*. From the time he was twenty-seven until he was thirty-two, Moser was in the studios at Taliesin, during those years (1923–1928) when Wright was almost totally without commissions and was famous only as a precursor or father of modern architecture. But if Moser could have gotten little from Wright's design process at this particular time, he had also had other earlier career connections. Like Neutra and Moser's close friend, William Lescaze, he had studied under his father, Karl Moser; then, upon his return to Switzerland in 1928, Moser had a whole series of colleague associations that could have served as catalysts. The results can be seen in his later, stronger designs. Werner Moser was the third of Wright's employees to earn his reputation outside the United States.

During that period of famous designs in the mid-to-late 1930s, not a single one of Wright's apprentices emerged with the power of their master, even though several established excellent regional reputations or became important writers or museum curators. The only architect who worked for Wright at this time who would be judged important enough for inclusion in the Macmillan encyclopedia was Alden Dow [B5]. It happens that Dow was with Wright very briefly, for five months in 1933, two years before the burst of activity created by the commission for Falling Water. He joined Wright when Wright began to take in paying pupils and was working on his utopian scheme "Broadacre City."

Wright was invigorated by a belated but growing recognition of his genius in the architectural press. He had never been forgotten in Europe, but Moser's article, a series of seven articles written by various authors republished in book form in 1925 by H. T. Wijdeveld, editor of the Dutch periodical *Wendingen,* and the following year a book edited by H. De Vries generated renewed interest in his designs. Finally two Americans looked hard at Wright's work (possibly because they knew his reputation abroad). Henry-Russell Hitchcock wrote a monograph on Wright, published in France in 1928, and the editor of *Architectural Record* paid Wright handsomely for the brief but influential series of articles "In the Case of Architecture" published in 1927. Paradoxically, Wright was close to destitution at that time and his career seemed finished. But he began to be invited to lecture, write, criticize, and review his and others' work; he published his autobiography in 1932 and he opened Taliesin as a communal school.

A tremendous generation of fresh publicity, upon occasion, is followed by an architect's best work. This activity sparked a new period of stunning design strength paralleling the 1900–1909 decade. It is tempting to speculate that Alden Dow's presence at that time might have been a variant on the mechanics of fame. However, Dow was extremely wealthy and this was the depths of the Depression. He was able to begin his career and establish his own reputation with a dramatic modern house for himself at the time when most architects were desperately unemployed.

Most of the pupils and employees during the period of Falling Water (1935–1939) at Bear Run, Pennsylvania, and the Johnson Wax Headquarters building (1936–1946) at Racine, Wisconsin, did not become more than regionally well known. Curiously, a number became known as writers. Kevin Lynch's writings and persuasive theories on city planning and architecture, much more than his actual designs, garnered his reputation. Lynch was at Taliesin at a peak time, 1937–1939. Elizabeth Mock—later a curator at the Museum of Modern Art—and Frederick Gutheim were also there, and, like Lynch, are known as authors. The son of the client for Falling Water, Edgar Kaufmann, Jr., was another apprentice who became a major architectural critic and historian. However, there were as many as forty young people at Taliesin at any given time after Wright began his school in 1932, asking $1,000 in tuition (in the Depression) and requiring cooperative work in the kitchen and in the fields where crops and their food were grown.

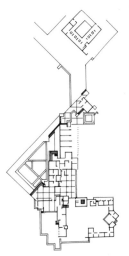

Wright: Taliesin West,
Scottsdale, 1938–1959

Wright's ego continued to inflate at that time, and the distance between master and apprentices became too great for any real two-way communication. Edgar Tafel remembered:

> What a presence he had! He shot out electricity in every direction. . . . Many apprentices were afraid of him. . . . Very, very few of Mr. Wright's students continued the relationship while still retaining their own identity in architecture. . . . Here was the giant to look up to, the creative source to draw from and give form and character and clarity to what, someday, might be my own ideas. I didn't think I could emulate such a giant, or anyone for that matter. I didn't believe my ideas were especially creative or original. . . . On the other hand, I was never one to copy or parrot what I found around . . . Mr. Wright had no hesitation at all about firing anyone—draftsman, contractor, or client.[32]

The other two employees famous enough to be given entries in the Macmillan encyclopedia were, again, foreign-born, and worked for Wright in the late 1940s—while Taliesin West was well underway at Scottsdale, Arizona. The Guggenheim Museum in New York had already been designed but construction had not yet begun. One of these men was Paolo Soleri [C6], who has generated his own cult. Trained in Italy and possessing a Ph.D. from Torino, Soleri worked for Wright from 1947 to 1949. He was both shy in manner and a fiercely self-confident young man in his late twenties, who had as strong a self-image and commitment to reshape society through architecture as did the eighty-year-old master. Some say that Soleri disliked Wright, but affection has little to do with the ability to see oneself in the same role. In the case of Wright's employees and students, it seemed better for the future of the younger person if there was no question of awe or worship. Even while Soleri was with Wright, he began to attract attention through his proposal for an unusual curving envelope of a bridge he called "The Beast" which was exhibited under the aegis of Elizabeth Mock, at the Museum of Modern Art. In 1951 Soleri joined with another Taliesin graduate, Mark Mills, in Arizona, and soon after formed his own and even more ambitious version of that communal institution. As director of the Cosanti Foundation, he planned to create an environment for 3,000 people on 860 acres. Since that time, he has had more than "2,500 students and professionals of all ages, races, and backgrounds . . . in [his] experimental workshops and seminars."[33]

The internationally known Jørn Utzon was also at Taliesin in 1949. But paralleling the experiences of Schindler and Neutra, by that time the Danish-born Utzon had already been strongly influenced by several major figures. In Denmark, after having studied under Steen Rasmussen and Kay Fisker, he had worked for Gunnar Asplund in Sweden and then was employed by Alvar Aalto in Finland. The course of his career perfectly exemplified the mechanics of fame. It is no surprise that he won the international competition for the Sydney Opera House, Australia, in 1956, four years after he had his first commission. He was good, he was talented, he had courage; but he also had the luck to be, not once but repeatedly, in the right place at the right time.

In practice for sixty-six years, Wright, America's greatest architect, had hundreds of employees, pupils, and (early on) close associates. In his own employment by Silsbee and Adler & Sullivan, the mechanics of fame had worked in Wright's favor. However, Wright was exceptional indeed in American history, and the fact that so few of his employees achieved a measure of fame (four outside of the United States) is unusual. The fact that there were so many who did not become more than regionally famous has a great deal more to do with his particular and powerful personality and with the way he ran his office than it has to do with the timing of their association with him. It is clear that, whatever their innate talent, few of these younger people were able to equate their talent with Wright's. They did not receive the boost that Neutra got from Loos, Mendelsohn, and Schindler or that Utzon got from Rasmussen, Fisker, Asplund, and Aalto before encountering Wright. Most of Wright's employees did not experience that transference of design power that can be seen in so many other cases in history.[34]

Wright, however, was fortunate in the timing of his entry into Sullivan's firm and in his own unshakable self-confidence. His future design potential was augmented by his early career experience. The proof of this phenomenon is much more convincing when the careers of other giants like Sullivan, Richardson, Gropius, or Louis Kahn are documented.

SIX

Henry Hobson Richardson

Even though he was born in Louisiana, Richardson's architectural roots were European, in part. Like Neutra, Gropius, Mies, and Eliel Saarinen, Henry Hobson Richardson [A24] served his apprenticeship in Europe. After graduation from Harvard University with a liberal arts degree, Richardson entered the Ecole des Beaux-Arts in Paris in 1860. Henry-Russell Hitchcock's classic biography, *The Architecture of H. H. Richardson and His Times,* gives an extensive verbal picture of the French architectural world of the 1860s.[1] Henri Labrouste was at work on his additions to the National Library; the Louvre was undergoing expansion; and Charles Garnier's Opera House was soon to be begun.

Richardson was accepted into the atelier of Jules-Louis André, the 1847 Grand Prix winner, and it is of some interest to note that at that time, 1860, André entered the competition for the new Opera House. Although his entry did not win, it did indicate a certain amount of self-confidence on André's part at that time. When the outbreak of the American Civil War left the once-wealthy Richardson pressed for funds, André—who had taken over Henri Labrouste's atelier when the famous architect began to devote himself totally to his practice— was able to persuade Théodore Labrouste, Henri's brother, to give Richardson a half-time position. In a letter to his fiancée, dated July 18, 1862, Richardson said: "I am now engaged in studying a Hospice des Incurables pour Hommes et Femmes. It is quite a monument, to contain 2,000 persons—invalids, a large church, nuns and nunnery— in fact, a hospital of first importance, the total cost being two millions of dollars. Monsieur Labrouste has put into my hands the correspondence he had with the government, and told me to study it as I thought best. I rarely see him. I work at his house, but in a room entirely to myself—private. . . . [I] never see a person unless I go into Monsieur Labrouste's room to speak to him . . ."[2]

Year of Birth **Chart 3. Richardson and McKim, Mead & White and their connections.**

1820 + △
EIDLITZ

1830

+
Gambrill

+
R. STURGIS

△
RICHARDSON

1840

BABB
COOK WILLARD   MEAD
McKIM

1850

PRICE   L. Warren
                                    Rutan

C. Eidlitz   +
WELLS   WHITE
MASON   Coolidge

1860 △
Gmelin   CARRÈRE
C. GILBERT   Heins HASTINGS   Brown   SHEPLEY
          BRAGDON LaFarge   HOWARD GREENE
BACON   YORK   MAYBECK   GREENE
HELMLE A. KAHN SAWYER   WARREN BOSWORTH +
1870   WETMORE   POLK
CORBETT   ALDRICH   +
              POPE MORRIS DELANO MIZNER Morgan MULLGARDT

Voorhees   HARMON   HOFFMAN
1880   △   +
       Fouilhoux   Doyle   SHREVE   Severance PURCELL
                                    LAMB VAN ALEN +
                                                    GOODWIN
WALKER FERRISS
1890   I KIESLER   HOFMEISTER
                                      REINHARD   WURSTER
       +
       HARRISON
1900
       BELLUSCHI
                                                   Bernardi
                                            +
                                            Will
1910
+   YEON DE MARS
YAMASAKI

Employment	——————→	NAME ON THE INDEX OF FAME
Partnership	— — — — — — —	Name not on the Index of Fame
Mentorship	····························	
European training	△	Connects to others on another chart +

Mariana Van Rensselaer, Richardson's contemporary biographer, said, "I remember his saying that (at all events for a certain period) he worked half his days at getting his education and only half at earning his living. . . . At one time he acted under Hittorf in superintending the construction of various railroad stations. . . ."[3]

Unfortunately, most of Richardson's correspondence home was lost in a fire, and these years in his career are not well documented, though records of his work at the Ecole have been found. If Richardson did indeed work for Jacques-Ignace Hittorf, this was the time when Hittorf's most famous work, the Gare du Nord (1861–1865), was under construction. Richardson did manage to continue his studies under André while employed and enjoyed telling a "vivid, enthusiastic, humorous" report of his having been jailed for participating in a student protest march over the Ecole's decision to rehire the famous Viollet-le-Duc.[4] Obviously, at this point, Richardson was not in the avant-garde.

Théodore Labrouste had become a specialist in hospitals, and

Richardson undoubtedly regarded him as a major architect. Like his more famous brother, and like André, he had been a Grand Prix winner—the annual award that gave one outstanding student funding for five years' study in Rome. However, in the 1860s he was not designing anything that later critics would consider to be out of the ordinary. If Richardson had any firsthand acquaintance with the more interesting and daring Henri Labrouste, it is not on record, nor does there seem to be any influence from him on Richardson's own work. Nevertheless, Richardson could not but be aware of the work of André's friend and his employer's brother at the time Henri Labrouste was working on the second of his two celebrated libraries—the Bibliothèque Nationale (1862–1868), now considered one of the early monuments in the development of Modern architecture.

All of Richardson's biographers agree that his work was relatively undistinguished for the first few years after his return to the United States in 1865. He settled in New York, worked briefly for a builder, designed fixtures for Tiffany, and then, when he got his first commission through the good offices of a Harvard classmate, shared an office with Emlen Trenchard Littel, an architect who favored a rather bland Victorian Gothic style.[5]

Richardson married early in 1867 and built a house for his bride on Staten Island. That same year he entered the competition for the Equitable Life Assurance Building in New York (1868–1871). Richardson's entry was not successful, but he did manage to meet one of the winning partners—George B. Post (at that time in association with Arthur Gilman [A6] and Edward Kendall). With the help of Post, Richardson—a vital man who loved good food and good company—became a member of the artistic and intellectual society of New York. Post is also credited with introducing Richardson to both of his future partners—Charles Gambrill and John La Farge, the painter.[6]

George B. Post [A14] was on the threshold of his fame: his work on the Equitable Building in 1867 had "a remarkable effect on Post's career."[7] He was a much better designer than his place in textbooks would suggest because the great early historians of American architecture turned their attention so firmly to Chicago rather than New York. He and Gambrill had been in Richard Morris Hunt's atelier together and formed a partnership in 1860, interrupted by Post's service in the National Guard and resumed from 1864 to 1866. Gambrill and Richardson shared a loose partnership from 1867 to 1878, when Gambrill left to practice for the two remaining years of his life with H. Edward Ficken in New York. Post's friend John La Farge teamed with Richardson for the decoration of the interior of Trinity Church in Boston, and he also had some influence on the entire design since it was La Farge who suggested the tower of the Old Cathedral of Salamanca as the prototype for the church's splendid fat tower.

Post was not Richardson's only influential friend, nor his only colleague experiencing the first years of his fame. His neighbor on Staten Island turned out to be Frederick Law Olmsted [A14]. Olmsted was an exciting friend and associate. He listed himself in the New York Directories as "Sailor, Farmer and Landscape Architect. Co-Designer Central Park, Prospect Park, etc."[8] When they met, Olmsted was forty-five to Richardson's twenty-nine. Olmsted had evolved into a landscape architect over a long period of time.[9] He had traveled extensively—to Canton in 1843, in Europe in 1850, and in many parts of the United States. He had been a writer and publisher of note and the co-founder of the Union League Club in New York in 1862. Olmsted and Richardson met in 1867, when Olmsted was several years into his work on the design of Central Park (1857–1876). The Richardson and Olmsted families became close, even vacationing together. When Richardson moved to Brookline, Massachusetts, in 1874, the Olmsteds soon followed and lived a few houses away. Post and Olmsted were in the springtime of their fame and it appears that Richardson's motivating sparks may have come from his colleagues rather than from a connection with an employer earlier—though there was a possibility of something of this sort occurring if he did work for Hittorf.

Richardson's Office

Richardson's first assistant was the eighteen-year-old Charles Rutan. Hired in 1869, he progressed from office boy to partner and one of the principals in Richardson's successor firm, Shepley, Rutan & Coolidge. Given equal ability and ambition, however, a young designer who stays only a few years with a master is more apt to benefit in terms of personal fame than one, like Rutan, who stays on. Financial security and commercial success are not the issues in this study. Fame is of a different nature and has more to do with dynamic design and successful experimentation than with financial success. Rutan would become highly successful in conventional terms, and Shepley, Rutan & Coolidge was a nationally regarded firm. But not one of these three ex-Richardson employees became independently noted in architectural history. They stayed on (as did Elmslie with Sullivan and, as will be seen, those who became additional partners in McKim, Mead & White). They might, or might not, have had the same potential for textbook fame as did the bright employees who struck off on their own, but they let the essential moment to move on slide by.

It was a different story when Richardson hired McKim in June of the following year. At twenty-three, Charles Follen McKim [A24] had an impressive background. His family was well connected. He attended Harvard (for one year) and then began his training in 1867 with Russell Sturgis before leaving for the Ecole. Although McKim's apprenticeship to Sturgis was so eclipsed by his later employment by Richardson that it has never been of much interest, even that connection was at a propitious time in terms of the mechanics of fame.

Russell Sturgis [A10] had nearly as impressive a background as did Richardson. He was the son of a prosperous Maryland merchant. After receiving a degree from the City College of New York, Sturgis worked in the office of the German-trained and Upjohn-trained Leopold Eidlitz [A10] in 1858 at the time of Eidlitz' first major commission, the American Exchange Building (1857–1859) in New York. Then Sturgis left for several years of professional training in Europe, not at the Ecole but in Munich, almost as prestigious a center as Paris. Upon his return, he joined in partnership from 1863 to 1868 with Peter Bonnet Wight just after Wight had won the commission for the National Academy of Design—in competition against entries by Richard Morris Hunt, Leopold Eidlitz, Jacob Wray Mould, and Ware.[10] Thus Sturgis had both an employer connection and a colleague connection in his own early career. Wight had been working for Augustus Bauer and Asher Carter in Chicago in 1858 (apparently missing Dankmar Adler as a co-worker). In 1861 he was in the Union Army when he entered the competition. After sharing an office with Sturgis, by 1871 he had returned to Chicago, where, as a partner in Carter, Drake & Wight, he became John Wellborn Root's acknowledged mentor.

Wight: National Academy
of Design, New York,
1861–1865

During the time that Charles McKim was working for Sturgis, Wight was also in the office. Sturgis was in the process of producing his *own most celebrated design,* Farnam Hall (1869) on the Yale University campus in New Haven. This building demonstrated an unusual simplicity and clarity for the period and is often illustrated in American architectural history surveys. It is curious that these intersections of well-known architects inevitably take place at the time when the building to be *illustrated* in future surveys is being designed and built, even though the architect may produce other praiseworthy buildings that are rarely illustrated. For example, Sturgis designed a series of houses built a few years later in New York that were also atypical and interesting—like Farnam Hall—but these have been generally ignored. Thus McKim was off to a good start; Farnam Hall was the right building in terms of his own potential fame.[11]

His father, Miller McKim, and Frank Furness' father were close friends. The senior Furness advised that the young Charles be sent to study at the Ecole des Beaux-Arts. Charles McKim was admitted to the

Sturgis: Farnam Hall,
New Haven, 1869

Ecole in 1868 and remained in the atelier Daumet for three years. Upon his return, his father had arranged to have him work either for Frank Furness or for Olmsted & Vaux. According to my theory it is possible that McKim would have benefited from either association at that time—although it was a bit late in Olmsted's office and a little early in Furness' office for the torch to have been passed. However, McKim made his own arrangements and returned to Sturgis' office, though only for one month.

When Richardson hired McKim, he was working on the Brattle Square Church (1870–1872) to be built in Boston. As a recently trained Ecole graduate, McKim was placed in charge of the renderings and drawings. This design was seminal, the moment in Richardson's career when his mastery of large simple massing and volumes first appeared. His mature style—reduction of ornament, juxtaposition of large forms, and sense of material and structure—began to emerge. Hitchcock said that "the most professional quality of the work of 1870–72 is probably due in considerable part to the fact that, in McKim, Richardson had at last a properly trained draftsman who, in the French fashion, knew how to translate sketched ideas of plan and façade composition into finished drawings. In the previous years all the drafting was either done by untrained assistants, or by Richardson himself, never a happy arrangement for a designing architect who must deal primarily with his problem as a whole." [12]

> The years between 1870 and 1877 are perhaps the most important of Richardson's career. They established him justly as the most brilliant architect of his day. Later he was to do far more work and far more finished work. But the series of buildings built between the time he was thirty-two and the time he was forty have a freshness that is later lost. . . . [In these works] we can piece together his personal style step by step, almost as he found it himself. . . . The course of his genius was rising. Had his career ended here, books would hardly have been written about his architecture. [13]

"The course of his genius was rising"! Others lend support to the thesis that there are very creative moments in a career—moments when imagination and confidence coincide. What has been missed by most historians is the impact of "rising genius" on others who witness it.

The Richardson scholars—especially Hitchcock, James F. O'Gorman, and Theodore Stebbens—have revealed much about the Richardson office and its methods. The impression one gets is that it was an office where a sort of formal camaraderie existed, very different from that of either Wright or Sullivan, a place where the employees not only felt deep respect for their master but felt comfortable in his

COMPETITIVE DESIGN FOR TRINITY CHURCH, BOSTON.

Plate 3. Early rendering of Richardson's Trinity Church, Boston, 1871. (Van Rensselaer, Henry Hobson Richardson and His Works*)*

presence. But as his fame grew so did the size of the staff, and Richardson was never as close to his later assistants as he was to those who helped him on the Trinity Church project.

McKim did the renderings for the competition entry for Trinity Church (plate 3) in the spring of 1872. At that time Stanford White, fluent draftsman and artist, with no formal training whatsoever in architecture but a year of instruction in drawing by John La Farge, was taken on by Richardson at Olmsted's urging. White learned architecture directly from Richardson. That same year McKim left to form his own firm with William R. Mead and William B. Bigelow. (Mead had been trained in Sturgis' office after McKim left for France; Bigelow was a colleague at the Ecole.) However, McKim continued to do work for Richardson as well, at least until Richardson moved his office to Brookline, Massachusetts, in 1874. Thus both McKim and Stanford White were with Richardson at the most powerfully dramatic time in Richardson's career. Their presence certainly may have contributed to Richardson's surge of design strength, but Trinity Church was designed primarily by Richardson and not by his assistants. The difference between the drawing that won the competition and the finished

TRINITY CHURCH, BOSTON.

Plate 4. Trinity Church, 1872–1877, Boston, as completed. (Van Rensselaer, Henry Hobson Richardson and His Works*)*

Ware & Van Brunt: Memorial Hall, Harvard, Cambridge, 1865–1879

building (plate 4) is striking and graphic proof of the change that occurred at that time—comparable to the sudden improvement already noted in Sullivan's work on the Auditorium a few years later.

Soon after Trinity Church was completed, Richardson was accepted as a leading designer by the profession at large. Stanford White left for a trip to Europe and Richardson named Langford Warren to replace him as chief draftsman. The following year the thirty-year-old MIT graduate George Foster Shepley [A8] moved over from Ware & Van Brunt's office [A9], where he had worked on their one famous building, Memorial Hall. Charles Coolidge [A5] also entered the office after Richardson's first burst of publicity settled into fame. O'Gorman quoted W. A. Langston's description of the office in the 1880s, when Langston was an employee with Shepley and Coolidge:

Richardson designed, the head draughtsman or draughtsmen executed his design, and the junior draughtsmen made from it the working drawings and specifications. There was, of course, much mutual consultation, criticism and advice. . . . [The controlling idea was] often done in bed where the state of his health obliged him to spend much of his time. A plan 2 or 3 inches square embodied his idea. The ultimate result of his study was inked in over the mass of soft pencil marks with a quill pen, and sometimes principal dimensions were figured. That was usually the end of his work on paper.[14]

Richardson lived for only seven years after White left, but it was during that time that he designed his masterpieces—the Ames Gate Lodge, the Stoughton House, the Allegheny County Courthouse and Jail, and, of course, the Marshall Field Building in Chicago. Though these are splendid, full-bodied, and stylistically the most influential of his works, no spectacularly creative architects emerged from the staff—that is, no one the historians would consider a major architect. The names of forty-one men are recorded as having worked for Richardson, proving that not every architect who works for a famous designer will automatically have a claim to fame himself.[15] Many of these employees were MIT graduates, some had been trained at the Ecole, and several, we must assume, were quite talented young men. Naturally most of them worked for Richardson after he had become famous and had expanded his office staff to about twenty people in order to handle the large number of commissions that resulted. Though some of the names are still familiar to architectural historians, Heins and La Farge [A3], for example,[16] none became as famous as McKim and White—not even the three favored employees who took over the projects upon Richardson's untimely death from Bright's disease—Shepley, Rutan, and Coolidge.

George Shepley married Richardson's eldest daughter and their son, Henry Richardson Shepley, eventually became one of the inheritors of his grandfather's practice. Shepley, Rutan & Coolidge finished the work in progress, including the master plan for Leland Stanford University (1883–), the Ames Building in Boston (1892), and the Chicago Art Institute (1897). The firm name changed as major partners changed, and it continued to prosper.[17]

The strongest of their employees, in terms of architectural history, worked for Shepley, Rutan & Coolidge in these first few years, when the firm was experiencing its first overwhelming challenge. The younger of the two Greene brothers, Henry Mather Greene [A15], worked for Shepley from 1891 to 1895 and later stated that Shepley had taken a personal interest in his work. Henry Greene had recently graduated from MIT and had also worked in the Boston firms of William Chamberlain and Stickney & Austin. His brother, Charles Sumner Greene [A15], served his apprenticeship to Winslow & Wetherell, a firm that had passed its prime, but he also worked for Langford Warren—the man who had taken White's position under Richardson.[18] The Greenes established their own celebrated practice in Pasadena, California, and these links to the Richardson line, albeit weak, are noteworthy since so much emphasis has been placed on the importance of the manual training program they had before they entered MIT. It is not just the fact that Henry Greene worked for Shepley, Rutan & Coolidge that matters; he was an employee at the time these architects found themselves as designers and were working on the buildings for which they would be most noted.

John Galen Howard [A8] was employed by Richardson just before he died and continued in the office of Shepley, Rutan & Coolidge working on the Warder House. He left very soon, in 1887, and worked for a year for Caukin & Haas in Los Angeles and then spent one year in Paris. When he returned he worked for McKim, Mead & White from 1889 to 1891, under White's supervision when the firm was completing the last of the early projects that created its fame—the Boston Public Library. In 1891, using money he borrowed from McKim, Howard left for the Ecole des Beaux-Arts.[19] In 1899 he won fourth place in the Hearst-sponsored competition for a plan for the University of California. When the Frenchman who placed first, Emile Bénard, reneged on supervising its implementation, Bernard Maybeck—then a professor and the promoter of the competition—suggested Howard as project architect. Howard moved to California and became head of the school of architecture at the university in 1903. It was at this point that William Purcell and Julia Morgan worked for Howard. Howard had talent; he placed fourth out of 230 applicants in the entrance exams for the Ecole. But it seems fair to point out that he had six years of office training by Richardson, Shepley, and White beforehand. In fact, the time he spent with these three architects—in two cases during significant early years—may be the key to his own successes as well.

Still another early Shepley, Rutan & Coolidge employee eventually established his practice in California, but he was better known in 1910 and 1915 than he is today. Louis Christian Mullgardt [A4], like the Greene brothers, was from St. Louis. He worked for Shepley, Rutan & Coolidge from 1887 to 1891 and just missed Henry Greene and John Galen Howard. But like Howard he moved about, working for architects whose names appear in the lower rankings in the Index of Fame.[20] By 1911 he was featured as an "Architectural Innovator" in the *Architectural Record*, and in 1915 was being celebrated for his most published work, the Court of Ages at the Panama-Pacific Exposition in San Francisco.

The dates of Alfred Hoyt Granger's employment by Richardson are not on record, but, given his age, it had to be late in Richardson's career. He also stayed on with Shepley, Rutan & Coolidge, and had some training at the Ecole as well. By 1898 he was in Chicago, in partnership with his brother-in-law, Charles Sumner Frost.[21] Granger became important enough that he was the single architect chosen for the jury for the $100,000 international competition for the Chicago Tribune Tower in 1922. In 1926 Granger took on a young partner destined for fame, John O. Merrill, the Merrill of Skidmore, Owings & Merrill (SOM). Granger was not only a connector of some importance, he was a major promoter of Wright in his early fame. It is curious, with all this, that Granger is not known for his own designs.

George R. Dean, like Granger a member of what Wright called "The Eighteen" in Chicago, worked for Shepley, Rutan & Coolidge in 1889–1891 before going to Paris. On his return in 1893 he entered their Chicago office. Others of Wright's circle also had had jobs with that branch of the firm.

But, without question, the most famous employees to graduate from Richardson's office were Charles McKim and Stanford White, there when he broke free from his "relatively undistinguished" early design ability.

SEVEN

McKim, Mead & White

Sturgis: Farnam Hall,
New Haven, 1869

William Rutherford Mead [A7] was the commonsensical and prosaic partner of the three, the essential stabilizer for the flamboyance and energy of Stanford White [A17] and the cautious and strong personality of Charles McKim [A24]. Although Mead never worked for Richardson, and thus missed out on McKim's and White's experience, Mead did work for Russell Sturgis [A10] at the right time. After graduation from Amherst College, he entered Sturgis' office in 1868 as a paying student (after McKim had left). He rose rapidly from pupil to paid employee. Although Mead cited Sturgis' chief draftsman, George Babb [A4], as his personal mentor,[1] and not the principal of the firm, these sparks of power—weak or strong—seem to have very little to do with direct personal instruction or friendship. Again, only one of Sturgis' buildings is normally illustrated in surveys of American architectural history, Farnam Hall (1869) at Yale University. A tough and simple building, remarkably undecorated for the time, the hall depended upon its massing and materials rather than abundant applied ornament to give it distinction. This was the building Sturgis worked on while Mead was his employee.

But Mead was impatient with the apprenticeship system and stayed less than two years. He sailed to Europe in 1871 and spent a little over a year in Italy, taking lessons at the Accademia di Belle Arti in Florence. He returned to New York with the intention of resuming his work with Sturgis. But, he said, "Sturgis was out of town, and I made a call upon Mr. McKim in his new offices in this same building. I found that he had a quantity of work to be finished before closing with Gambrill & Richardson, and with the two or three country houses he had on hand, he was very much in need of assistance, so we at once made an arrangement that I should help him out."[2]

Soon Mead and McKim, along with William B. Bigelow, became

partners. In 1874 McKim married Bigelow's sister but, four years later, when the union ended, Bigelow left the partnership. McKim, greatly disturbed by the divorce, went to Europe with Stanford White but stayed just two weeks, leaving White to travel alone. When White returned in 1879, probably intending to rejoin Richardson, he decided to stay in New York and join McKim and Mead in partnership instead.

White proved to be a catalyst for the other partners. McKim had been struggling along since 1872, trying to find his way in the profession. But suddenly the mix was right (and their social connections, though already enviable, were augmented by the éclat of the social lion White). In the first few years of this partnership, McKim, Mead & White produced most of its best-known buildings: the Bell House (1881–1882) in Newport and the Low House (1887) in Bristol, Rhode Island; the Villard Houses (1883–1885) in New York; and the Boston Public Library (1887–1892).

Each of the men contributed to the partnership. Mead, for example, "possessed an instinctive sense of scale and proportion, a grasp of architectural planning, which was of the greatest value to the firm. But he gave little time to designing. . . ."[3] He served as office manager and thus was in close contact with the staff. He also served as the engineer, but "when he spoke up about his partners' work they took strict notice for he was seldom wrong. . . ."[4]

White was the powerhouse and worked on many more commissions than did his partners. His energy and flexibility served as a perfect foil for McKim's meticulous attention to details:

> Many said that White never seemed to stop, and yet there were quiet times. Often, on short winter days, after the light had failed and the lamps were lit, the partners would quietly puff cigars while studying each other's work, commenting and making suggestions.
>
> Compared to White, McKim was a strict traditionalist, sending his assistants to scour the large office library (perhaps as many as 2,500 volumes at its peak) for precedents to corroborate a detail under study. Conversely, White would use any arrangement, material or detail that seemed to suit the situation. . . .[5]

One of the employees was more specific about White's method. Albert Randolph Ross remembered that "White's designs were conceived spontaneously; and he was little bothered by precedent or formulas. In directing his draughtsmen he expressed his thought always with a pencil rather than by discussion. After covering, often-times, yards of tracing paper with alternative suggestions for work under consideration, he would eliminate all but two or three of the most pleasing and turn these over to his draughtsmen to 'do something'—which he would either reject at sight or (if this 'something' was found favorable) use as the basis of future study."[6]

The draftsmen were assigned to one of the principals rather than to the firm as a whole. Charles Herbert Moore wrote a biography of McKim in 1929 that included an appendix with over 500 names of architects employed by McKim, Mead & White. This extensive list supports the assertion that it is the employee who works for an architect at the beginning of his or her fame who is the most apt to become famous. Very few of these 512 names have any significance at all today beyond a local level. Nevertheless, some thirty architects of note were trained in this office, and, with only a few exceptions, they were in the firm while the four buildings listed above were underway.[7] The three principals worked together for less than thirty years; Wright's practice lasted more than twice that long. Walter Gropius and Marcel Breuer, with all the famous students they had at Harvard, did not sire so many celebrated architects.

To attain the kind of fame I have been describing—fame based on one or more powerful designs that heralded a new direction within the profession—the employee must not remain with the famous architect for very long, no more than five years. A study of the later partners in the firm of McKim, Mead & White bears out this assertion. However prosperous and successful they may have been, none of the later partners—William Mitchell Kendall, Teunis van den Bent, Burt Fenner, James Kellum Smith, William S. Richardson, and Lawrence Grant White—built personal reputations. Generally they played it safe. In addition, it should be noted that, of this group, only Kendall had joined the staff before 1887. There is almost always a direct correlation between the date of entry into the office and a later reputation—though by no means does just being an employee at an early date guarantee fame.

Cass Gilbert [A17] was an employee from 1880 to 1883; Arthur Page Brown from 1882 to 1884; Carrère and Hastings [A15] were there from 1883 to 1884 and Henry Bacon [A15] began work for them in 1885. Other employees who have received some attention from architectural historians include Joseph Wells [A3], there at the beginning. York and Sawyer [A6], Magonigle [A5], and Arthur Loomis Harmon [B6] were there later, in the 1890s. John Russell Pope [A15] and Wallace Harrison [B16] were even later, Harrison very late, but with several other employers of note.

Taking these better-known employees in order of their hiring, the name of Joseph M. Wells [A3] is known primarily to architectural historians. He had begun his training in the office of Clarence Luce, who was only one year older than Wells. Wells may have been a student of Richard Morris Hunt [A22] at some point, but he was an employee of Peabody & Stearns [A6] just as the firm completed the Mutual Life Insurance Company Building (1874–1875) in Boston. He was hired by McKim and Mead before Stanford White joined the firm in 1879. Wells had a difficult personality, reserved and shy, cynical yet witty, but he seems to have been accepted by the three partners on an almost equal footing. Wells had been in the office for about four years when the commission for the Villard Houses (1883–1885) was received from a wealthy relative of McKim's. The fact that Wells suggested that the building be modeled on a High Renaissance Roman palazzo has been on record for some time, an unusual occurrence since it is quite rare to find information about an employee's contribution to a major design. Both McKim and White were absent from the office much of that year and White had left "Wells, Cass Gilbert, Clark, Harlow, Whidden, Chamberlain and Hazlett" in charge of his work.[8] Wells and the client, Villard, became fast friends. The Villard Houses were both bold and understated, dignified in contrast to the exuberance of the High Victorian styles and imitation Loire Valley chateaux then going up in New York City. They were seminal in the introduction of a refined Renaissance Revival into the United States. Wells was apparently offered a partnership but became ill and died at the age of thirty-six. Whatever Wells' role was in fact, the Villard Houses established McKim, Mead & White in the forefront of academically correct design and were the first of this type not only in America, but possibly in the world.

McKim, Mead & White: Villard Houses, New York, 1883–1885

In 1880, also at the very beginning of the partnership, the bouncy and self-assured Cass Gilbert [A17] was employed as part of "a ten-man firm, including the partners."[9] Gilbert had been apprenticed at seventeen to an architect in St. Paul, Minnesota, A. M. Radcliff, and then attended the two-year program at MIT in a class of thirteen students.[10] After graduation in 1880, and with letters of introduction written by William Ware, Gilbert had hoped to work for a major London architect. But his trip to Europe provided him with no offers, and he was back in America the same year. On his return, he could have sought employment with one of the large and successful firms like George B. Post & Sons or the Eidlitz office, and perhaps he did. But, instead, he joined a very young group, McKim, Mead & White, who had not done much except a bit of innovative residential work. Gilbert stayed with McKim, Mead & White for three years and then returned to St. Paul to set up practice.

McKim, Mead & White: Boston Public Library, Boston, 1887–1898

Even though they temporarily take us away from McKim, Mead & White as the subject, Gilbert's career and his own employees' careers serve as further illustration of the thesis. In 1884 he joined in partnership with James Knox Taylor, an MIT classmate, who may have been employed by George B. Post [A14]. Their partnership dissolved in 1892, and shortly thereafter Taylor became the supervising architect of the U.S. Treasury Department.[11] From 1897 to 1912 he was in charge of the construction of all customhouses, post offices, and federal buildings (a rather surprising honor for a relatively untried architect).

Gilbert won the commission for the splendid Minnesota State Capitol (1895–1903) at the age of thirty-six. Two years later another competition, the U.S. Custom House in New York (1897–1907), was awarded to Gilbert; the New York building was more significant for Gilbert's rise to fame because, oddly enough, state capitols constructed after the Civil War never interested the fame makers or the contemporary professional press as much as did buildings in major cities. Soon after Gilbert won the Custom House, he began to work on the Broadway-Chambers Building, which also was featured in the press at the time.

Gilbert had been in McKim, Mead & White's office just as these designers developed into surprisingly fresh inventors of a new stylistic direction. Gilbert was a superb follower of that direction. His most famous employee, Harvey Wiley Corbett [A11], was with him from 1901 to 1903 when Gilbert began to achieve his national reputation.[12] Corbett's name may not seem especially famous today; however, he was one of the thirty-three architects chosen by the editors of the 1968 *Encyclopaedia Britannica* to represent the most important designers in America even though he was never favored by the major architectural historians responsible for establishing most of our famous names. Gilbert employed Corbett just after Corbett returned from training at the Ecole des Beaux-Arts (an opportunity that Gilbert himself missed).

Gilbert: Custom House, New York, 1897–1907

Corbett set up his own practice in 1903 and, as is usual for most young designers, had a slow start. He was a pleasant, friendly man, highly respected by his professional colleagues and he took on the added challenge of conducting an atelier in New York in order to expose young American architects to the methods of the Ecole des Beaux-Arts. Over the years he had several partners. Frank Helmle [A5] had been a McKim, Mead & White employee later than Gilbert, in 1890, after that firm had grown very large. In 1912 Helmle, Corbett & William H. MacMurray (business partner) was established. Four years later the firm's Bush Terminal Building (1916–1917) "marked Corbett's debut as an influential designer and theorist."[13] Wallace Harrison was in Corbett's atelier at that time, while working for McKim, Mead & White during the day. Harrison is the final subject of this chapter, but for now it should be noted that Harrison would re-place Helmle when Helmle retired and was Corbett's partner during the first few years that they worked on Rockefeller Center. Corbett rose to such prominence that he not only was involved in Rockefeller Center, but in 1929 was named a director of planning for the 1933 Chicago World's Fair, sharing the overall organizational problems with Raymond Hood, Paul Cret, and Arthur Page Brown, Jr.

While McKim, Mead & White's employee, Cass Gilbert, is the subject at hand, two other Gilbert employees deserve mention. Antonin Raymond, Wright's employee who would become famous in Japan, was mentioned earlier as having worked for Gilbert on the Woolworth Building (1911–1913) in New York, Gilbert's internation-ally discussed skyscraper, the one most people associate with his name. By the time of its construction Gilbert's staff had grown to over a hundred. Hugh Ferriss [A8] included his work for Gilbert at that time in his biographical data. If neither Gilbert nor Ferriss has a par-ticularly famous name today outside of the profession, it is due to the powerful propaganda of the architectural historians who documented the rise of Modern architecture before the 1960s and who demanded glass and exposed steel and also to a lack of recognition from the Mu-seum of Modern Art in the 1930s. At one time Ferriss and Corbett were very well known indeed in America for their part in the develop-ment of the skyscraper. Ferriss had a degree in architecture from Washington University in St. Louis. He started working for Gilbert in 1912, one year after graduation, and stayed until 1915. Ferriss' talent as a renderer was as great as that of Marion Mahony Griffin, Harvey Ellis, or Alexander Jackson Davis, and he was so much in demand by other architects to do their presentation drawings that, rather than becoming a building designer himself, he established his name as the primary artist of the American skyscraper.

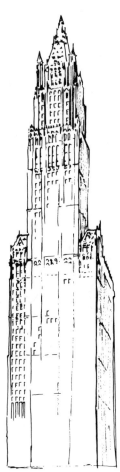

Gilbert: Woolworth Building, New York, 1911–1913

Before Cass Gilbert left McKim, Mead & White, the firm had be-gun to expand. In 1882 and 1883, while the most important of the early commissions were beginning, several young designers were employed who later founded their own successful firms, or in some cases, became well-known authors, critics, and professors.[14] Two more graduates of the Ecole des Beaux-Arts arrived in the office in 1883. John Mervin Carrère [A15] and Thomas Hastings [A11] met as co-workers in the office during the time that the Villard Houses were being built. Within two years Carrère and Hastings formed their own partnership when they won the sumptuous commission for an enor-mous resort hotel complex in Florida from Flagler, a member of the congregation of Hastings' father's church. Carrère was twenty-nine and Hastings was twenty-seven when they began work on the Ponce

Carrère & Hastings:
Ponce de León Hotel, St.
Augustine, 1885–1889

de León, the Alcazar, and the Casa Monica in St. Augustine. These hotels were to be the first major designs in a somewhat Spanish idiom (mixed with Byzantine styling) and they were well covered in contemporary journals. Their major assistant for this seminal project was the twenty-five-year-old Bernard Maybeck [A15].

Maybeck was the son of a New York City woodcarver who apprenticed him to the furniture firm that was his own employer and then sent him to Paris to study "in the studio of the owner's brother."[15] Instead, Maybeck entered the Ecole des Beaux-Arts; he was in the same atelier that Richardson had attended long before. Maybeck's roommate in Paris was Thomas Hastings. Maybeck was a delightfully offbeat sort of person, talented and well-loved. Carrère & Hastings hired him soon after beginning the first job, the buildings that launched the partnership—still another instance of an early connection, though this was more nearly one of colleagues than of employers and employee.

When the hotel was completed, Maybeck moved to Kansas City in 1889 and joined briefly in a loose partnership with Ambrose James Russell, another classmate from the Ecole. Next he was associated for a short time with the English-trained Ernest Coxhead in California and with McKim, Mead & White–trained A. Page Brown on the Crocker Building (1891) and Brown's building for the Chicago World's Columbian Exposition.[16] From 1894 to 1903 Maybeck was a professor at the University of California, where he expanded his course in descriptive geometry into a department of architecture. At the outset, in 1894, he also conducted seminars in his home. Harvey Wiley Corbett's very first association with a potentially famous architect had been as one of the students in these informal seminars that Julia Morgan also attended before she became the first woman to enter the Ecole des Beaux-Arts. Maybeck's first commission was Hearst Hall (1899) on the Berkeley campus and it was through him that Julia Morgan made the spectacular contact that resulted in her major Hearst commissions.[17]

Maybeck's work, like his career, was extraordinary and varied, but always forceful. Even though his Hearst Hall and the First Church of Christ Scientist (1912) were unique, his Palace of Fine Arts for the San Francisco Panama-Pacific Exposition (celebrating the opening of the Panama Canal in 1915) has become a major landmark, and his numerous residences in the San Francisco area bear his distinctive personal stamp, his national reputation came very late in his life. Corbett and Morgan seem to be his best-known pupils or employees, although there was significant colleague interaction during his career.

Carrère & Hastings had other employees of note—in fact, during their lifetimes they were more famous than Maybeck. Almost immediately after receiving the hotel commissions, they won the major trophy of their career, the New York Public Library (competition won in 1897; built 1902–1911). They were now also leaders in this "new" style, in direct competition with their employers of four years earlier, McKim, Mead & White. Two firms spun out of their office through employees at that time: Shreve, Lamb & Harmon [B10] and Delano & Aldrich [A11].

In 1906 they hired a young Cornell instructor, Richmond H. Shreve; in 1911, the year the library opened, a young graduate of Williams, Columbia, and the Ecole, William Frederick Lamb, joined the firm. Shreve and Lamb proved to be an exception to the rule that those who stay on in an office and become partners will rarely make an independent name for themselves. In this case, they inherited the firm when Hastings retired in 1920 (Carrère died in 1911). But, like Shepley, Rutan & Coolidge, they changed the firm's name. Then when Arthur Loomis Harmon, a McKim, Mead & White graduate, joined the partnership in 1929, he was able to activate his partners' latent design conviction. In 1930 Shreve, Lamb & Harmon began work on the Empire State Building.[18]

Carrère & Hastings: New York Public Library, New York, 1902–1911

In 1901 Carrère & Hastings hired William Adams Delano and in 1902 Chester Holmes Aldrich, an Ecole graduate. Again, this was while the New York Public Library was the commission at hand. Delano left briefly to attend the Ecole des Beaux-Arts, and one year later Delano and Aldrich formed a partnership of their own, with an important commission, the Walters Art Gallery (1904) in Baltimore. Delano & Aldrich became important enough to become another rival to McKim, Mead & White, and to Carrère & Hastings as well.[19] The architects of Grand Central Station and the Chrysler Building were among the employees of Delano & Aldrich. But one of the most interesting employees was with them quite late, too late in terms of the theory I have been exploring. This was William W. Wurster [B10], who worked for the firm from 1923 to 1924. Wurster is the first exception to the rule to surface thus far and one of the very few who seems to have found his power without the advantage of "timing." During high school Wurster worked for E. B. Brown in Stockton, California. From 1920 to 1922, after graduation from the University of California under Howard, he was employed by Charles Dean in Sacramento. Although Delano & Aldrich are in the textbooks, they are hardly "famous" and were not at the threshold of their reputations when Wurster was their employee. Wurster set up his own office in 1929, but even by 1927 he had received notice in an issue of *House Beautiful* and its award for "Carpenter architecture," for his Gregory farmhouse. By 1944 Wurster was dean at MIT and instrumental in Alvar Aalto's commission there. By 1950 he was head of architecture at his own alma mater.[20]

This has been a long detour from McKim, Mead & White in 1883, by way of Gilbert, Carrère & Hastings, and their employees. Even though these sidetracks may be confusing, they are germane to my thesis. Let me emphasize again that it usually was the first major work—the first work to be heralded in architectural histories—that spawned strong designers. White left Richardson only two years after Trinity Church was completed and Richardson's fame was established. In ten years not only had McKim, Mead & White begun the Boston Public Library and Villard Houses, but Carrère & Hastings had also had their most important commissions. Soon Gilbert would be soaring to fame. By the time of the great New York skyscrapers, nearly every one of their major designers had roots that traced back to either the early years of McKim, Mead & White or to Upjohn and Eidlitz.

I want to say again that the kind of fame I have been discussing has little to do with financial success; at any one time there are hundreds of prosperous big firms that are rarely mentioned in textbooks. What I am talking about results from the kind of originality and boldness that attracts the attention of critics and historians and has little to do with financial success. Of course, the converse is not necessarily true; several of the architects mentioned in textbooks became quite wealthy in their practices.

Although the number of McKim, Mead & White employees destined for fame began to thin after 1883—even before the Boston Public Library cemented the fame of the firm in 1887–1898—several are worthy of discussion. Henry Bacon [A15] left the University of Illinois in 1884 and entered the office in 1885. Bacon was talented enough that while working for McKim, Mead & White, he won a Rotch Travelling Scholarship and left in 1889 for two years' travel in Europe, where he found a fellow architect with whom he would explore the villages and monuments. Though Henry Bacon was only three years his senior, Albert Kahn [A15] felt that Bacon became his teacher, mentor, and guide to architectural understanding—a colleague-colleague connection.[21] Henry Bacon returned to McKim, Mead & White from 1891 to 1897 and served as McKim's representative on site at the World's Columbian Exposition. Bacon's name entered architectural history when McKim secured the commission for the Lincoln Memorial for his protégé—a project that won Bacon the Gold Medal, the highest honor of the American Institute of Architects.[22]

Other McKim, Mead & White employees of note include Paul Gmelin[23] and John Galen Howard [A8], whose later pride in his posi-

Shreve, Lamb & Harmon: Empire State Building, New York, 1930–1933

Price: Chateau Fronte-
nac, Quebec, 1892

Goodhue: Nebraska
State Capitol, Lincoln,
1920–1932

Howells & Hood: Chi-
cago Tribune Building,
Chicago, 1922–1926

tion under White indicates that of all his heroic employers it was then, in 1889, that he received whatever design power he had. In 1890 Edward P. York was hired and, in 1891, Philip Sawyer. They stayed for several years before they formed their partnership in 1898. Like Delano & Aldrich, York & Sawyer [A6] was a prestigious firm in terms of the assessment of contemporaries though not particularly important to historians.[24] At about this same time H. Van Buren Magonigle [A5] worked for McKim, Mead & White after having moved from office to office—Rotch & Tilden, Calvert Vaux, and Charles C. Haight had employed him. He was thirty-seven before he established his own practice. All of these slightly later employees showed little of the creative force of Gilbert or Carrère & Hastings, although there are some exceptions. Arthur Loomis Harmon [B6], the lead designer of the Empire State Building (1931), was employed in 1902 and was the principal assistant for the expansion of the Metropolitan Museum of Art.

John Russell Pope [A15], the son of an artist, first worked for Bruce Price [A13] in about 1890 at the time Price was producing his most famous works. Tuxedo Park (1885–1900), New York, and the Windsor Station (1888–1889) in Montreal were being finished and the Chateau Frontenac Hotel in Quebec (1892) was about to be undertaken.[25] Pope then studied at Columbia and cited William Ware as an early mentor. An outstanding student, Pope was awarded a McKim scholarship to the American Academy in Rome in 1895 and upon his return became McKim's assistant in the atelier McKim conducted for Columbia University. He won a second scholarship, the Schermerhorn, in 1896, which allowed him to attend the Ecole.

On his own by 1903, Pope's practice in time became international in scope (though he was either ignored or derided by the writers who helped create Modern architecture). Both the Jefferson Memorial (1934–1941) and the National Gallery of Art (1937–1941) in Washington were completed after his death.[26]

Finally, Wallace Harrison [B16] was a McKim, Mead & White employee who was much too late in terms of receiving any direct inspiration from them. When he was employed, in 1916, McKim had been dead for seven years and White for ten. Only Mead, the least colorful of the original partners, was alive. Three years later Harrison left to enter the Ecole des Beaux-Arts but returned to the firm and then won the Rotch Travelling Scholarship, which took him back to Europe. During his stay in New York he had attended night classes conducted by Harvey Corbett, and Corbett was on the Rotch jury the year Harrison was chosen.

When Harrison returned the second time, he became a drafts-

Rockefeller Center archi-
tects: Rockefeller Center,
New York, 1929–1938

man for Bertram Grosvenor Goodhue [A18], discussed later as part of
the Renwick dynasty. But it is important to note that, even though
Goodhue's fame had been initiated much earlier, this was a late burst
of creativity—a variant on the mechanics of fame that will be seen
again with the T. U. Walter–Richard Morris Hunt connection and with
Walter and Strickland. This was the time of Goodhue's Nebraska State
Capitol, nationally one of the most celebrated buildings of the decade.
Then Harrison worked for Raymond Hood [B19], also discussed later.
Hood, it happens, was trained in the office of Cram & Goodhue, the
year of its first commission of note. But Harrison was with Hood at the
first hour of Hood's own rise to fame, for it was Hood's design that won
the international competition for the Chicago Tribune Building in
1922. Harrison worked for Hood from 1924 to 1926 while the building
was under construction. Next he was in the office of Harvey Wiley
Corbett [A11].

Thus, though Harrison was too late to participate in the early
success of his employers at McKim, Mead & White, he had two other
chances to watch an architect find his power, first with Goodhue and
then with Hood. Harrison had an astonishing sense of timing. He
joined Corbett, Helmle & MacMurray in 1927. Within two years they
were working on Rockefeller Center, in concert with several others
including Reinhard & Hofmeister,[27] Benjamin Wistar Morris, and Raymond Hood. When Hood died in 1934 there was a general realign-
ment of partners, and Harrison joined in partnership with Hood's former partner, Jacques André Fouilhoux.

Fouilhoux has never received much attention from historians or
the press, but he is quite interesting. Educated at the Sorbonne and
the Ecole Centrale des Arts et Manufactures (Eiffel's and Jenney's
school), he came to the United States in 1904 at the age of twenty-five,
and thus had some working experience behind him. He was employed
by Albert Kahn on Kahn's first highly publicized commission, the
Packard Motor Car factory, from 1905 to 1908.

Kahn: Packard Motor
Car Plant, Detroit,
1905–1908

In 1909 Fouilhoux moved to Portland, Oregon, where he practiced for a time with Morris Whitehouse. From 1916 to 1919 Fouilhoux
was in partnership in New York with Frederick Augustus Godley, a
Yale, MIT, and Ecole graduate. In 1920 he went to work for Raymond
Hood, and was with Hood from the time of his explosive publicity for
the Chicago Tribune Building through Hood's growing acceptance
and mastery of the modern idiom, like the McGraw-Hill Building
(1929–1931) by Godley, Hood & Fouilhoux. He was an engineer but
was present so often when his employer or partner took a giant step
forward that it makes one wonder if he may not have served as the

catalyst. In partnership with Harrison from 1935 to 1945, he not only worked on the Rockefeller Center but helped to design the Trylon and Perisphere (1939), the symbols of the New York World's Fair.

Max Abramovitz [C5] had degrees from the University of Illinois and Columbia and attended the Ecole on a fellowship in 1932 and 1933. He was a protégé of Corbett's protégé, Frederick Kiesler.[28] In 1934 he went to work for Corbett, Harrison & MacMurray and continued with Harrison & Foilhoux for seven years.[29] When Fouilhoux was killed in a building accident, Harrison invited Abramovitz into partnership. Harrison & Abramovitz were awarded the supervision of the United Nations Building (1949–1950), which, even without their work on Lincoln Center (1959–1966), would have assured their place in American architectural history. One of their employees during World War II was Minoru Yamasaki [C9].[30]

Edward Durell Stone [B10] had begun his career in the office of Shepley, Coolidge & Bulfinch in 1926. The following year he also won a Rotch Travelling Scholarship. When he returned in 1929 he joined Schulze & Weaver while the firm was working on the Waldorf Astoria Hotel. By 1930 he had moved over to Corbett's firm, then beginning to play a part in Rockefeller Center. In his autobiography Stone proudly notes that, in a quarrel among the Rockefeller associates, he sided with Corbett and Harrison against Hood; since several of his biographers state that he worked for Hofmeister and for Hood & Fouilhoux, it can be supposed that he was in fact a minor draftsman for the group. His memory of supporting Corbett and Harrison was important to him, however, and in 1934 he was officially in their employ.

Stone was trying his hand at private practice in 1935, and at that time employed Gordon Bunshaft [C9],[31] another Rotch Travelling Scholarship winner. Stone's Mandel House (1935) in Mt. Kisco, New York, caught the eye of the Board of the Museum of Modern Art. Harrison was a member of the board and suggested Stone as the designer for their proposed building, to serve in partnership with Philip Goodwin [B7], an older architect who was also a member of the board.[32] Stone was also supported by the museum president, A. Conger Goodyear, for whom Stone was designing a vacation house in Old Westbury, Long Island, in 1935–1936. Bunshaft left to join Skidmore and Owings in 1937, and Stone's fame was assured when the Museum of Modern Art was finished in 1939.

In 1964 Wallace Harrison and Max Abramovitz set up independent practices and continued to prosper, with Harrison given the chairmanship of the 1964 New York World's Fair. However, their most celebrated designs were the early ones done in partnership, and it

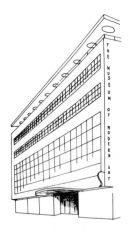

Stone & Goodwin:
Museum of Modern Art,
New York, 1936–1939

was then that their most famous employees emerged from their office—just as had been the case for so many others in American history.

Many of the names of other employees are known locally or even regionally. But none are as well known as those discussed above.[33]

EIGHT

Latrobe and His Descendants

From the time of the American Revolution to the period of the Civil War, the connection of one famous architect to another more closely resembles a family tree than a web. Nevertheless, the fact remains that when the torch was passed from an architect to an employee, it was usually at the time that the first significant design was the project at hand. The exceptions were similar to a few thus far noted. The same sort of response occasionally occurred when two colleagues worked together at the time when one proved himself noteworthy, or, in a few cases, during a late flash of power after a relatively long period of less interesting designs. The Bulfinch line had several branches, eventually leading to Town & Davis and to such architects as Russell Sturgis (and thus to McKim and Mead). The Latrobe line was more direct, through Strickland to Walter to Hunt, and from Hunt's five students to the whole interconnected fabric of the best-known architects of the latter half of the nineteenth century.

Benjamin Henry Latrobe [A23] was the son of a prominent English Protestant minister who was superintendent of the institutions in Ireland and Great Britain controlled by the Moravian church. Latrobe's mother was a Pennsylvanian Moravian who had been teaching in England in one of the boarding schools supported by the church, all of which maintained extremely high educational standards. In the past there has been much speculation about Latrobe's background, but Samuel Wilson, Jr., has provided much needed information on that subject:

> In September 1776, Latrobe [at the age of twelve] left England to study at the Moravian Pedagogium at Niesky in German Silesia, and then at the Moravian seminary at Barby in Saxony. An unconfirmed family tradition states that he spent three years at the University of Leipzig and served briefly in the army of Frederick

Year of Birth   **Chart 4. The Latrobe line.**

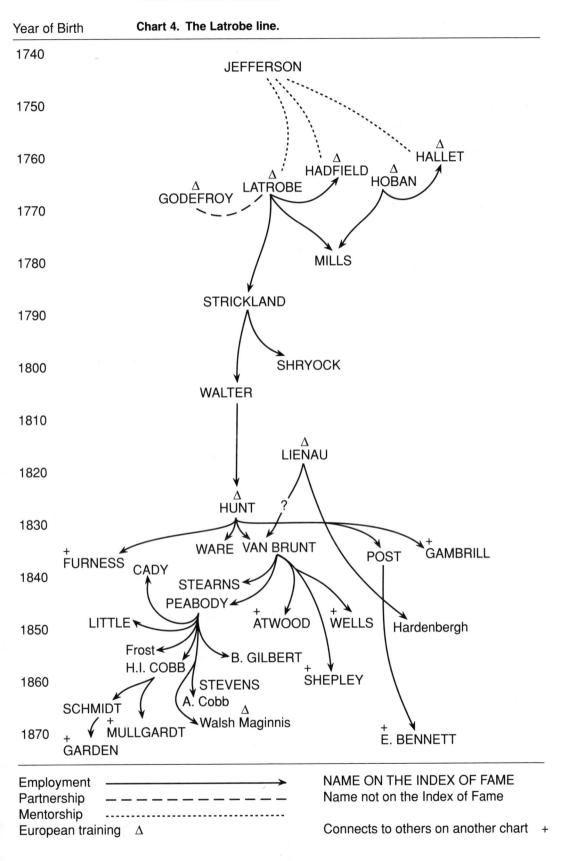

Employment	—————————→
Partnership	— — — — — — — — —
Mentorship	··················
European training	Δ

NAME ON THE INDEX OF FAME
Name not on the Index of Fame

Connects to others on another chart   +

the Great. . . . While still in Germany, Latrobe showed an interest in engineering, observing the levee systems and flood control works along the Elbe and other rivers. Much of his final year abroad was spent traveling in Germany, France, and Italy, a trip that strengthened his idea of becoming an architect and that also influenced his later works. Latrobe returned to England in 1784 an accomplished mathematician, linguist, musician, watercolorist, writer, and advocate of political and social reform.[1]

However, it is still not certain that Latrobe did or did not work for the engineer John Smeaton, designer of the Eddystone Lighthouse (1756–1759), canals, bridges, windmills, and watermills. Smeaton's fame was established long before Latrobe could have been his employee. But whether or not he was employed by that famous man, Latrobe's interest and competence in such engineering projects as the Philadelphia Waterworks (1798) and his important canal and dock designs indicate an excitement about engineering on his part.

Latrobe did work for the English architect Samuel Pepys Cockerell. Latrobe described the projects Cockerell completed while he was in that office: "While I conducted Mr. Cockerell's office in 1791 and 92 he was surveyor to the Admiralty, and built the long new range of buildings then carried up. . . . He also built the great range of Stores and Slaughterhouses belonging to the Victualling board at Deptford."[2] Like Théodore Labrouste, Richardson's employer, Cockerell worked primarily on government commissions, but unlike Labrouste he was described as "memorable for originality rather than quality and he can hardly be said to have developed a consistent style. . . . [He was] clearly dissatisfied with the dull good manners of later eighteenth-century architectural taste but lacked the large vision or the scholarship to establish an alternative within the framework of the classical tradition. His principal buildings, then, are not the dull Admiralty House, Whitehall . . . but bizarre follies such as the neo-Norman Tickencote church, or the neo-Indian Sezincote."[3] Even though Cockerell was not particularly good, Latrobe may well have been influenced by his daring.

In 1791 Cockerell founded an exclusive dinner club for architects that was limited to twelve members. The youngest of the twelve was John Soane.[4] Scholars have combed Latrobe's papers for mention of Soane and found nothing, even though Latrobe's buildings show the influence of Soane's best work. The only positive statement that can be made in terms of Latrobe's "connections" is that he did work for Cockerell, an inventive and strong designer, and that he obviously knew the work of the more famous Soane at the time Soane had begun work on the Bank of England (1788–1833), his most famous project.

Latrobe opened an office in London and built up a practice, worked on the building of the Surrey Canal, and acted as surveyor of public offices in London. Distress over the death of his first wife led him to immigrate to America in 1795, where he first settled in Richmond, Virginia. Tall, handsome, charming, and generous, the highly sophisticated Englishman quickly became a member of the local society. He won his first commission, the Richmond Penitentiary (1797), in competition and proved his credentials as an engineer and architect.

Latrobe soon paid a visit to Pennsylvania to meet his maternal relatives, the Antes family, and to establish his claim to the land that had been left to him at his mother's death. While he was visiting Philadelphia, he attended a dinner party where he was encouraged to sketch his idea for the planned Bank of Pennsylvania (1799–1801). That brief sketch won him the commission that would establish him as America's finest architect. In December 1798 he moved from Richmond to Philadelphia, not only to supervise the construction of the bank but to design a public water system (1799–1801) for the malaria-ridden city and to design Sedgeley (1799), a Neo-Gothic house—which reminds us that, four years later, his former employer, Cockerell, also was an early experimenter in the Romantic mode. Sezincote, designed for Cockerell's brother-in-law in 1803, was an odd combination of a classic pavilion, an onion dome, Indian pinnacles, and large windows with quasi-Gothic fanlights—stylistically ahead of the much more famous Brighton Pavilion done later by Nash for the prince regent.[5] Unfortunately, Latrobe's Sedgeley did not survive long enough to permit a close comparison to the later building by Cockerell, but its existence does prove that Latrobe was receptive to his employer's desire for originality.

Latrobe met Thomas Jefferson [A23] in 1798. Jefferson had a lifelong interest in architecture and was a fine designer in his own right. He was impressed with Latrobe's ability. When he became president in 1801, he personally assumed almost total control over federal building projects and was able to give Latrobe some extremely important commissions. His first task for Latrobe was "to design a great covered dry dock for the Navy. Although Congress failed to make the appropriation for its construction, Jefferson was so impressed with Latrobe's design and obvious ability that in March 1803 he appointed Latrobe as surveyor of the public buildings of the United States and charged him with the completion of the Capitol (1803– 1817)."[6] Even though Latrobe was quarrelsome about architectural matters and had a considerable ego about his professional training and status, he apparently respected Jefferson's own talent; they became friends and colleagues.

Jefferson had spent many years working out the final appearance of his home, Monticello, in Charlottesville, Virginia. Before he went to France, Jefferson relied upon illustrated publications to learn the fundamentals of architecture, especially the works of Serlio and Palladio. In France he had firsthand acquaintance with much more advanced designs and "also made the acquaintance of several of the great contemporary architects in France. From these men he gained a clearer idea of the methods of the practicing professional architect; and from this time on he used the freer medium of the pencil [rather than the unprofessional use of the pen], and the more exacting system of attaining proper proportions by means of coordinate paper."[7] This makes it clear that Jefferson did not simply admire buildings but also entered the architects' studios to observe the techniques of the profession. In his correspondence, he recorded his impressions of those Parisian buildings he admired: Ledoux's city gates and the Pantheon-like domed wheat market, la Halle au Blé (1782–1787), with its dazzling quantities of glass set in an umbrella of wooden ribs, designed by Jacques G. Legrand and Jacques Molinos. He also wrote home about his admiration for Pierre Rousseau's Hôtel de Salme (1781–1810), which he later used as the model for the second story of Monticello. In each case, the French architect was at that moment being celebrated for his first highly publicized work.

It is perhaps stretching the point to claim that Jefferson himself had an experience much like those we have been noting. At that time, he not only was inspired by these French architects—he in turn inspired other young architects. Both John Trumbull and Charles Bulfinch visited Jefferson in Paris and were advised by him on architectural matters. George Hadfield of England and Etienne Hallet of France became his protégés. And from that time on Jefferson was a much more daring and accomplished designer. A radical and powerful change occurred in his design ability during his stay in Paris, and this can be seen in two drawings of the façade of Monticello: the first done in 1771, the second in 1803, drawn by Robert Mills (plates 5 and 6).

In about 1801 or 1802 the young Robert Mills [A22] spent an extended period as a guest at Monticello when it must have been in an uproar of rebuilding. At that time, after considerable reevaluation, Jefferson was taking down parts of the first design and constructing the brilliant final solution. Thus Mills was in a position to benefit in

Plate 5. Jefferson's drawing of Monticello before he went to France. (Courtesy of the Coolidge Collection, Massachusetts Historical Society)

Plate 6. Robert Mills' drawing of Monticello as revised. (Courtesy of the Coolidge Collection, Massachusetts Historical Society)

terms of his own design courage. Jefferson recommended Mills to Latrobe, who then employed him for about five years.

Mills had been educated at Charleston College in South Carolina and he had been working for James Hoban [A13] in Washington at the time he met Jefferson.[8] In 1792 Hoban had won the Jefferson-sponsored competition for the design of the President's House (the White House) and supervised its construction until 1800.[9] Hoban also took over as supervisor of the building of the Capitol in 1798 when George Hadfield was dismissed because he was unable to work with its amateur designer, William Thornton [A18]. Not only was Robert Mills in the right place at the right time in terms of Jefferson's design career—he was with Hoban on the only assignments that tie Hoban's name into American architectural history.[10]

Hoban: President's House, Washington, 1792

Even more impressive was Robert Mills' employment by Benjamin Latrobe at about the time when the Bank of Pennsylvania was completed. Jefferson had given Latrobe the major commissions of the Capitol and the additions of porticoes to the White House. While Mills was still his assistant, Latrobe began work on his finest extant design, the Baltimore Cathedral (1804–1818).

By 1806 Mills was beginning to get his own commissions, though he continued to work with Latrobe until 1809. It seems odd that nothing is known about any of his employees, students, or protégés. He evidently inspired no famous architect, but then again no one building by Mills could be regarded as seminal. His career continued to spiral upward from the time of his Monumental Church (1812) in Richmond, the Washington Monument (1815–1829) in Baltimore, and his fireproof building in Charleston (1822).[11] The commission for the Washington Monument (1833–1884) came just before his appointment as federal architect from 1836 to 1842, when he designed the present U.S. Treasury Building (1838–1842) and the Patent Office Building (1839) in Washington. Mills is one of the very rare deadends in the chain of connections of famous architects, though he personally gained on three counts in his own apprenticeship years.[12]

Latrobe: Bank of Pennsylvania, Philadelphia, 1798–1801

Along with the conscientious and hard-working Mills,[13] Latrobe took on a young and talented apprentice, William Strickland [A20]. Strickland's father was Latrobe's head carpenter on the Bank of Pennsylvania and then was rehired by Latrobe to be his clerk of the works on one of his canal projects. But the relationship between Latrobe and the younger Strickland was stormy. Latrobe found the boy both delightful and irritating. However, it was Strickland and not the steadier Mills who would continue the Latrobe line down to Frank Lloyd Wright and others. Strickland had a very intermittent career in terms of the buildings that made him famous. At the age of twenty he was

Latrobe & Godefroy: Baltimore Cathedral, Baltimore, 1804–1818

ready to strike out on his own, but for the next ten years he made most of his income from painting, surveying, drawing maps, illustrating books, and painting theatrical scenery. He entered several competitions and finally won the commission for the Second Bank of the United States (1818–1824) in Philadelphia, one of the buildings that would mark him as of major importance in American architectural history. Latrobe's entry placed second. After winning, he changed the design somewhat to incorporate some of Latrobe's ideas and Latrobe became furious with his former student. Nevertheless, this commission launched Strickland, and he received eighteen other projects almost immediately. He had two pupils in his office at that time, Samuel Honeyman Kneass, who is now totally unknown, and Gideon Shryock [A7], who became an important Kentucky architect.[14]

Strickland: Second Bank of the U.S., Philadelphia, 1818–1824

The next important Strickland design—one that would later be featured in architectural history textbooks—was his Philadelphia Exchange of 1832–1834. In the ten years between his two most famous buildings, no apprentice or employee of note emerged from his office. However, from 1830 to 1831, just before the Exchange was constructed, Strickland employed one of the students he had taught at the Philadelphia Franklin Institute. Thomas Ustick Walter [A19] was hired by Strickland in much the same sort of arrangement that he himself had experienced. Walter's father was the master bricklayer on Strickland's first major project, the Second Bank. However, Walter actually was trained in his father's profession and was not the mere boy apprentice Strickland had been. Then there was a hiatus after this burst of activity: from 1838 to 1845 Strickland was "architecturally idle," except for an occasional minor project.[15]

Strickland: Philadelphia Exchange, Philadelphia, 1832–1834

After working in Strickland's office, T. U. Walter immediately won the competition for the county prison of Philadelphia and, three years later, the competition for Girard College against entries that included designs by William Strickland, Isaiah Rogers, Town & Davis, and John Haviland (like Strickland, a former teacher at the Franklin Institute where Walter had studied).[16] By 1835 Walter had also won another nationally advertised competition for a building in Charleston. Famous in the 1830s, Walter proceeded to do little of interest during the following decade.[17]

But one quite famous architect "connected" to Walter late in Walter's career when he again began to produce an outstanding design. After a fallow decade, in 1851 T. U. Walter was named architect of the United States Capitol and was in charge of the construction of the present dome (1855–1865) and the extensions of the north and south wings (1851–1859).[18] Though inspired by the dome of the cathedral in St. Petersburg (1840–1842)—which had its own antecedents—and,

Walter: Dome of the U.S.
Capitol, Washington,
1855–1865

Lefuel: Louvre addition,
Paris, 1854–1880

thus, not totally original, this dome and the additions introduced full-blown Beaux-Arts styling to America in one of its most visible and important monuments. At least two scholars have been studying material on Walter's role in the design, looking for the reason why he made so many enemies among his professional colleagues at that time. Records of Walter's commission for the Capitol are curiously ambiguous, and even the author of the recent biography of Richard Morris Hunt seemed bemused by the lack of exactness in the records of Hunt's role in Walter's office. Nevertheless, the fact remains that Hunt [A22] was employed by Walter in 1855 immediately after Hunt's return from Paris, at the moment in Walter's career when he showed new power after a period of relatively uninteresting designs. This connection with Walter has been all but ignored in surveys because writers like to emphasize Hunt's role as the first native-born American to attend the Ecole des Beaux-Arts in Paris. Hunt also served his apprenticeship in Paris.

There were twelve years between Hunt's entry into the Ecole des Beaux-Arts and his return to the United States. In Paris Hunt studied with Hector Martin Lefuel and entered the Ecole in Lefuel's atelier. Hunt also worked for Lefuel for a few months. "Early in 1854, his patron, Lefuel, was made architect to the emperor Napoleon III, and director of works of the new structures being built to connect the Tuilleries and the Louvre. . . . In April, 1854, Lefuel invited Richard to join his staff as Inspecteur des Travaux at an annual salary of two thousand francs. . . . In his work on the Louvre extensions, Richard joined a massive endeavor, one of the great building projects of the nineteenth century—the remaking of the city of Paris."[19] The senior architect was soaring; the junior architect was employed at just that moment. It was not Lefuel's first major award, but it was his most potent.

Upon his return to America, Hunt was employed only briefly by Walter. Nevertheless, he did have this connection with the Latrobe dynasty in addition to a significant employer in Paris. It was not just that he worked for Walter, who had worked for Strickland, who worked for Latrobe. In every case, these conjunctions had been within a year or so of the design of a major landmark. Henry Van Brunt gave Hunt's eulogy at the 1895 convention of the American Institute of Architects:

> In the autumn of 1858, three earnest aspirants for architectural knowledge applied to Hunt, who had then just completed the Tenth Street Studio Building in New York, to take one of the studios himself and install them as pupils. One of these applicants, our present honored vice-president, George B. Post, had just graduated from the Engineering School of the New York University; the other

two were Charles D. Gambrill and myself, who, since their graduation at Harvard four years before, had been pursuing the study of
architecture under the somewhat discouraging conditions which
then prevailed.

With the noble generosity of the true artist, Hunt granted our
request and equipped one of the studios for our use. Early in the
following year we were joined by William Ware . . . and subsequently by Frank Furness, . . . and by Edmund Quincy and E. L.
Hyde, who never practiced our art. . . .

His own studio and home at that time were in the old University Building on Washington Square. Here he lived as a bachelor in
spacious and lofty apartments, filled with the spoils of foreign
travel. . . .

His criticisms of our poor attempts were pungent and severe,
but so genial and picturesque that every visit left behind it not only
an enduring inspiration but an atmosphere quickened by his energy and illuminated by his inexhaustible humor. For he was as
much a comrade as a master.[20]

Architectural historians have made much of the fact that Hunt
had five students, all of whom found a niche in history, and that Hunt
was the first American-born architect to attend the Ecole. Hunt was
only a few years older than his pupils, but he had enormous self-
assurance and confidence in his ability and training and, like so many
other inspiring teachers, was a man of considerable energy. Both the
daring of his Griswold House in Newport, Rhode Island, and the sophistication of the Studio Building itself were noted in the first chapter
in the discussion of Frank Furness' career. The pattern is becoming
so obvious that it should no longer seem curious that later, when Hunt
was fully established, no other pupils or employees achieved such renown.[21] The Tenth Street Studios had been an instant success, rapidly
filled with artists as well as Hunt's own pupils. The five young men in
Hunt's atelier were talented, well-to-do, and socially connected, and
three of them had already worked in other architects' offices before
they joined with Hunt.

George Browne Post [A14] was one of the three who first asked
for instruction. Fresh from New York University, he stayed from 1858
to 1860, as did Charles Gambrill, but Gambrill had four years of previous apprenticeship experience after his graduation from Harvard.
Post and Gambrill formed their own firm in 1860. With the outbreak
of the Civil War, Post joined the National Guard as a captain, but was
back at work with Gambrill from 1864 to 1866, when he joined very
briefly in a different partnership with Samuel Mead. Post established
his reputation by his part in the Equitable Life Assurance Building
done in association with Arthur Delavan Gilman [A6]—a major architect at that time—and Gilman's partner on that project, Edward H.

Kendall.[22] From that time on Post's commissions came readily, and his Western Union Telegraph Building (1873–1875) assured his early fame. By the time of the World's Columbian Exposition (1893), Post had one of the most important practices in the United States and was Hunt's near equal. His Produce Exchange in New York (1881–1885) was a particularly strong design and preceded the stylistically somewhat similar and much more famous Marshall Field Building by Richardson and Adler & Sullivan's Auditorium Building, both in Chicago. From 1896 to 1899 Post was president of the American Institute of Architects.[23]

Hunt: Studio Building,
New York, 1857–1858

Gambrill did not live long after he left his partnership with H. H. Richardson and not a great deal is known about his potential. William Robert Ware [A9] had graduated from Harvard in 1852 and then served an apprenticeship to Edward Clarke Cabot.[24] Ware was in Hunt's studio for the briefest period of all, from 1859 to 1860—yet he was the member of the group who was most affected by Hunt's teaching method. In 1860 he established his own office in Boston and from 1863 to 1865 conducted an atelier of his own. The Massachusetts Institute of Technology had been incorporated in 1861; by 1865, when it opened, Ware was organizing its future architectural program. After a trip to Europe in 1866 to observe firsthand the methods of the Ecole des Beaux-Arts, classes began in 1868 with just a few students. (Sullivan was there in the fifth year of its existence. Silsbee must have been among the first of the students.)

Henry Van Brunt [A9] said in the eulogy that from 1854 to 1858 he "had been pursuing the study of architecture under the somewhat discouraging conditions which then prevailed." If it is true that he worked for Detlef Lienau [A8] during those years,[25] it would be one more case of a young man who did not admire his employer but who did gain something from the connection in spite of his feelings. At that time, Lienau—born in Denmark and educated at the Royal Architectural College in Munich—was one of the few American architects to have received formal academic training. If the information in Withey and Withey's *Biographical Dictionary of American Architects (Deceased)* is correct, Lienau was a student of Henri Labrouste.

Labrouste conducted an atelier at the Ecole des Beaux-Arts from 1830 to 1856, and his first famous building, the Bibliothèque Ste.-Geneviève (1843), is known to nearly all architects as a dramatic leap forward in the graceful and skillful use of iron—one of the turning points in the history of architecture. Lienau arrived in America in 1848 at the age of thirty and established a successful practice, though his work never appealed very much to architectural historians. However, there is no reason to believe that Lienau actually worked for Labrouste and, as has been noted already, to have been a student of a famous architect does not seem to be as effective as to have been an employee, unless there was an unusual closeness between the teacher and the pupil. Nevertheless, if Van Brunt did work for Lienau, he would have left just as Lienau's first major work, the Schermerhorn House (1859), was underway.[26]

Van Brunt was trained by Hunt for about two years and then joined the Union Army at the outset of the war. By 1863 he had joined Ware in partnership, though it was Van Brunt who carried the greater load as the designer in the firm. Within a short time they had their most famous commission, Memorial Hall (1865–1879) at Harvard. Four employees in their office at that time not only took their own places in architectural history but formed bridges to the Burnham and Richardson firms: Charles Atwood, Robert Swain Peabody, John Goddard Stearns, Jr., and George Foster Shepley.

Ware & Van Brunt: Memorial Hall, Harvard, Cambridge, 1865–1879

As noted earlier, Shepley [A8] replaced White in Richardson's office in 1880 and eventually headed the successor firm. Charles Atwood [A8] began with Ware & Van Brunt just as the firm received the Memorial Hall project in 1865. After three years he left to attend Harvard's Lawrence Scientific School and then returned to the firm until 1872, when he set up his own practice in Boston. Three years later Atwood moved to New York and from 1879 to 1881 worked in association with John B. Snook on houses for the Vanderbilt family. (John Wellborn Root had been one of Snook's assistants between 1870 and 1871.) In 1884 Atwood won first prize in a competition for the Boston Public Library, although his design was not built and McKim secured the commission a few years later. When Root died in 1891, Daniel Burnham asked Atwood to become his design partner for an enormously important project—the coordination of the architecture for the World's Columbian Exposition. Charles McKim advised against this collaboration because, though Atwood was likable and talented, McKim believed that he was emotionally unstable. Unfortunately, Atwood died of a drug overdose a year or two after the exposition closed. Nevertheless, Atwood was responsible for over sixty structures at the fair and his Fine Arts Building (1893) was the only building chosen to be replicated in more permanent materials. Rebuilt from 1929 to 1940, it now serves as the Museum of Science and Industry.

Two more employees on Memorial Hall became well known. Robert Peabody [A6] was a classmate of Charles McKim's at the Ecole. Upon his return to Boston, Peabody worked for Gridley James Fox Bryant [A8], who will come up later as part of the Bulfinch dynasty. This was the time of Bryant's best-known work, the Boston City Hall, done in association with Arthur Gilman. When Peabody was hired to

Bryant & Gilman: Boston
City Hall, Boston, 1861–
1865

work on Memorial Hall, he met Ware & Van Brunt's chief draftsman, John Goddard Stearns, Jr. Stearns had a degree from the Lawrence Scientific School and had been with the firm from the outset. In 1870 the partnership of Peabody & Stearns was established and it not only prospered, but produced its own roster of successful graduates. Although none established a major place in history, quite a few of the Peabody & Stearns employees at least found a niche.[27]

Ware & Van Brunt also prospered, even though Ware himself put most of his energies into teaching at MIT. When Ware moved to New York in about 1881 to establish an architecture department at Columbia University, Van Brunt moved to Kansas City to join in partnership with a former employee, Frank M. Howe. Although Van Brunt continued to be an important architect throughout his life and although both George B. Post and Richard Morris Hunt became not only very prosperous but famous with their colleagues, those employees who emerged from these offices to establish major reputations were all with them early in their careers. The direct line of succession from Latrobe to Hunt fanned out weblike and connected to Burnham, Richardson, Sullivan, and their descendants.

Most of the important members of this network were brought together for the 1893 World's Columbian Exposition. As chief of construction, Daniel Burnham convinced the directors of the fair that it would be best if he personally selected the major participating architects. Recall that there were several thousand people in America at that time who claimed to be architects. Burnham chose nine firms: Richard Morris Hunt; Hunt's previous employees George B. Post and Henry Van Brunt; Van Brunt's ex-employees Peabody & Stearns and their ex-employee, Henry Ives Cobb, with Ware & Van Brunt's Charles Atwood, now Burnham's partner, as designer-in-chief. Two of the other architects selected by Burnham were his own former employer, William Le Baron Jenney, and Jenney's former employee, Louis Sullivan. Finally, the last of the major architects chosen, and one of the most important, was Charles Follen McKim (who was tied to this group; though it was not of importance to McKim's future ability, he did work for the fifth Hunt student, Gambrill).

Burnham was praised for achieving a geographic balance with firms from Boston, New York, Kansas City, and Chicago.[28] It is true that he knew for a fact that these men could work together in harmony, but it is equally true that this was a very tight fraternity with Burnham himself the only real outsider. Yet Burnham's partner, Root, was connected directly to the Renwick line and indirectly to the Bulfinch dynasty, as was Burnham himself. The employer-employee relationship is too consistent to be ignored in the creation of major designers.

NINE

The Bulfinch and Renwick Lines

Well-bred young ladies of the later eighteenth century were expected to develop some skill on a musical instrument or as a singer and to master ornamental needlework. Wealthy young men, like those in Charles Bulfinch's family, cultivated a refined taste in architecture and collected illustrated volumes on the subject, occasionally designing houses for their friends. Bulfinch [A22] had the best education available in America at that time and ample means to be a gentleman for life when he left for a year and a half tour of Europe. He had no premonition of the fact that, soon after he reached the age of thirty, he would have to make a career of architecture and become an architect for hire—though, in fact, Bulfinch was rarely paid enough in that role actually to support himself and his family.

He visited Thomas Jefferson in Paris at the time when Jefferson was undergoing a transition in his understanding of architectural design, even visiting architects' offices, studying their techniques with newly invented graph paper and learning to master the pencil. Bulfinch was shown the buildings that Jefferson found exciting and inspiring. He urged the young man to travel the route he had taken through southern France and then go to Rome. Although Bulfinch followed his advice, he spent most of his time in England, where he admired the work of Robert Adam and William Chambers. It is doubtful that he went as far as Jefferson did and visited these men with the intention of learning their specific methods.[1]

Upon his return to Boston in 1787, Bulfinch drew up an elevation and plan for a new State House for Massachusetts—though its construction would not begin for some time. Five years later he designed his first house, for Joseph Coolidge, one of his wife's relatives. The in-

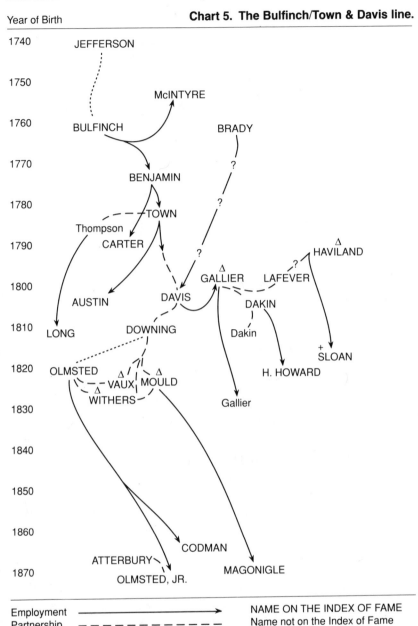

Chart 5. The Bulfinch/Town & Davis line.

Employment	———————————▶	NAME ON THE INDEX OF FAME
Partnership	— — — — — — — — — —	Name not on the Index of Fame
Mentorship	··························	
European training △		Connects to others on another chart +

fluences of his European observations are evident in his next design, also completed in 1792, the Joseph Barrell House in Charlestown, Massachusetts. Functionally planned, with an elliptical salon, it was "epochal."[2] The following year Bulfinch began an ambitious project that would prove to be the financial disaster that forced him to become a professional architect. Tontine Crescent (1793–1795), probably inspired by the terrace houses in Bath, England, was an urbanistic design consisting of sixteen houses with a 300-foot-long common pal-

Year of Birth  **Chart 6. The Bulfinch/Upjohn line.**

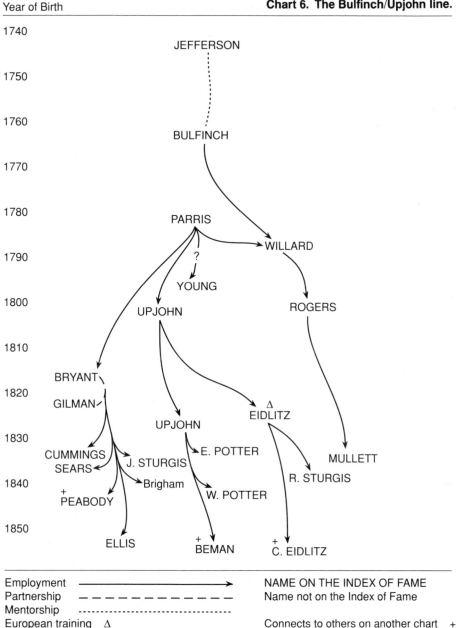

Employment ——————→	NAME ON THE INDEX OF FAME
Partnership — — — — — — — —	Name not on the Index of Fame
Mentorship ························	
European training Δ	Connects to others on another chart +

atial façade curved in a crescent around a grassy area. In 1795 construction finally got underway on the Massachusetts State House. The State Capitol, the Tontine Crescent, and the Harrison Gray Otis Houses (1796–1805) are the buildings that first established Bulfinch as an important and worthy architect. In the course of his career Bulfinch would change Boston from a backwater late-medieval town to an elegant and sophisticated little city. His reputation grew to the point that he was considered no less than equal to Latrobe as a de-

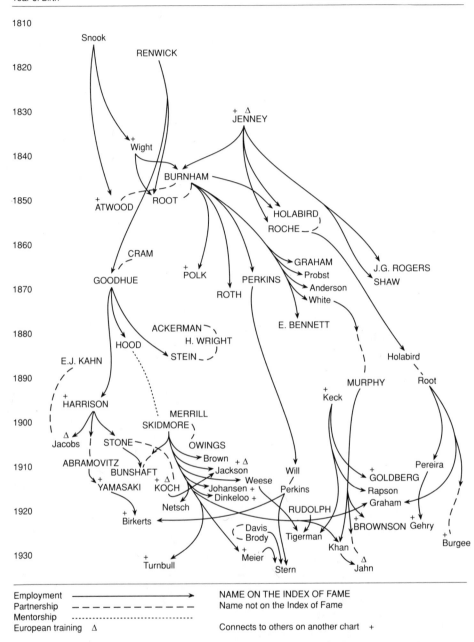

Chart 7. The Renwick lines.

Year of Birth

Employment	⟶
Partnership	– – – – – – – –
Mentorship	··············
European training	Δ

NAME ON THE INDEX OF FAME
Name not on the Index of Fame

Connects to others on another chart   +

signer. These early triumphs correspond exactly with Bulfinch's employment of Asher Benjamin and Samuel McIntire.

Several historians have noted Bulfinch's stylistic influence on McIntire, but few mentioned that McIntire actually worked for and with Bulfinch on one of these early buildings. Samuel McIntire [A16], twelve years Bulfinch's senior, was described by Fiske Kimball as "a modest craftsman and sober citizen, who never travelled more than a few miles from his native town," Salem, Massachusetts.[3] He was the typical New England carpenter-builder of the period in that he depended upon such books as Batty Langley's *Treasury of Design* (1740) for ideas on styling: like many of the men who entered the competition for the United States Capitol in 1792, McIntire submitted an entry derived from illustrations of books produced in Europe. However, after Bulfinch's return from Europe, McIntire was quick to see the freshness and elegance of Bulfinch's first houses. Kimball stated that "Bulfinch made the first designs, and McIntire the final ones, for the lavishly decorated Derby mansion begun in 1794 (destroyed in 1815)."[4] As I have said, it is not important that the employee work on the masterpiece produced by an employer; it is only important that he work with the employer during the time that the masterpiece is being conceived, built, or completed. Thus, though McIntire did not work on the Massachusetts State House (1795–1797) or the Tontine Crescent, he did work for Bulfinch during the time that those buildings were being constructed.

Bulfinch: Massachusetts State House, Boston, 1795–1797

For McIntire this event matured his talent, made him more decisive, and added elegance to his own work. The Pierce-Nichols House (1782) and the Gardner-White-Pingree House (1804–1810) in Salem are often illustrated to demonstrate, by comparison, McIntire's new strength and assurance after the 1790s (plates 7 and 8). It can be argued that it was not just a matter of McIntire's observing Bulfinch's buildings, but that he was personally able to sense and absorb Bulfinch's own period of maturing by close contact. Even though by this time in American history there were "more than 100 builders in Boston" alone,[5] McIntire and Benjamin both stand out—though McIntire was certainly of less interest than Bulfinch himself.

Asher Benjamin [A14] was also a builder, from Hartland, Connecticut. He had little experience with European design innovations before he was hired to erect "a circular staircase in Bulfinch's Connecticut Statehouse in Hartford in 1795. This contact with Bulfinch, and with the Neo-classical style, had a profound effect upon Benjamin's entire career. He became a follower of Bulfinch, and in 1801 he moved from the Connecticut River Valley to Boston, where he practiced until 1845."[6] Within two years of his professional contact with Bulfinch, Benjamin was emboldened to write the first builder's guide to be published in the United States. He was only twenty-five, and this and subsequent books by Benjamin would have more to do with his fame than would his actual buildings.

Benjamin: Center Church, New Haven, 1813–1814

No employees' names are on record as having worked for Samuel McIntire. But Asher Benjamin conducted a school for young men who wanted to learn his trade. One of the pupils in Benjamin's school from 1805 to 1806, when his book was establishing Benjamin's reputa-

Plate 7. Samuel McIntire's Pierce-Nichols House, Salem, Massachusetts, 1782. (Courtesy of the Essex Institute, Salem, Mass.)

tion, was Ithiel Town [A14], the son of a Connecticut farmer. By the time that Benjamin had the commission for the lovely Center Church on the green at New Haven (1813–1814), Town was employed as his principal assistant, and a number of authors have credited its design to Town himself.[7]

In 1814 Town proved that he had considerable design talent, evident in his Trinity Church (1814) in New Haven.[8] Town had trained himself to be both an architect and an engineer (not uncommon in the profession in the early nineteenth century). In 1821 he published a description of a lattice truss that he had invented and patented, a considerable improvement in bridge-building techniques at that time. This document was republished in 1825, 1831, and 1839, and the invention made Town wealthy. In addition, since he traveled about the country to promote his system, in the process he made contact with numerous potential clients for architecture as well as for bridges.

Plate 8. Samuel McIntire's Gardner-White-Pingree House, Salem, Massachusetts, 1804–1810, showing the change in McIntire's work after Bulfinch's return from England. (Courtesy of the Essex Institute, Salem, Mass.)

Ithiel Town moved to New York City in 1826 and joined in partnership with Martin Euclid Thompson [A3]. Thompson had just completed the Bank of the United States in New York, a fine classic building important enough that its façade has been incorporated into the courtyard entrance to the American wing of the Metropolitan Museum of Art.[9] It was Thompson's most celebrated work, one that must have had a considerable impact on Town. This is perhaps another example of the kind of connection I have discussed previously, a conjunction of colleagues.

It was at this time that the young Alexander Jackson Davis [A18] was hired. A highly talented artist, Davis may have studied painting under John Trumbull.[10] But it was another painter, "Rembrandt Peale, who told him he was fated to be not a painter but an architect."[11] Before joining Town, Davis had been in the office of Josiah Brady [A4]. Brady had been in practice in New York before Davis was even born, but his early work was not impressive. His Second Trinity Church (1788–1791) was a naive and amateurish Neo-Gothic affair. Brady's talent matured late, but by the 1820s his St. Thomas (1824–1826) was executed in correct Doric Neo-Greek and, several years before Richard Upjohn's famous Trinity Church, Brady's Second Unitarian Church (1826) was done in good English Perpendicular Gothic styling. Davis worked for Brady just after this surge of design ability, in 1826 and 1827.[12]

At this time he began to work for Town & Thompson and was promoted to partnership almost immediately. Thompson left to re-establish a separate practice in 1830 and never again equaled the 1820s designs. Town did not remain interested in the firm of Town & Davis for long himself. He dropped out from 1835 to 1842, when he returned for one year shortly before his death. But from 1830 to 1833 the air in the office of Town & Davis must have crackled with excitement. Town had a large circle of friends who were clients but also others who were artists, writers, and architects; he had amassed a library of approximately 11,000 volumes that was a magnet for many in those years before public libraries. By 1840 Ithiel Town had been immortalized by the painter Thomas Cole, who portrayed him as the lounging figure in the foreground of the enormous composition *The Architect's Dream*. However, it was not Town, a highly capable architect, but Davis who became the principal design partner.

Town & Davis: U.S. Custom House, New York, 1833–1851

Alexander Jackson Davis continued to be of major importance in terms of experimenting with new architectural styles, shifting from the Greek Revival into much more Romantic modes in the 1840s. But much of his best work was done in the first few years of this partnership: the United States Custom House (1833), New York University (1833), and Colonnade Row (1836) in New York City, and the North Carolina State Capitol (1833–1834) in Raleigh. James H. Dakin [A5] entered the office as an employee in 1829 just as Davis assumed his role as partner. In 1832 Dakin was also promoted to partnership, though he stayed for only one year in that capacity. He is credited with the design of the chapel at New York University (1833–1835), but his reputation rests more on the buildings he did in the South.[13] His brother, Charles Dakin, also worked for Town & Davis in the first years of Davis' fame.

So did James Gallier, Sr. [A5]. Gallier was the son of a Dublin builder and had been an employee in the office of Sir William Wilkins, the architect of the National Gallery (1834–1838) in London. However, Gallier arrived in New York before Wilkins' most famous building was begun. He was hired by Town, Davis & Dakin and he and the Dakins immediately became fast friends.

Gallier briefly set up in partnership with Minard Lafever in 1833 and 1834 but then left with his family to accompany Charles Dakin to New Orleans where they practiced together from 1834 to 1839, with James Dakin joining them in 1835.[14] Thus it was at the outset of Alexander Jackson Davis' career that his office spun off its stars. Town & Davis continued to be a large and prosperous firm. Draftsmen paid to work there, although there were always some on salary, but only one later employee became of enough interest to architectural historians even to be mentioned in textbooks, and only as a minor aside. Josiah Cleveland Cady [A4] was with them in the early 1860s, well after their initial projects and after he had been trained by Peabody & Stearns.

There was a lateral connection in the 1840s between Davis and his friend Andrew Jackson Downing [A11]; Davis did a number of the illustrations for Downing's successful books. Downing was not an architect but he nevertheless influenced architectural design as an architectural critic and writer with the publication of his *Treatise on Landscape Gardening* (1841), *Rural Cottages* (1842), and *The Architecture of Country Houses* (1850). These books were instrumental in shifting American taste from the Greek Revival to much more Romantic styles and helped create the desire for pastoral landscapes. Downing must also be given most of the credit for urging the establishment of Central Park in New York (begun several years after his accidental death at the age of thirty-six).[15] The Downing-Davis connection was one of colleagues, and it is strange that all of Davis' significant connections were with his contemporaries so that the chart of the lineage from Bulfinch to Davis fans out without progeny.

Likewise, James Gallier's partnership with Minard Lafever [A12] is Lafever's only direct link to the Davis group, though James Dakin as well as Gallier provided drawings for Lafever's 1833 book. Lafever had begun as a carpenter, and in this capacity worked on the stairs of John Haviland's Grecian Arcade (1826–1827) in New York. This might lead us to assume a link between Lafever and Haviland [A14] except that Lafever wrote that this staircase was "executed by the Author some time after the building was in use."[16] There is no record of a personal connection between Lafever and Haviland at that time. It would be pure speculation, based on Lafever's use of a book written by Haviland's recent former employer, James Elmes of London, that would hint of any interaction with Haviland when he was in the first flush of success in America.

Although Lafever became active as an architect in New York, it was his books that made his name nationally known. His first book, published in 1829, *The Young Builder's General Instructor*, showed "uncertainty, lack of confidence, a self-conscious originality like early Soane's 'amateurishly indecisive country house designs'" [17] with which Soane had begun his own career. Lafever's second book, published in 1833 when he intersected with Gallier and his friends, was quite a different matter. Lafever was involved in a conjunction of extremely able colleagues, all at the outset of their careers. (I see this as yet another example of the sort of power generated in the early years of the Schindler and Neutra association.) *The Modern Builder's Guide* of 1833 not only had better-drafted illustrations, it demonstrated that

Plate 9. An illustration by Lafever published in The Young Builder's General Instructor, *pl. 43, 1829. (Courtesy of the Avery Architectural and Fine Arts Library, Columbia University in the City of New York)*

Plate 10. An illustration by Lafever published in The Modern Builder's Guide, *pl. 75, 1833, showing the change in his work after his contact with other creative designers. (Courtesy of the Avery Architectural and Fine Arts Library, Columbia University in the City of New York)*

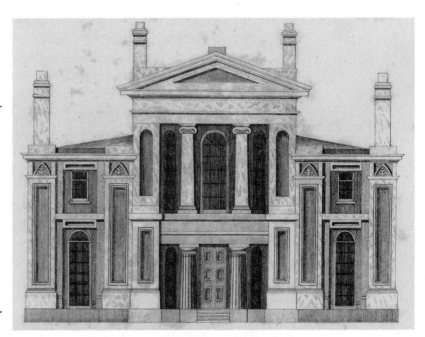

FRONT ELEVATION FOR A COUNTRY RESIDENCE.

Lafever had fully matured in terms of his handling of proportions, spacing, and ornament (plates 9 and 10). More than one writer has commented upon the improvement and polish of the 1833 book over the first. Talbot Hamlin said of the three books published in 1829, 1833, and 1835 that "his artistic progress from the crudity of the first to the polished restraint of the last is amazing in so brief a period. . . . The second and third contain probably the most exquisite and the least archaeological of all American Greek Revival detail—personal, inventive, restrained."[18]

Lafever, Gallier, Dakin, Davis, Town, Thompson—all interlock in this period between 1829 and 1835. The younger men were at the threshold of major careers; Town and Thompson had just proved themselves in the mid to late 1820s. It is true that there were not a great many architects in New York at that time and ambitious young men of taste gravitated to each other and sought employment with the best designers in the city. But surely the people who were employees or associates later in these men's careers had their own measure of talent and ability! It is particularly important to note again that only those architects in Town & Davis' office at the beginning—Dakin and Gallier—became important enough in their own right to be considered relatively famous.

Clearly, something extraordinary happens at a specific moment in the careers of those architects who eventually become famous— the contact with another in a professional capacity (not generally as a student) transmits conviction, power, and design strength. Lafever's later partners and employees remain unknown,[19] and none of Town & Davis' later employees became famous. The seeds of genius are cast at an early period.

There was a second line of succession from Bulfinch. It began with Alexander Parris [A14], who worked for Bulfinch on his Lancaster Meetinghouse, which was under construction in 1816 and 1817. This building has been singled out by historians as the beginning of a new stage in Bulfinch's career, "a simpler and more monumental style."[20] In that respect it fits the formula. Parris was promoted and then "served as executive for Charles Bulfinch in the building of the Massachusetts General Hospital" from 1818 to 1823.[21]

Bulfinch: Lancaster Meetinghouse, Lancaster, 1816–1817

If, indeed, what we have been tracing thus far is beginning to look like a formula for fame, it does not quite work in the case of Alexander Parris' employees. All of Parris' best-known employees were with him *after* his reputation was fully established. He is best known for the Sears House (1816) and Faneuil Hall Market (Quincy Market, 1823–1826) in Boston and the First Unitarian Church of

Quincy (also called the Stone Temple, 1828). The Sears House was done at the time he first worked for Bulfinch; the two other designs came just after his completion of his assignments for Bulfinch.

Ammi B. Young, Gridley James Fox Bryant, George Dexter, and Richard Upjohn all worked for Parris in the 1830s, not during the time his masterworks were produced. In this case, we must look for colleague inspiration. Young [A9] had already learned the building trade, taught by his father, and was in practice by 1830 with a number of commissions before he connected to Parris. "He received some instruction from the Boston architect Alexander Parris, but probably not before the late 1830s."[22] Since the Vermont State House (1833–1836) was built to Young's designs and, like his Boston Custom House (1837–1847), was a bold and well-proportioned essay in the Greek Revival style, this "instruction" is a bit difficult to understand. Nevertheless, that the two designers did connect has come down to us as a fact. By 1842 Young was working for the Treasury Department. Appointed the first supervising architect of the U.S. Treasury Department (1852–1862),[23] Young was in charge of many post office and federal buildings of great merit, among them the handsome Galveston Custom House of the early 1860s. Young had a talent that should have been given more notice by the writers of general architectural surveys. Although, perhaps, he was never an employee of Parris, Young may well have been stimulated by his colleague.

The names of two of the three actual employees of Alexander Parris are well known in Boston. George Minot Dexter built up a substantial practice and was elected president of the American Society of Civil Engineers in 1850. The other man, Gridley James Fox Bryant [A8], had an enormous practice in the middle of the nineteenth century, with at least 152 buildings finished before 1872.[24] Bryant had worked for Parris for five years before he established his own office in 1837. Although he designed many different types of buildings, it was his rugged granite warehouses that caused Sigfried Giedion to praise him in his influential book *Space, Time and Architecture*, published in 1941. However, except for Giedion's book, Bryant & Gilman's Boston City Hall (1861–1865) was more usually illustrated in books on architecture in the United States. This was an early example of the soon to be popular Second Empire or General Grant style. Bryant's best-known employees were with him at that time.[25]

Bryant & Gilman: Boston City Hall, Boston, 1861–1865

Before exploring Richard Upjohn's relationship to Parris when Upjohn was in his office, it should be noted that still other prominent New England architects intersected with Parris at this time. Charles Bulfinch had hired Parris' close friend and former assistant, Solomon Willard [A8] to carve architectural ornament for the Massachusetts

State House and to make a model of his design for the United States
Capitol. Shortly after this contact with Bulfinch, Willard won the 1824
competition for the Bunker Hill Monument (1824–1842) and for the
Bank of the United States (1822–1824) in Boston.

In 1822 Willard hired Isaiah Rogers [A12], a Massachusetts-born
architect who had already won a competition for a theater in Mobile,
Alabama. They became associated in 1826 and remained together until 1848, when Rogers moved to Ohio. Rogers' international reputation
was established in 1830 when William Harvard Eliot published a description of Rogers' extraordinary Tremont House in Boston, the first
of its kind, a palatial hotel of the sort soon demanded by every large
city in the world. Tremont House immediately made Rogers a major
architect with commissions in half a dozen states.[26]

Without question, it was Parris' employee, Richard Upjohn [A21],
who was able to pass design power on to others. Upjohn had been
trained by a builder and cabinetmaker in England and came to America at the age of twenty-seven. After moving about and securing few
commissions either in New England or in Washington, D.C., Upjohn
settled in Boston and worked in Parris' office from 1834 to 1839, doing
some work for Parris and some for himself. He was near bankruptcy
when his fortune suddenly changed with two events. The first was the
design of a house for a wealthy client from the old Boston family,
the Gardners, in 1835. The second was the experience of working in
Parris' office. Though Parris himself was a little past his most dramatic work, his close friends and students were receiving their first
national publicity. It is easy to guess that Upjohn was able to experience a colleague connection at this time. Before the decade ended, he
was more famous than any of the others.

Church attendance was important to Upjohn; his grandfather
and his father-in-law were clergymen, and Upjohn himself grew almost fanatically religious over the years. He had become friendly with
the minister of Boston's pre-Richardson Trinity Church. Because of
this friendship, when the minister was called to serve Trinity's sister
church in New York City, he asked Upjohn to draw up a plan for a remodeling of the existing New York building. However, the vestry was
persuaded to change plans and gave Upjohn permission to design a
new church instead. Trinity Church (1839–1846) in New York is featured in most architectural history surveys both as early and as the
prototypical American version of fine Gothic Revival. Many commissions followed, for houses as well as churches, and Upjohn was
launched in his career.

The present American Institute of Architects (AIA) was founded
in his office in 1857, and Upjohn was elected its first president, a posi-

Upjohn: Trinity Church,
New York, 1839–1846

tion he held until 1876. Over the years he had numerous employees, but it was the men who worked for him on Trinity Church who would pass the torch on to others.[27] Upjohn's own son, Richard M. Upjohn [A6], joined him in the office two years before Trinity was completed. Leopold Eidlitz [A10] was hired that same year, 1843. Eidlitz was born in Prague and trained in Vienna and immediately upon his arrival in the United States he became one of Upjohn's three German assistants on Trinity. Eidlitz' own practice began soon after, in 1846, with the design of St. George's Church in New York, a work he completed in partnership with Otto Blesch, a winner of a Grand Prize in Munich and possibly one of Upjohn's other assistants. Blesch stayed in America only briefly, but Eidlitz' St. George's, like Trinity, was a popular success and was followed by some thirty other church commissions, a suitably exuberant house for P. T. Barnum (1846–1848), and many other projects, including a number of large commercial buildings. The most exciting of his projects was never built. This was the radical proposal, done with the inventor James Bogardus [A14], for a suspended iron and glass pavilion submitted for the 1853 competition for an exhibition hall for New York's fair. By 1883, when he was in association with H. H. Richardson on the New York State Capitol, Eidlitz was the better known of the two architects.

Eidlitz had maintained a successful practice for ten years when he employed Russell Sturgis [A10] in 1858. There were quite a number of projects in his office at that time, but I would argue that what little celebrity Sturgis gained as a designer did not grow from the Eidlitz connection but was more likely the result of the surge of conviction he showed just after he joined with Peter B. Wight when Wight had just completed his prize-winning design for the National Academy. Sturgis carried the Bulfinch-Parris-Upjohn line down to his employees, Mead and McKim.

Eidlitz' son Cyrus continued the name of the firm successfully into the twentieth century. His head draftsman at the time he assumed command in 1899 was Andrew McKenzie, and one of his other employees then was Stephen Voorhees. Their future partner, Paul Gmelin, moved over from McKim, Mead & White's office, as did Ralph Walker [B7] later. These men became partners and changed the name of the firm, with Ralph Walker emerging in the 1930s as "the architect of the century" in the minds of his professional colleagues and the AIA. Thus Eidlitz' successors bound the two lineages together and Bulfinch and Latrobe became direct professional ancestors of many of the famous architects in America.

James Renwick, Jr. [A23], was sixteen years younger than Upjohn and is the only major American architect of this period who appears to spring from nowhere. But it must be noted that his father, a professor at Columbia, exerted an unusually strong influence on his son's career. Though unknown today, he was once considered to be one of the country's foremost engineers. "He was also an expert astronomer and mineralogist, a leading art collector and patron, a prolific author on both scientific and historical subjects, as well as an accomplished artist, architectural historian, and amateur architect who found time to supervise the construction of buildings for friends. . . . He not only trained his three sons as engineers but, whenever necessary, unhesitatingly used his influence to further their careers."[28] However, even if we accept the idea that Renwick rose phoenixlike to fame with only this connection to another noted older architect, he did employ two men who became famous themselves.

After graduation from Columbia at eighteen (not especially unusual at that time), Renwick worked as an engineer on the Erie Railroad and on the Croton Aqueduct. He was twenty-four when he was chosen the winner in the competition for the design of Grace Church (1843–1846) in New York. This established his national reputation. Three years later his entry in the competition for the design of the Smithsonian Institution in Washington won that major commission. At that time his knowledge of historical styles had been gained through books and his well-traveled father's instruction. Although he did not visit Europe until the 1850s, the church, with Upjohn's Trinity, was one of the first correctly executed Gothic Revival designs in America; the Smithsonian was a more awkward blend of Romanesque motifs, but Renwick was in the American avant-garde in terms of shifting style preferences. Later he also worked in Italianate and French styles.

Renwick also does not fit very well in the pattern that I have been describing in a second respect. The two architects employed by him who later achieved fame were not in his office during the generation of these early and highly publicized designs.[29] Neither John Wellborn Root nor Bertram Goodhue could have possibly worked for Renwick then. Root was born in 1850 and Goodhue in 1869. In fact, the only architect who is known to have been in Renwick's office in the early years is relatively unknown outside of Cincinnati—James K. Wilson, the designer of the Isaac M. Wise Temple (1866) in that city, and Wilson also worked for Upjohn.

However, as Goodhue later pointed out, Renwick always took a personal interest in his apprentices. His first famous assistant was John Wellborn Root [A20], the son of a Georgia merchant. Because of

Renwick: Renwick
Gallery (Old Corcoran),
Washington, 1859–1861,
1870–1871

Buckhout & Snook:
Grand Central Station,
New York, 1869–1871

the Civil War, he was sent to England at the age of fourteen in order to finish his schooling. Though accepted to Oxford, he returned to America and was a prize-winning student in engineering at the New York University. Upon graduation, Root went to work for Renwick in 1869, as a student without pay. At that time St. Patrick's Cathedral was still under construction (1859–1879), and the completion of the Corcoran Gallery (1859–1861, 1870–1871) was underway in Washington. Together with Grace Church and the Smithsonian, these are the designs popularly associated with Renwick's name. In fact, the Corcoran Gallery, the first one, has been renamed for its architect.

In 1870 Root became superintendent of construction for John B. Snook during the time that Buckhout & Snook's old Grand Central Station was being built. Then Root moved to Chicago after the fire of 1871 and became head draftsman for Carter, Drake & Wight for two years. Asher Carter was a generation older than Renwick; he supervised the erection of Renwick's early Second Presbyterian Church in Chicago (1849?–1851). How he came to Renwick's attention is speculation, but it might be remembered that Carter was a connector of sorts as Adler's employer, as Wight's employer and then his partner, and as the employer of Burnham and Root. Wight, of course, connected to Sturgis and indirectly to Mead. It was Peter B. Wight whom Root cited as his mentor.

Daniel Hudson Burnham [A23] had a more erratic start into the profession; nevertheless, he was not only present at Carter, Drake & Wight in 1872, but had been in William Le Baron Jenney's office at the beginning of the design for Jenney's Portland Block.

Root and Burnham were as complementary in their way as the sober Mead had been with his two red-headed partners. Root is described as having little ambition, though the evidence of his employment indicates otherwise. Burnham had real talents as a hearty salesman-businessman that overshadow his image as a designer. He was not a disciplined scholar or intellectual, and his schooling had been a struggle. His first job was as a clerk in a store. In 1868 he became one of Jenney's draftsmen but left before the end of the year for an unsuccessful venture in Nevada where he failed in a mining scheme. He tried to be elected to the Illinois Senate but failed, and by the time of the fire in 1871 he was back in Chicago in partnership with Gustave Laureau. Then Root and Burnham met in the office of Carter, Drake & Wight and the following year they established their firm.

The outgoing Burnham got along well with both clients and his fellow architects. By 1884 he was the first president of the Western Association of Architects; in 1891 he became the national president of

Jenney: Portland Block,
Chicago, 1872

the American Institute of Architects. Although Root has been some-what overpraised as a designer—he was able to produce some un-gainly buildings upon occasion—the combination of Burnham, Root, and the economy-minded, no-nonsense Chicago businessmen pro-duced some of the first major monuments of commercial design in the United States and had impact on Europe as well.

The Montauk Block (1883), the Rookery (1885), and the Monad-nock Building (1889–1891) all were designed by Burnham & Root with Root as the principal designer; but when Root died of pneumo-nia in 1891, Burnham continued as a leading architect. Charles At-wood [A8] (trained by Ware & Van Brunt) came from New York to join Burnham in 1891, finished the design of the Reliance Building (1891), and did much of the work for the 1893 exposition. However, he died shortly thereafter. Burnham's next major partner was Ernest R. Graham [A6], an employee who had joined the office in 1888 while it was still creating its reputation. Emery Roth was also an early em-ployee, from 1890 to 1893, before establishing his own highly success-ful firm.[30] Dwight Perkins [A6], mentioned earlier in connection with Wright, Marion Mahony, and John Galen Howard, was a high-ranking employee at this same time.

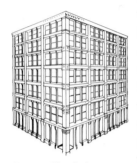

Jenney: First Leiter
Building, Chicago, 1879

Many of Burnham's employees, like Roth, became skilled at the design of large commercial buildings and cognizant of the methods of operating big offices.[31] Willis Polk [A14] was an experienced architect when he worked for Burnham as head of the firm's San Francisco office. Polk was first trained by his father and then by Henry Van Brunt and Frank Howe, who were also in Kansas City at the time. He had also worked for Arthur Page Brown in New York before Brown moved to California. Polk is normally featured for his glass-faced Hallidie Building (1918) in San Francisco, possibly the first glass front in the world. His own employees made names for themselves as well: Addison Mizner [A7] was with him from 1893 to 1897 and later be-came the architect of great vacation mansions in Palm Beach, Florida. Maybeck and Polk were closely associated at one time.

Burnham & Root: Mon-
tauk Block, Chicago,
1880–1883

But Burnham & Root's most famous employee was their first, William Holabird [A19]. The son of a general, he had two years' train-ing at West Point, where engineering was stressed. He went to work for Jenney in 1875, the last of the famous Jenney employees. Holabird honed his skills as an engineer as he watched Jenney design the first Leiter Building (1879), a significant step toward true skyscraper con-struction. Holabird then worked for Burnham & Root only briefly, probably in 1879 or early 1880, just as they were gearing up for the Montauk Block.

In 1880 Holabird struck out on his own, setting up practice with Ossian C. Simmonds. Martin Roche [A9] left Jenney's office and joined them, but within a year Roche was promoted to partnership. Simmonds left in 1883, and Holabird & Roche soon produced the Tacoma Building (1886–1889), a project known for its technical innovations.[32] This firm also prospered over the years with some of the same kind of clients that Burnham & Root served.

Burnham & Root and Holabird & Roche had a number of successor and spin-off firms, but it is somewhat difficult to follow the connections because of each firm's various permutations and, in addition, an interweaving with the Mies van der Rohe descendants in the 1950s and afterward. Burgee was a principal in Holabird, Root & Burgee when Philip Johnson took John Burgee as partner in the late 1960s.[33]

Another major line of descent came from the fact that Bertram Grosvenor Goodhue [A18] was employed by Renwick, Aspinwall & Russell in 1884. He was only fifteen, but in his autobiography he claimed to have been trained personally by James Renwick, Jr.—who would have been sixty-six at that time but was still dominating the office. The spires of St. Patrick's Cathedral were being added, but it was not a time of any creative significance otherwise. Thus, unlike Root, who saw a significant early building being erected when he got to Chicago, Goodhue was not a prime example of the mechanics of fame in his own training. Nevertheless, he was well trained and by the age of twenty-two won first prize in a national competition for a cathedral for Dallas, Texas. Goodhue needed the backing of an established office to complete the project and was able to join the firm of Cram & Wentworth in 1892. A national economic depression in 1893 prevented the church from actually being built, but Goodhue continued his partnership until 1913.

Ralph Adams Cram [A18] also had a weak connection with an employer during his apprenticeship to Rotch & Tilden. The Boston firm was not on the cutting edge in design matters.[34] However, the name of Arthur Rotch is familiar to all young Massachusetts architects. As a graduate of the Ecole des Beaux-Arts, Rotch felt that the sons of his state should have the opportunity to study abroad and, at his father's death in 1882, he and his family founded the Rotch Travelling Scholarships, awarded annually to a student or young architect working or studying in the state of Massachusetts or a native-born son. Cram believed that he would have been the first recipient, except that he was disqualified on a technicality. But he was in the office at the time of this event, and the sudden prominence of his employer, though having little to do with the man's design talent, must have had some effect on the young employee. Arthur Rotch is also interesting in view of Cram's reputation as a medievalist, since, in the 1870s, Rotch was employed on the restoration of the chateau of Chenonceau under Viollet-le-Duc. But it is a relatively weak link in the chain of connections.

From 1885 to 1886 Cram served as the art critic of the *Boston Evening Transcript;* in 1886 he was a finalist in two architectural design competitions, for the Boston Court House and for the expansion of Bulfinch's Massachusetts State House.[35] He was twenty-seven when he organized the firm of Cram & Wentworth with Charles Francis Wentworth, who died seven years later. Goodhue joined him in 1892 and was Cram's partner almost from the outset of Cram's active career. As is so often the case, it was about a decade before their first major commission was undertaken. In 1903 they won the competition for the West Point chapel and entered the ranks of nationally famous architects.

Cram & Goodhue: Chapel, West Point, 1905

Cram was formerly credited with the design of the chapel and the slightly younger Goodhue was thought to have been the assistant. But Richard Oliver's research proves that it was otherwise, with Goodhue the designer. In 1903 Goodhue moved from Boston to take charge of the New York office that would supervise this project and Cram remained in Boston. "Saint Thomas Church (1906–1913) in New York was the last collaborative effort between Goodhue and Cram."[36] Even though it was Cram and not Goodhue who was chosen to be given a full entry in the 1968 *Encyclopaedia Britannica*, most would agree that Goodhue was by far the more famous designer.[37]

In 1904 Raymond Hood [B19] went to work for Goodhue. The following year he left to attend the Ecole des Beaux-Arts and, upon his return in 1906, went back to Cram & Goodhue's New York office. He was fired in September, though he claimed that he did not know why. Hood then went to work for Henry Hornbostel. Hornbostel had been at the head of his class at Columbia and had attended the Ecole des Beaux-Arts. Although he did do drawings for McKim, Mead & White, he did not serve an apprenticeship to a famous architect but, rather, with the Ecole in his background, he set up practice himself. He won first prize in 1904 for the design of Carnegie Institute of Technology; when Hood was employed he was working on this and the Soldiers and Sailors Memorial (1907) in Pittsburgh. Hood became the chief designer in his New York office in 1907. After a second tour at the Ecole, Hood returned again to Hornbostel's office from 1911 to 1914. By that time Hood was ready to strike out on his own, but for financial reasons he had to continue working for other firms as well, like that of

Godley, Fouilhoux & Barber in 1916 and again in 1919. Even as late as 1920 Hood was not considered a successful architect.

In 1922 ten firms were invited to submit entries in an internationally advertised competition for a new building for the *Chicago Tribune*. The prizes were so attractive—$50,000 to the winner and $20,000 to the second-place entry—that 258 designs were submitted from over twenty different countries.[38] One of the invited firms was the winner; the Harvard and Ecole-trained John Mead Howells [A11] had been one of those so chosen and he had asked Hood to join him in preparing the entry. Although Hood has been given the lion's share of the credit, Robert Stern has convincingly argued that Howells was "definitely a designer" of the winning entry.[39] Fouilhoux joined Howells & Hood on the Chicago Tribune Building (1922–1924), and, as mentioned earlier, after working for Goodhue on Goodhue's last major commission, Wallace Harrison was employed by Hood in 1924.

In the twelve years between 1922 and Hood's death at the age of forty-three, his reputation as a skyscraper designer soared as he progressively moved away from historicist ornament on his tall buildings. He changed partners constantly, though Fouilhoux was always one of them. The 1924 American Radiator Building was done with Godley and Fouilhoux, the Daily News Building (1929–1930) with Howells and Fouilhoux, the McGraw-Hill Building (1929–1930) with Fouilhoux, and Rockefeller Center in concert with a whole assembly of architects.[40] By 1928 he was so highly esteemed that he was chosen one of the major commissioners for the 1933 Chicago world's fair, the Century of Progress.[41]

Louis Skidmore [B15] was in Europe on a Rotch Travelling Scholarship from 1926 to 1929. Specifically how Hood first made him his protégé is not on record. But one of Hood's partners had been on the Rotch jury that selected Skidmore, and it is probable that Hood and Skidmore met at that time. Hood was also in Europe when preliminary plans for the Century of Progress were needed in 1929. He located Skidmore in Italy traveling with his friend Carl Landefeld. Another young man, Alfred Bendiner, had joined them and later wrote that Hood found the group and said, "Landy, get the hell up to Paris and get Skid and Joe Judge and Roorda and start some sketches for the Chicago World's Fair. . . . I'll see you in Paris."[42] It was a fortuitous accident. Another bright young man was in the right place at the right time. Frank Roorda and Carl Landefeld became Rockefeller Center architects under Hood. Skidmore, whose only apprenticeship had been with the relatively large firm of Maginnis & Walsh in Boston,[43] was named assistant general manager of design and construction for the Century of Progress (under Hood). According to Bendiner, Skidmore was able to take the ideas submitted by Paul Cret, John Holabird, Hood, and others and coalesce them into a master plan for the fair.

Not only was Skidmore employed during those hungry years for other young architects—he was also developing the skill to work with large numbers of designers, an ability that later characterized the firm of Skidmore, Owings & Merrill (SOM). In addition, the Chicago fair put Skidmore in contact with about 700 corporations, not a bad set of contacts for a young architect. The development supervisor of the fair was Skidmore's brother-in-law, Nathaniel Owings.[44]

After the exhibition was dismantled in 1935, Skidmore and Owings joined in partnership and acted as consultants for the upcoming New York World's Fair (1939–1940). In 1937, before Merrill came, Gordon Bunshaft [C9] became their employee (after being in Edward Durell Stone's [B10] employ at the time he began the Museum of Modern Art). Bunshaft became a full partner in 1946 and is best known as the designer of SOM's seminal Lever House in New York. John O. Merrill, Skidmore's classmate at MIT, became the third principal in 1939.

During World War II SOM managed as many as 400 employees, all of whom were working on government projects. One of these was Oak Ridge, Tennessee, a town for 75,000 people. Thus the experience gained on the two fairs was augmented by other tremendous jobs and in the postwar period SOM continued as a large team-design firm. Although the name of the firm remained unaltered, there were eventually many partners.

SOM had a number of noted employees. William S. Brown entered the office in 1939, took 1940 off as the winner of the Schermerhorn traveling fellowship, and returned to the firm in 1941. John Dinkeloo was with the firm from 1942 until 1950. At that time he moved to Eero Saarinen's office, then occupied with its first major commission, the General Motors Complex in Warren, Michigan. In 1961 he and Kevin Roche, a Mies ex-employee, succeeded to the Saarinen practice. Vincent George Kling worked for SOM in 1945. Walter A. Netsch, Jr., was hired in 1946 and became a partner in 1955. Bruce Graham [C4] first worked for Holabird & Root in 1949–1951 and became a SOM partner in 1960. John Johansen worked for his former teacher, Marcel Breuer, and then SOM before establishing his own practice in 1948. Stanley Tigerman worked for George Fred Keck, then for SOM from 1957 to 1959, for Harry Weese at the time of the Arena Stage in Washington, D.C., and finally for Paul Rudolph in Rudolph's most famous period. William Turnbull, Jr., was an SOM employee before he joined in partnership with Charles Moore, Donlyn Lyndon, and Richard Whitaker in the design and construction of Sea Ranch (1966) in California—their seminal commission. Edward Bassett was a product of both the SOM and Saarinen offices. Richard Meier worked for SOM in 1959–1960, but left to enter Breuer's office from 1960 to 1963.

The Bulfinch and Wright lines have perhaps come to an end, but the Renwick line, as well as the Gropius, Breuer, Mies, Saarinen, and Kahn lines, will surely continue on into the future if the mechanics of fame remain unchanged.

TEN

The European Immigrant Masters in the Twentieth Century

Behrens: AEG Turbine Factory, Berlin, 1908–1909

Walter Gropius, Ludwig Mies van der Rohe, and Eliel Saarinen had established their careers and were in their fifties when they came to the United States; Breuer was thirty-five. They became magnets for the restless young men and women who were searching for a new direction in architecture.

Gropius and Mies had first met while working for Peter Behrens. Behrens was approximately the same age as Frank Lloyd Wright and achieved his fame in architectural history at about the same time that Wright produced his Prairie School masterpieces. In Behrens' case, he was one of the first designers to be given total control over all of the industrial products and design needs of a large company—the stationery, advertisements, and light fixtures as well as the office and factory buildings—for the Allgemeine Elektricitäts Gesellschaft (AEG), the German equivalent of America's General Electric. Although many of these designs are of interest, it is his Turbine Factory (1908–1909) in Berlin that is considered his major contribution to the development of Modern architecture.

Walter Gropius [B19] served as Behrens' chief assistant on this building and then set up his own practice shortly thereafter, with Adolf Meyer.[1] Almost immediately they received a commission for the Fagus Shoelast factory (1911–1912) in Alfeld-an-der-Lein, Germany. This was an amazingly strong statement of the emerging stripped Modern styling, much more interesting than a factory a few blocks away that Gropius designed later. Not only did they take Behrens' glass curtain-wall a step further—they had the courage visually to remove the corners of this building, with glass-enclosed stairways, thus revealing the relatively thin skeletal system. They were even braver than Behrens, who had added masonry piers to the corners of the

Year of Birth   **Chart 8. Gropius and Mies and their descendants.**

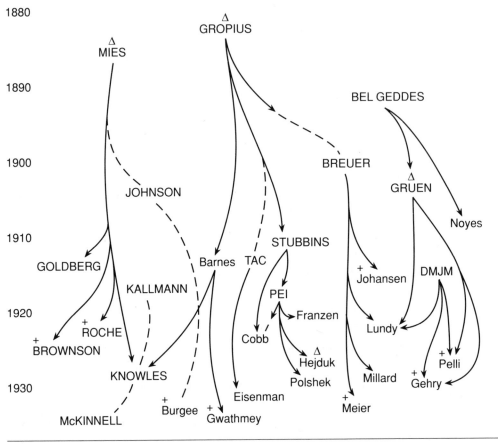

Employment	⟶	NAME ON THE INDEX OF FAME
Partnership	– – – – – – – – – –	Name not on the Index of Fame
Mentorship	· · · · · · · · · · · · · · · · · · ·	
European training	Δ	Connects to others on another chart +

AEG building in order to make it appear more stable and natural to a public unaccustomed to steel supports.

Ludwig Mies van der Rohe [B19] also worked for Behrens at that time; in fact he stayed two years longer than did Gropius, from 1908 to 1911,[2] when he left to set up his own practice with much more modest commissions. As mentioned in the first chapter, Le Corbusier was also briefly in Behrens' office, though shortly after the completion of the AEG Turbine building rather than during its design.

Not only hostile public taste but World War I and the subsequent economic situation in Germany kept commissions to a minimum for these ambitious architects. However, Gropius was able to establish his international fame when he designed the building for his school, the Bauhaus (1925–1926), when it made its major move to Dessau. It was at that specific time that Marcel Breuer [B19] was promoted from being Gropius' student to a position as a member of his faculty. While the building was under construction, Breuer made his own bid for a place in history with the design of the first successful Breuer chair. It was not his first chair design; he had been trying for several years, but earlier attempts had been clumsy and none had the éclat of the 1925 chair. Though he had been in close contact with Gropius for five years, Breuer found his power at the same time that Gropius demonstrated his fullest strength and at the same time that he could be considered an employee rather than a student.[3]

Gropius: The Bauhaus, Dessau, 1925–1926

Breuer: Breuer chair, 1925

In 1927 the German Werkbund, an organization of avant-garde designers, sponsored an exhibition of low-cost housing, the Weissenhof Housing Settlement at Stuttgart. Mies was the vice-president of the Werkbund and chose a number of the most advanced European architects as designers: Gropius, Le Corbusier, Bruno Taut, Hans Scharoun, J. J. P. Oud, himself, and others. The exhibition established these men in the forefront of the new movement.

Gropius and Breuer each left the Bauhaus in 1928 to set up separate practices in Germany. Breuer had even fewer commissions than did Gropius and with Hitler's rise to power they both immigrated to England, Gropius in 1934 and Breuer a year later.[4] Gropius entered into a partnership with Maxwell Fry, Breuer with Francis Reginald Stevens Yorke. For most of his career Mies had been nearly without commissions. Even though Mies' work in 1929 on the German Pavilion for the World's Fair in Barcelona and the Tugendhat House in Brno, Czechoslovakia, eventually brought him fame, at the time only his colleagues recognized his brilliance. In 1930 Mies took over the directorship of the Bauhaus from Hannes Meyer, at Gropius' request. Mies moved the faculty and students to Berlin, where it struggled along until it was closed by the Nazis.

Few Americans attended the Bauhaus under either Gropius or Mies. However, Bertrand Goldberg [C4], whose reputation was established by the twin-towered Marina City in Chicago (1960), was Mies' student in 1932 and 1933 and then returned to Chicago to work for George Fred Keck just when Keck produced the second of his extraordinary exhibition houses for the Century of Progress exhibition in Chicago (1934).[5] Three years later Goldberg won praise for his design of Suitland, Maryland (1937–1944), and an inventive ice-cream shop in Chicago (1938).

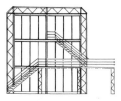

Keck: Crystal House, Chicago, 1934

Gropius, Mies, and Breuer all immigrated to the United States in 1937. A whole new start came for both Gropius and Breuer when Walter Gropius was invited to join the Harvard architecture faculty in 1937 and was able to bring Breuer with him. In 1938 Gropius became

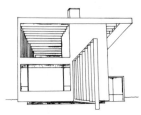

Gropius & Breuer:
Gropius House, Lincoln,
1937–1938

the chairman of the department, and for three years, from 1938 to 1941, Gropius and Breuer also formed a design partnership. At that time they designed a house in Lincoln, Massachusetts (1937–1938), for Gropius and also a house for Breuer. In the originality of these houses and those to follow—they were the first "International Style" houses to be seen in that region in America—and in their masterful control of design elements, Gropius and Breuer exhibited a fresh and exciting burst of creativity.

It was these first few years in the United States and at Harvard that produced the most famous of their American students. In fact, quite a few of the names associated with them as students at that time were actually employees. As a teacher, the younger man, Breuer, was closer to the students than was Gropius as director, although Breuer did not stay as long on the faculty.

One of their first pupils was only four years younger than Breuer himself, and he was as much a colleague as a student (and never an employee). This was Philip Johnson [C13], who took advantage of their arrival to reenter Harvard in 1940 in order to prepare himself as an architect rather than just as a major architectural critic. In the ten years since his graduation as a classics major, Johnson had been a very active promoter of European Modernism, including the work of Gropius and Breuer. Johnson, Henry-Russell Hitchcock, and the director of the Museum of Modern Art, Alfred Barr, Jr., had sponsored not only the famous 1932 show that gave us the title "The International Style," but also the exhibition "The Bauhaus" in 1938. As was also the case in Johnson's promotion of Mies in 1947, this kind of support and publicity often seems to generate new confidence in the person being featured. Gropius and Breuer both were hitting a new stride at the time Johnson was with them as a most unusual student. When Johnson graduated in 1943 he was one of the rare students who did not have to turn in drawings, models, and plans for a final thesis, but instead could afford to finance the building of his project—a small house—and have it photographed by Ezra Stoller. Although Johnson was an exceptional case, he was certainly ripe for the contact he made at that time.[6]

Hugh Stubbins [C5], among other things the architect of the highly visible Citicorp Building in New York, was not, in fact, a Gropius and Breuer student. He was Gropius' assistant. Stubbins had received his architectural degree from Harvard in 1935 and went to work for Royal Barry Wills.[7] Then, while working for the Birmingham, Alabama, firm of Miller, Martin & Lewis, Stubbins was offered the 1939 Wheelwright traveling fellowship and, at the same time, the position of Gropius' aide at Harvard. Significantly, Stubbins chose the second option. The employer-employee relationship is of more value than that of student and teacher in terms of future fame, and although travel is, indeed, important to the development of an architect, this employment by Gropius tied Stubbins into the system we are study-ing. An early work by Stubbins, a housing development at Windsor Locks, Connecticut (1942), and Stubbins' own house in Lexington, Massachusetts, attracted the attention of the press. I. M. Pei [C11] was his employee then. Stubbins remained on the faculty until 1954, as-suming the chairmanship for one year when Gropius resigned from teaching in 1952.

Eliot Noyes was one of Gropius' very first students. He graduated from the Harvard School of Design in 1938 and the following year was named the first director of the Museum of Modern Art's Department of Industrial Design. He held that position until 1945, when he worked briefly for Norman Bel Geddes,[8] and then entered Breuer's office just as Breuer struck out alone in full-time practice in New York. When Noyes set up his own firm, one of his own employees was Peter Millard.[9]

Edward Larabee Barnes had a degree in architectural history from Harvard when he reentered the university for his professional degree in architecture under Gropius and Breuer. However, again, Barnes was not only their student—he was employed by them during the period when they were in formal partnership. There is no ques-tion that he was a talented young man. Barnes had won the Milton-Harvard award in 1938 and the Sheldon traveling fellowship in 1941. However, with the outbreak of World War II he was unable to profit from the second honor. Perhaps it was actually to his advantage that, like Stubbins, rather than travel to Europe, Barnes worked for the two masters instead. In 1948 he opened his own office in New York; he consistently produced excellent work and gained a solid reputation among his professional colleagues. Barnes did not, however, design in the spectacular and dramatic fashion that the historians find most photogenic, and his "fame" is not as pronounced as some of Gropius' and Breuer's other apprentices and students. Nevertheless, two archi-tects who are currently in the spotlight were his employees: Jacquelin Robertson and Edward Knowles. Knowles then went to work for Mies & Johnson at the time of the Seagram Building before he became a major award winner as a partner in the team that won the competi-tion for the new Boston City Hall.

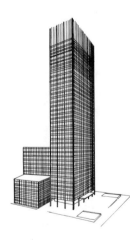

Mies & Johnson: Sea-gram Building, New York, 1954–1958

John Johansen became one of the more startling and dramatic designers. He received his degree from Harvard in 1941 and also worked for Breuer—and for SOM in its early years as well. Johansen established his own practice in 1948 and for a few years worked more or less in the International Style. But by the mid-1950s he had begun to experiment with heavily sculptural forms achieved with sprayed concrete. He then moved to chunky, brutal assemblages of concrete poured in geometric shapes. From that time forward, one never knew quite what to expect next. His Charles Center in Baltimore, the Goddard Library at Clark University, and the Mummers Theater in Oklahoma City all received attention from the architectural press. However, I am not aware of any of his employees at those times who later became famous.

Gropius' classes were limited to about 16 students per semester. Since he taught for fourteen years at Harvard, more than 400 people can claim to have been trained by Gropius. About 20 of these have achieved various measures of recognition in their own right as designers; since they are nearly all still in practice, their future fame is still quite uncertain. We can never judge the staying power of a contemporary architect's reputation. One of these noted students was Lawrence Halprin, who had already focused on botany and was interested in landscape design when he entered the program under Gropius. In 1949 he began to establish himself as a nationally known leader in the field of landscape architecture. The Argentine-born Eduardo Catalano was another student. He graduated in 1945 to become a master of dramatic structures.[10]

Ieoh Ming Pei [C11] was a student a little later. He had come to America from China in 1935 and received a bachelor of architecture degree from MIT in 1940, winning a traveling fellowship that same year. He had worked for John M. Gray in Boston in 1939, while the office was designing the Gulf Oil Building in Atlanta, Georgia. In 1941 he was hired by the engineering firm of Webster & Stone, and then from 1943 to 1945 he worked for William Lescaze [B13]. However, he returned to seek a master's degree in architecture from Harvard and was a student from 1945 to 1946, the year before Breuer left for full-time practice.

Pei was employed while at Harvard, not by either Gropius or Breuer, but by Hugh Stubbins at the period in Stubbins' career when he was first gaining the attention of the architectural press. Upon his second graduation Pei was invited to join the Harvard faculty in 1946 and taught there for the next two years; in this respect he worked for Gropius. In 1951, while a member of the Zeckendorf firm of Webb & Knapp, Pei won the Harvard Wheelwright Fellowship. He also rejoined Lescaze as an associate. Finally, at the age of thirty-five, Pei established his own firm.

The Mile-High Center in Denver gave Pei his first national recognition. While this building was being designed, Ulrich Franzen was

Pei: Mile-High Center,
Denver, 1954–1959

one of Pei's employees (from 1950 to 1955). John Hejduk, like Franzen a Harvard graduate, worked for Pei immediately after Mile-High was completed, from 1956 to 1958.[11] James S. Polshek, who became dean at Columbia, was with Pei in 1955 and 1956 and also worked for Franzen. Finally, Henry N. Cobb, still another Harvard graduate and also a graduate of Stubbins' office, became Pei's most important partner and, with Pei, was able to live through the embarrassment of the endlessly dropping glass panels of the John Hancock Building in Boston (now stabilized) and to emerge famous with the addition to the National Gallery of Art in Washington. In the 1970s Cobb took over as chairman of Harvard's architectural program.

Though there are very few exceptions to the in-office contact of famous architects, Paul Rudolph [C14] rose to fame with only a "student connection" to Gropius or Breuer. Rudolph entered the graduate program in 1941 and claimed to be influenced as much by another teacher, Gropius' colleague the engineer Konrad Wachsmann, as by the master himself. Unlike the other most successful graduates of that program, he never worked for a famous architect. Rudolph left to serve in the shipbuilding arm of the United States Navy, returning to graduate in 1947. He joined in partnership with a much older Florida architect, Ralph Twitchell, and within a short time was receiving attention from the architectural journals for his experimentation with new structural systems and materials in small Florida houses. The year 1955 saw the beginning of Rudolph's major commissions—the Riverview High School in Sarasota (1955–1959) and the Jewett Art Center at Wellesley College (1955–1959).

In 1957 Rudolph was appointed to the chairmanship of the architecture department at Yale University and, in the early 1960s, he and Eero Saarinen were the most discussed of the younger architects in America. Rudolph's vigorous Yale Art and Architecture Building (1958–1962) was receiving praise from such critics as the *New York Times'* Ada Louise Huxtable (later rescinded). It was not his first celebrated work, but it certainly was the one to get the most attention. Charles Gwathmey, Jacquelin Robertson, Richard Rogers, and Der Scutt were in his master's class at that time. Stanley Tigerman was Rudolph's employee.[12]

Finally, Huson Jackson, after working for Charles Eames in St. Louis, attended Gropius' and Breuer's first classes at Harvard. Jackson then worked for Carl Koch [C3], another Harvard graduate, but one who had served an apprenticeship under Sweden's famous Sven Markelius and also worked for Edward D. Stone [B10]. Ronald R. Gourley entered the Harvard Design program just before Breuer left to practice. Though neither Jackson nor Gourley is especially well

Rudolph: Art and Architecture Building, New Haven, 1958–1962

Le Corbusier: Villa Savoye, Poissy, 1929–1930

known nationally, in 1958 they became partners of an internationally celebrated architect, Josep Lluis Sert [B8].

Is it possible that Sert may have become a particularly strong designer *because* he had an especially important apprenticeship where he gained this magic? Sert was born and educated in Barcelona and in 1929 he was employed by Le Corbusier at the time that the Villa Savoye was the project in his atelier and the time that his dormitory for Swiss students at the University of Paris was in the design stage.

Sert became an active member of the Congrès internationaux d'architecture moderne (CIAM) almost from its inception. CIAM was organized by Le Corbusier and Sigfried Giedion in 1928 and not only Gropius but many of the most progressive architects at the time were members, including Richard Neutra in America. Sert returned to Spain in 1930 and seven years later was given the commission for the Spanish Pavilion where Picasso's *Guernica* was exhibited at the Paris World's Fair. In 1938 he was asked by CIAM to write a book on its theory of city planning, and he immigrated to the United States in 1939 with this project in hand. Sert finished *Can Our Cities Survive?* in 1942 (though it was not published until after the war). That same year he was elected president of CIAM, a position he held until 1956. When Gropius decided to concentrate on his practice rather than continue teaching, Sert left his partnership in the city planning firm of Wiener & Schulz and took the position of head of the Harvard Graduate School of Design.[13]

Several times in his career, Breuer was inspired to produce fresh works that received attention. The success he achieved in Germany with his chairs was repeated in America with his house designs at the beginning of his Harvard appointment. Three years after Breuer moved to New York in 1946 he was commissioned to design an exhibition house for the Museum of Modern Art, and a monograph on Breuer and his work was published in conjunction with the display of the house. At that time, Victor Lundy, a former student, was in Breuer's employ. Lundy then worked in association with Victor Gruen and with Daniel, Mann, Johnson, Mendenhall in California. But in the late 1940s Breuer had not yet produced the buildings that would be featured in history surveys. For example, when William Jordy wrote a chapter on Breuer's Ferry Cooperative Dormitory at Vassar College (1951) in Volume 4 of *American Buildings and Their Architects* he began with the statement that "it is easily passed over because it exists in the limbo of the all-too-familiar and the not-quite-historical."[14]

But Breuer's largest and most published commissions were finally underway: St. John's Abbey in Collegeville, Minnesota (1953–1961); the UNESCO Building in Paris (1960–1969); and the Whitney

Breuer: Exhibition House, Museum of Modern Art, New York, 1949

Museum of Art in New York (1963–1967). Richard Meier was Breuer's employee at that time. Meier also had worked for SOM and for Davis, Brody & Associates. The latter were featured by Robert A. M. Stern in his *New Directions in American Architecture* (1969) and Robert Stern, a Yale graduate, was Meier's employee when Meier was getting established.

Richard Meier was one of the two major colleague connections for Michael Graves. Graves was at Harvard under Sert and his early employment is never mentioned. However, when interviewed, Graves said that he felt that his inspiration came not from his employer, but rather, as in the case of Eames and Saarinen and Schindler and Neutra, grew out of the excited dialogs that occurred between himself and Richard Meier when they were both starting out as very young professors at Princeton in the 1960s. At that time Graves was also working in a close informal partnership with Peter Eisenman, producing competition entries every year from 1963 to 1966.[15]

Harvard produced an exceptional number of attention-getting architects during the period when Gropius and Breuer were on the faculty. With only a few exceptions the record proves that those young men who were actually employed by one or both of these teachers (or their recent ex-employees) gained even more from that experience than from their classes. Of course, one assumes that employers hire their most promising pupils and thus there is a question of cause and effect. However, the more holistic learning process that occurs in a working office is of more value than the university design studios— the young employee can gain more from observing the master at work than from attempting to understand the professor's criticisms, which are inevitably personal and focused on the student, not the teacher. Gropius, who has been described as extraordinarily charismatic, though shy and almost inarticulate when speaking,[16] undoubtedly would have been more influential in the office than in the classroom in terms of benefit to the single individual.

"Mies does not talk easily," Peter Blake explained in 1961 when he presented a recorded conversation with Mies van der Rohe at a conference which focused on the four "great architects" Gropius, Mies, Wright, and Le Corbusier.[17] Philip Johnson said, "Gropius stressed teamwork, but Mies was alone. Gropius spread the gospel; Mies will never make a speech, and never write an article."[18] It is no surprise, therefore, that those young people who came in contact with Mies in his office where they could observe him designing are the ones whose names are familiar today although, even there, Mies preferred to work by himself. Mies' students, on the other hand, though capable and competent architects, were not candidates to receive that

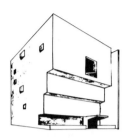

Breuer: Whitney Museum, New York, 1963–1967

strange surge of design power that occurred in some of his employees present at the right time.

Several events in America had brought Mies' name up in the 1930s. He had been one of the architects whose work was shown in the 1932 exhibition of International Style architecture at the Museum of Modern Art and was a favorite of Philip Johnson. Johnson wanted the museum to hire Mies to design a new building in New York, the commission that was awarded instead to Goodwin and Stone. The Stanley Resors, owners of an advertising firm, learned of Mies through Johnson and invited Mies to design a house in Wyoming (never built). Finally, Henry T. Held, then president of the Armour Institute of Technology in Chicago, brought Mies to the United States in 1937, the same year Mies' former colleagues moved from England to Harvard. Held said:

> I had the privilege of inviting one of these creative individuals, Mies van der Rohe, to take a position in this country. I invited him largely on the recommendation of John Holabird, a leading Chicago architect, who said, "I don't know Mies van der Rohe, but the Barcelona Pavilion and one or two other things that he has done are outstanding." And, he continued, "after all, even if we don't know too much about this fellow, he's so much better than any of the people you could get to head a school of architecture, why not take a chance?"
>
> So we invited Mies, and after some time he accepted the post. . . . He couldn't speak English . . . [but] soon went to work to rebuild the architectural curriculum at the Institute. He was joined by Ludwig Hilderseimer, Walter Peterhaus, and by two Americans who were former students of his in Germany, Rogers and Priestly. In a very short time, I.I.T. became the only American school of architecture where the teaching was in German.[19]

An architect who was also a member of the Board of Trustees had been planning to design a new campus for the school at the time it was undergoing its name change from Armour to the Illinois Institute of Technology (IIT). When he died suddenly, Mies was given this impressive task and, with it, began to build his reputation as an American designer. The curriculum itself was "rigid and formal," since, as Mies put it, "I was just thinking to find a method which teaches the student how to make a good building. Nothing else."[20]

In 1946 Philip Johnson mounted an exhibition of photographs of the still relatively unknown work of Mies van der Rohe at the Museum of Modern Art and wrote an accompanying monograph, published the same year. Mies' most celebrated American work followed shortly *after* this conjunction. He seems to have responded to the publicity with greater force—just as Wright did in the early 1930s and as Kahn

Mies: Lake Shore Drive
Apartments, Chicago,
1948–1951

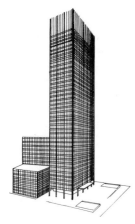

Mies & Johnson: Sea-
gram Building, New York,
1954–1958

did in the 1950s. The Lake Shore Drive Apartments (1948–1951) in Chicago and the Dr. Edith Farnsworth House in Plano, Illinois (1946–1950) signaled Mies' final mastery of his style at the same time that Philip Johnson was completing his own first famous work, his Glass House. Again we have two colleagues (though a generation apart in age and experience) forcing each other into creative peaks. Finally, though most of the design was by Mies, Philip Johnson was actually Mies' partner on the one building most likely to be called to mind when the late work of Mies is mentioned, the Seagram Building in New York (1956–1958).

Two employees on Mies' most famous highrises have made their own national reputations: Kevin Roche and Edward F. Knowles. Kevin Roche [C5] was first trained in Ireland and then did postgraduate work at IIT. He was employed by Mies in 1948 and 1949, just as the Lake Shore Drive buildings were being designed. However, Roche then went to work for Eero Saarinen, an equally important contact. Knowles was employed by Mies & Johnson in 1955 and 1956 when the plans for the Seagram Building were emerging. He then worked for Barnes in 1959 and 1960. Immediately thereafter, in partnership with Gerhard Michael Kallmann and Noel M. McKinnell, he won a highly publicized commission for the new Boston City Hall in 1961.[21] If there was magic at work in any contacts with the reticent and silent Mies, then Roche, Knowles, and Goldberg are examples of the spell. For each the timing was splendid.

Few of Mies' students or employees graduated to design flamboyant or pyrotechnical buildings, the sorts of structures that are particularly attractive to the architectural press and hence likely to generate fame. Fazlur Khan did graduate work under Mies before he became a major engineering designer of the spectacular Sears Tower (1970–1974) and equally monumental John Hancock Center (1965–1970) in Chicago done by the firm of SOM—perhaps he died too young. Reginald Malcolmson and Jacques Brownson are said to be Mies' protégés. Brownson moved from being a student to the faculty at IIT from 1948 to 1957. He set up practice as well in 1952 and from 1957 to 1966 was an associate of the C. F. Murphy firm in Chicago. Malcolmson followed the same pattern at first. He studied under Mies in 1947 to 1949 and was on the faculty from 1949 to 1959 and was Mies' assistant from 1953 to 1958. In 1964 Malcolmson was appointed dean at the University of Michigan. Myron Goldsmith worked for Mies and then took over his practice for a while when Mies retired. Helmut Jahn did not arrive in the United States until 1966, after Mies retired. However, he studied with Myron Goldsmith and with Fazlur Khan at IIT and then joined C. F. Murphy in 1967 while its first spectacular buildings were going up. C. F. Murphy was actually one of the heirs to the Burnham firm but had close connections with Mies and many Mies ex-students in the office staff. The firm that finally succeeded to Mies' practice is "a partnership of his former associates and his grandson [which] still flourishes under the name Fujikawa, Conerato, Lohan."[22]

Unlike Mies, Breuer, or even Gropius, Eliel Saarinen [A20] had had a vigorous and attractive practice in Finland for over twenty years before he arrived in the United States in 1923. As early as 1900 Saarinen had begun to win international recognition, and his reputation was fully established by 1914, though not as a member of the avant-garde. His second place entry in the *Chicago Tribune* competition of 1922, which was won by Howells & Hood, generated so much interest that it influenced the styles of buildings by architects as different as Bruce Goff and Harvey Corbett, and Raymond Hood as well. The American architectural climate seemed right for Saarinen and so he came with his family, which included his thirteen-year-old son Eero. However, as John Jacobus, Jr., points out, "a comparison of the Cranbrook buildings of the 1920s and 1930s with the earlier Helsinki Station reveals little or no intensification or development of a personal style, but instead only an overall simplification or generalization of forms that are ultimately derivative."[23]

Therefore, it follows that although Eliel Saarinen taught and employed young architects from 1925 on at Cranbrook Academy and in his practice, because he took no dramatic new roads, no famous employees or students would have emerged from his contact. Nevertheless, one of his students did achieve success.[24] But it is interesting to look at all of the connections involved. Florence Schust was an orphan who showed talent as a boarding student at Kingswood, the girl's school connected to Cranbrook. She was taken under the wings of Eliel Saarinen and his wife, traveling with them in the summers. Trained in architecture at Cranbrook, she graduated from the Architectural Association in London in the late 1930s and returned to study under Mies van der Rohe at IIT, where she got to know him well as a personal friend. Her first employers were the partnership of Gropius and Breuer in Cambridge at that fertile time when they were showing the strength and self-assurance of masters of modern architecture while much of the profession in America was still unsure of the direction to take. A year later she went to work for Harrison & Abramovitz and then began to design for the Knoll furniture firm. In 1946 she married Hans Knoll, a pacesetter in the field of interior furnishings, and became largely responsible for matters of design as well as a partner in the firm.[25]

In 1937 and 1938 there was a conjunction of colleagues at Cranbrook that generated the fireworks of creativity. Charles Eames [C8] had been in practice as an architect in St. Louis for a decade. His background included an unsuccessful start as an architecture student in the late 1920s at Washington University in St. Louis. In 1929 he visited the Weissenhof housing development exhibition in Stuttgart, where he saw work by Mies, Gropius, Le Corbusier, and others. Deeply affected, he found his Beaux-Arts training incompatible with his new vision of architecture. He worked for the St. Louis firm of Trueblood & Graf and in 1930 was a partner in the firm of Gray & Eames and then in Eames & Walsh with Robert Walsh. In spite of the Depression he received some work, the John Philip Meyer House (1935–1938), for example, and "built and furnished all the ceremonial decorations for some churches in St. Louis."[26] It was at that time that Huson Jackson was his employee.

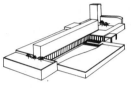

Saarinen & Saarinen:
Smithsonian Project,
1939

These attracted Eliel Saarinen's attention and Eames was invited to join the faculty at Cranbrook; "a bond was forged. . . . Eames' genius began to open up."[27] Charles Eames arrived in 1937 and stayed until 1941. Eero Saarinen [C18] was also at Cranbrook at that time. After studying sculpture in Paris in 1929 and 1930 he graduated from Yale, where he won the Charles O. Mecham traveling fellowship from 1934 to 1936. He had joined Cranbrook as an instructor in 1936 and "wherever Charles and Eero were together their minds struck off sparks, a spontaneous exchange of ideas that lasted until Eero died."[28]

It was a three-way exchange between Eames and both the son and the father. In 1939 Eliel and Eero Saarinen (with J. Robert Swanson) won first place in the Smithsonian Gallery of Art competition (unfortunately, because of the war it was not built). Their Crow Island School in Winnetka, Illinois, of the same year, done with Perkins & Will, would be featured by the Museum of Modern Art. Charles Eames won awards in all categories that very same year in the Museum of Modern Art's Organic Design Competition. The following year he won again. The year 1939 proved the impact of a connection between colleagues. In 1942 Eames and his wife, Ray Kaiser Eames, who was also a designer, moved to California, where their Case Study houses, begun in 1945, reached an international press. For the rest of their lives the Eameses worked brilliantly in many design media—film, furniture, stage, graphics, but these are almost their only essays into pure architecture. Significantly, this great leap of strength occurred in these first years after the meeting of the Saarinens and Eames.

Who were the students at Cranbrook and the Saarinen employees in the period between 1938 and 1945? One was Edmund Bacon, who became a national figure as an urban designer. Ralph Rap-

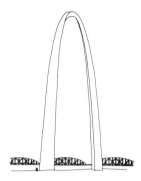

Saarinen: Jefferson Memorial Arch, St. Louis, 1949

son was a student on scholarship for two years at that time. He later designed embassies in Stockholm and Copenhagen in the 1950s and the Tyrone Guthrie Theater in Minneapolis (1961–1963) and headed the school of architecture at the University of Minnesota. Harry Weese graduated from MIT in 1938 and won a fellowship to Cranbrook. In 1941 he joined in partnership with another Saarinen student, Benjamin Baldwin (an associate of Louis Kahn on Kahn's last commission many years later). Weese was on his own by 1947 and on his way to recognition. Gyo Obata was a Cranbrook student at the very end of this period, in 1945–1946. For the next three years he was employed by SOM and today is a partner in Hellmuth, Obata & Kassabaum.[29]

But the other well-known architects associated with the Saarinen name were in Eero Saarinen's office at the time that his personal reputation soared after his father's death in 1950. Bassett, Birkerts, Dinkeloo, and Venturi were all hired between 1949 and 1951, the years when Saarinen's fame increased dramatically. He had just won the St. Louis arch commission and his firm was handling the enormous General Motors Technical Center complex (1951–1955) in Warren, Michigan. Edward Charles Bassett worked for Saarinen from 1951 to 1955 before becoming an important designer for SOM. Gunnar Birkerts arrived from Germany in 1949 and first was employed by Perkins & Will and then joined Saarinen in 1951. He moved on and worked for Minoru Yamasaki during the time that Yamasaki designed the concrete vaulted terminal building for the St. Louis airport that first brought him attention. Birkerts himself would design as spectacular a structure as those done by his former employers when he produced the Federal Reserve Bank building in Minneapolis (1968–1972) carried by hugh catenary curves.

Saarinen & Saarinen: GM Technical Center, Warren, 1951–1955

The young man in Saarinen's office from 1950 to 1953 who would unquestionably be the most famous and most influential in architectural thought was Robert Venturi [C6], but Venturi had an equally significant connection because he left to work for Louis Kahn at just the time when Kahn was starting to generate attention.

Cesar Pelli, Helmut Borcherat, Anthony Lumsden, and Paul Kennon all were hired by Saarinen slightly later in the 1950s, when the office grew large with Saarinen's many commissions. But many of these men not only had other famous employers—like Borcherat with Frank Lloyd Wright—they stayed on after Saarinen's sudden death of brain cancer in 1961, when Roche and Dinkeloo took over the practice and completed the TWA and Dulles terminal buildings, the CBS building, and the John Deere headquarters. A similar thing happened when Richardson died: Shepley, Rutan & Coolidge changed the name of the firm and the architects had to prove themselves.

Yamasaki: St. Louis Air Terminal, St. Louis, 1951–1956

John Dinkeloo had moved to Saarinen's office from SOM in 1950. At about the same time Saarinen hired Kevin Roche, who had just been working for Mies when the Lake Shore Drive Apartments were being designed. By 1955 Roche was Saarinen's chief assistant. Paul Kennon, who became head of Caudill, Rowlett & Scott (CRS), was among the employees who stayed on for the first years of the successor firm and personally worked on Roche & Dinkeloo's Oakland Museum (1961–1968). This and the Ford Foundation Building (1963–1968) in New York were their first and, in my opinion, their best designs as a team. They were the buildings that launched Roche & Dinkeloo. Cesar Pelli left in 1964 to become head designer for Daniel, Mann, Johnson, Mendenhall (DMJM), an enormous commercially successful firm in California though unheralded in terms of fame. Pelli then worked for Victor Gruen from 1968 to 1977 before becoming the dean at Yale University. Anthony Lumsden spent ten years with Saarinen and Roche & Dinkeloo before he also joined DMJM in 1964.

Roche & Dinkeloo: Ford Foundation, New York, 1963–1968

For the final proofs of this hypothesis that the design of an early significant building will have been in the office, about to be begun, or very recently completed at the time a young and ambitious architect is employed by another who has found a place in architectural history we must look at the career of Louis Kahn and the timing of his employees' presence in terms of his fame.

ELEVEN

Louis Kahn

The example of Louis I. Kahn [B13] underscores the claim that a magic spark may pass from one famous architect to a bright and talented employee at a specific moment in their careers—the moment when the senior architect undergoes a dramatic surge of design strength. Kahn is particularly interesting as a case in point because for him the road to fame was so long. He was in practice for years before he attracted the attention of the profession.

Kahn was born on an Estonian island in the Baltic and was four when his parents brought him to Philadelphia. Though poor, he attended the University of Pennsylvania from 1920 to 1924, supporting himself by playing the piano and organ in local movie theaters and by working as a draftsman for Hewitt & Ash,[1] and for Hoffman & Henon in Philadelphia. Although he was better than average, he was not seen as a brilliant student by either John Harbeson, his first-year design teacher, or Paul Cret, his senior year professor.[2] After graduation he was employed by the city architect, John Molitor. In 1927 he worked for William H. Lee. None of this work or educational experience boded well for Kahn's eventual fame.

After a trip to Europe in 1928 Kahn was hired by his former professor, the Philadelphia architect Paul Philippe Cret [B7]. Kahn worked on the drawings of the Folger Shakespearean Library in Washington, D.C. This was by no means Cret's first important design; it had been years since he had inaugurated his reputation as a designer with his prize-winning entry for the Pan American Union Building (1907) in Washington.[3] In fact, Cret was near the peak of his fame. Cret was one of the designers selected at that time to initiate the planning for the Century of Progress exhibition in Chicago (along with Hood and Corbett). He also had the commission to redesign the campus and add numerous buildings for the University of Texas. Ten

Year of Birth   **Chart 9. Saarinen and Kahn and their descendants.**

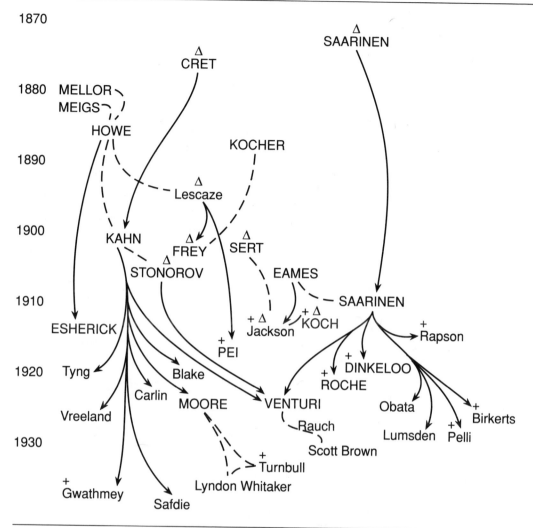

Employment —————————————▶   NAME ON THE INDEX OF FAME

Partnership   — — — — — — — — — —   Name not on the Index of Fame

Mentorship   ·····································

European training   Δ   Connects to others on another chart   +

years later, in 1938, he was the Gold Medal winner of the American
Institute of Architects, an award that comes only after a reputation has
been solid for decades. According to my hypothesis, Cret's influence
on Kahn's future fame would have been slight, whether he had substantial influence on Kahn's design style at that time or not.

Cret had long been a close friend of George Howe [B16], another
Philadelphia architect who would become a powerful factor in Kahn's
career a number of years later. At the time that Kahn was working in
Cret's office in 1929 and 1930, Cret's colleague, Howe, was rocketing

to fame. Like so many other Philadelphians, Howe's background included study at the Ecole des Beaux-Arts and a local apprenticeship. From 1913 to 1916 he was an employee of Furness, Evans & Company. However, Frank Furness was not even alive at that time, and it had been many years since the firm had produced notable work. Allen Evans was the head of the firm and he invited Howe to join him as a partner. Howe left in 1916 and teamed up with Walter Mellor and Arthur Meigs. Mellor was a graduate of Haverford and the University of Pennsylvania under Cret. He had worked for the local architect Theophilus P. Chandler.[4] Arthur Meigs had no formal training in architecture whatsoever and was one of the last of the breed of "gentleman architects." The Mellor, Meigs & Howe [B8] partnership lasted until 1928 and turned out a great number of charming period pieces—comfortable, large, romantically styled homes, but hardly the sort of architecture that avant-garde historians and critics of the next several decades would find of interest.

Quite suddenly George Howe entered a period of transition in terms of the direction his designs would take. In 1929, after creating four different schemes for a large building for the Philadelphia Savings Fund Society (PSFS), "all surprisingly modern,"[5] Howe sought and found a new partner.

Born in Switzerland, William Lescaze [B13] had studied at the polytechnical school in Zurich from 1915 to 1919. Neutra was also there as a student, but there is no mention of an acquaintance between them. Lescaze cited his professor Karl Moser as his mentor.[6] From 1919 to 1920 Lescaze worked for Henri Sauvage in Paris, an architect devoted to the problems of low-cost housing although at that time he had commissions for theaters and much of his best-known work would be done a few years later. Lescaze came to America in August 1920 with Karl Moser's son, Werner Moser. Moser went to Wright; Lescaze stayed in New York one week and left for Ohio, where he was employed by Hubbell & Benes, a firm that had just done the Cleveland Museum of Art (1916) in a well-executed Neo-Classical style—hardly what one would have supposed would attract Lescaze. However, he stayed with them for two years before he set up practice alone in New York.[7] He designed a bus terminal and the Edward A. Normal House, neither of which was particularly innovative.

When Lescaze joined Howe in 1929, he brought the commission for the Oak Lane Country Day School near Philadelphia to the firm, a project that would be featured in the press as an advanced design. However, it was the PSFS Building in Philadelphia that made the team of Howe & Lescaze famous and, in the long run, Howe was to be the partner that gained the greater reputation, in large measure because he was American-born, unlike so many of the architects who were being promoted as leaders of a new Modern direction. How much of the design of PSFS was Howe's, how much was Lescaze's, will probably never be known. But this connection of colleagues was fruitful. The building was praised by the proponents of Modern styling even before construction was begun and in 1930 Howe & Lescaze worked on schemes for a building for the Museum of Modern Art, the mother of the intense movement to promote the International Style. It was never built, but Howe became active in that fledgling institution. The PSFS Building was heavily featured in the 1932 Museum of Modern Art exhibition that became the seminal event in effecting a change of direction for architecture in this country.

Riding high at the time, Howe, who had considerable personal wealth, financed a new journal for the Philadelphia-based T-Square Club. It was in that club in 1931 that Kahn met the hero-colleague Howe, while Kahn was still basically an unimportant and in fact rather uninteresting Beaux-Arts designer.[8]

The PSFS Building was completed during the depth of the Depression, but Howe managed to continue his practice. Though he never again produced a masterpiece, his reputation remained and he was invited to be a juror on a number of major competitions.[9] Kahn, on the other hand, had no work whatsoever. He organized, or was one of the organizers of, "a group of unemployed architects called the Architectural Research Group, chiefly to study housing design."[10] Kahn was not unusual in being out of work; the 1930s were dismal for the architectural profession, although it is true that Wright, Neutra, Schindler (and others on the West Coast) had the luck to get good commissions. Nevertheless, in 1935 Kahn joined the AIA and began a rather unpromising private practice at the age of thirty-four.

Le Corbusier: Villa Savoye, Poissy, 1929–1930

Federally supported public housing was one possible source of work for architects during the Depression and World War II. In 1940 George Howe asked the still unknown Kahn to be his partner in the design of government housing, and late in 1941 they were joined by Oskar Stonorov [B5], a man with an impressive background. The sculptor Aristide Maillol and the architect André Lurçat were among Stonorov's teachers, but he also worked for Lurçat during the early years of his practice. Robert Stern states that he worked for Le Corbusier; others say he did not.[11] But he was, without question, in close contact with Le Corbusier in the late 1920s. He was the translator of *Le Corbusier und Pierre Jeanneret* in 1930 and, with Willy Boesiger, edited *Le Corbusier et Pierre Jeanneret, oeuvre complète, Vol. I: 1910– 1929* (though it was not published until 1937).

Upon Stonorov's arrival in the United States in 1929, he was em-

ployed by McKendree Tucker and Albert Howells, Jr., as design con-
sultant for the Sam T. Weyman Biological Laboratory at the Highlands
Museum, North Carolina—one of the few "American" works featured
in the 1932 Museum of Modern Art exhibition catalog. By 1930 he
was in partnership with another German-born immigrant architect,
Alfred Kastner, for the Carl Mackley Houses (1933–1935) in Juanita
Park near Philadelphia. Together they entered the competition for the
Palace of the Soviets in 1932 and won second prize.[12]

In 1938 Stonorov had worked for George Howe on a children's
playground for the New York World's Fair. With Stonorov's interest in
low-cost housing, it was natural that, when Howe began to receive de-
fense housing commissions, he asked Stonorov to join as a third partner. Howe, Stonorov & Kahn's Carver Court (1942) at Coatsville, Pennsylvania, received accolades from the Museum of Modern Art, which
assumed that Stonorov was the main designer. In 1942 George Howe
left to assume the highest government post in architecture, supervising architect of the Public Buildings Administration, which, as Stern
points out, was a highly influential position even though little was actually built.[13] Kahn was as yet virtually untried as an individual designer and still not really comfortable with the anti-Beaux-Arts design
philosophy of the Modernists. Stonorov and Kahn remained together
until 1948 but nothing earthshaking came out of the partnership.[14]

George Howe continued to be considered a leader, even though
he designed little of significance. When the war ended Howe traveled,
was the professional advisor for the St. Louis Jefferson Memorial
competition in 1946, which Eero Saarinen won, and then from 1947 to
1949 was the first Modernist to be chosen to be the resident architect
at the American Academy in Rome. At the same time, Kahn was invited to become a visiting critic at Yale University, where he rapidly
established a reputation as a fine teacher and made still more significant colleague connections with Philip Johnson, who was a critic on
and off, with Vincent Scully, the writer and architectural historian
who would become primarily responsible for Kahn's early publicity,
and with Buckminster Fuller, who apparently had a direct influence
on Kahn's ideas.[15]

When Howe's tenure at the American Academy ended in 1950 he
saw to it that his former partner was awarded the next fellowship and
exchanged places with Kahn in a fashion, by becoming the new head
of the architectural program at Yale, partly through Kahn's suggestion.
The impact of ancient Roman ruins on the Beaux-Arts-trained Kahn
was obviously overwhelming even if he tended to deny the fact later.
So was the implied recognition of his potential that the fellowship and
his new professorial status conveyed. It was late, Kahn was entering

his fifties, but he was finally ready to become a powerful designer. He had role models for fame in Howe, in Stonorov's connection to Le Corbusier and Lurçat, and in the people he had met at Yale. Upon Kahn's return to Yale two years later, he shared in the glow of his colleague and mentor. It had been two decades since the PSFS Building had made Howe famous, but he was still riding the top waves.

Philip Johnson [C13] was just beginning to receive attention at that time for his Glass House (1949–1950) in New Canaan, Connecticut. He began "to direct the attention of students, architects and critics alike to Kahn's work . . . and urged him to greater design . . . encouraging Howe to back Kahn for the Art Gallery commission."[16] This is quite amazing. Kahn was still nearly unknown as a designer at that time although he had been an architect for twenty-five years. With the Yale Art Gallery addition, helpful recommendations from Howe and Tyng, and vigorous promotion by Scully, Kahn began to reveal his full design strength. Today the addition is so much less interesting and impressive than the buildings that Kahn began designing in 1957 to 1959 (the Richards Medical Building was begun in 1957, Salk in 1959, and the Unitarian Church in 1959) that it is fortuitous that Kahn's colleagues saw his potential. However, at that time, it was a tentative move away from the glass-and-steel aesthetic of the International Style into something with more monumental substance.

Johnson: Glass House, New Canaan, 1949–1950

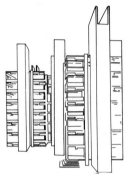

Kahn: Richards Medical Laboratories, Philadelphia, 1957–1964

As I have said previously, it is not unusual to find that a famous architect's employees or associates who stay with him over the years remain in his shadow. Kahn's two major associates are well known to their former students, but not outside of academia. Robert Le Ricolais (1894–1977) had been in the same atelier at the Ecole des Beaux-Arts that George Howe was in. He worked closely with Kahn, as did the engineer Auguste Komendant. Komendant later bitterly commented on Kahn's office. "It was typical of Kahn not to give credit to any one of his associates . . . Kahn never allowed anyone in his office, or even in the university to become his successor. . . . There were many talented young architects in Kahn's office . . . but he was afraid of their domination and let them go. . . . The most brilliant ones worked for Kahn one or two years and after that usually established their own offices or became professors."[17] The fact that they stayed briefly has echoed quietly through many of the case studies thus far presented. Mills was with Jefferson briefly. McKim worked for both Sturgis and Richardson for a relatively short time. Hunt was Walter's employee for only a few months. Sullivan moved in and out of Furness' and Jenney's offices within a year. There are numerous instances of this quick touch that surely indicate a measure of ambition and self-confidence. It seems that five years is the maximum time that a famous architect ever worked for another famous architect and, if it were not for Wright, even that appears excessive.

Robert Venturi [C6] was born in Philadelphia and studied from 1943 to 1950 at Princeton, where he proved to be a brilliant student. His first employment was in Philadelphia, where he worked for Kahn's ex-partner Oskar Stonorov. Next he was employed by Eero Saarinen [C18] at the time the General Motors buildings were establishing his national reputation. Then, from 1954 to 1956, Venturi was a Fellow at the American Academy in Rome, where, like Kahn, he was strongly influenced by the architecture of Rome itself. In his case, the impact on his future work came not from the great axial geometries of the brick and concrete ruins, but from his heightened sensitivity to the meaning and sophistication of mannerism in architecture, its delightful jokes and its twisting or bending of the rules of classicism. When he returned to Philadelphia, he started teaching at the University of Pennsylvania and Princeton. He also worked for Kahn when Kahn returned to that city from Yale in 1957. Venturi began independent practice two years later, in 1959, and in 1966 became a truly major figure in the profession with the publication of *Complexity and Contradiction in Architecture* by the Museum of Modern Art. It is nearly impossible to judge the future fame of one's contemporaries, but both Kahn and Venturi will certainly remain in books about American architectural history.

Charles Moore [C6] is about as well known and influential as Venturi. Moore was also considered a brilliant student at Princeton, where he received the first Ph.D. in architectural history ever awarded at that university, combined with a master's of architecture. Princeton was not his first choice for his graduate studies, nor had he gone there in the hope of studying with Kahn. In fact, Kahn arrived back in the area two years after Moore first enrolled.[18] Though Moore was older than the other graduate students and often was their instructor as a teaching assistant to Enrico Perussutti and, in time, to Louis Kahn, he actively interconnected with such students as Hugh Hardy, Donlyn Lyndon, and William Turnbull as well as his colleague Robert Venturi—another case of sparks flying. When asked about his mentors, Moore first mentioned Jean Labatut and Perussutti, his professors, but also spoke of his contact with Kahn. I asked him to be more specific—"did you ever actually work for Kahn?"—since there is nothing in his usual biographical information that indicates this connection.

He decided that perhaps he did. In 1958 Moore was Kahn's teaching assistant for an advanced design course at Princeton and one night a week he would take the entire thesis class to Philadelphia to have Kahn discuss their projects in Kahn's own office (with the work in progress surely in evidence). Although Kahn continued to produce more and more beautiful buildings, 1958 was the seminal year when he found his full power. Venturi was there; Moore was there. Granted they were both brilliant and ambitious, as were most of the other famous architects. These two leaders in the profession can also be charted in the family tree. The timing of these connections is amazing: it has to be more than coincidence.

Though Venturi and Moore are the most famous today, there were other important employees who worked for Kahn in the 1950s. Anne Griswold Tyng has yet to become especially well known on her own. She began with Kahn & Stonorov in 1945 and stayed with Kahn until 1954. Even though they were very close colleagues, according to my theory, this was, first, too early a contact with Kahn and too late with Stonorov, and too long altogether. Earl Paul Carlin, on the other hand, was Kahn's assistant on his first publicized project, the Yale Art Gallery addition, and from 1954 to 1955 Carlin worked for Paul Schweikher,[19] at the time Schweikher was dean at Yale, as did Peter Millard. The Carlin-Millard partnership was formed in 1955 and by 1961 their fire station in New Haven was well publicized. Charles Gwathmey worked for Kahn, for Venturi, and for Tom Vreeland between 1956 and 1959 while attending the University of Pennsylvania. He became a competition winner at Yale in Paul Rudolph's classes and won a Fulbright scholarship in 1962. From 1968 to 1970 his firm was Gwathmey & Henderson; in 1970 he joined with Robert Siegel, a Barnes ex-employee, to form the award-winning firm of Gwathmey/ Siegel.

Thomas R. Vreeland, Jr., was employed by Kahn from 1954 to 1959. He became chairman of the architecture school at the University of New Mexico. Moshe Safdie, a Kahn employee, startled the architectural profession by winning the commission for Habitat (1967) in Montreal at the age of twenty-nine. Romaldo Giurgola was a colleague rather than an employee of Kahn's from 1954 to 1966.

Kahn's later assistants and employees may yet prove themselves to be nationally celebrated designers. William Porter, Carlos Vallhonrat, and Marshall Meyers were major assistants in the 1960s. At that time students on distant campuses were almost worshipping Kahn. However, people closer to him, who had known him in earlier years, were aware of a Wrightian posture that came with his fame.[20] Is it this change in personality, even a subtle change, that explains why the talented architects who are in contact with a master while he is still thrilled by his first major recognition, and before he has wrapped himself in the mantle of the born genius or guru, are the architects who are apt to receive the message that they also may succeed with a bit more confidence and strength? Presumably many of the young designers who were with Kahn in the 1960s were talented, even brilliant. Those who were with him at the takeoff point have become current stars.

TWELVE

The Loners

Who among America's famous architects cannot be included on a chart of employer-employee or active colleague intersections? Of the numerous American architects given the more than one column of comment in the *Macmillan Encyclopedia of Architects* there are five who do not have a professional connection to one or more of the others in the Index of Fame: Pierre L'Enfant, Bruce Goff, James Bogardus, Buckminster Fuller, and Ernest Flagg. (The Newsom brothers of California, by a fluke, make this seven. They were exuberant late-nineteenth-century designers rather like Nicholas Clayton and others, to whom the editors agreed to give several pages.)

Of the 247 names in the Index of Fame, 228 could have had their names drawn in on chart 1, though this would have made it entirely unreadable. Of the more than 200 designers cited by a minimum of three surveys of American architectural history, only 38 had no direct career link to the mainstream in terms of a famous employer or employee or close association with a significant colleague early in a career. I call them "loners." Even more surprising, on the list of loners on table 3, only 19 did not have an employer, employee, or partner among others on the list of loners. Several of the others were of interest to only a few of the authors and editors whose works were used to compile the Index of Fame. In 6 cases there is no readily available record of the office in which they were trained.

Ten of the loners practiced early in American history. The most famous of these early loners was Pierre Charles L'Enfant [A18], who came to America in 1777 as a volunteer infantry lieutenant in the French colonial troops. He served with honor under George Washington and—after the war—was given the task of remodeling the building called Federal Hall in New York so that it would provide an appropriate background for Washington's inauguration. While this was in

Year of Birth   **Chart 10. The Philadelphia and Rhode Island connections.**

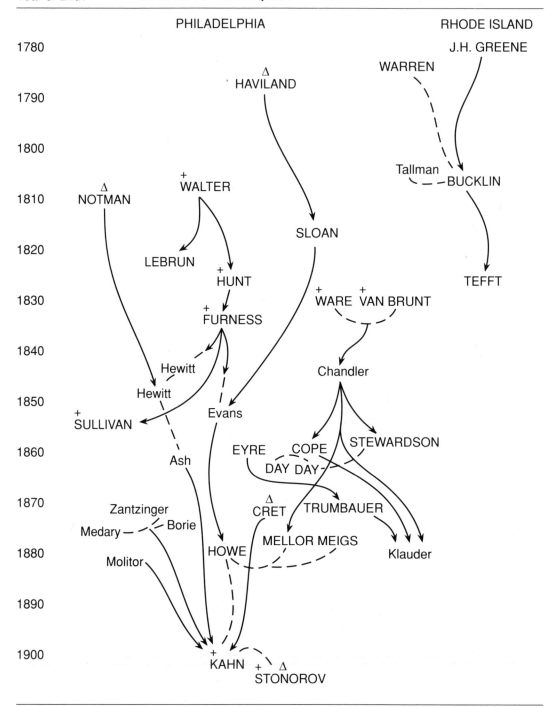

PHILADELPHIA   RHODE ISLAND

1780   J.H. GREENE

                                              WARREN
                                    Δ
                                 · HAVILAND
1790

1800

                                                              Tallman
                          +   BUCKLIN
                       WALTER
              Δ
1810   NOTMAN

                                              SLOAN
1820
              LEBRUN
                    +
                  HUNT   TEFFT

                    +   +   +
1830   FURNESS   WARE VAN BRUNT

1840
            Hewitt

          Hewitt
1850   Evans   Chandler
        +
       SULLIVAN

                                                  EYRE   COPE   STEWARDSON
1860
                    Ash   DAY DAY

                                              Δ
1870   Zantzinger   CRET   TRUMBAUER
      Medary — Borie
                                    MELLOR MEIGS
1880   Molitor   HOWE   Klauder

1890

1900   KAHN   +   Δ
                                STONOROV

Employment	———————————▶	NAME ON THE INDEX OF FAME
Partnership	— — — — — — — — —	Name not on the Index of Fame
Mentorship	································	
European training	Δ	Connects to others on another chart +

Table 3
Loners in the Index of Fame

Thornton, William	A18	Gentleman architect	MORE RECENT LONERS	
L'Enfant, Pierre Charles	A18	Foreign training	Fuller, Buckminster	B13
McComb, John, Jr.	A13	Trained by his father	Wurster, William W.	B10 Employed by Delano &
Ramée, Joseph Jacques	A11	Foreign training		Aldrich but late
Mangin, Joseph			Goff, Bruce	B7
François	A11	Foreign training	Johnson, Reginald	B4
Platt, Charles A.	A11			
McArthur, John, Jr.	A10		CAST-IRON SUBSET	
Flagg, Ernest	A9	Ecole des Beaux-Arts	Bogardus, James	A14
Emerson, William Ralph	A9	(minor connection—A.	Gaynor, John P.	A4
		Cobb)	Kellum, John	A4
Hooker, Philip	A8		Hatfield, R. G.	A3
Buffington, Leroy	A8	(employed Harvey Ellis)		
Jay, William	A5	Foreign training	RHODE ISLAND SUBSET	
Hoadley, David	A5	Local fame	Warren, Russell	A8
Hunt, Myron	A5		Bucklin, James C.	A7
Johnston, William L.	A5	(employed by Walter??)	Greene, John Holden	A6
Manigault, Gabriel	A5		Tefft, Thomas	A6
Atterbury, Grosvenor	A5			
Ittner, William B.	A4		PHILADELPHIA SUBSET	
Lowell, Guy	A4		Eyre, Wilson	A8
Smith, George			Notman, John	A8
Washington	A4		Day, Frank Miles	A7
Newton, Dudley	A4	May have been an agent	Cope, Walter &	
		of Peabody & Stearns	Stewardson	A6
de Pouilly, J. B.	A3	Foreign training	Trumbauer, Horace	A5
Van Osdel, John	A3	Local fame		

process in 1788 and 1789, he wrote to Washington asking to be employed as the designer of the new capital city and was granted the commission in 1791.

We know only a little about L'Enfant's professional background. It is believed that his father was a tapestry designer, a painter, and a professor at the Academie Royale de Peinture et de Sculpture in Paris and that L'Enfant attended that school in 1771. L'Enfant obviously considered himself eminently prepared for his projects but rapidly encountered trouble with the various governmental committees that he dealt with. It is amazing that his grandiose scheme was permitted to influence the development of the capital city to the extent that it actually did (although several scholars believe that Jefferson was equally involved with the design). Not only the Washington plan but also L'Enfant's design for a house for the wealthy Robert Morris proved overambitious. He seemed to have no understanding of the sizable costs his designs demanded. His plan for Paterson, New Jersey, also went unused; the Morris house was never completed; and L'Enfant died of poverty after years of wrangling over his unpaid fee for the Washington plan.

As mentioned earlier, L'Enfant's fame emerged in 1909 at the time McKim and Burnham took over the project of developing the

Mall into the sort of formal composition L'Enfant originally had envisioned. While ridicule had been his lot in his own time, in the end, L'Enfant's plan made him one of America's most famous architects. If the plan was essentially his, then he was a strong designer. leaping ahead of his American contemporaries, without any known connection to an employer, employee, or professional colleague. But if Jefferson was closely involved in the plan, then L'Enfant should not be classed as a loner since this was the exciting and emergent period in Jefferson's architectural career.

Joseph Jacques Ramée [A11], who also appears in the Index of Fame, was in the United States for only about five years. Whether his prior experience in France supports my hypothesis needs to be learned. I discount him due to his short tenure in the United States. He left no famous apprentices behind in America when he returned to Europe.

William Thornton [A18] and Gabriel Manigault [A5] were two other early loners. They were self-trained gentlemen-architects and, by definition, could not have been connected through an apprenticeship to someone famous. Unlike Bulfinch or Jefferson, they did not have employees or design associates who found their own places in history.[1] Manigault had been trained as a lawyer in London before he arrived in Charleston, South Carolina. William Jay [A5], a Savannah, Georgia, architect, received professional training in England. Like Ramée, Jay remained in America for only a few years. He returned to London in 1824. Likewise, Jacques Nicholas Bussière de Pouilly [A3] arrived in America with a professional background, although his claim to have been trained at the Ecole des Beaux-Arts in Paris is not substantiated by the listing of students published in 1894.[2] He settled in New Orleans and—like McComb, Ramée, Jay, and Manigault—his fame is real primarily in the city where he built rather than on a national level. David Hoadley, John Van Osdel, and William Ittner also tend to be only of local interest. So, also, is Philip Hooker [A8], better known in the Albany area than he is in general. Hooker was a native-born American and the son of a carpenter-builder. "His buildings, more derivative than original, characterized by conservative design, skilled massing, and refined elegance of decoration and detail, reveal his familiarity with a broad range of neo-classic styles."[3] Two were partners: Mangin & McComb [A11]. Not only Joseph Mangin but four others of these early loners came to America as adults after training in France. The nature of their apprenticeship experiences is unclear.

Four of the apparent loners in the Index of Fame worked with cast iron. Sigfried Giedion introduced the name of James Bogardus [A14] into historical surveys. Although not an architect but an inventor and businessman, he became famous for his production of cast-iron fronts. R. G. Hatfield [A3] was subsequently included in surveys because he designed the Venetian architectural detail of the Baltimore Sun Building (1851) for Bogardus,[4] although Hatfield and his brother did more traditional work as well—in New York City. John Kellum [A4] was the designer for the cast-iron A. T. Stewart store (1859) in New York (later Wanamakers). John P. Gaynor [A4] worked for Bogardus' chief rival, Daniel Badger, when he designed the cast-iron façade of the Haughtwout Store (1857) also in New York. If these 4 men are added to the others discounted above, that leaves only 27 loners out of 247 names from a period covering more than two hundred years. Given that Ramée, Mangin, and Jay stayed in America for only a few years, this number is even more astonishing.

There are other architects who might easily be considered loners except for the fact that they had threads of connections to each other.[5] The Index of Fame includes the names of a group of Rhode Island architects who connect to each other in the same manner thus far described, and this is also true of John Notman, Horace Trumbauer, Walter Cope, the Stewardson and Day brothers, and Wilson Eyre—all Philadelphia architects. The connections to Furness, Haviland, Ware & Van Brunt, Howe, and Louis Kahn are distant but can be charted (chart 10).[6]

Wilson Eyre [A8] is celebrated mainly for his residential designs in Philadelphia. For a while he worked in a style close to the Shingle Style of New England of the 1880s. He was born in Florence, Italy, of American parents and attended school in Europe, Canada, and Newport, Rhode Island (where the Shingle Style was born). Eyre attended MIT briefly and then worked for the young James P. Sims in Philadelphia beginning in 1877 and then, when Sims died in 1882, inherited the practice. Eyre was active in the Philadelphia AIA, a founder of the T-Square Club, and of *House and Garden* as well as its editor at one point. He also served as a professor at the University of Pennsylvania. By the time he worked on the Free Museum of the University of Pennsylvania (1893–1926) he was associated with Frank Miles Day and Cope & Stewardson. So Eyre, like most of the Philadelphia architects, was part of a network of professional connections, although at some distance from the major establishment.

Two Philadelphia designers do seem to have been true loners. William L. Johnston [A5] died at the age of thirty-eight, just before the site was cleared for the building that gave him his place in history, although the Jayne Building (1849) was mentioned because it related to Louis Sullivan, who had seen the building twenty-four years after its completion. It was a surprisingly tall building for masonry construction and had great quantities of glass and other design features that appeared many years later on Sullivan's Wainwright and Reliance buildings. Johnston did a few other buildings in the 1840s in Philadelphia, but when he died of tuberculosis Thomas Ustick Walter took over the work on the Jayne Building. Very little is known about Johnston's training and activities, but George B. Tatum speculated that he might have become a major designer if he had lived.[7] He was both daring and inventive.

John McArthur, Jr. [A10], was first cited in a survey as an anti-hero. When Hitchcock wrote his first major plea for a new aesthetic in 1929 he chose the Philadelphia City Hall (1874–1894) by McArthur to illustrate the ultimate in bad taste—the extreme against which enlightened architects should react. This building, with its encrustation of columns, cornices, and dormer windows, and the surprising slip in scale between its tightly detailed body and loosely detailed tower, was McArthur's only really important work.[8] Though Hitchcock thoroughly disliked the building, it was a vigorous and strong design, hardly avant-garde, but definitely up-to-date in terms of American styles at the time it was designed.

Three other loners in the Index of Fame may or may not connect by way of apprenticeships. Myron Hunt [A5] never revealed in which specific offices he first worked. All his biographies state that he worked in Boston and Chicago from 1890 to 1894 and then traveled in Europe for two years. Hunt was in Chicago from 1896 to 1903 and was one of the Steinway Hall group that included Frank Lloyd Wright—which certainly should be counted as a connection of sorts. However, stylistically he was conservative, as seen in his Huntington Art Gallery and Ambassador Hotel in Los Angeles where he practiced after 1903. Reginald Johnson [B4] and George Washington Smith [A4] were also cited for their work in California, not always favorably since they worked in Spanish Revival styles that have only recently returned to favor. Biographical information on Johnson is scanty, but the Pennsylvania-born Smith studied at Harvard, worked for Newman, Woodman, & Harris in Philadelphia, and then spent a number of years abroad. He was forty when he designed his first house. In the past, none of these men was considered very important and space allotted to actual descriptions of their work in history surveys generally is very brief indeed.

Five of the remaining loners had enormous advantages in terms of client contact. Two were from great wealth; three had the highest intellectual and social contacts. They are discussed below in the section on family advantages: Ernest Flagg, Charles Adams Platt, Guy Lowell, Grosvenor Atterbury, and William Ralph Emerson. Emerson, like Eyre, entered surveys when Antoinette Downing, Hitchcock, and Scully all called attention to the Shingle Style. Vincent Scully was also responsible for spotlighting another loner, Dudley Newton, even though he was not at all sure that Newton was the actual designer of the building he wished to discuss—the Sturtevant House (1872) in Newport, which Scully christened as a good example of the Stick Style, which preceded the Shingle Style. Little, indeed, is known of this particular loner. Scully speculated that he may have been serving as an agent for one of the other more important designers, like Peabody & Stearns.[9]

There are only three more loners in the Index of Fame: Buckminster Fuller, Bruce Goff, and Leroy Buffington. Buffington [A8], like McArthur, entered history as an antihero. He was a strong but inconsistent designer, quick to pick up ideas from the professional journals.[10] He began civil suits in 1892 with a claim to have invented the skyscraper. He was not granted a patent and later he was ridiculed by the historians who were championing Jenney's role in the development of steel-framed office buildings, but it was this that made Buffington's name familiar. Buffington did have an employee who is also in the Index of Fame, Harvey Ellis [A5]. Ellis had one year at West Point and then worked for Arthur Gilman in 1875 when Gilman had already established his reputation. Ellis met Richardson at that time and was impressed by him and his work on Trinity Church, but did not join his office staff. Instead, from 1879 to 1885, he joined in partnership with his brother Charles in Rochester, New York, where he designed the Federal Building (1884–1889). At that point Ellis began to shift from firm to firm in the Midwest. First he worked for Buffington, and he also did renderings for Mould & McNichols in the Minneapolis area. Later he was with the European-trained Edmund Eckel and his partner George R. Mann in St. Louis. Finally, Ellis did drawings for Gustav Stickley, the publisher of the little journal the *Craftsman*. Both Buffington and Ellis had talent. Neither one became famous on the strength of his designs.

The remaining two loners were considerably more interesting designers than were most of the others just discussed. Both were mavericks. R. Buckminster Fuller [B13], like Bogardus, was an inventor. Since he was never trained in architecture that kind of apprenticeship connection was impossible.[11] His partnership with his father-in-law, the McKim-trained James Monroe Hewlett, was important to Fuller, but their production of fibrous building blocks can hardly count as a colleague connection. Hewlett was well placed socially. During his lifetime he was considered important by his colleagues, but he certainly was not famous in the minds of historians.

Fuller was a tireless promoter of his inventions and by the 1930s had the support of the Museum of Modern Art. He wrote, he lectured interminably, and he carried the model of his Dymaxion house in his car for years and exhibited it whenever possible. By 1932 he had attracted the attention of *Architectural Forum*. Like Wright, he considered himself to be a genius. Students followed him around in crowds after his lengthy lectures, absolutely rapt and convinced that they were in the presence of another Leonardo da Vinci. Part of the reason Fuller became so famous was that architectural historians saw him as continuing the experiments of the nineteenth century that they so greatly admired: the Crystal Palace, Machinery Hall in Paris, the Eiffel Tower.

By the 1950s Fuller was a professor at Ivy League schools and in contact with the famous architects on these faculties. It was then, in 1952, when his dome for the Ford company first made him commercially accepted, that he is said to have had a considerable influence on Louis Kahn. Fuller reached his pinnacle of success when his geodesic dome was chosen to represent the United States at the Montreal World's Fair (1967). Fuller had a different personality than Wright's, softer and more lovable, yet, even so, he was of a similar mold—an original—and no follower has yet become famous.

Bruce Goff [B7] had no academic training in architecture. He was born in Kansas and taken to Tulsa, Oklahoma, as a child. He was only twelve when his father apprenticed him to the local Tulsa firm of Rush, Endicott & Rush where Goff learned his trade. By the time he was twenty-two he was their chief designer for the Boston Avenue Methodist Church (1926–1929). Although his early work did not look like that of Frank Lloyd Wright, people told him that it did, and Goff hunted up illustrations in journals and then wrote Wright for counsel on possible professional schools. Wright, of course, advised him to avoid all architectural schools and generously sent the young admirer a set of the precious Wasmuth volumes. Wright and his ex-employee Barry Byrne both did work in Tulsa in the late 1920s, and Goff met Wright in 1927. He saw more of Wright in later years but never actually worked for him.[12]

Goff had none of Wright's tectonic sense of structure and materials—nor did he understand Wright's powerful spatial sequences. What Goff had in common with his hero was a desire to be completely and totally original. There is a measure of the spectacular in every Goff building. Goff taught in Chicago and Oklahoma with a number of students as followers. Thus far only one disciple has been spotlighted (though not to the extent of being famous)—Herbert Greene.

These are the loners as defined in this book, those designers deemed important enough to be mentioned in three or more surveys who did not have—or are not known to have had—close contact with others in the Index of Fame. Nearly half of them were active in the early nineteenth century; three were in this country for only a short time; there is no specific information available about the professional training of ten of these men; thirteen of the loners can be grouped in subsets of connections; finally, only three of the thirty-four names are really well-known. The 247 names in the Index represent an infinitesimally small number of those Americans actually in practice since 1776. That such an enormous percentage of these same people were professionally—and meaningfully—connected raises many questions about conventional explanations of fame.

The importance of an in-office experience has been somewhat overemphasized—as though it were the only stimulant to dynamic and creative design. By no means is the apprenticeship or colleague connection the exclusive stimulant to heroic design. In actual fact, it is often a building and not a person that opens an architect's eyes to exciting future possibilities. Sullivan's response to Richardson's Marshall Field Building in Chicago is well documented. Charles Eames remembered the impact on him of his visit to the Weissenhof exhibition in Stuttgart and how fresh and astonishing possibilities were opened to him, and this was several years before he made his contact with the Saarinens. Buildings in Paris and in France revealed a new direction to Jefferson. Charles Moore's early essay, his own house of 1961, was, without question, a response to Louis Kahn's design for the Jewish Community Center in Trenton, New Jersey. Venturi's discovery and reinterpretation of sixteenth-century Mannerist buildings and the more or less ignored work of Edwin Lutyens were fundamental to his own architectural theories.

In addition several architects achieved prominence without the specific experience of an exciting apprenticeship. For example, Louis Kahn worked for Paul Cret a number of years after Cret first showed his design talent; Richard Upjohn was similarly connected to Alexander Parris—though both Kahn and Upjohn subsequently had major employees present when their own first major works were being designed. Neither Belluschi nor Wurster fits the pattern well. Paul Rudolph studied under Gropius and Breuer during their second period of acceleration, but he did not work for either of his teachers. Nevertheless, what was true for the most famous architects—Gropius, Mies, Sullivan, McKim, White, and Frank Lloyd Wright—was also true for a large majority of other architects who achieved a measure of fame: the apprenticeship connection at a specific moment in the career of the employer.

PART II

Conventional Wisdom about Architects' Predispositions for Fame

THIRTEEN

Connections: Family, Friends, Schools

The Architect's Family

Architects—like artists, lawyers, doctors, and many other professionals—have an advantage if they are born into wealthy, prestigious families. Mothers, fathers, uncles, aunts, brothers, and in-laws can provide the kind of financial support—the best schools, European travel—and social connections, especially friends and acquaintances who may be potential clients, that supplement the advantage gained through a fortunate apprenticeship. Marriage to a woman from a prosperous and socially well-placed family is a frequent occurrence in the lives of famous architects. The architect who intends to become famous must, at the very least, gain access to wealthy, highly educated clients who are eager to back experimental or dramatic designs. Wealth itself is not always as important as social prestige. A number of famous architects were the sons of ministers or rabbis who, although not wealthy, had considerable prestige in the community and served congregations that were often well-to-do. Quite a number of architects were relatively affluent in their youth or apprenticeship years. A few were born to wealth that was later lost, but grew up with the contacts their families had established earlier. Several architects noted in their capsule biographies that they were "of Mayflower descent."

Thomas Jefferson was by no means poor. At the age of fourteen he inherited considerable acreage when his father died. "Charles Bulfinch's father was one of the great physicians of his day; his mother was the daughter of one of the city's richest and most influential merchants."[1] John Trumbull, the son of the governor of Connecticut, sometimes dabbled in architecture, though painting was much more important to him. Like most well-to-do architects, all three of these men attended the finest schools in America and were able to afford the pleasures of travel in Europe. They were members of an American social elite by birthright, and many of their designs were financed by clients who were also long-time friends or relatives.

Benjamin Latrobe's family belonged to the circle of friends around Samuel Johnson in London. His mother, a third-generation descendant of Pennsylvania settlers, had property and extensive social connections in the area around Philadelphia. His father held a high position in the Moravian church of England and Ireland. Historian Alan Gowans adds the following credentials: "his mother, born in Bethlehem, Pennsylvania, granddaughter of a German baron who had been abbot of a Roman Catholic monastery; his father born in Dublin, son of a French count."[2] (However intriguing the Catholic abbot-baron and the count may be, these seem to be the sort of genealogies that Americans were likely to have attributed to themselves in the nineteenth century.) After coming to America as a bereaved widower, Latrobe married into a prominent and wealthy family. His wife was the daughter of the partner of Robert Morris, the man whose wealth had financed the American Revolution. Her father's and Morris' fortunes declined (Latrobe's ventures into investments also were disastrous), but the social contacts remained. Mrs. Latrobe was a lifelong friend of Dolly Madison, and in the later years, when things were going badly for her husband, she used this relationship to ask Madison, then president, for work for Latrobe.

Alexander Parris was born to a prominent New England family. However, he was just three years old when his father died, leaving him with little money. Thus he did not become a gentleman-architect like Jefferson but was forced to serve an apprenticeship with a carpenter and builder. For the most part, gentlemen-architects and carpenters dominated the profession at that time. William Thornton, the winner of the competition for the design of the United States Capitol in 1792, was born in the West Indies and, when his father died, was sent to Scotland to be educated as a physician, a profession that apparently did not interest him and that he never practiced. Gabriel Manigault was trained in London as a lawyer and practiced design as a hobby. He designed houses for his friends and relatives and is best known for the Joseph Manigault House (1800) in Charleston, South Carolina, but he took on larger commissions as well—the City Hall, for example. William Jay also worked in Charleston and in Savannah. His first major work was the Richardson-Owens-Thomas House for a wealthy man related to Jay's family by marriage.[3]

Other nineteenth-century architects also gained immeasurably from family connections. George Hadfield made his contact with

Thomas Jefferson through his sister Maria Cosway, who was an important member of Jefferson's social set in Paris. He was said to be the protégé of the queen of England and of Lady Chesterfield, which, if true, put him in very high social circles indeed. As the designer of the portico of Arlington, the Curtis-Lee mansion overlooking Washington, D.C., he appears to have maintained some social standing in America as well. Robert Mills was the son of Anne Taylor, a member of an old Charleston, South Carolina, family; his father was born in Scotland. They saw to it that their son received a classical education at Charleston College,[4] which in the late eighteenth century indicated a family with position.

Solomon Willard was the great-grandson of the noted preacher Samuel Willard, vice-president of Harvard College. Though Willard's father was simply a carpenter and cabinetmaker, the name held prestige. James and Charles Dakin were from an old upstate New York family of established reputation; they were quite young when their father died and were raised by their guardian, a carpenter by profession. Isaiah Rogers was of Mayflower descent. His father was a shipbuilder in Plymouth, Massachusetts. William Le Baron Jenney's father was a prosperous whaling ship owner who lived in Fairhaven, Massachusetts; while he was young, Jenney accompanied his father and traveled to California, the Philippines, and the South Seas.

Henry Hobson Richardson's great-grandfather was Joseph Priestley, a dissenting clergyman, an important writer, and the discoverer of oxygen. Priestley spent the last ten years of his life in America, where his sons had already immigrated. Richardson was born on a Priestley sugarcane plantation in Louisiana. His "father was a prosperous businessman who died when Richardson was sixteen. At this time his mother . . . married Mr. John D. Bain, a partner in her brother's large hardware business."[5] Richardson was not only able to attend Harvard, where he was invited to join several prestigious clubs, but he lived in some elegance in Paris until his funds ran short because of the Civil War. When he made the move from New York to Boston in 1874, he chose to settle in Brookline, which was also the location of many of his wealthy Harvard classmates. Hitchcock, Richardson's biographer, claimed that this move was a necessary component of Richardson's success. "For the architect the practical consideration of working where the biggest and most varied commissions are to be had is not merely a matter of earning the most money: it is the necessary basis for any adequate practice of the art at all."[6] Richardson enjoyed entertaining his friends and loved to dine out in supper clubs. It is not incidental to his eventual fame that many of his commissions came through these same friends.

James Renwick's father was a well-traveled professor and a man of considerable education and talent. The family had wealth and owned valuable land in New York City. Grace Church, Renwick's first architectural commission and the building that put his name in the history books, was built on land his mother owned. While that commission was won in competition, it is hard to believe that the Renwick name bore no weight in the decision. In fact, Renwick's father was quite active in promoting his son's talent. The Renwick family had relatives among the Clintons, Hamiltons, and Russells of New York, and several of the younger men in these families became architects of moderate note.

Other New York architects included George Browne Post, who traced his American ancestry back to 1639; James Aspinwall, Renwick's partner, whose wife was related to the Renwicks; and the Potters, Edward and William, grandsons of a man who not only had amassed a fortune, but was the president of Union College. One of the other Potter brothers was the bishop of New York; another also became president of Union College. Edward Potter's first commission, for Union College, came through his grandfather's influence. Henry Avery was the son of a wealthy art connoisseur. Stanford White's roots went back to 1632 in America, and his ancestors founded several towns. There were financial problems about the time White began his apprenticeship, but his parents were distinguished and he had been wealthy in his youth. His colorful father, Richard Grant White, was a music and drama critic and had a wide circle of influential friends.

Ernest Flagg [A10] was the "ambitious and shrewd" grandson of Commodore Vanderbilt and the son of the rector of the socially elite Grace Church.[7] His aunt, Mrs. Cornelius Vanderbilt, paid for his education at the Ecole des Beaux-Arts, and Flagg began a successful practice at the age of thirty-four. He designed many important New York buildings, including the Singer Building and Tower (1896–1908) and the bland but academically correct second Corcoran Gallery of Art in Washington, D.C. (1892–1897). Charles Adams Platt [A11] was a late manifestation of the wealthy gentleman-architect. He began designing houses for friends at the age of forty-two and his background was painting, etching, and garden planning, not professional architectural training.

Grosvenor Atterbury [A5] was another architect who developed his practice independent of a connection to another in the Index of Fame except as a colleague of Olmsted in the design of low-cost housing. However, the large residences he also designed were for wealthy clients socially connected to his family.

William Ralph Emerson [A9] was related to the great essayist. He worked for Jonathan Preston in Maine, became his partner from 1857 to 1861, and then took Carl Fehmer in partnership from 1864 to 1873. His employee Albert W. Cobb was with him in about 1880 when Emerson was producing his most significant Shingle Style houses. Cobb also worked for Peabody & Stearns, and his future partner, John Calvin Stevens, was with McKim, Mead & White in 1882, a vital moment in that firm. Thus, in an indirect way, Emerson could have been added to the chart of connections. Samuel Breck Parkman Trowbridge, Isaac Newton Phelps Stokes, and H. Van Buren Magonigle all bore their lineage in their names and Stokes' family was notably wealthy. William Adams Delano and Chester Holmes Aldrich also bore distinguished names. Stephen Voorhees, one of the New York City skyscraper architects of the 1920s, was the descendant of ancestors who arrived in 1660. John Russell Pope was the son of an artist who traced his family back to the 1630s and grew up with wealth. Bertram Grosvenor Goodhue's lineage on both sides also went back to the first settlers. Goodhue Livingston's forebear, Robert Livingston, was involved with Thomas Jefferson in the Louisiana Purchase. Joseph Wells, McKim, Mead & White's early assistant, though not wealthy, was a descendant of Samuel Adams.

Quite possibly the man with the greatest advantage over all of those born in the second half of the nineteenth century was not in the Index of Fame. William T. Aldrich was the son of a powerful senator and the brother of the president of Chase Manhattan Bank and ambassador to Great Britain; his sister was the wife of John D. Rockefeller.

Charles Sumner Greene and his brother, Henry Mather Greene, were descendants of families that "participated in the origins of the United States; among their forebears were such distinguished Americans as Generals Christopher and Nathaniel Greene, Benjamin Franklin, Cotton Mather, the Reverend Richard Mather, and Senator Charles Sumner."[8] The names of the second-echelon New England–born architects similarly read like a social register of the area: Cabot, Clark, Lowell, Cummings, Sears, Longfellow, Emerson.

Buckminster Fuller was the fifth generation of Fullers to attend Harvard, although he did not stay to graduate.[9] His great-aunt was Margaret Fuller of the transcendentalist movement. In 1917 Fuller married the daughter of James Monroe Hewlett of Hewlett, Long Island, an architect who had served his apprenticeship with McKim, Mead & White. Hewlett was president of the Architectural League of New York from 1920 through 1921; president of the Society of Mural

Painters in 1922; vice-president of the AIA in 1928; and the director of the American Academy in Rome from 1932 until 1935.[10]

Family connections benefited Philadelphia architects like Biddle and Trowbridge. All three partners of Mellor, Meigs & Howe were from old, wealthy families. Frank Furness' brother Horace became a Shakespearean scholar and professor at the University of Pennsylvania and was on the university's building committee at the time Furness was selected to be the architect for the University of Pennsylvania Library (1888–1891). His older brother, the artist William Furness, had met the architect Richard Morris Hunt through Hunt's artist-brother in Paris. Hunt visited William in Philadelphia, and it was at that time that Frank Furness decided that he also wished to be an architect.[11] Frank Furness' second partner, Allen Evans, was very well-to-do.

Cass Gilbert's family was prominent in Ohio and St. Louis and, although his father died when Gilbert was nine, he grew up "financially secure though not affluent."[12] Farther south, Addison Mizner was a descendant of Sir Joshua Reynolds, had Gold Rush money, and was world-traveled as a child. John Mervin Carrère, son of a wealthy Baltimore coffee-merchant, was born in Rio de Janeiro and was also a world traveler in his youth. Another Baltimorean, Bruce Price, did not serve an apprenticeship to a famous architect although he did have employees who became famous to varying degrees. While a student at Princeton, Price's father's death cut his formal education short, and he returned to Baltimore to learn through apprenticeship in the local firm of Niernsee & Nielson. Price retained his social connections and became moderately celebrated in later years.[13]

Though he was never a wealthy man, Charles McKim's father, Miller McKim, belonged to a set that included Lowell, Emerson, Whittier, Holmes, Olmsted, and others. Charles McKim's first partner and, for a few years, his brother-in-law was the son of a prosperous cotton merchant with intellectual connections to Henry James, Bret Harte, and Julia Ward Howe. McKim's second partner, Mead, was the son of a member of the New England "aristocracy." William Rutherford Mead's father was a well-to-do lawyer surrounded by an artistic social set. Mead's nephew, the architect John Mead Howells, was the son of an author of note and Mead's brother was a socially popular artist who settled in fashionable Newport, Rhode Island. Stanford White was the most colorful of the partners and had been brought up in the highest circles of New York intellectual society and became a social lion himself. John Jay Chapman, Augustus Saint-Gaudens, and Addison Mizner were his close friends, and Frederick Law Olmsted became his mentor. White's flamboyant charm attracted attention and he was a great favorite of society, until he was murdered by a jealous husband in 1906.

The young McKim, Mead & White firm might never have become famous without the sophisticated clients it had from the beginning. Mead's first commission came from a Harvard classmate; the firm's first commission was the design of the exclusive Newport Casino in Rhode Island (1879). The Villard family was tied to McKim by marriage, and the Villard Houses in New York and the Boston Public Library, where McKim had personal friends on the Building Committee, were McKim, Mead & White's bids for national fame in the mid-1880s. One or more of the three partners belonged to every prestigious club in New York City.

George Howe's appointment as the first chairman of the junior advisory committee of the infant Museum of Modern Art, in 1929, surely resulted as much from his social contacts and wealth as from his standing as a designer at that time. Edward Durell Stone, the architect for the museum's building, had "a leisurely affluent youth."[14] His partner, Philip Goodwin, a beneficiary of the J. J. Goodwin estate, belonged to the Knickerbocker, University, and Yale clubs in New York City and was on the board of directors of the Museum of Modern Art.

John Wellborn Root was indeed well born. His father, a northerner, had moved to Lumpkin, Georgia, where he established a mercantile business and married the daughter of a prosperous plantation owner. They then moved to Atlanta, where he made a fortune as a blockade runner during the Civil War. Daniel Burnham's ancestors had arrived in 1635. When Burnham was nineteen, his father, a prosperous wholesale drug merchant, was the president of the Chicago Mercantile Association. Thomas Eddy Tallmadge was the nephew of the second Mrs. Marshall Field. William Holabird was the son of a general, and Henry Van Brunt's father was a navy commander. Both Charles Sumner Frost and Alfred Granger were sons-in-law of the president of the Chicago and North Western Railroad.[15] William Purcell was raised by his grandfather, the editor of the periodical *Interiors*.

It has become less common in the twentieth century to point to a parent's social and financial standing when writing brief biographies of architects; however, the connections still can be found. Hugh Stubbins is a descendant of the first governor of Virginia. Charles Willard Moore traces his ancestry back to early New England. Alden Dów was the son of the founder of the Dow Chemical Company; Victor Gruen's father was a prominent lawyer in Vienna. Philip Johnson's father was also a lawyer with considerable means.[16] Johnson was given valuable shares of stock by his father when he was in his twenties and was not only able to amass an exceptional art collection, but was able to build six exquisite little buildings for himself on his estate in New Canaan, Connecticut. Ieoh Ming Pei is the son of a Cantonese banking family; John Johansen's parents were both artists; Joseph Esherick's uncle, Wharton Esherick, was a sculptor and an associate of Joseph's employer, Howe, and his professor Cret. Charles Gwathmey is the son of a major artist.

For many architects, a wife with social graces and social contacts has been an unquestionable asset. Daniel Burnham married the wealthy Sherman daughter in Chicago in 1876 just at the beginning of the practice of Burnham & Root. When Wright first began his practice, his first wife helped establish his image as a man of "fine taste and discrimination." At that time he was still honing the country boy out of his image. He began "to cut a figure in quiet Oak Park," a suburb of Chicago. "He kept a good riding horse" and participated in horse shows. "He and his wife gave parties whose 'artistic' air more or less overcame their suburban acquaintances; every winter, Mr. and Mrs. Wright took season tickets for the symphony in Chicago; Mrs. Wright . . . sponsored a kindergarten society in Oak Park . . . Wright began his collection of objects of art." [17] (All this while running up considerable debt.) Wright's sexual liaisons and eventual divorces severely damaged his reputation after 1909 and, in large measure, were the factors that reduced his commissions for many years.

Sometimes social connections seem to be more important than talent for an ambitious young architect. It is impossible, for example, to avoid speculation about Wallace Harrison's true talent. Not only was he always in the right office at the right time—in a roundabout way, Harrison was an in-law of the Rockefellers through his wife. Harrison's long friendship with Nelson Rockefeller was immensely significant to his career. Not only Rockefeller Center itself, but the United Nations Building (1946, supervising architect) and Lincoln Center (1962–1965) were Rockefeller-backed operations. During World War II Harrison "joined Nelson Rockefeller at the State Department." [18]

Not only did Richard Morris Hunt marry into wealth—his whole career was studded with advantage. He "always took pride in his American birth and in the knowledge that his ancestral roots were deeply planted in American soil. Since the early seventeenth century, Hunts had been leaders in politics, community service, and business in New England. . . . They lived comfortably, even luxuriously." [19] Hunt's father was a prominent lawyer, banker, landowner, and politician who died when Hunt was four years old. His mother decided to move with her children to Beacon Hill so that his brothers could be prepared for Harvard and he could attend the Boston Latin School. Five years later they moved to Europe: Paris, Italy, Switzerland. Their mother was generous with her funds, and after completing his studies at the Ecole des Beaux-Arts, where his work was "rather undistinguished,"[20] Hunt and a friend made the full-scale Grand Tour, including Egypt, Syria, Turkey, and Palestine as well as Greece and the rest of Europe.

Upon his return from his apprenticeship in France, he settled in New York. "Although Hunt was not rich . . . he had ample means. His social position was a respected one."[21] And as Henry Van Brunt mentioned in his eulogy (cited earlier), Hunt had amassed an impressive collection of art objects and a library before he returned to the United States. Hunt rented a studio in the New York University building, and a remarkable group of creative people were in the building at that time: Samuel F. B. Morse, Alexander Jackson Davis, Samuel Colt, a number of major American painters, and others of interest, including "Joseph Howland, the son of a wealthy merchant . . . [who] would in a few years be Hunt's brother-in-law and patron."[22] With very few buildings to his credit but with a powerful mother, wealthy wife, and patrons, Hunt was invited to join both the Union League Club and the Century Association, "a social stronghold of men of distinction and wealth."[23]

Hunt's wife, Catherine Clinton Howland Hunt, had inherited a fortune amassed by her father whose worth, in about 1845, was "estimated to be around $250,000."[24] On their honeymoon, Hunt and his wife stayed briefly with the Griswold family in Paris. "At this time the Griswolds concluded the arrangements with Hunt for the design and construction of a summer house in Newport . . . "[25] (This Griswold house was the important early design that probably inspired Frank Furness when he was Hunt's employee in the 1860s.)

The Clerical Connection

Architects from wealthy, old families usually have easy access to clients. But fathers in the ministry, though often not wealthy, also have provided a number of architects with wide client contact. William and Edward Potter have already been mentioned as the brothers of the Episcopal bishop of New York and the grandsons of a powerful man. Richard Upjohn was the grandson and son-in-law of Episcopal clergymen. Charles Coolidge Haight's father was the assistant rector of Trinity Church in New York and a trustee of Columbia University from 1843 to 1847. Haight's earliest major works were St. Luke's Cathedral in Portland, Maine (1868–1877) and Hamilton Hall at Columbia (1880). Benjamin Wistar Morris, one of the first architects employed on the design of Rockefeller Center, was of a pre-revolutionary family and the son of the bishop of Oregon. Richmond Shreve, one of the architects of the Empire State Building, was the son of the dean of the Cathedral of Quebec.

Benjamin Latrobe and William Jay were the sons of dissenting preachers. Charles Bulfinch, Raymond Hood, and Daniel Burnham were grandsons of ministers. Alexander Jackson Davis was the son of a theological bookseller and publisher of religious materials. William Robert Ware's father was a Unitarian minister, and Robert Peabody's father was the Unitarian minister of the prestigious Kings' Chapel in Boston that Bulfinch's grandfather had built. (Peabody's mother's family was of old Boston wealth.) Thomas Hastings, of Carrère & Hastings, was the son of a Presbyterian minister, and the firm's first commission came from the entrepreneur Flagler, while Flagler was a member of the father's congregation. Eliel Saarinen was a minister's son in Finland, and Ralph Adams Cram's father was still another Unitarian minister. (Cram converted to the Episcopalian church.) The Reverend William Howard Furness was also a Unitarian minister and an intellectual with a wide circle of interesting associates. The Reverend James Miller McKim, a Presbyterian, an ardent abolitionist, and the editor of the *Pennsylvania Freeman*, was a close friend.

Dankmar Adler's father was a liberal rabbi, first in Detroit and then in Chicago. Adler designed at least two synagogues in Chicago—the Sinai Temple (c. 1876) and Anshe Ma'arev for his father in 1882. Because Albert Kahn's father was an itinerant rabbi, Kahn's early major commissions came from large manufacturers and he had little advantage from a stable congregation. Frank Lloyd Wright's father was an itinerant Baptist and then Unitarian preacher as well as a music teacher, and, again, this did not lead to connections through a father's congregation. However, his uncle Jenkin Lloyd Jones was a Unitarian minister in Chicago and Wright did gain access to clients through his congregation. Not only did Wright also find his first employer through his uncle's contact, but it was in his uncle's church that he met the socially well-placed young woman who became Wright's first wife.

Fathers in the Building Trades

Of the architects in the Index of Fame whose parental occupations can be found in biographies, nearly all of those who were not the sons of socially well-placed men were apt to be the offspring of men in the building or engineering trades. Their fathers were housewrights, carpenters, surveyors, engineers, and architects. Only a few of the most famous architects came from this stock, however. It was more difficult for these men to obtain major commissions than it was for those who had longstanding friendships with wealthy or influential clients. (Even many design competitions were by invitation only.)

Many architects joined their fathers' offices. Some are well-known relationships: John McComb, Jr. and Sr. in New York City; the sons of Latrobe, Hunt, Upjohn, Eidlitz, Burnham, Root, Holabird, Olmsted, Brown, Wright, and Saarinen—though only two, McComb and Eero Saarinen, became as famous or more famous than the father. There are other sons who may have achieved financial success but were hardly noticed by the historians: Cass Gilbert, Jr.; the Roths; LeBrun's and Post's sons; Dankmar Adler's sons; Richardson's son-in-law and grandson; Martin Roche's son, for example.

Walter Gropius' father, though trained as an architect and supervisor of the Berlin Housing Authority when his son was born, was primarily a successful tapestry dealer. Gropius' great-uncle was an architect, director of Prussian art education, and the director of an Arts and Crafts school in Berlin. Another uncle owned an estate in Pomerania and in 1906 permitted the young Walter to design houses for his workers while he was still a student in Munich. Mies came from a family of stonemasons. R. M. Schindler's father was a wood and metal craftsman. ("His mother, a milliner, was one of the few women awarded the Austrian Golden Cross of Merit for services to her trade,"[26] and turn-of-the-century hats were very nearly miniature architectural projects.)

Thomas Jefferson learned several architectural skills from his father, who was a surveyor. Not so well known are the builder or architectural backgrounds of the following: McIntire (carpenter), Hooker (builder), Strickland (carpenter and clerk of the works for Latrobe), Upjohn (surveyor), Shryock (architect), Walter (bricklayer for Strickland), Bryant (engineer), Howard (builder), Polk (architect), Gill (builder), Lamb (builder), Kump (architect), Buffington (engineer), and Schmidt (engineer). Donlyn Lyndon is the son of the architect Maynard Lyndon, who was considered an important young designer in the 1950s. John McArthur and Minoru Yamasaki had uncles who were architects. George Fred Keck's grandfather was a cabinet-maker. Maybeck's father was a woodcarver. In some cases, the sons were able to obtain clients through their father's professional contacts. Many had their father's help in securing their apprenticeships to more famous architects.

Although these family connections—especially wealth or a milieu that included contact with potential clients—reinforced the likelihood for success, they are not exclusive to famous architects. The same sort of background can be found for many a designer who, though possibly quite successful in terms of number and scope of commissions, never ventured to execute the sort of design that attracted the attention of the press. Family background or support has much less bearing on that sort of fame than does the fact that so many who have been singled out for attention worked for or with another famous architect.

College Acquaintances

Table 4 shows that a few schools have dominated in terms of having been attended by famous or moderately famous architects: Harvard, the Massachusetts Institute of Technology, Columbia, Yale, the University of Pennsylvania, and Cornell, followed by state universities in Illinois and California, and then Princeton. Yet before 1895 Harvard, Yale, and Princeton did not offer courses in architecture. However, they did give their future architects an advantage that even the Ecole des Beaux-Arts could not provide—client contacts. These were the schools for the children of the wealthy and, from the time of Charles Bulfinch on, they were preeminent in producing graduates who became America's financial, political, and social leaders—the members of boards and committees—exactly the sort of clients that go hand-in-hand with major commissions for public and commercial buildings as well as large and dramatic summer homes in Newport, Rhode Island or palatial mansions in large cities—the stuff of architectural fame.

Richardson's first biographer, Mariana Van Rensselaer, was quite frank about the fact that it was Richardson's classmates and fellow club members at Harvard who were essential, later, as his clients. His first important chance came through the invitation from a college friend to join a restricted competition for a church in Springfield, Massachusetts. Many of his subsequent designs were also done for clients he had known well in college. His Harvard contacts surely had something to do with his commissions for Sever Hall (1878–1880) and Austin Hall (1881–1883) on the campus. Ware, Van Brunt, Jenney, Silsbee, Peabody, McKim, and others had this same sort of client advantage through their attendance at Harvard. Of course, equally helpful classmates were found at Yale, Princeton, Amherst, and similar schools.

Students who enter architectural programs with an academic background in some other subject have an advantage that goes beyond their greater intellectual breadth. A close look at the lists of students at the various schools shows many names on two and even three different rosters, and the tables would be excessively long if all the first colleges attended by famous architects were listed. Unfortunately, now, in terms of potential client contacts, it is normal in many excellent public institutions for students to enter professional programs as freshmen; the restricted and time-absorbing curriculum rarely permits many classes or even much in the way of social club work outside the school itself. Friends are apt to be those who also spend the night in the design studios working on architectural projects. If architectural studies are postponed to graduate-level work, students have more ample opportunity to make social and intellectual contacts that may benefit their future careers. The programs at Yale and Harvard are graduate-level and many of the entering students have already established friendships with future leaders outside the profession. The University of Pennsylvania is an Ivy League college, but for most of this century the architecture program was at the undergraduate level with just the limited client contact that is typical of public schools. It is interesting to note that few famous graduates emerged from Penn until the post–World War II period, when most of the names listed were, in fact, graduate students.

Professional Connections

Another factor that should not be overlooked in terms of the network of connections charted in the first part of this book is that Harvard, Yale, MIT, Penn, and Princeton have names that attracted famous architects to try their talents as teachers when offered positions. These same professors maintained active practices and were quite likely to hire their own favorite students. This was the case with Gropius and Breuer at Harvard's Graduate School of Design and with Mies at IIT—as demonstrated earlier—and it was also the case with numerous other architects. In 1947 the students at Yale were in contact with Edward D. Stone, Louis Kahn, Paul Schweikher, Carl Koch, and Gardner Dailey. In the next decade a student might attract the attention of Paul Rudolph or Buckminster Fuller or Philip Johnson or Louis Kahn. By no means all Harvard and Yale students of the 1940s and 1950s became famous—but many of those employed by one of these professors who was just beginning to generate publicity did so.

Thus young architects who attended prestigious universities began their careers with important employer contacts. It was, and to a large extent still is, a closed system. Men like Eero Saarinen who were not teaching at the time would get on the phone and call Yale or Penn professors when they were seeking additional employees. It is this sort of mentorship by a professor that really counted in terms of a

Table 4
Schools Attended by Ten or More of the Architects
Discussed in This Study

MASSACHUSETTS INSTITUTE OF TECHNOLOGY

Francis Chandler	Charles Coolidge	Guy Lowell
J. Lyman Silsbee	Cass Gilbert	Marion Mahony Griffin
Arthur Rotch	Henry Ives Cobb	Robert P. Bellows
Langford Warren	George F. Shepley	Thomas Tallmadge
Arthur Little	George Heins	William Aldrich
Edmund Wheelwright	C. Grant La Farge	Raymond Hood
A. W. Longfellow, Jr.	Richard Howland Hunt	Lawrence Kocher
Glenn Brown	Robert Spencer	Ralph Walker
A. D. F. Hamlin	John Galen Howard	John Staub
William Aiken	Richard E. Schmidt	John Merrill
George Mann	William B. Faville	Louis Skidmore
Charles Sumner Frost	Dwight Perkins	Morris Lapidus
William Chamberlain	Alfred Hoyt Granger	Edward D. Stone
Louis Sullivan	Myron Hunt	Gordon Bunshaft
Herbert Jacques	Charles Sumner Greene	William Caudill
James Knox Taylor	John Mead Howells	Harry Weese
Wilson Eyre	Welles Bosworth	I. M. Pei
Ion Lewis	Howard Van Doren Shaw	Walter Netsch
William Whidden	Henry Mather Greene	Stanley Tigerman

HARVARD INCLUDING THE LAWRENCE SCIENTIFIC SCHOOL
AND THE GRADUATE SCHOOL OF DESIGN

John Trumbull	John Stewardson	Huson Jackson
Charles Bulfinch	Charles Wetmore	Bertrand Goldberg
William Robert Ware	I. N. P. Stokes	Edward L. Barnes
Henry Van Brunt	John Mead Howells	Lawrence Halprin
Charles Gambrill	Guy Lowell	Eduardo Catalano
William L. Jenney	Pierce Anderson	I. M. Pei
H. H. Richardson	F. L. Olmsted, Jr.	John Johansen
John G. Stearns	Robert P. Bellows	Paul Rudolph
J. Lyman Silsbee	George W. Smith	Landes Gores
Robert S. Peabody	George Howe	John Carl Warnecke
Theophilus B. Chandler	Harold Bush-Brown	Anne Tyng
Walter Cook	R. Buckminster Fuller	Ulrich Franzen
Charles F. McKim	William W. Wurster	Victor Lundy
Charles Atwood	Edward D. Stone	Frank Gehry
A. W. Longfellow	Philip C. Johnson	John Hejduk
John Calvin Stevens	Eliot Noyes	Peter Eisenman
Edmund Wheelwright	Carl Koch	Michael Graves
Charles Coolidge	Hugh Stubbins	Robert Siegel
Henry Ives Cobb	Harry Seidler	

COLUMBIA

James Renwick, Jr.	Chester Aldrich	Morris Lapidus
Charles C. Haight	William Delano	Alden Dow
Walter Cope	John Russell Pope	Robert A. Jacobs
Thomas Hastings	Albert Doyle	Max Abramovitz
S. B. P. Trowbridge	Arthur Harmon	William Brown
Whitney Warren	Clarence Stein	Vincent Kling
Henry Hornbostel	William Lamb	Romaldo Giurgola
I. N. P. Stokes	Ely Jacques Kahn	Peter Eisenman
Goodhue Livingston	Philip Goodwin	Noel McKinnell
James M. Hewlett	Talbot Hamlin	Robert A. M. Stern
Benjamin W. Morris	Andrew Reinhard	

Table 4
(*continued*)

YALE

Frederick L. Olmsted	Charles Collens	Earl Paul Carlin
Walter Cook	William Delano	Thomas Vreeland
James Gamble Rogers	Frederick Godley	Stanley Tigerman
Howard Van Doren Shaw	Paul Schweikher	James Polshek
Clarence Zantzinger	Eero Saarinen	Marshall Meyers
Egerton Swartwout	Benjamin Thompson	Jacquelin Robertson
		Robert A. M. Stern

PENN

Emlin T. Littel	Milton Medary	Peter Blake
Frank Miles Day	Alfred Githens	Anne Tyng
Emlyn Stewardson	Henry Wright	Erhman Mitchell
Percy Ash	Francis Keally	Denise Scott Brown
George B. Page	Louis I. Kahn	John Rauch
Clarence Zantzinger	Joseph Esherick	Charles Gwathmey
John Molitor	Eduardo Catalano	

CORNELL

Arthur Page Brown	John W. Root, Jr.	Lawrence Perkins
Edward York	Pietro Belluschi	Edmund Bacon
Walter Bliss	Nathaniel Owings	Lawrence Halprin
Richmond Shreve	Philip Will	Peter Eisenman
William Purcell	Robert Alexander	Richard Meier

PRINCETON

Bruce Price	David Adler	Robert Venturi
James Brown Lord	Benjamin Baldwin	Hugh Hardy
Stephen Voorhees	Landes Gores	William Turnbull
Arthur Meigs	Charles Moore	Donlyn Lyndon

CALIFORNIA, BERKELEY

Julia Morgan	William W. Wurster	John Funk
Harvey Corbett	Theodore Bernardi	Ernest Kump
A. Page Brown, Jr.	Vernon De Mars	Gyo Obata
Gardner Dailey	Gregory Ain	

ILLINOIS

Henry Bacon	George Fred Keck	Cesar Pelli
William Drummond	William Keck	Fazlur Khan
Walter B. Griffin	Max Abramovitz	
Albert Fellheimer	William Pereira	

graduate's future career. (There is an interesting parallel to the mechanics of fame for designers. Famous professors of architectural history begot other famous professors, from Berenson to Sir Kenneth Clark, and Wölfflin to Giedion and Jencks. A chart of the connections between the famous architectural historians would look much like chart 1, with only a few loners—like Vincent Scully, who by now has generated his own descendants.)

These schools also attracted academically celebrated architects—that is, those architects featured by textbook writers—as deans. Howe, Gropius, Mies, Moore, Wurster, Sert, Harris, Rudolph, Giurgola, Pelli, and Cobb are but a few of the acclaimed architects who became deans or chairmen. A great many of the younger candidates for fame who are not yet in the Index of Fame are professor-architects with important fame makers as their colleagues on the faculty—the textbook authors. Because of the fraternal nature of the star system in architecture, these people bring others from their own set to join the faculty. It can seem exclusive, even incestuous, to the able professor or designer who is outside the clan. Upon close inspection, even an "unknown" new name in the academic limelight is discovered already to have become a member through an apprenticeship or close association with one of the others.

The interrelationship between George Howe, Philip Johnson, and Louis Kahn is a case in point and bears repeating. In the late 1940s Kahn had not produced much of significance but gained a reputation as a good teacher (as had Le Ricolais and Labatut, two professors who were his associates and just about as well known). He was a visiting critic at Yale at the time Howe was awarded the position of resident architect at the American Academy in Rome for the years 1947–1949—the first "modern" architect to be so honored. Howe secured a fellowship for his former partner, and Kahn went to Rome (and so did Howe's former employee, Louis A. McMillan, and Kahn's former employee, Robert Venturi, at a later date). In turn, Kahn was given credit by Charles Sawyer, who was then serving as the dean at Yale, for suggesting that Howe be named the new head of Yale's architectural school. Kahn was backed by Howe's one-time colleague at the inception of the Museum of Modern Art, Philip Johnson, and Howe took over. At Johnson's urging, Howe got the commission for the Yale Art Gallery addition for the almost untried Kahn.[27] Then Johnson, who was a frequent visiting critic at Yale, and Vincent Scully, the celebrated young architectural historian on the faculty, actively promoted the Art Gallery as a great design. In this they received the aid of Robert A. M. Stern, one of their students and a Johnson protégé, then serving as editor of Yale's *Perspecta* journal.

FOURTEEN

Self-promotion and Publicity

Self-promotional activity has been a fact of architectural history since the beginning of the Renaissance. Architecture is an art, but it is also a marketed product, and even wealthy architects have need for clients. The architect can, of course, design buildings for his own use—Philip Johnson built six for himself—but even that is a way of attracting the attention of potential clients.

Some architects become known principally through the books they have written. Robert Venturi and Andrea Palladio, for example, are alike in that their work is widely known in the profession by many who have never entered much less seen a building they designed. They both wrote important theoretical works, illustrated with their own designs (and designs from earlier times). Other celebrated architects have become famous before any building actually was constructed. The words "publication," "publicity," and "fame" are so closely related that it is hard to conceive of architectural fame without both the printed word and photographs or drawings.

One route to fame, sometimes taken by less verbally skilled architects, is the display of drawings, or, at a more advanced level, the organization of an exhibition of drawings and, if possible, photographs of built designs. This was Richard Morris Hunt's action when his proposals for gates for Olmsted and Vaux's Central Park were not accepted. According to his biographer, Hunt was a tedious public speaker and did little writing but

> in the spring of 1865 he put the plans and elevations of his works for the park on exhibit at the National Academy of Design, and the following year published a little book which included the plans, illustrations of the gateways, and an extended favorable analysis of

the works by his friend William H. Hoppin (who signed himself "Civic"), a critique that had originally appeared in the *New York Evening Post*. The Hunt designs were also shown in various shop windows and showcases in the city, and reproductions of the drawings were sold. . . . The public response to the proposed gateways was largely negative.[1]

However, in terms of eventual academic fame, a negative reaction by the public does not seem to matter. Originality and distinctiveness are characteristics that are apt to seem strange to the general public, but these are exactly the qualities that attract the fame makers.

There are several means of architectural promotion:

1. Illustrated lectures (Sullivan, Wright, Gallier, and others) and modest exhibitions, like that by Hunt, on a local level.

2. Articles about the architect's work in local and regional publications by the architect or his or her friends.

3. Articles in professional journals.

4. Exhibitions *with* published catalogs (especially those of the Museum of Modern Art).

    a. Broad surveys of contemporary work, like *The International Style, Built in USA, 40 under 40*.

    b. Shows featuring a limited number of architects, like *The Chicago 7, Five Architects*, or MOMA's *1932 Modern Architects*.

    c. One-man shows (Richardson, Sullivan, Wright, Mies, etc.).

5. Articles in the popular journals (*Time, Ladies' Home Journal*, etc.).

6. Monographs, biographies, and sometimes autobiographies (although there are clear exceptions to the effectiveness of this form of publicity).

7. Inclusion in a select group of textbooks—more than two texts.

Two of the most famous architects born in America were also the most active self-promoters in American architectural history. In addition, they benefited from promotion by their colleagues and professional connections. Louis Sullivan adopted the persona of a misunderstood loner, but this was patently untrue. It is true that he, Wright, and many of the others we now revere were designing against the mainstream of popular and professional taste. But for a while Sullivan reaped the rewards of promotion. Even before he went to work for Adler, his ornamentation of the interior of Johnson & Edelmann's Moody Tabernacle had created enough of a stir among the congregation that the art critic of a Chicago newspaper went to investigate and published a favorable account. Sullivan's self-promotion was well underway in 1885 when he read a paper entitled "Characteristics and

Tendencies of American Architecture" before the local Western Association of Architects. It was also published in London in the *Builder's Weekly Reporter* that same year, quite a feat for a twenty-nine-year-old architect.

Most of Sullivan's lectures and articles, and there were a number, were published in regional trade journals with limited readerships. The fifty-two "Kindergarten Chats," for example, were not published in book form until 1934. But Sullivan had been featured in the major professional journal *American Architect and Building News* in 1889, and one year after the World's Columbian Exposition of 1893, Sullivan was mentioned not only in *Scribner's* but in the French journal *Revue des Arts Décoratifs*. His work had been favored by the major American architectural critic Montgomery Schuyler and he was well enough known in 1900 that A. D. F. Hamlin—a Columbia professor—elected to include one of his designs in his list of "The Ten Most Beautiful Buildings in the United States." Sullivan chose dramatic titles for his lectures and articles. The year after the spectacular and influential World's Columbian Exposition of 1893, Sullivan pleaded for "Emotional Architecture as Compared with Intellectual: A Study in Objective and Subjective." The most important of these lectures of the 1890s was "The Tall Building Artistically Considered" (1896).

Frank Lloyd Wright was a full participant in all the aspects of self-promotion and, in addition, was indebted to his associates for much of his early publicity. Wright's reputation actually preceded his outstanding work. Before 1900 Wright was speaking to local, civic, social, and professional bodies, as well as engaging in the activities that brought him into contact with wealthy potential clients: horse shows, regular attendance at the opera, dinner parties.[2] Wright had a dominant role in the Chicago Architectural Club, which put on annual exhibitions with profusely illustrated catalogs. He was a founder of that chapter of the Architectural League of America and active in Hull House as well as the Arts and Crafts Movement. The "Eighteen" architects in his circle energetically published each other's work in regional and national periodicals.

H. Allen Brooks discovered the first article about Wright in the first issue of *House Beautiful* in 1897, at that time a Chicago-based periodical. It was unsigned, but two years later the same magazine published an article by the Ecole des Beaux-Arts–trained Alfred Granger on Wright's studio and home in Oak Park. Wright shared an office with the man who really launched his career in terms of fame—Robert Spencer, an MIT graduate like Granger. He had already contributed a photograph of Wright's entry to the Luxfer competition (won by Spencer) to the press, but it was Spencer's major article "The

Work of Frank Lloyd Wright," published in the *Architectural Review* (Boston) in 1900, with Wright's willing cooperation in providing dozens of plans and illustrations, that really launched Wright.[3] Another architect in the same group, George R. Dean, published Wright's speech "The Architect" in *Brickbuilder* in 1900. These two 1900 items led to Wright's major breakthrough, a feature story in *Ladies' Home Journal* in 1901.

During the first decade of the twentieth century Wright was bathed in accolades. In 1906 *House Beautiful* devoted the leading article in three issues to Wright. There were 87 illustrations in the March 1908 issue of the *Architectural Record* accompanying an article on Wright's work. In 1907 Wright was given a solo exhibition at the Chicago Art Institute. By the end of this first decade of attention Wright's ego had swollen out of bounds. In this he duplicated his "Lieber Meister," Sullivan. And in both cases their popularity immediately fell off in America.

Other architects in this Chicago group were also active in both self-promotion and promotion of their associates. However, several of the receptive publications had limited readership. The Prairie School received significant recognition by the *Western Architect* even after 1911. "In 1912 articles appeared by Purcell on Griffin, and by Griffin on his plan for Canberra. . . . In 1913 an issue was devoted to the work of Purcell and Elmslie, the architects themselves preparing the layout, marginal decorations, text, captions . . . . In 1914, the March issue was devoted to George W. Maher and the April issue (with text by Purcell) to Spencer and Powers." Arthur Heun's work was "profusely illustrated in P. B. Wight's article 'Melody Farm, the Country Home of J. Ogden Armour,' *Architectural Record* 39, 1916, 96–121. . . . Howard Shaw's own house was illustrated in *Inland Architect and News Record* in 1899 and again in 1904."[4] This mutual activity explains why H. Allen Brooks can say that "Wright's publicity was far in excess of his local prominence."[5]

For a while interest in Wright waned. He was fifty-five in 1922 when the Tokyo Hotel was finished, normally a prime year for most famous architects, even early for many. But, as mentioned in chapter 2, quite suddenly, beginning in 1925, Dutch, French, and American editors and writers showed renewed interest in Wright. This revival culminated in Wright's autobiography, and he became a sought-after lecturer at various universities at the end of an extremely bleak period in his career. This activity and publicity sparked a new period of powerful design growth, and, with the Museum of Modern Art's 1938 exhibition of photographs of Falling Water, he reemerged as the dominant American architect and achieved world-wide fame. However, his later work rarely matched that of the first decade after the publicity of the later 1920s and 1930s—a period that paralleled that of 1901 to 1909.

A corollary in the mechanics of fame is that recognition can trigger the genius that in turn makes fame possible. Just as a certain kind of apprentice can cheer a designer on to greater heights, so a burst of publicity may inspire him and bring about a period of special creativity. Wright's career was like that of several other famous architects in that his greatest strength came just *after* major publicity and eventually fell off in quality even though publicity continued. It is significant to note that only with recognition in 1900 and 1901 did Wright suddenly synthesize his design ideas and begin to produce real masterpieces. He had been in practice for seven or eight years, but his best work *followed* this burst of attention and lasted another eight years. This pattern—creative production following publicity—was repeated in other careers—those of Walter Gropius, Mies van der Rohe, George Howe, and Louis Kahn, for example.

In several instances, publication precedes an architect's really outstanding work. The act of publishing generates a burst of self-confidence in actual design and, since much great architecture is essentially bold architecture, the designer is emboldened further by the event. In this, the response is similar to Richardson's accelerating talent after he won the commissions for the Springfield and Brattle Square churches with his real genius emerging *after* his publicity for Trinity Church.

Several authors have noted this occurrence in the lives of the architects they were studying. Jacob Landy even draws a parallel between Minard Lafever's enhanced ability *after* his first publication and this same occurrence that the historian Sir John Summerson discovered in Sir John Soane's career.[6]

Walter Gropius began with advantages that neither Wright nor Mies had. One early advantage was that his "father had been head of the Berlin Art School and Director of Education in Prussia."[7] His father undoubtedly had contacts that enabled Gropius to attract the attention of potential clients. Gropius' first major commission was completed when he was twenty-five years old. Two years later he wrote an article on the development of modern industrial architecture that was published in the 1913 *Jahrbuch des deutschen Werkbundes*. Gropius did not speak comfortably or fluently in public but he was a prolific writer and tireless organizer. Reyner Banham commented wryly in *Age of the Masters* that "none has so consistently hidden his own light under a bushel of collaborators while never escaping public notice for a minute."[8] The same author reported in *Theory and Design in the*

First Machine Age that the "Bauhaus produced 14 books between 1925 and 1930" and that Gropius, as head of the Bauhaus from 1918 to 1928, was the initiator of this sort of steady promotion.[9] In addition, Gropius "developed a new type of exhibition in which every modern technique of display was called into service."[10] However, it was a long time before Gropius was admired beyond the fringes of a quite select group of advocates of Modern architecture.

Ludwig Mies van der Rohe: An Annotated Bibliography and Chronology by David Spaeth traces the publicity and self-promotional activities of this architect who seemed to be the quietest of the giants. Mies, the stonemason's son, was the slowest to receive substantial commissions, although he had two notices as early as 1910 for a house he designed. By 1921 Mies was director of architectural exhibitions for the Novembergruppe and had begun to publish his projects for glass skyscrapers. "He was active as a propagandist. He was among the founders of the magazine *G* which was devoted to modern art. . . . It was principally in the annual exhibitions of the Novembergruppe that his early modern projects appeared."[11] In the role of director of the Werkbund exhibition at Stuttgart in 1927, Mies displayed his own work as prominently as that of other architects. By 1930 he had taken the directorship of the Bauhaus, but his Barcelona Pavilion and Tugendhat House, which were so celebrated in the later part of this century, passed almost unnoticed in 1930.[12]

Mies and Gropius fully participated in promotional activities in Germany before the rise of Hitler. Gropius' *The New Architecture and the Bauhaus* was translated into English and published in 1935, while he was working in England. Gropius was also the source for the title of *The International Style*, the famous Museum of Modern Art book (1932), which, according to Henry-Russell Hitchcock, one of its authors, was drawn from the title of Gropius' *Internationale Architektur*.[13] Gropius, Breuer, and, in time, Mies were indebted for their fame in America to the Museum of Modern Art.

In 1938 the museum sponsored an exhibition of the work of Gropius and Breuer that complemented a recently published book by Gropius just before they designed their first American house. Philip Johnson had long been an admirer of the work of Mies van der Rohe. Although he lost out in influencing the MOMA board to select Mies as the architect for its building in 1936, Johnson produced a monograph on Mies and an exhibition of his work in 1947. In each case—Wright, Gropius and Breuer, Mies—the work that *followed* this sort of attention was more significant than the work that they had produced in the several years preceding this exposure.

A surprising number of the men in the Index of Fame tried their hands at writing as well as design. Several "how-to" books have been available through the AIA to aid in self-promotion. Because advertising one's self is frowned upon, the suggestions are nonspecific, aimed at architects' promotion of architects in general. For example, one offered a full-page reproducible advertisement about the advantages of hiring an architect. Another explained "How to place a series of pictures and captions about good and bad environmental features in local papers." An architect could try the following offerings: "Selling Architectural Services," "Conducting Winning Presentations," "Public Relations Aids," and "How to Prepare Professional Design Brochures" (277 pages). Advertising may be against the rules, but self-promotion is a long-standing tradition that has roots in European practices. In the United States, many architects from Asher Benjamin onward have published books.

Architects usually take one of two approaches to publication. A number of architects are compelled to put their theories in print. The fact that this may also make the author known may be thought of as an innocent side effect. The manifesto was nearly a prerequisite in the early part of the twentieth century for architects who wished to declare their independence from historicism. This is the Albertian approach.

In America Sullivan was the most outspoken writer of this sort, although Wright ran him a close race. Gropius, Mendelsohn, Neutra, and other immigrant architects were fluent theorists also, almost equal in persuasiveness to France's Le Corbusier, whose lyrical polemics were read like an Epistle to the Romans. But many lesser architects also felt compelled to verbal expression. These manifestos should be taken as sincere attempts on the part of their authors to enlighten their readers. As Conrad Jamison has said,

> It is naive to assume that an interested belief system also requires interested motives, still less that these motives must be self-conscious or conspiratorial. The contrary is more likely to be the case. Before an ideologue can convince someone else, he must first of all convince himself: without an idealistic impulse he could fail before he begins.
>
> The Modern Movement brings not just an aggrandizement of architecture, but of the architect as well: like it or lump it, the two go hand in hand, and not by accident but by design. Whomever else the Modern movement has served, there can be no question about the most immediate beneficiary: the architect himself.[14]

The Palladian method, often just as sincere, goes a step further in terms of self-promotion. The theories are illustrated by the author's own work. Venturi's *Complexity and Contradiction in Architecture* is in a sense two books. The first is theory based on examples from architectural history; the second is the theory applied in his designs. Some readers have accepted the first and rejected the other.

For early American architects, self-promotion most often took the form of handbooks and similar "how-to" books: Asher Benjamin's *The Country Builder's Assistant* was published in 1797, when he was twenty-five. More books followed in 1806, 1814, 1830 (seventeen editions), and 1843. Ithiel Town's *A Description of Ithiel Town's Improvement in the Construction . . . of Bridges . . .* of 1814 was reprinted in 1825, 1831, and 1839. Solomon Willard published *Plans and Sections of the Obelisk on Bunker's Hill*. Mills abandoned a book on theory but did write *The American Pharos; or Lighthouse Guide* (1832), *Designs for a Marine Hospital* (1837?), and *A Guide to the Capitol of the United States* (1834). In the 1840s Strickland published reports on his engineering projects and the tomb of Washington at Mt. Vernon.[15]

John Haviland has not been discussed up to this point except peripherally as a possible employer of Lafever and one of the contestants in competitions. Haviland's publications had much to do with his eventual fame and, in this, he patterned himself on his former employer in England, James Elmes, who built his own reputation with the second book that he wrote, *Metropolitan Improvements or London in the Nineteenth Century* (1827), mentioned earlier as strongly influencing Lafever's 1829 guide. Almost immediately upon arrival in America, Haviland put together a three-volume builder's guide based on the Philadelphia-born Owen Biddle's *The Carpenter's Assistant* (1805), published the year before Biddle died at the age of thirty-two. Haviland's version contained the first plates of the Greek Orders published in America. Haviland's international notice came from his publication of his winning design for the Philadelphia penitentiary in 1824.[16] Finally, in 1833, Haviland put together yet another builder's guide. Samuel Sloan, his carpenter at that time, wrote four of his own later but then turned to journalism and published the first architectural periodical in America from 1868 to 1870.

James Gallier, Minard Lafever, Richard Upjohn, Alexander J. Davis, A. J. Downing, Calvert Vaux, Frederick Withers, Henry Austin, and Thomas U. Walter all wrote, or attempted to write, builder's guides and articles. Builder's guides eventually went out of style and architects turned to other genres. Leopold Eidlitz wrote a monumental book of architectural theory, published in 1881. Hunt's thirty-six-page pamphlet on his designs for the Central Park gateways appears to be his only attempt at publication. Of course, he had beneficial social ties to his clients and thus did not need to advertise once these were established. His student, Professor Ware, wrote as well as lec-

tured on architecture, and his partner Henry Van Brunt was a prolific author whose most important contribution was the translation of
Viollet-le-Duc's *Entretiens* in 1875. William Le Baron Jenney wrote
one book, with his partner Sanford Loring. *Principles and Practice of
Architecture* was published in 1869, at the same time that the Portland
Block initiated his fame. Both the book and the building were fresh
when Jenney had the cluster of employees who would achieve future fame.

Russell Sturgis, the employer of McKim and Mead, not only
wrote for the journals, but also published a collection of articles written by John Wellborn Root the year Root died. (Sturgis' former partner, Peter B. Wight, had become Root's mentor.) Wight had published
an essay and photographs on his own award-winning National Academy of Design and in 1869 he produced an eight-page tract *Remarks
on Fireproofing Construction* two years before the Chicago fire. In his
later years he was a regular contributor to the *Architectural Record*
and *Inland Architect* and Russell Sturgis became more widely known
as an author than as a designer.

Other nineteenth-century books by major architects include the
publication of three sketchbooks by Robert Peabody, who also wrote
many articles for *Harper's*, *Atlantic Monthly*, and *American Architecture* beginning at the time that the Peabody & Stearns practice was
only getting underway. John Wellborn Root began seeing his articles
published in 1883 when the Montauk Block, Burnham & Root's first
major work, was finished. The first project of Carrère & Hastings,
which Maybeck supervised, was well publicized upon its completion,
not only in advertising brochures by Flagler, but also in the professional journals. (Neither architect had yet reached thirty.) Maybeck
also wrote, proudly, of his Palace of Fine Arts in 1915.

Ralph Adams Cram had been an art and music critic before he
established his architectural practice. He wrote *Church Building*
(1899) before his firm received its first significant commission. Several lesser Beaux-Arts architects did not resist the urge to write.[17] The
Modernistic skyscraper architects also wrote; Ely Jacques Kahn,
Harvey Corbett, Hugh Ferriss, and Paul Frankl were authors.[18] Norman Bel Geddes wrote *New Horizons* in 1932, not long after he established his own office. In 1927 Fuller published *4-D*, which featured his
light and inexpensive megastructure, and continued to write throughout his career.

William Lescaze, Howe's partner on the PSFS building, was the
author of a number of articles and three books. Eric Mendelsohn began publishing works in 1919 at the time he got his first commission,
for the Einstein Tower. Neutra's *Wie Baut Amerika* was published in

1926 just as he was beginning the Garden Apartments in Los Angeles and establishing his career. Josep Lluis Sert's *Can Our Cities Survive?* came out before his American career was really underway. Victor Gruen was writing in the 1920s. Oskar Stonorov, who would become Kahn's partner, was an editor of the first volume of Le Corbusier's *Oeuvre Complète* and a translator of *Le Corbusier und Pierre Jeanneret* with W. Boesiger in 1930. Several of the architects who are discussed most often in architectural schools today are writers almost as much as designers—Robert Venturi, Charles Moore, Peter Eisenman, and Robert A. M. Stern. Like Sullivan, Wright, Gropius, and Mies, they have benefited from promotion by their colleagues as well.

Professional Journals and Group Efforts

American periodicals of a generalized nature occasionally ran pieces on architecture during the first half of the nineteenth century and fairly often at a later period. As early as 1844 the *North American Review* carried a well-written article by the young architect Arthur Gilman supporting eclecticism. William Rutherford Mead, of McKim, Mead & White, was the brother-in-law of William Dean Howells, editor of *Atlantic Monthly*.[19] It was in *Atlantic Monthly* that Henry Van Brunt's early and complimentary article about Richardson appeared in May of 1879 while the partnership of McKim, Mead & White was just being established by two of Richardson's protégés.

By the 1880s architectural periodicals had become an important organ of the profession. From the beginning these journals were under the domination of the same architectural establishment discussed throughout this book. For a brief time members of the newly founded American Institute of Architects in New York were published in the *Crayon*. Among its articles was an exchange between the very young Henry Van Brunt and Leopold Eidlitz on the virtues of the use of cast iron, with Van Brunt taking the affirmative position. One periodical, which survived for several years, managed to maintain its independence from the establishment. In fact, the New York– and Chicago-based *American Builder* (1868–1895) was "specifically hostile to architects," and directed toward builders.[20] This was not so for most of the others that succeeded.

Neither Hunt nor Richardson had need to write in order to call attention to themselves. Others within their immediate circle of colleagues served as their promoters. However, "Richardson's name as editor appears in an editorial note at the beginning of the first volume of what is more accurately entitled *The New York Sketch-Book of Architecture*; also . . . Montgomery Schuyler later asserted that McKim

really served as de facto editor."[21] The first illustration in the first
issue of this periodical was Richardson's design for the Hampden
County Courthouse in Springfield, Massachusetts. "The early work of
George B. Post, who had been Richardson's predecessor as Gambrill's
partner . . . is also illustrated in the *Sketch Book* with an exceptional
design of the mid-seventies . . . a domed Renaissance building . . .
which prefigures McKim's Columbia Library."[22] George Babb's work
was also included in the *Sketch Book*; Babb actually worked for
McKim and Mead after serving as Mead's mentor in Sturgis' office.
McKim was only twenty-seven when the *Sketch Book* was begun, and
it lasted only three years. However, one of its other editors, Montgomery Schuyler, "returned repeatedly in his later essays to the buildings,
the men, and the implicit ideals illustrated in its pages."[23]

William Rotch Ware, a nephew of William Robert Ware (Hunt's
apprentice, Van Brunt's partner), was the editor of the first professional journal able to sustain itself. The *American Architect and Building News* was Boston based and lasted from 1876 to 1938. At first it was
published weekly, and the first illustration in the first issue was a
building by Richard Morris Hunt, several years before he hit his
stride. The editors, Ware and Wadsworth Longfellow—a Harvard,
Ecole, and Richardson product—provided many illustrations of European architecture and favored what was then called "the Queen Anne
style," but any architect was welcome to send in properly prepared
illustrations of his or her work.[24]

In the first year of publication, the *American Architect* featured
another Hunt graduate in its December 23 and May 13, 1876, issues.
Frank Furness, however, ceased being of interest to the magazine
about 1880. In 1888 Theodore Minot Clark assumed the editorship
and kept the Richardson line in the forefront, since he had himself
been a Richardson employee before serving for eight years as a professor at MIT. For a while Furness found recognition in other journals. Other "periodicals such as *The Brickbuilder* or Philadelphia-
based *Architectural Era*, among professional journals, and the *Scientific American*, among general magazines, did carry his work from
time to time. Criticism began to run against him in the nineties."[25]

Montgomery Schuyler and the architect Russell Sturgis became
highly influential architectural critics, and Sturgis continued to promote his ex-employer, Eidlitz, his ex-partner, Wight, and his ex-
employees, McKim and Mead, but also Wight's protégé, John Wellborn
Root. Later, because of Lewis Mumford's heavy reliance on the writings of these men when he turned to architectural criticism in the
early 1920s, this network fed directly into the sequence established
by the fame-making critics of this century. For example, Nikolaus

Pevsner used a quotation from Sturgis to reinforce the Modernist position: "Things might be better, if architects were allowed to build very plainly for a while. . . . If the architects were to fall back upon their building, their construction, their handling of materials as their sole source of architectural effect, a new and valuable style might take form."[26]

Montgomery Schuyler was as important as Sturgis, though, as is the case with Sturgis, "selective quotation had magnified our impression of his prescience."[27] He was a minister's son, born in Ithaca, New York. He attended but did not graduate from Hobart College, where he studied literature. His career began on the news desk of the *New York World*, where he was a literary reviewer. But he came under the influence of Wight and Sturgis and in 1874 joined the editorial staff of the Richardson-McKim *Sketch Book*, while continuing to write for other periodicals and newspapers as well. In 1885 he became managing editor of *Harper's Weekly* for two years and from 1883 until 1907 was also on the editorial staff of the *New York Times*. The *Architectural Record* was established in 1891, and Schuyler contributed articles regularly for the next twenty-three years. While with *Harper's*, he had published Richardson's drawings for the Allegheny County Courthouse and Jail in Pittsburgh. He liked not only the work of Richardson, but that of Charles Coolidge Haight, and was a close personal friend of Leopold Eidlitz. However, it was mainly Schuyler's interest in skyscrapers and bridges that made him seem a prophet to later writers. His praise for Sullivan and Chicago commercial buildings has kept Schuyler's name alive.

The *Architectural Record* was founded in 1891. One of the major editors of the 1920s, Charles Harris Whitaker, was a close friend and advisor to the critic Lewis Mumford. He edited the *Journal of the American Institute of Architects* from 1913 to 1928 and was the principal mentor for a group that included Mumford, Clarence Stein, Henry Wright, Frederick L. Ackerman, and Catherine Bauer (who later became Mrs. William W. Wurster). Editors sometimes moved from journal to journal and were likely to maintain their interest in certain architects in the process (narrowing the field of possibilities for some aspiring designers). The *Brickbuilder* began its life in 1892 and in 1917 changed its name to *Architectural Forum.* In 1913 Russell Whitehead took over the editorship of the *Brickbuilder* after serving in the same capacity on the *Architectural Record.* Then in 1930 he became the editor of *Pencil Points*, which existed under that title from 1920 to 1945, when it became *Progressive Architecture.* During the late 1920s A. Lawrence Kocher was an associate editor of the *Record* and provided a receptive climate for the emerging International Style. He was professionally associated with Albert Frey in the early 1930s and Frey's former employer had been the most vocal of all the champions of this fashion—Le Corbusier. Kocher himself was an early member of CIAM. He became editor of the *Record* from 1928 to 1938.

The editor of *Architectural Forum* in the 1930s, Howard Meyers, and Edward Durell Stone, the architect of the building of the Museum of Modern Art, were, in Stone's words, "inseparable friends."[28] Naturally enough, Stone was featured in *Forum* after completing the museum, but he also won the *House and Garden* Grand Prize that same year and this publication was allied to *Forum*.

Various important critics did their first writing for these professional journals. Among them was James Marston Fitch, an associate editor of *Architectural Record* from 1936 to 1941. After service in the Air Corps, he was technical editor for *Architectural Forum* from 1945 until 1949, when he took over as architectural editor for *House Beautiful*. At the time when Jane Jacobs was an editor of *Architectural Forum*, her enormously influential *Death and Life of Great American Cities* (1961) was published—one of the first antihero outcries, or at least antihero in contrast to what had become so common as other journalists lauded the Modernist masters. Ada Louise Huxtable wrote for the professional journals in the period between her position as assistant curator at the Museum of Modern Art, under Philip Johnson, and her assumption of the role of architectural critic of the *New York Times*. Peter Blake, a former employee of Chermayeff and of Stonorov & Kahn, left the staff of the Museum of Modern Art to become editor of *Architectural Forum* and then of *Architecture Plus*.[29] Considering the connections these editors and writers had to several of the most progressive institutions and architects of the time, it is amazing, in retrospect, to scan their journals. Only a fraction of what they published would also appear in the surveys written by the historians. (Of course, Fitch, when he evolved from journalist to historian, did include his favorites in his books, though many of them were mentioned only briefly.) Smaller regional magazines had a much better record of forecasting the future fame of architects. However, many of these journals had a quite limited readership and have been distorted in importance by citations in later writings.

The Prairie School's major organ, the *Western Architect*, was one of these small journals and it is nearly impossible to locate today. A journal called the *Craftsman* is also cited regularly by historians. It was published by the furniture designer and manufacturer Gustav Stickley, an adherent of the English Arts and Crafts Movement. Although it was published in New York state, the magazine was anything but regional. It published Sullivan's Owatonna Bank and was interested in the group that revolved around Sullivan in Chicago. Stickley discovered the work of Greene & Greene on the West Coast. He also promoted Irving Gill (who had been born in Syracuse) and Harvey Ellis (who had practiced in Rochester from 1879 to 1885 and would work for Stickley later). Mumford discovered this journal early in his writing career and used it, as well as selections from Schuyler, as source material in his early essays.

These smaller journals were important to that minority of architects who were developing modern architecture. The *Western Architect* published Eliel Saarinen's "A New Architectural Language for America," in 1923, and the scheme he proposed for the development of the Chicago lakefront was published in *American Architect* and also in the *Architectural Review* that same year (1923 was also the year that Saarinen was appointed director of Architecture and City Planning at the University of Michigan).

William Wurster's commissions followed his discovery by *House Beautiful* in 1927, but it was the more regionally directed *California Arts and Architecture* and *Arts and Crafts* that introduced Harwell Harris' designs in 1935. Fitch began to promote his work, and Harris was featured in *Architectural Forum* by 1937. The Entenza house, in Santa Monica, was designed by Harris for the editor of *Arts and Architecture* in 1937. Entenza and his magazine backed the Case Study Houses by Charles Eames, Eero Saarinen, and others in the early 1950s.

The web of influence in professional promoting is summarized and made clear by the case of George Howe. Howe received his first publicity for a house he rented and remodeled on his return from his studies at the Ecole des Beaux-Arts in Paris. It was illustrated in an article in *Architectural Record* in November 1914.[30] Six years later the *Record* featured his house "High Hollow" in an article written by Howe's friend Paul Cret. This was reprinted by Howe's firm in *A Monograph on the Work of Mellor, Meigs and Howe* in 1923. Then Howe burst into prominence in 1930. He had teamed up with William Lescaze, who had come to the United States several years earlier with Werner Moser. Moser wrote "Design for an Office Building," published in *Architectural Record* in 1930, which featured the PSFS building while it was still in its early stages of construction.[31] Howe was a financial backer of the short-lived *Modern Architecture USA* in the early 1930s,[32] and also of the *T-Square Journal*, and as president of Philadelphia's T-Square Club he wrote the preface to the first issue in 1930. This journal had a circulation of 4,000 in 1932, and contributors included Neutra, Johnson, Le Corbusier, Schindler, Bel Geddes, Buckminster Fuller, and the young Louis Skidmore—all destined for fame.[33] In 1932 the name was changed to *Shelter, A Magazine for Modern Architecture*, and "Philip Johnson helped Howe in financing it since he wanted to publish a packet of items entitled 'International Architecture.'"[34]

That was the year of the now famous Museum of Modern Art exhibition "Modern Architecture" with the accompanying books *The International Style* and *Modern Architects*. Howe was one of the very few American architects featured in *Modern Architects* and he was also on the editorial board. "The Museum of Modern Art hired a publicist to have Howe's and Lescaze's resignations from the Architectural League on the front page of the *New York Times*, Sunday 28 February, 1932."[35] Although Howe designed little else of significance after PSFS, his fame was assured.

While dean at Yale, several years later, Howe largely underwrote the first issue of that school's journal *Perspecta*, the leader of a new genre.[36] The success of *Perspecta* inspired a number of other architectural schools and spawned a wave of high-quality academic journals. Harvard's amateurish *Connections* (edited by Charles Jencks at the same time that Robert Stern produced one of the most brilliant of Yale's journals) was replaced by a much more impressive publication, and other institutions have sponsored their own periodicals. Naturally enough, there is an in-house tendency in most of these. Authors are often members of the individual faculties. While *Perspecta* was ascendant the articles were almost exclusively written by Yale professors or visiting critics.

It is still early to know how effective these academic journals will be in establishing lasting fame for those they feature. Unquestionably, Louis Kahn's reputation was launched by Yale's celebrated architectural historian, Vincent Scully, in *Perspecta* while Kahn was at Yale. Buildings have been "discovered"—like the Maison de Verre (1929–1931) in Paris by Pierre Chareau, an architect whose work in New York after 1940 certainly did not class him among the famous immigrant designers. In acknowledging the role of professional recognition in establishing fame one must keep in mind the thousands of other architects who also were being featured by the national professional journals—only a few achieved fame. While a contributing factor, this is not the most important aspect of their rise to a place in history.

FIFTEEN

Other, Weaker Patterns

Design Competitions

Many a reputation has first been established through competition entries, built or unbuilt, and even second- and third-place entries can enhance one's status. Competitions were the established method for selecting architects for governmental buildings for many years, beginning with Jefferson's 1792 competitions for the United States Capitol and the White House.[1] National reputations have been established on the strength of one winning design, such as that by Kallmann, McKinnell & Knowles for the Boston City Hall in the 1960s. However, with the growing elaboration of design presentations, competitions have often become inordinately expensive to enter today. This frequently prevents beginning firms from participation.

In the first several decades after the American Revolution, nearly all buildings, other than houses, involved competitive design. These competitions were, apparently, fully open to all who might be interested, and for that reason several architects of these early years became famous even though they had no career connections to anyone else. Usually, however, they were known only for that one building. This was certainly true of Joseph François Mangin. And his partner, John McComb, Jr., is well known in New York City, but nationally known only for his part in the competition they won—the New York City Hall (1802–1812).

Several architects of the federal period are noted only for their part in the first buildings of Washington, D.C. We do not know the specific academic or professional background of Etienne Hallet, who won second prize in the U.S. Capitol competition in 1792 and was Hoban's assistant for a while. William Thornton is occasionally mentioned for other work than his winning design (and the problems he caused in its execution), especially after the American Institute of Architects purchased his Tayloe House—the Octagon—for its national headquarters early in this century. Thornton had won a competition for a library in Philadelphia even before he was awarded the Capitol.

In 1797 Benjamin Latrobe won his first American commission in competition for the Richmond Penitentiary.[2] William Strickland also won his first major building, the Second Bank of Pennsylvania, in competition in 1818.[3] Since competitions often exist outside the usual network of connections, it is sometimes possible for a talented loner to obtain a commission that would normally go to a well-connected major designer. For example, Philip Hooker, a local architect in Albany, won the design of the Albany City Hall (1829) over Town & Davis, Lafever, and Isaiah Rogers. Haviland won the commission for the Eastern Penitentiary (1823) in Philadelphia seven years after his arrival in the United States and established a considerable reputation in the process. Strickland's pupil T. U. Walter also received his first commission through a competition for a prison design three years before he won the important Girard College competition.[4]

Church boards frequently chose to conduct "invited" competitions for their new buildings, a practice that was often followed for civic buildings as well. In those cases, the architects who were personally known to members of the boards were in an advantageous position. Thus client contact was a factor even in the apparently democratic process of competitions. Renwick's first commission, for Grace Church, is a case in point.

From about 1840 to 1890 competition awards became somewhat less noticeable in the careers of the academically famous, and self-promotional activities—lectures, exhibitions, articles, and books—correspondingly more frequent. Design competitions did not cease, however.[5] Witness Richardson's important invitations from former classmates to submit entries for the churches that launched his career. He was no stranger to competitions—he lost the one for the Library of Congress in 1874. Even at the height of his fame in 1883, Richardson still participated in, and lost, competitions such as that for the Young Men's Association Library in Buffalo, awarded to Cyrus Eidlitz, the son of Leopold.

Nearly all state capitols began with design competitions, and a surprisingly large number of famous nineteenth-century architects entered these and did not win. For example, Richardson entered drawings by McKim in the Connecticut State Capitol competition that was won by Richard Mitchell Upjohn, the son of the more famous Richard Upjohn.[6] However, the juries for these commissions were dominated by politicians (and all too frequently there were later problems of corrupt management). The winners did not have to please the taste of architects, but the public. Now virtually forgotten, Elijah E. Myers, a close friend of Philadelphia's Samuel Sloan and perhaps his employee, mastered the problem of winning these competitions. He won three: Michigan (1871–1888), Texas (1883–1888), and Colorado (1886–1908). But, for the most part, biographical data on the famous in this period mentions few competition-won commissions until Cass Gilbert, at the age of thirty-six, launched his career with the Minnesota State Capitol (1895–1903).

Gilbert was by nature competitive and a super-salesman. He designed the Minnesota building after leaving a partnership with his former classmate from MIT, James Knox Taylor. In 1897 Taylor began a fifteen-year term as supervising architect of the U.S. Treasury Department; soon after he took command, the AIA was able to insist that governmental structures be awarded by competition. However, Taylor was a major judge and in the competition for the New York Custom House in 1899 Gilbert's winning entry was signed. There was a flurry of excitement about collusion, but this was never proved. This building and the Broadway Chambers building (1901–1907), more than the capitol, made Gilbert nationally prominent. Hitchcock and Seale's study of American state capitols indicates that there was also some question of favoritism in the selection of Gilbert for the St. Paul commission.[7]

Toward the end of the nineteenth century competitions for individual buildings again became important for talented young architects. In 1892 the competition for the Cathedral of St. John the Divine was won by Christopher Grant La Farge and George Heins, who had both worked for La Farge's father's associate, Richardson. But the church was plagued with problems, and perhaps it would be better if their reputation rested on St. Matthews (1893) in Washington, D.C. Ralph Adams Cram took over the commission for St. John. Cram had begun his own career by winning a competition for a Boston Courthouse (1886), but much more important was his winning entry for the chapel at West Point, New York, in 1903, a building that was actually designed by his partner Goodhue. Even before he joined Cram, Goodhue had won first prize in a competition for the Cathedral of Dallas (never built) when he was twenty-two. Goodhue's ultimate commission, the Nebraska State Capitol, was also won in competition.

When Wright was twenty-six, he generated his first publicity over a losing entry for the Milwaukee Public Library and Museum. If either the illustration in Mark Peisch's *The Chicago School* or Hitchcock's article in *Perspecta 1* is to be believed,[8] this was a typical Beaux-Arts composition, not as interesting as its prototype, the Fine Arts Building just completed by Atwood for the World's Columbian Exposition. Though the design had no particular distinction, Wright struck a dissenting posture and was able to attract the attention of a reporter for the Chicago paper to air his views. Wright and Robert Spencer both entered a competition sponsored by the Luxfer Prism Company. Spencer won. Wright's entry was disqualified because he was named to the jury. Then Spencer sent Wright's entry to *Inland Architect*, where it was published anonymously in 1898. Thus Wright alone and with the help of his colleague was able to get publicity even for competition entries that had not succeeded.

Paul Cret entered a great many competitions, many more than the seven he won, but nevertheless won his first major project, the Pan American Union (1907), when he was thirty-one. Walter Burley Griffin won an international competition for the design of the city of Canberra in Australia. One of the most visible competitions was that for the Chicago Tribune Building in 1922. The winners, Howells & Hood, with Hood regarded as designer, became celebrities in the popular press. Eliel Saarinen's second-place entry was the one that the professional architectural journals of the day found exciting. On the strength of the reputation this gave him, and the $20,000 second prize, he immigrated with his young son to America. This was certainly not his first competition, however. In Finland he had won two before he graduated from college and was a veteran of many prizes. Eliel and Eero Saarinen entered and won several competitions in the late 1930s, as did their young associates. Eero was twenty-eight when he won the St. Louis Jefferson Memorial prize with his enormous stainless steel arch.

Prize money brought Richard Neutra to America, and then together Neutra and Schindler entered the competition for the League of Nations headquarters. Although they did not win, their entry received recognition. Oskar Stonorov and Alfred Kastner, who was trained in Germany, won second prize in the international competition for the Palace of the Soviets in 1932.[9] While they were in their thirties, Gregory Ain—Neutra's employee—won a Guggenheim grant for a study of low-cost housing in 1940 and Alden B. Dow—from Wright's office—was awarded the Gold Medal for Domestic Design at the 1937 Paris Exposition. Paul Rudolph won a number of prizes: first prize in the Rorimer competition sponsored by the American Institute of Designers in 1940; a foreign travel scholarship; the 1952 AIA award of merit; and in 1954 "Outstanding Young Architect" in an international competition in São Paulo, Brazil. The less-heralded Landis Gores, Johnson's partner from 1945 to 1951 and a former classmate, won first prize in that same competition. Jørn Utzon, with Wright briefly, won the international competition for the Sydney Opera

House. Romaldo Giurgola and Erhman Mitchell placed second in the 1962 Boston City Hall competition. Two years later they won the.AIA National Headquarters competition (their design was not built) and in 1979 the Australian Parliament building race.

The conclusion is clear: competitions are not only a means for receiving work, they are an ingredient in many architects' formula for fame. Even losing entries can be used to garner publicity. Yet competitions—whether won or lost—are not a necessary ingredient of fame.

Scholarships and European Schools

If eventual fame were basically a matter of the right schools and teachers, then every year should have graduated at least ten to fifteen famous architects, but, of course, even though the lists in the school tables were impressive, it was rare that more than one person every other year or so became even moderately famous. Almost without exception, these people went to work for famous architects after their graduation or became employers of others who would be more famous than themselves.

A key issue with regard to schooling and eventual fame might well be: with whom did one spend the long design studio hours? The quality of one's peers may weigh the scales in favor of stronger design. Whereas a highly motivated student, anywhere, will be able to educate himself or herself successfully, the competitive and usually well-prepared students in prestigious schools stimulate each other to greater achievement. Immense differences can be found in architectural education, one design studio being dynamic with friendly competition whereas in another the students are lethargic. More than in most disciplines, architecture students learn as much from each other as from their professors. However, Wright, Mies van der Rohe, Buckminster Fuller, and Bruce Goff—the latter three were professors—had neither college degrees nor technical school degrees. A college degree was not absolutely mandatory for success.

The Ecole des Beaux-Arts was clearly important for Americans from about 1860 to about 1930. The list in table 5 includes employers' names in many cases because the best-known so often worked for a previous graduate, or, if not for an Ecole product, for such men as Frank Furness, Ware & Van Brunt, or Daniel Burnham, who were part of the establishment featured later by architectural historians. While there were a good many Ecole graduates who never became famous, the proportion of famous names in the first decades of the American pilgrimage is impressive. Ten Americans were enrolled in the 1860s, twenty-six in the 1870s, and twenty-five in the 1880s. The most fa-

Table 5
American Students at the Ecole des Beaux-Arts

1820s
Jacques Bussière de Pouilly
1830s
RICHARD MORRIS HUNT (Lefuel, Walter)
HOLLAND C. ANTHONY (Hunt)
Arthur Dexter
Francis Peabody
1860s
HENRY HOBSON RICHARDSON (T. Labrouste)
ROBERT S. PEABODY (Bryant, Ware & Van Brunt)
EDMUND ECKEL (employer of Ellis)
WALTER COOK (Babb)
WILLIAM BIGELOW (Richardson)
CHARLES McKIM (Sturgis, Richardson)
Frederick Allen
Edward Kendall (Bryant)
Frank W. Chandler (Peabody & Stearns, Ware & Van Brunt)
Theophilus Chandler (Peabody & Stearns)
Alfred Greenough
Douglas Smyth
Morris Belknaps
1870s
WILLIAM ROTCH WARE
ARTHUR ROTCH (Viollet-le-Duc)
EDWARD TILDEN
HENRY AVERY (Sturgis, Hunt)
A. D. F. HAMLIN (McKim, Mead & White, Ware & Van Brunt)
CHARLES I. BERG (Cady)
LOUIS H. SULLIVAN (Furness, Jenney, Adler)
Edward Kent
A. Wadsworth Longfellow, Jr. (Richardson)
Edmund Wheelwright (McKim, Mead & White, Peabody & Stearns)
George F. Newton (Peabody & Stearns)
George Healy
Lusk Webster
Lindsley Johnson
Edward Wilson
Elliot Bassett
J. C. Hornblower
Edmund Willson
Henry Philipps
Rudolph Daus
1880s
ERNEST FLAGG
CLARENCE BLACKALL (Peabody & Stearns)
E. MASQUERAY (Hunt)

E. D. LINDSEY (Hunt)
JOHN CARRÈRE (McKim, Mead & White)
THOMAS HASTINGS (McKim, Mead & White)
JOHN STEWARDSON (Furness, Chandler)
L. C. BERG (Cady)
BERNARD MAYBECK (Carrère & Hastings)
RICHARD H. HUNT (Hunt)
William Boring (McKim, Mead & White)
Walter Cope (Chandler)
James Russell
George R. Dean (Shepley, Rutan & Coolidge)
T. H. Randall (Richardson)
S. B. P. Trowbridge (Post)
George Cary
Alfred Gould
Temple Snelling
P. H. Field
Arthur Tuckermann
C. W. Wheelwright
Vernon Wright
C. B. Perkins
C. C. Lane
Dudley Hale
George de Gersdorff
Emile Baumgarten
Edgar Josselyn
J. Marshall Shirk
1890–1894
EDWARD P. CASEY (McKim, Mead & White)
JOHN GALEN HOWARD (Richardson, Shepley, Rutan & Coolidge, McKim, Mead & White)
WHITNEY WARREN (Carrère & Hastings)
HENRY HORNBOSTEL (employed Hood)
JOHN MEAD HOWELLS (Stokes)
PHILIP SAWYER (McKim, Mead & White)
C. F. GOULD
I. N. P. Stokes
James Gamble Rogers (Jenney)
Alfred Granger (Richardson)
J. R. Coolidge
Walter Chambers
Harry Donnell
Arthur J. Dillon
Abner Haydel
Robert Potter
J. H. Freedlander
John Howe
Charles Butler

Evarts Tracy
Edson Perkins
Robert Kohn
Charles Weeks
Nathaniel Wyeth
Richard Walker
Edward Denby
AFTER 1894
T. M. Robertson (Post, Potter)
Welles Bosworth (Shepley, Rutan & Coolidge, Carrère & Hastings)
Benjamin Wistar Morris (Carrère & Hastings)
J. J. B. Benedict (Carrère & Hastings)
Donn Barber (Carrère & Hastings)
Chester Aldrich (Carrère & Hastings)
Pierce Anderson (Burnham)
George Kelham (Trowbridge)
Kenneth Murchison (Hood)
Julia Morgan (Polk, Howard)
John Bakewell (Brown)
Harvey Corbett (Gilbert)
Charles Collens (Peabody & Stearns)
Edward Bennett (Burnham)
Grosvenor Atterbury
J. Stewart Barney
Guy Lowell
John Russell Pope (McKim, Mead & White)
William Delano (Carrère & Hastings)
William Aldrich (Carrère & Hastings)
Alfred Githens (Carrère & Hastings, Gilbert, McKim, Mead & White)
Paul Philippe Cret
Robert Peabody Bellows (Peabody & Stearns)
Raymond Hood (Goodhue, Hornbostel)
William Van Alen (Clinton & Russell)
Clarence Zantzinger
David Adler
Hubert Burnham (Burnham)
John Root (Burnham)
Clarence Stein (Goodhue)
Ely Jacques Kahn
William Lamb (Carrère & Hastings)
Philip Goodwin (Delano & Aldrich)
John Holabird (Holabird & Root)
George Howe (Furness & Evans)
Frederick Godley (Lowell)
Wallace Harrison (McKim, Mead & White, Corbett, Goodhue, Hood)
Max Abramovitz (Harrison)

Note: This list was compiled in part from claims in individual biographies and is not an official roster. Biographies that state only "studied in Paris" were not considered for this list. The names printed in capital letters were found in David de Penanrun, Roux, et Delaire, *Les Architectes élèves de L'Ecole des Beaux-Arts 1819–1894.* Names of students listed in the book but not otherwise mentioned in the present study are in italics. The firms for which the architects worked are in parentheses.

mous of these would be Richardson, McKim, Sullivan, and Maybeck, but Robert Peabody, Frank Chandler, Edmund Eckel, Arthur Rotch, Edmund Wheelwright, John Carrère, Thomas Hastings, John Galen Howard, and Whitney Warren all had successful and important practices and apprentices of note upon their return. By the 1890s the enrollment of Americans exploded to 110. At that point the percentage of graduates with familiar names sharply declined. The later entries on the table indicate only those architects discussed in this study who attended after 1894, but a surprising number of the most important twentieth-century skyscraper designers are on the list.

As important as it was, the Ecole was not the only source for ideas from Europe. Jenney and the impressive but unheralded Fouilhoux had graduated from the Ecole Centrale des Arts et Manufactures in Paris and brought a particularly strong training in experimental engineering back to the United States. Munich and London attracted several American architects. And the generation of German and Swiss architects born in the 1880s and 1890s had a major effect not only on styling but on American educational instruction as well. But I persist in the belief that the famous architects who attended European institutions received more from their apprenticeships than from their professors, unless they also were employed by their professors. Their schooling preconditioned them to be receptive, but their contact with employers or colleagues (at a given moment) created their power. There were and are numerous graduates who, with identical training at the most prestigious of these schools, did not become famous, and there were essentially self-educated architects who did so. Whether they were academically trained or office-trained, their success was assured only if they worked for someone else with some degree of renown.

If not every graduate from the "right schools" became famous, one might conclude that only the best of these were chosen. If one defines the best students as those who win scholarships and fellowships, then a list of major graduate scholarship and fellowship winners should be full of familiar names. Surely these people must have been among the most promising young architects within the establishment. However, though there are thirteen architects on the Rotch Scholarship roster who found a pedestal (or a small niche) in history, there are seventy-four who did not (see table 7). The American Academy Fellows since 1945 have included Robert Venturi and Michael Graves in the list of forty-nine names, but who else?[10] (The most recent winners on the list must be at least thirty-eight years old at the time of writing, but that is still young in terms of fame.) In other

Table 6
Location of Other Foreign Institutions Attended by Architects Discussed in This Study

MUNICH	**STUTTGART**	**BAUHAUS**
Detlef Lienau	Paul Gmelin	Marcel Breuer
Russell Sturgis	Cyrus Eidlitz	Bertrand Goldberg
Walter Cook	Gunar Birkerts	
David Adler		**ROME**
Walter Gropius	**PARIS**	Pietro Belluschi
Eric Mendelsohn	Pierre Charles L'Enfant	Romaldo Giurgola
Helmut Jahn	William Le Baron Jenney	Thomas Vreeland
	Jacques André Fouilhoux	
VIENNA	H. Craig Severance	**ARGENTINA**
Leopold Eidlitz	Eero Saarinen	Eduardo Catalano
R. M. Schindler	Thomas Vreeland	Cesar Pelli
Frederick Kiesler	George Hellmuth	
Paul Wiener	William Turnbull, Jr.	**IRELAND**
Richard Neutra		Kevin Roche
Victor Gruen	**LONDON AND ENGLAND**	
	George Hadfield	**HELSINKI**
BERLIN	Jacob Wray Mould	Eliel Saarinen
Charles Reichardt	Calvert Vaux	
Henry Fernbach	Frank Miles Day	**PRAGUE**
Walter Gropius	Florence Knoll	Antonin Raymond
Eric Mendelsohn	Peter Blake	
	Denise Scott Brown	**WARSAW**
ZURICH	Gerhard Kallmann	Matthew Nowicki
Richard Neutra	William Van Alen	
Werner Moser	Peter Eisenman	**DACCA**
William Lescaze		Fazlur Khan
Albert Frey		
Oskar Stonorov		

words, these represent the cream of the students at the time they applied. Those who worked for an important person before or after residence in Europe or, in a few instances, had a stimulating colleague interrelationship were the ones likely to become famous.

Robert Venturi was awarded a fellowship to the American Academy in 1956. He had been a brilliant student at Princeton and graduated summa cum laude and Phi Beta Kappa in 1947. He stayed for the degree of master of fine arts and won an AIA student award in 1949. Kahn was the architect in residence at the American Academy in Rome, and Jean Labatut of Princeton held that position in 1953, 1959, 1964, and 1968. Venturi worked for Oskar Stonorov, for Kahn, and for Eero Saarinen before and after his trip to Rome, where he was deeply affected by his stay and was the first fully to understand and explain Italian Mannerist architecture. His book *Complexity and Contradiction in Architecture* (1966) was one of the fruits of his visit and not only heralded the new mannerisms currently in vogue, but made Venturi's name nationally known at the beginning of his career. Michael Graves said in an interview with the author that he was profoundly moved by his stay at the Academy, in fact almost gave up architecture for painting at the time he was there in 1960 to 1962.[11] There were forty-seven others so honored who have not yet become famous.

Charles McKim founded the American Academy in Rome in 1894 and throughout his adult life gave a great deal of his income to promising young architects. The McKim scholarship was but one of a number of scholarships given to particularly impressive students or apprentices. However, many of these were not open to every graduate of brilliance. There were various restrictions on the McKim, Rotch, Matchem, Schermerhorn, Wheelwright, Warren, Stewardson, and other fellowships that permitted students to travel and study in Europe, though nearly all were won in competition. They reflect the tradition of the Prix de Rome so fiercely sought by French students at the Ecole des Beaux-Arts, which American students were not permitted to try for. Eero Saarinen and Paul Schweikher were Matchem Fellowship recipients at Yale. Hugh Stubbins, I. M. Pei, and Paul Rudolph were all Wheelwright Scholars at Harvard. The Schermerhorn award was restricted to Columbia University graduates. William S. Brown (Ohio State and Columbia) was given the award after he had begun to work for Skidmore, Owings & Merrill. This was not exceptional. Quite a few graduates had already begun their apprenticeships.

The Rotch Travelling Scholarship was established as a memorial to Benjamin Smith Rotch in 1883 by his son and other members of that wealthy family. Arthur Rotch had attended Harvard, then MIT, and finally the Ecole, serving his apprenticeship to the then elderly Viollet-le-Duc. The award—closely allied to the Boston Society of Architects, which Rotch also believed in—stipulated that the recipients were to be "the architectural youth of Massachusetts" with at least a minimum record of study or professional practice in Massachusetts.[12] Thus many of the winners were graduates of MIT and Harvard since, for years, these were the professional schools in the state. But twelve of the recipients were employees of members of the Boston Architectural Club (now called the Boston Architectural Center), which was sponsored by MIT and Harvard.

The first winner, Clarence H. Blackall, was an apprentice at Peabody & Stearns. (It was noted earlier that Cram, in Rotch's office at that time, complained that he was eliminated on a technicality, but he did not say whether he competed and lost later.) Blackall became the designer of the Copley Plaza Hotel in Boston. But even with the enormous support implied by the award itself, and the backing of the Boston Architectural Club, only a fraction of the names on the roster are well known today. Henry Bacon, an AIA Gold Medal winner for the Lincoln Memorial and McKim's protégé, was elected in 1889. Ralph

Table 7
Rotch Scholarship Winners to 1979

1884	Clarence H. Blackall*	1914	Ralph Johnson Barchelder	1950	Robert L. Bliss
1885	Samuel W. Mead*	1915	Frederick R. Witton	1951	Bruce A. Abrahamson
1886	George F. Newton*	1916	Ralph T. Walker*	1952	Norman M. Klein
1887	Edgar A. Josselyn	1917	James N. Holden	1953	Richard C. Brigham, Jr.
1888	Austin W. Lord	1920	Robert M. Blackall	1954	Paul J. Carroll
1889	Henry Bacon*	1921	Frank S. Carson	1955	Robert T. Coles
1890	William T. Partridge	1922	Wallace K. Harrison*	1956	James E. Stageberg
1891	Robert C. Spencer*	1923	Isidor Richmond	1957	John I. Schlossman
1892	John W. Case	1924	Eugene F. Kennedy	1958	W. Byron Ireland
1893	Walter H. Kilham	1925	Walter F. Bogner	1959	Gardner Ertman
1894	H. Van Buren Magonigle*	1926	Louis Skidmore*	1960	Jack Chun
1895	Will S. Aldrich*	1927	Edward D. Stone*	1961	John O. Cotton
1896	Louis H. Boyington	1928	Ralph E. Winslow	1962	Thomas N. Larson
1897	Henry B. Pennell	1929	Charles S. G. Pope	1963	James T. Flynn
1898	Louis C. Newhall	1930	Barnett S. Gruzen	1964	Harry F. Eagan
1899	Louis W. Pulsifer	1931	Carney Goldberg	1965	John Wilson Cuningham
1900	William L. Welton	1932	Carroll Coletti	1966	Dennis Walsh
1901	William L. Mowll	1933	George S. Lewis	1967	William E. Roesner
1902	James F. Clapp*	1934	Nembhard N. Culin	1968	James Sandell
1903	Edward T. Foulkes	1935	Gordon Bunshaft*	1969	Michael Buckley
1904	Frederick C. Hirons	1936	Leon Hyzen	1970	Gary Lowe
1905	William D. Crowell	1937	John A. Valtz	1971	John Sheehy
1906	Leroy P. Burnham	1938	Malcolm C. Robb	1972	Richard Green
1907	Otto Fælten	1939	William E. Hartmann	1973	Valdis G. Smits
1908	Israel P. Lord	1940	George R. McClellan	1974	Craig D. Roney
1909	Horace G. Simpson	1941	J. Martin Rosse	1975	Nelson Scott Smith
1910	Joseph McGinniss	1946	Melvin Coates Ensign	1976	Philip Dangerfield
1911	Niels H. Larsen	1947	Dale C. Byrd	1977	Patrick M. Sullivan
1912	Charles C. Clark	1948	Victor A. Lundy*	1978	Ernest F. Cirangle
1913	William L. Smith	1949	Edward H. Bullerjahn	1979	Glenn Matsumoto

Source: The Rotch Travelling Scholarship, p. 81.
*Architects discussed in this study.

Walker, a graduate of MIT and an employee of James Ritchie in Boston, won in 1916. He returned to work for McKim, Mead & White and then joined Voorhees and Gmelin (Paul Gmelin trained in Stuttgart) to become a Modernistic skyscraper designer. H. Van Buren Magonigle won in 1894. An employee of Rotch & Tilden, he became quite celebrated in about 1915. Robert Spencer, Wright's colleague, was an MIT graduate who served his apprenticeship period with Wheelwright & Haven and then won the scholarship while with Shepley, Rutan & Coolidge in 1891. Upon his return, he joined the firm's Chicago office before he established his own practice. Wallace Harrison and Edward Durell Stone won the Rotch Scholarship in the 1920s, and Stone then worked for Harrison. Louis Skidmore was on a Rotch Travelling Scholarship at the time he was favored by Raymond Hood and subsequently employed (or, in one case, sponsored) the following Rotch winners: Gordon Bunshaft, William Hartmann, and Victor Lundy.

These eleven men are the only well-known architects of the

ninety winners since 1884 and they always were proud of the honor and mentioned the award in even the briefest descriptions of their careers. From the assembled information on career patterns, it seemed that the scholarship alone might have been proof of their eventual design ability, regardless of whom they worked for. The same assumption seemed likely for the American Academy Fellows. However, these two samples show a very small percentage of winners who became important enough to be included in textbooks. It is obvious that scholarship prizes are not the pivotal event—no matter how beneficial in terms of expanded educational horizons and important professional contacts—but one event in a series that *had* to include a connection during early employment in order for the architect to achieve fame as a strong designer.

Organizations and Institutions

Three organizations come to mind as potentially significant fame makers: the American Institute of Architects, the Museum of Modern Art, and the Congrès Internationaux d'Architecture Moderne. The first of these, the AIA, had surprisingly little success in promoting its younger members, those who showed signs of having dramatic and outstanding talents. The Museum of Modern Art (MOMA) was considerably more influential. But even MOMA was not all powerful. Of the three, CIAM—which influenced the museum—eventually was the most effective.

The AIA

The American Institute of Architects is the dominant professional organization for registered architects in the United States. Its national headquarters are in Washington, D.C., and there are numerous state and local chapters. It is primarily a service organization and about 40 percent of all American architects are members. This body had a very ragged start and did not become strong or effective until late in the nineteenth century.

It was not until 1836 that there were enough practitioners in any one city to organize a meaningful body. One of the aims of the first such venture was to separate themselves as "architects" from the great number of builders, who were apt to list themselves as architects in city directories, but the line between the two professions was certainly not clear at that time; several of the founders of the first attempt at a national organization were once "builders." The elder statesmen—Asher Benjamin, Alexander Parris, Ithiel Town, and

William Strickland—represented Boston, New York, Philadelphia, and Washington. Benjamin's and Parris' two protégés, Isaiah Rogers and Ammi B. Young, were present and, by that time, establishing national reputations. John Haviland of Philadelphia and Minard Lafever, then of New York, were also present, as was Thomas Ustick Walter—Strickland's former employee. Alexander Jackson Davis, Town's partner, completed the group.[13] They named themselves the American Institution of Architects but, perhaps because of problems of distance, this first group did not last as a body for more than one year. But, at the beginning, the organization consisted of a closely knit group of architects. However, Bulfinch, Mills, and Willard were not present, nor were the Rhode Island designers, Russell Warren and John Greene. The Dakins and Gallier had left for the South. Richard Upjohn had not yet proved himself but, like several of the others who were absent, may have been invited. There were thirteen men in all, ten of whom are now considered to have been leaders in the profession at that time.[14]

Two decades passed before a second attempt to form a professional society was undertaken, this time with more success. The current organization was born at a meeting in Richard Upjohn's office in New York in 1857. Again there were thirteen members present, and again many of them were the leaders of their profession.[15] James Renwick was not involved, but Hunt, fresh from Europe, and the recently emigrated Mould, Vaux, and Withers were present. Davis and Walter were the old guard. For several years this remained a New York group, but by 1867 the members had decided to hold a national convention and named themselves the American Institute of Architects. Even when AIA began to expand with chapters in 1869 and 1870—it had twenty-two by 1887—for most of the nineteenth century it remained closely affiliated with leaders who would also be featured as leading designers by later historians. In 1876, when Upjohn finally abdicated as the president, Richard Morris Hunt took over in New York. T. U. Walter was the president in Philadelphia and Peter B. Wight in Chicago. Charles McKim soon became active in the organization and Henry Van Brunt and George B. Post, Hunt's former pupils, would have terms as national presidents. At about the time the original founders died off, the organization began to elect less important architects as its administrators—a circumstance that undoubtedly affected its role in championing daring new designs. The operational structure was completely reorganized, and the focus became more clearly a matter of policies, standards, and rules, involving such matters as unfair competitive acts, licensing, and architectural education.

The AIA was not the only professional organization for architects. For example, the Philadelphia Institute of Architects began in 1861. The Boston Architectural Club was founded in 1867, and there was a large and active Western Association of Architects (which amalgamated with the AIA in 1889). In New York City itself a second professional organization was formed in 1881, the Architectural League, which put on exhibitions with prizes and illustrated catalogs. Chicago's Architectural League also was very active at the end of the nineteenth century. None grew so large or dominant as the AIA, however. By 1930 there were over 3,000 members in the AIA, and the very size of this organization—its democratic inclusiveness—ensured that it would lose all traces of an elite fraternity of the most important designers.

The AIA and similar groups provided a forum for discussions, an audience for lecturers, and often a place to exhibit the work of their members. Cincinnati, Cleveland, Minneapolis, Pittsburgh, and other large cities at the turn of the century had professional organizations that exhibited the work of their members to the public and to critics. However, most of the publicity produced by these exhibitions was ephemeral in terms of the exhibitor's eventual fame (although those involving Wright in Chicago were highly effective since foreign architects, visiting Chicago, were introduced to his work in this way).

Architects and critics did, and still do, keep an eye out for such exhibitions and especially for their accompanying catalogs. It was a local exhibition of the work of Neutra and Schindler that prompted the final rupture between Wright and Schindler in the late 1920s, after Wright saw an item in the accompanying catalog stating that Schindler had been in charge of Wright's office while Wright was in Japan. An exhibition that George Fred Keck, Paul Schweikher, and others initiated and mounted in Chicago was responsible for an invitation to show their designs at the Museum of Modern Art, "and the first commissions came shortly after."[16] Much more recently, the spectacular rise to prominence of the "New York Five"—Eisenman, Graves, Meier, Gwathmey, and Hejduk—came in large measure after the Architectural League of that city sponsored an exhibition and catalog of their drawings. Robert A. M. Stern, a peripheral member of the five, a sort of five-plus, was also active in this organization and mounted an exhibition entitled "40 under 40," which may have done as much for his own reputation as for the other thirty-nine exhibitors. Under the leadership of Stanley Tigerman, a group of Chicago architects has been active in the promotional activities of exhibitions with catalogs.

Local AIA chapters and other professional groups provided showcases and sometimes financial support, although often the architects involved had to put up the necessary money for the catalogs and

Table 8
AIA Gold Medal Winners to 1983

1909	Charles Follen McKim	1958	John Wellborn Root
1911	George Browne Post	1959	Walter Gropius
1923	Henry Bacon	1960	Ludwig Mies van der Rohe
1925	Bertram Grosvenor Goodhue	1962	Eero Saarinen
1927	Howard Van Doren Shaw	1967	Wallace K. Harrison
1929	Milton Bennett Medary	1968	Marcel Breuer
1938	Paul Philippe Cret	1969	William Wilson Wurster
1946	Louis Henry Sullivan	1970	R. Buckminster Fuller
1947	Eliel Saarinen	1971	Louis I. Kahn
1948	Charles Donagh Maginnis	1972	Pietro Belluschi
1949	Frank Lloyd Wright	1977	Richard Neutra
1951	Bernard Ralph Maybeck	1978	Philip Johnson
1953	William Adams Delano	1979	Ieoh Ming Pei
1956	Clarence S. Stein	1981	Josep Lluis Sert
1957	Louis Skidmore	1982	Romaldo Giurgola
1957	Ralph Walker, Centennial Medal of Honor	1983	Nathaniel Owings

exhibitions. But normally the group efforts of these organizations had very little impact. In the 1950s the local chapters of the AIA began to publish illustrated guides to the architecture of their cities (including their own buildings), and the national organization began to present glossy photographs of the award winners of all their various chapters in the *Journal of the American Institute of Architects*—one means whereby a young practitioner could get his or her first national publicity. The most innovative of these may well attract the attention of architectural critics and writers who reach a wider audience. But as a fame maker per se, the American Institute of Architects usually responds after the fact and not as an initiator on the national level. A large proportion of its membership is not interested in avant-garde designers while they are still in their early years and unproved commercially. The bulk of the membership is concerned with that workaday world wherein they must satisfy the typical client.

By the time an architect is awarded the supreme accolade, the Gold Medal of the American Institute of Architects, he has no need for a fame maker (table 8). At that point, he is probably elderly and lucky to be alive. In some cases, the medal is awarded posthumously.

CIAM

The Congrès Internationaux d'Architecture Moderne, CIAM, was effective in its role as fame maker. In large measure this was because one of the founders was the extraordinarily influential architectural historian, Sigfried Giedion—although one can hardly discount the impact of the writings of other founders, especially those of Le Corbusier. Giedion was born in Switzerland and was a student and protégé of Heinrich Wölfflin, an equally famous historian, in

Munich.[17] His thesis, published in 1922, had been concerned with late Baroque architecture and Romantic Classicism. But the year following its publication, Giedion visited the Bauhaus when Gropius and his designers put on a week-long exhibition of their work in Weimar. Giedion was instantly converted by the show and its director.

Even though he was not an architect, Giedion was a major instigator of CIAM. He wrote a selected group of Europeans to invite them to an organizational meeting at a chateau in Switzerland owned by Helène de Mandrot, who wished to become a patroness of modern architecture. Giedion wrote that the first congress was "concerned with the aim of establishing a programme of action to drag architecture from the academic impasse and to place it in its proper social and economic milieu."[18] The dogmatic tenor of Giedion's words reminds us that these were highly unorthodox attitudes at that time. Giedion and his allies hated the Ecole des Beaux-Arts and its products. They did not even have sympathy for the sleeked-down Modernistic styling of Goodhue's capitol at Lincoln, Nebraska. The congresses were organized to bring likeminded designers together to work on set problems like low-cost housing or city planning concepts. They also gave a number of relatively isolated avant-garde designers a network and contact with their counterparts elsewhere. The purpose was to provide "an ideological basis and professional support."[19]

Members were invited to join only with the approval of those already enrolled. For many young designers, their participation in the organization led to a "de facto rupture . . . with their elders, even though it was not deliberate."[20] For example, Peter Behrens, Hendrick Berlage, and Auguste Perret were not present, but their pupils were there. Le Corbusier was a founder; Gropius and Sert joined in 1929, when Alvar Aalto also attended. Karl Moser was the first president. The congresses, which met only ten times in twenty-eight years,[21] attracted several members from America. Richard Neutra spoke at the 1930 meeting in Brussels, and A. Lawrence Kocher, an editor of *Architectural Record*, was an early member. These men were serious, sincere, and had the highest aims. Their intent was not overtly self-promotional but rather the promotion of a totally new architecture that they truly believed would create a better society. But, of course, they kept up with each other's work. No one served as a fame maker for the others so handsomely as did Giedion.

The year of the first CIAM meeting at La Sarraz, Switzerland, Giedion had written *Bauen in Frankreich: Eisen, Eisenbeton*, which celebrated French pioneering in steel and concrete construction. Thus Giedion was as committed to French progressive design as to the Bauhaus and was already championing Le Corbusier and his forerunners—Auguste Perret, Tony Garnier, and the engineer Freyssinet. Equally important, in terms of lasting fame and the style of architectural histories to follow, this was the first major book to pick up the threads of history first isolated by the founder of the German Werkbund, Hermann Muthesius. In 1902 Muthesius had selected the Crystal Palace of 1851 in London, the Eiffel Tower (1887–1889), the Machinery Hall built for the same Paris exposition, and the two libraries by Henri Labrouste as the direct ancestors of modern architecture. He was also the first to speak of "the 'failure' of the Chicago Centennial to maintain the standards set by earlier exhibitions."[22] Muthesius also was closely involved with the English Arts and Crafts Movement. Giedion now added the French designers and Le Corbusier, Gropius, and others to this sequence. This was not entirely a whim since there was, in fact, considerable stylistic influence in the chronology.

Between the first and second CIAM meetings, Giedion wrote the introduction to *Le Corbusier et Pierre Jeanneret, oeuvre complèt* (largely a self-promotional work by the architect—translated into German by Louis Kahn's future partner, Oskar Stonorov). But Giedion did not concentrate solely on French architects; in 1931 he was the author of *Walter Gropius*, which was published in Paris. Soon after Gropius arrived in America, he brought Sigfried Giedion to the United States, and it was Giedion's first lecture series at Harvard in 1939 that evolved into *Space, Time and Architecture*, a celebration of the men and ideas that made up CIAM. For a few years after its publication this book was in combat with the view held by the majority of architects, who neither appreciated nor understood the sort of architecture and city planning that CIAM and Giedion championed. But no single architectural history book has had greater impact.

Space, Time and Architecture was a visually exciting book at a time when students were assigned texts like Kimball and Edgell's *History of Architecture*, a book with uninspiring type and layout, small— really miserable—illustrations, and a text that simply petered out somewhere around 1910. Talbot Hamlin's somewhat more attractive but no more progressive *Architecture through the Ages* had its plates separated from the text. *Space, Time and Architecture*, a title hinting of kinship to Einstein, was designed with wide margins on heavy glossy stock and included full-page and half-page glamorous photographs by photographers who were sympathetic to the ideology of CIAM. Although it was a slow process, the book gradually converted students and then architects and ultimately the public to accept the CIAM positions.

Giedion did not stop there. After World War II he wrote *A Decade of New Architecture*, which reviewed the work of CIAM members between the fifth (1937) and sixth (1947) congresses. Josep Sert became the CIAM president in 1942. He had been the chief writer of *Can Our Cities Survive?*, which was essentially a restatement of the Athens Charter, the CIAM doctrine created at the tenth congress when the members sailed as a group to Athens in 1933. CIAM was never blatantly intended as a self-promotional venture but rather as a much more rigorous and disciplined intellectual association. However, because of publications and especially because there was a major historian/critic in their midst, it became an effective organization for fame making.

The Museum of Modern Art

The Museum of Modern Art was founded one year after CIAM as a gallery to display avant-garde paintings and sculpture.[23] It soon became a key selector and prime publicist for certain architects who would sustain national attention over several decades. The museum's architectural exhibitions were particularly effective in generating fame when they were limited in scope—say, to one, five, or ten architects—and when the exhibition had an accompanying catalog or related book published at about the same time—or, as was the case with Robert Venturi, when it simply published an important book. Publications must be stressed because exhibitions without catalogs were not so influential. It was the abundant high-quality photographs and stylish typography that reinforced the strongest bids for fame.

The people behind the productions of the MOMA form a fraternal group. When the subject was architecture, they pivoted around Philip Johnson, who acted as both paid and unpaid director of architecture for a number of years. One major historian and textbook and survey writer was constantly involved in the background—Henry-Russell Hitchcock. Thus, like CIAM, the museum had its own potent historian/fame maker.

From the time of its founding until 1943, Alfred H. Barr, Jr., was the director. Only twenty when he received his undergraduate degree from Princeton in 1922, he was awarded a master's degree in art history one year later. In 1923, as an instructor at Vassar, he was already excitedly teaching about such painters as Wassily Kandinsky, the Bauhaus professor, and the following summer Barr visited Europe to seek out the newest work. He had in common with the Bauhaus philosophy a conviction that all art is interrelated and included architecture and crafts in his definition of art.

In 1924 Barr won a fellowship to Harvard, where he came in

contact with Professor Paul Sachs, the man who taught museum cura-
torship and was the director of Harvard's Fogg Museum. Sachs, who
was enormously impressed with Barr's brilliance and scope, became
his powerful mentor. Barr was invited to become an instructor at his
alma mater in 1925, but the following year accepted the position of
associate professor (at twenty-four) at Wellesley, which took him back
to the Harvard scene. One year later he spent the winter in Europe
and visited the Bauhaus while Gropius was still its director. He saw
the modern housing project by Oud in Holland and spent time in Rus-
sia with members of the Russian avant-garde. When he returned to
Wellesley, Sachs persuaded the infant Museum of Modern Art to ap-
point Barr its director with a substantial salary and travel expenses.

Henry-Russell Hitchcock, born in 1903, was a New Englander
proud of his descent from the Mayflower passengers. He received his
bachelor's degree from Harvard in 1924, winning a traveling fellowship to study European brickwork.[24] He returned to become a Harvard
tutor in fine arts. In 1926 he discovered Le Corbusier's writings while
on a third summer in Europe, but he said it was the summer of 1927
before he had his first real awareness of modern architecture. He
sought out Gropius, Mies, Oud, and Le Corbusier, and other European
architects who were busily writing manifestos on the new architecture. Even in 1926, when he was asked to write an introduction for a
French edition of Wright's work, he knew of the flurry of reawakened
European interest in Wright's early work.

In 1927 he moved to Vassar, and at that time he had his first article published in America, in *Hound and Horn*, a "little" magazine
published by one of his Harvard students, Lincoln Kirstein. Later
Philip Johnson claimed that it was this article, "The Decline of Architecture," that first interested him in architecture. By 1928 Barr and
Hitchcock had become close friends.

With such enthusiastic young teachers in their midst, it is not
surprising that a group of Harvard students became caught up in the
excitement about the changing worlds of painting, sculpture, and architecture. Calling themselves the Harvard Society of Contemporary
Art, Inc., they mounted exhibitions of avant-garde work from such
artists as Alexander Calder and Buckminster Fuller, who contributed
a model of his 1927 Dymaxion House. Between 1929 and 1931 they put
on twenty-one such shows. Philip Johnson was no more than a peripheral member of that group. He had entered Harvard with the class
of 1927 and majored in classics, not art or architecture. His graduation was delayed because of a three-year illness; by that time, in 1930,
he knew both Barr and Hitchcock well. That summer Johnson visited

Mies van der Rohe at the Bauhaus in Berlin and joined Hitchcock, Barr, and Barr's talented wife in Paris, where they were planning exhibitions for the Museum of Modern Art.

In 1929 several wealthy young people were appointed to serve as a Junior Advisory Committee for the Museum of Modern Art. George Howe (forty-four) was its first chairman—a sophisticated, personable "young" architect who was just beginning the designs of the PSFS building in Philadelphia that would proclaim him a modern architect. In 1930 the chairmanship was given to the really young Nelson Rockefeller, just out of Dartmouth. Rockefeller appointed Philip Johnson to his committee. Soon after this Johnson assumed the role of unpaid director of architectural exhibitions and demonstrated an innate talent for design. He mounted eight shows before he resigned in 1934 to go off on an aberrant pro-Nazi political safari.[25] Although Hitchcock was never actually an employee of the museum, he gave generously of his expertise for many years.

Both men were concerned with the subject of architectural forerunners in America as well as in Europe; they wanted to demonstrate that Modern architecture had evolutionary roots and was not just a momentary derangement, as it was so often viewed at that time. One of their early exhibitions brought back to America the German adulation of the work of Sullivan and Wright before 1910. "Early Modern Architecture: Chicago 1870–1910" was the theme, complete with catalog (1933). In 1936 Johnson returned and mounted an exhibition of the work of H. H. Richardson, against the advice of the board, which felt that he was a Victorian has-been in no way connected with contemporary design. The show corresponded with the publication of Hitchcock's major biography, *The Architecture of H. H. Richardson and His Times*, and "although the show did little for Richardson's popular reputation, the book revived and established his reputation as an American genius once and for all. It also established Hitchcock's reputation as an architectural historian beyond any question of doubt."[26] An early purpose of the Museum of Modern Art had already been abandoned; it was no longer "a kind of halfway house for art on its way from obscurity to immortality."[27] It was trying to help create that immortality.

The Museum of Modern Art of the 1930s is credited with introducing Modern architecture to American professionals, possibly more credit than it really deserves since several writers had already begun this proselytizing before 1932—in particular Hitchcock in his *Modern Architecture: Romanticism and Reintegration*, published in 1929. However, the 1932 exhibition "Modern Architects" was a highly ambitious undertaking, backed financially in part by Nelson Rockefeller's mother and Philip Johnson's father. It was also the first MOMA exhibition to travel to other cities. Though it was indeed seen by a great many people, it was also accompanied by two publications that solidified its impact: *Modern Architects* by Henry-Russell Hitchcock, Jr., Alfred H. Barr, Jr., Philip Johnson, and Lewis Mumford; and *The International Style* by Hitchcock and Johnson. Both were published by W. W. Norton in 1932; although they look alike, with similar heavy glossy paper and the same type style, the first, *Modern Architects*, was the catalog.

For at least a decade Modernist ideals continued to govern most of MOMA's architectural selections, and the resulting style did, eventually, become known as the International Style. The philosophy was close to that voiced by Le Corbusier, Gropius, and CIAM, and, as its proponent, the museum became enormously influential as other architectural critics and writers and architects themselves took up the call. As fame makers for individual architects—notably Gropius, Breuer, Le Corbusier, Neutra, and finally, Mies—MOMA succeeded.

However, it is surprising to find that several of the architects whom it championed in 1932 are virtually unknown today. The Bowman brothers were featured in *Modern Architects*—along with Gropius (Germany), Le Corbusier (France), Oud (Holland), Mies (Germany), and the Americans—Raymond Hood, Howe & Lescaze (Swiss), Richard Neutra (Viennese), and Frank Lloyd Wright.[28] Hitchcock wrote the essay on the Bowmans' designs for inexpensive housing and for modular and prefabricated units. The catalog included photographs of drawings of a small house, two city buildings, an executed interior, and a model for an apartment building (plate 11). The thin-skinned, glossy model looks similar to the advanced work done in the period following World War II, but it is even closer to the glass-skinned buildings by Cesar Pelli in the late 1970s. But this was not the direction in which architecture would move at that time. In fact, Hitchcock forecast the outcome in his essay: "The profession of architecture in America has hardly a place as yet for men like the Bowman Brothers who fit into no established category," even though this was "without question the most distinguished project for a city apartment house thus far worked out."[29] This suggests that there are creative persons whose ideas are out of step with even the most advanced of their contemporaries, to the degree that they do not become famous during their lifetime. They are out of place; they cannot connect to any establishment.[30]

Perhaps the depth of the Depression of the 1930s prevented any of the Bowmans' projects from being built. But most important in their eventual eclipse was the fact that their styling was so unlike that of the other eight candidates for fame. It might be significant that they

Plate 11. Model for the Lux Apartments by the Bowman brothers from the 1932 Museum of Modern Art catalog, Modern Architects. *(Courtesy of The Museum of Modern Art)*

had no stimulating apprentices or protégés and little other publicity. Until they were briefly discussed in Stuart Cohen's *Chicago Architects* and then by the critic Ada Louise Huxtable, the only mention of either architect in the national architectural press seems to have been a brief note on a projected design for the Charleston Civic Center in West Virginia, in 1956 (by Irving Bowman in partnership with Glen C. Hancock and Martens & Sons). However, like other architects with talent, they continued to be known locally.

The other book, Hitchcock and Johnson's *The International Style*, illustrated work by Clauss & Daub, Hood & Fouilhoux, Howe & Lescaze, Kocher & Frey, Neutra, and Oscar Stonorov's design for Tucker & Howells. Architects under the age of forty today probably would recognize only the names of Neutra, Hood, and Howe. Possibly they would also know of Lescaze and Stonorov—the latter because of recent interest in Louis Kahn and his background. Clauss, Daub, Tucker, Fouilhoux, Kocher, and Frey would be unfamiliar names outside of the areas where their buildings stand. In terms of lasting fame, therefore, only a portion of the MOMA's candidates succeeded well enough to be included in written general histories of American architecture. Even Hitchcock did not include all of these architects in his own ambitious survey of 1958, *Architecture: Nineteenth and Twentieth Centuries.*

George Howe was one of the architects featured in both books. The PSFS building was completed in 1932; as explained earlier, a number of important events occurred in Howe's life in 1930, which may have strengthened his confidence as a designer. The designs that he and Lescaze proposed for a possible new building for the museum in 1930 (illustrated in *Unbuilt America* and in Stern's *George Howe*) indicate that he had assuredly joined the Modernist fold at the time he was on the advisory committee. But, in terms of fame, it certainly did not hurt Howe to be a friend of the museum. The PSFS building featured in the 1932 exhibition would remain popular with architectural historians while contemporary structures in New York, including Hood's featured buildings, would largely be ignored until the 1960s and 1970s. Well-educated people who have no particular interest in architecture are quite surprised to discover that young architects (and even architectural historians themselves) frequently have no idea who designed the Empire State Building (Shreve, Lamb & Harmon) and the Chrysler Building (Severance & Van Alen), much less the roster of names of the designers connected to Rockefeller Center (Benjamin Wistar Morris; Reinhard & Hoffmeister; Corbett, Harrison & MacMurray; Hood, Godley & Fouilhoux; Edward Durell Stone; and others). With growing interest in exactly the architecture that was so studiously ignored by the writers involved with (or influenced by) the Museum of Modern Art, this lack may ultimately be redressed.

MOMA did create stars. An exhibition did not have to be popular or well attended; it was the publication that brought fame. The Gropius-Breuer show in 1938 was miserably attended, but it was accompanied by a book. The houses they built in Cambridge at that time were among their best designs and heralded the beginning of revived careers. A book by Johnson on Mies van der Rohe coincided with his 1947 show of the work of Mies. Within a few years Mies was to finish the Farnsworth house in Plano, Illinois, and the Lake Shore Drive Apartments in Chicago, which were to be much more celebrated than any of the work after 1931 that Johnson had displayed and written about. (Again, this is evidence that publicity seems to generate bolder design.)

In 1945 the first of two MOMA catalogs entitled *Built in USA* was published. It featured thirty-three designs and gave full biographies to fifty-eight of the architects listed in table 9. Forty of these names appeared in at least two general histories of American architecture—an

Table 9
American Architects Selected for *Built in USA—Since 1932*

Frank Lloyd Wright
John Funk
Gardner Dailey
Harwell Hamilton Harris
Walter Gropius & Marcel Breuer
John Yeon
Edward D. Stone
George Howe
Philip Johnson
Vincent G. Kling
William Lescaze
Gregory Ain
Carl Koch, Huson Jackson & Robert Kennedy
Harry A. Thomsen, Jr., & William W. Wurster
Vernon DeMars
Burton D. Cairns & Vernon DeMars
Hugh Stubbins, Jr.
Howe, Stonorov & Kahn
Richard J. Neutra
Eliel & Eero Saarinen; Perkins, Wheeler & Will
Franklin & Kump
Skidmore, Owings & Merrill
Lawrence B. Anderson & Herbert L. Beckwith
Burnham Hoyt
Philip L. Goodwin & Edward D. Stone
William A. Ganster & William L. Pereira
Albert Kahn and Associates
Mies van der Rohe; Holabird & Root Associates
George Howe & William Lescaze
Reinhard & Hofmeister; Corbett, Harrison & MacMurray; Hood & Fouilhoux
William Wilson Wurster
Raphael Soriano
John Stokes Redden; John Gerard Raben

impressive percentage, although less than half of the same designers are currently thought important enough to be mentioned in newer surveys. The second *Built in USA*, in 1953, is more contemporary, and about half of the featured American architects continue to generate interest (table 10). The selection committees for these two exhibitions are interesting. The 1945 group included Barr, Hitchcock, Johnson, Howe, Giedion, Talbot Hamlin, Catherine Bauer, and Edgar Kaufmann, Jr.—all connected either to a famous architect or to a network of historians. The other member was Serge Chermayeff, an early member of CIAM, a former partner of Eric Mendelsohn, the employer of Peter Blake (who also worked for Stonorov & Kahn and for MOMA). The 1953 committee included Hamlin, Howe, and Kaufmann from the 1945 committee, Peter Blake, John Johansen (a former employee of Breuer), Thomas Creighton, editor of *Progressive Architecture*, and the deans of the architectural schools at Harvard and the University of Pennsylvania.

Table 10
American Architects Selected for *Built in USA—Postwar Architecture*

Gregory Ain; Joseph Johnson, Alfred Day, Associated
Edward Larrabee Barnes
Donald Barthelme and associates
Pietro Belluschi
Marcel Breuer
Mario Corbett
Gardner A. Dailey and associates; Walter T. Steinberg associated
Charles Eames
Walter Gropius and The Architects' Collaborative
Harwell Hamilton Harris
Harrison & Abramovitz; Mitchell & Ritchey and Altenhof & Brown
Wallace K. Harrison and consultants
John MacL. Johansen
Philip C. Johnson; Landis Gores, associated
Kennedy, Koch, DeMars, Rapson & Brown
Ernest J. Kump
Maynard Lyndon
Eric Mendelsohn
Ludwig Mies van der Rohe; Pace Associates and Holsman, Holsman, Klekamp &
    Taylor; Sargent & Lundy, and Frank J. Kornacker, consultants
Richard J. Neutra
Igor Polevitsky
Saarinen, Saarinen and Associates; Smith, Hinchman & Grylls, Inc.
Schweikher & Elting
Skidmore, Owings & Merrill; Gordon Bunshaft, chief designer
Paolo Soleri and Mark Mills
Raphael Soriano
Twitchell & Rudolph
Frank Lloyd Wright
Lloyd Wright
John Yeon

In addition, such books as Hitchcock's *In the Nature of Materials: The Buildings of Frank Lloyd Wright 1887–1941* were directly tied to the shows. For the individual architect who wanted to be noticed, it was a major event to be included in an exhibition mounted by MOMA. Arthur Drexler, a subsequent director of architecture and design, ran ahead of the profession in several decisions about exhibitions and publications after 1956. The 1964 show "Architecture without Architects" heralded the growth of antihero revisionism. Venturi's *Complexity and Contradiction* (1966) was a landmark publication by MOMA that sanctioned what have now become the prevailing mannerisms in architecture. His exhibition of Ecole des Beaux-Arts drawings reflected the shift of taste occurring in architectural schools but was ideologically opposite to the earlier productions of the museum. Drexler invited the participants who had put together the Architectural League's "Conference of Architects for the Study of the Environment" (CASE), held at MOMA in 1969, to assemble an exhibition and criticism of the work of five architects who represented a New York school in its most dramatic form. Two of the five chosen to be exhibited had been the organizers of the conference—Michael Graves and Peter Eisenman. CASE occurred in 1969; the exhibition and book in 1972; by 1979 all five were heavily featured in the professional press, often with covers or full issues. Thus there is a time lag between stardom by MOMA and acceptance by the professional journals, and even history surveys published in 1979 were cautious about including them. Roth's *A Concise History of American Architecture* (1979) gave one paragraph to three of the five—Eisenman, Graves, and Meier—and omitted the other two. Although it is too early to tell in this instance, only a portion of the architects featured by the museum eventually became important enough to be included in general surveys. In Graves' and Meier's cases they may have profited greatly by the museum's sanction, which probably brought them important clients. MOMA also "helped to spawn the Institute for Architecture and Urban Studies," which has been dominated by Peter Eisenman.[31]

At the beginning, and even today, CIAM and MOMA were victorious fame makers; they introduced many talented architects to the public and the profession. But to make fame permanent, others must forge these names into place in architectural history. Fame, in its strongest definition, is the attribute of the person who makes history, whose actions are important enough to be recorded for the future.

SIXTEEN

The Historians as Fame Makers

It is obvious that historians must take much of the blame, or credit, for our recent view of America's architectural past. In their surveys they often focused on those architects they considered to be leading in the direction that became Modern architecture, thus assuring that some architects would be remembered while others, perhaps equally interesting, would not. These authors came upon the scene quite late; it was 1924 before the first real survey of American architectural history was published: Lewis Mumford's *Sticks and Stones: A Study of American Architecture and Civilization.*[1] In fact, a general interest in America's architectural past did not develop until slightly after the middle of the nineteenth century. The mood at that time was romantic and nostalgic, and architects looked back to simpler days, to the time of the anonymous cottages and farms of the early colonial period. No one ever expected to discover an internationally influential indigenous architecture in America; Europe had always been the fountainhead of major stylistic and theoretical movements in architecture and fashion.

In 1869 Richard Upjohn presented a lecture on American colonial architecture at the third annual meeting of the AIA. The sketching pilgrimage made by Charles McKim, William Bigelow, William Rutherford Mead, and Stanford White to Marblehead, Salem, Newburyport, and Portsmouth in 1877 was inspired by the simple geometrical volumes and weathered shingle skins of traditional New England and Cape Cod cottages. It was a pilgrimage that provided much of the inspiration for a truly American architectural development, the Shingle Style, which was for a brief time the latest fashion and attracted such architects as Richardson, Peabody & Stearns, Bruce Price, and others, including, of course, McKim, Mead & White. Articles began to appear on building of the colonial period, followed soon thereafter by a growing interest in the specific work of Bulfinch, Jefferson, McIntire, Latrobe, and other federal period architects. America began to develop its first architect-heroes.

Mount Vernon and the Alamo were saved for sentimental more than architectural reasons. But in the 1880s early churches and the houses of designers like Gabriel Manigault, William Jay, Samuel McIntire, and others began to be valued for their charm, and various grand early residences became objects of affection independent of the occupants who had lived in them in the past. Robert Peabody did a series of articles of "Georgian Homes of New England" published in the winter of 1877 in *American Architect and Building News.* Arthur Little, another Shingle Style architect and a former employee of Peabody & Stearns, not only wrote the first major book on early American architecture (1878), but took on the project of the restoration of Bulfinch's Harrison-Grey-Otis House in Boston. Within a decade architects like Joseph Lyman Silsbee, who had adopted the Shingle Style, began to produce awkward essays inspired by federal style houses. (Frank Lloyd Wright also gave both styles a try.)

The ever-generous Charles McKim helped the AIA to purchase the Octagon, the Tayloe House, in Washington, D.C. Because of this interest in a building by William Thornton, Thornton found a place in history as more than the self-inflated and testy winner of the 1792 competition for the U.S. Capitol. Although the Octagon was up-to-date at the time it was built in America, reflecting Thornton's interest in new geometrical room shapes, it was essentially only good upper-class vernacular architecture, inspired by illustration in books by men like Robert Adam in England. Nevertheless, Thornton was singled out, and the Index of Fame indicates that only Mumford, Hitchcock (1929), Giedion, Pevsner, and the Italian historian Benevolo did not consider him important enough to mention in their surveys of American architectural history. Thornton was, by definition, a loner in that he did not serve an apprenticeship to or employ an architect of note. It makes sense that self-trained designers like Thornton lived and worked during the federal period, a time when professional training was not essential for success.

When comprehensive surveys of American architectural history were eventually written in the twentieth century, authors tended to be somewhat more inclusive in their chapters on the colonial and federal periods than they would be when dealing with subsequent eras. Before the first group of comprehensive architectural histories were published in the 1920s, quite a lot of research had been amassed on this early period. Not only were there numerous articles, biographies, and books—Fiske Kimball's *Domestic Architecture of the American*

Colonies and the Early Republic (1922), for example—there were a considerable number of regional studies concentrating on the architecture of the colonial and federal eras. The nineteenth-century bias toward a romanticized view of the past meant that, for a generation or more after architects began to look at American architectural history, most people restricted their interest to the earliest periods.

Architectural history, as such, seemed so much more significant in Europe than in the United States that, when Americans began to write history textbooks at the end of the nineteenth century, authors like Russell Sturgis and A. D. F. Hamlin looked across the ocean for most of their material. By 1918 when George Edgell, professor of fine arts at Harvard, and his student Fiske Kimball wrote *A History of Architecture*, they were ready to include a few Americans in their roster.[2] They were quite selective and this survey was a basic text for decades, but even in the 1946 edition there was no building later than 1914 in the material on America.

There has been regional bias. The geographical location of an architect's practice not only was a factor in the likelihood of being isolated from contact with the establishment during training years but also greatly increased the probability that the architect's work, however interesting, would be overlooked by architectural historians. The first of the writers in the 1920s had quite a lot of archival information on the colonial and federal periods (eastern and southeastern states), but for the later periods they had to rely on articles in professional journals and regional periodicals. They also sought European publications for many of their data. Subsequent histories built on other histories, and it was rare that more than a portion of the judgments were based on primary sources or firsthand observation. For example, Lewis Mumford had not yet visited Chicago at the time he wrote *Sticks and Stones* (1924).

If the journalists were concentrated in only a few cities, so were the professors who became the architectural historians. They often taught in the same schools that dominated the profession, in Massachusetts, New York, the Philadelphia area, Virginia, Chicago, and Michigan (with California eventually developing its own fame makers, who had a tendency to lament that the work of that state was often ignored). Chances were slim that many architects outside of these core areas would interest fame makers. It did happen at times; when a building was truly spectacular or entirely original, writers were willing to consider men like Bruce Goff in Oklahoma. Matthew Nowicki's arena in Raleigh, North Carolina, put him in the textbooks,[3] and Pietro Belluschi attracted attention even before he designed the building that heralded the glass-skinned skyscraper style of the next decades—

the Equitable Building (1948) in Portland, Oregon. What happened was that each history tended to build on the ones before it, and the really persuasive fame makers severely limited the number of candidates they presented in their surveys.

Writers were quite frank about this. The introductions to most of the histories tabulated in the Index of Fame cited the previous authors (and, after 1932, the Museum of Modern Art publications). In a comparison of the entries in the Index of Fame, it is obvious that Mumford, Hitchcock (1929), Giedion, and Pevsner were in considerable agreement about whom to discuss and what should be omitted. Juan Pablo Bonta, a leading scholar in the new discipline of text-analysis, had a group of his students count the buildings discussed in Giedion's expansive *Space, Time and Architecture,* which thundered magnificently through four centuries. The students discovered that, in fact, Giedion dealt with only thirty-three works in any detail.[4] Lewis Mumford's approach, several years earlier, was equally selective, though the period he surveyed was shorter. The champion in this regard was Nikolaus Pevsner, whose American chapter in his 1948 edition of the *Outline of European Architecture* named only seventeen men (not added in the index of the book, but included in the text). Both Mumford and Hitchcock widened their horizons in later studies. Mumford's *The Brown Decades: A Study of the Arts in America 1865–1895* (1931) included several people he had not mentioned in his first survey. Hitchcock's interest in the work of Richardson (whose work he knew firsthand from his days at Harvard) led him to discover the designs of others in the same region. By the time his encyclopedic survey of nineteenth- and twentieth-century European and American architecture was published in 1958, his scope had expanded considerably, though, on the whole, the buildings he discussed were in a relatively limited number of geographic regions.

The connection between fame and being recorded in a number of histories or the *Encyclopaedia Britannica* is clear, although time can alter immortality, and heroes may change to antiheroes. Some designers are famous for a decade, and then interest seems to melt. For example, Harrie Lindeberg is relatively high in the Index of Fame. He had been with McKim, Mead & White for six years before he opened his own office in 1906. With commissions for such mansions as the P. D. Armour House in Lake Forest, Illinois, and the John S. Pillsbury House in Minneapolis, and several great houses for the oil and cattle barons in River Oaks in Houston, Lindeberg was very important in the press in the period before the Depression of the 1930s. Following World War II A. Quincy Jones received a lion's share of attention from the professional journals for his work in California; yet he was not included in even the minimum three surveys that covered that period. Paul Rudolph is rarely mentioned today, but in the late 1950s and early 1960s he was, with Saarinen, one of the most famous younger architects in America. We cannot forecast future interest in Michael Graves, who holds that same position at the moment and has yet to enter a later version of the Index of Fame.

As a rule, however, the Index of Fame shows that once a name is on record in several histories, it is quite likely to appear again. As tastes change, the appraisal may change. No matter how comprehensive a historian wishes to be, there will always be bias and, of necessity in order to make the book readable, a considerable degree of selectivity in the material presented in a survey. This narrowing of focus enhances the fame of those selected and diminishes the importance of those not included.

The most inclusive of all the books tabulated in the Index of Fame, Talbot Hamlin's 1926 survey and that by Burchard and Bush-Brown in 1961, were so democratic and comprehensive that little space was left in the text for analysis, and what resulted was essentially captioned photographs in the first and lists of names in the second book. Other historians concentrated on a particular set of designers whom they believed led to the architecture they personally endorsed as Modern. They restricted their content to a narrow set of forerunners and a few "bad examples" for contrast. They discussed American architectural history up through the Greek Revival period and then jumped to Richardson in the 1880s and overland to Chicago and the stripped-down commercial buildings of that city before 1893—exactly the work that had attracted European attention but certainly not the work that American architects of the first decades of the twentieth century would have considered to have been their heritage. Not only loners in remote cities, but the leaders of the profession in New York—men like George B. Post, Eidlitz, Haight, the Potters—and their equivalents in Boston or Philadelphia were ignored unless they had some connection to Richardson, Sullivan, or Root. Recent surveys are broadening their selections.

Lewis Mumford was the first successful American fame maker, not only because he was the first man to write a history that moved from the colonial period right up to the time of writing, but also because he was very selective and thought in terms of architects as either heroes or dolts. Mumford was a journalist, not an architect, and a disciple of the British biologist and sociologist Sir Patrick Geddes, who wrote on city planning concepts. By the time Mumford wrote *Sticks and Stones,* he was twenty-nine and active in the small group (fewer than twenty members) that called itself the Regional Planning Association of America and was guided by Whitaker, the editor of the journal of the AIA. The transition from Mumford's first book, *The Story of Utopias* (1922), to the second, which appeared to be a history of American buildings, was not surprising because the history was, in fact, an impassioned and biased view intended to bring about a radical change in architecture in the future, a new utopia.

He talked about people and rarely described any specific building, except for a few by Richardson (and he relied upon Mariana Van Rensselaer's biography with its full descriptions as his source). He emphasized ideas much more than substance, though for the early period he accepted the importance of Jefferson, L'Enfant, Bulfinch, Latrobe, McIntire, and McComb. However, he gave nearly equal weight to David Hoadley, a Connecticut architect (who was Town & Davis' agent in the 1830s). Although Mumford devoted more than eight pages of high praise to Richardson, he only mentioned Sullivan, not his buildings, and extolled Frank Lloyd Wright in one page. It is obvious that he had been enormously impressed by Van Rensselaer's view of Richardson; he was converted, as it were, in a decade when Richardson was certainly neither influential nor of general interest. But, since he had read Sullivan's autobiography, and was looking for heroes, it is strange that he was so little impressed at that time, especially because of his close association with Whitaker, who had published the autobiography in 1922 and 1923 and who, later, would dedicate his own history text to Sullivan. Mumford had begun to develop a list of devils and spoke negatively about Burnham & Root, the firm he associated with the World's Columbian Exposition held in 1893, a spectacle that he, and Sullivan before him, despised. So, too, Hunt, McKim, Mead & White, Henry Bacon, Carrère & Hastings, and John Russell Pope entered the first survey as architects with few redeeming virtues. (This was one year after Bacon received the Gold Medal from the AIA, and quite a while before Pope reached his peak of success.) Mumford introduced the name of Buffington into history texts, portraying him as the buffoon who had the nerve to patent a skyscraper construction technique (in Minneapolis) at the time the buildings were going up in Chicago. Of course, Mumford's heroes were above reproach.

It seems plain that Mumford was aware of the European view of what should be deemed significant in American architectural history. His survey came out before Henry-Russell Hitchcock went on his exploration of modern architecture in Europe. Hitchcock's *Modern Architecture: Romanticism and Reintegration* (1929) would carry on the torch that Mumford lit. But in the meantime Mumford's survey opened the floodgates. Not only were three other histories published before Hitchcock's, but an enormous number of books celebrating the work of various contemporary architects poured from the presses in the late 1920s.

The first of the histories of American architecture to follow *Sticks and Stones* was diametrically opposite in approach from that taken by Mumford. *The American Spirit in Architecture* (1926), by Talbot Hamlin, made an attempt to include a great many architects in practice and featured more than 148 architects as against Mumford's 27. The book was volume 23 of the heavily illustrated and encyclopedic series *The Pageant of America: A Pictorial History of the United States.* Of 337 pages, 178 were devoted to American architecture of the past and the remaining half tried to present a comprehensive overview of more recent work. For the most part it was done with captioned photographs and, for a student interested in less well known architects, this part is as rich in names as the later history by Burchard and Bush-Brown.

As a practicing New York architect and Columbia University professor, Hamlin had very definite views about his fellow architects. He had only a passing interest in what had been built in Chicago. He preferred McKim, Mead & White, devoting twenty-nine illustrations to their work. He also liked Goodhue (eighteen illustrations) and Richardson (seven illustrations). He was sometimes sharply critical, though the principles governing his praise and criticism are impossible to discern today. Normally his comments were effusive and he lavished words like "original," "lovely," "ordered informality," and "perfect" on so many buildings that seem quite dull that his comments on the four designs by Sullivan and two by Wright included among his 832 illustrations seem especially unsympathetic. He certainly missed as a forecaster of things to come.

When discussing the Auditorium Building, he scorned Sullivan's use of ornament, which he described as "a combination of geometric forms, Byzantine ideas, and some Richardson Romanesque details." The building, which was "famous for its size, careful design, and the novelty of its decorative forms," was original, but he said, "as is so frequently the case, originality unrestrained leads to disregard of structural logic."[5] Hamlin was kinder to the Wainwright Tomb in St. Louis, but it followed fairly closely the Beaux-Arts rules of symmetry and geometric massing that he understood. Of the Transportation Building (1893) the author said, "In scale the whole is masterly, and the ornament has delicate scintillating loveliness, though the reliefs below are strangely banal."[6] In the welter of mediocre work that Hamlin favored, his complimentary words for Sullivan were drowned in his effusions about other buildings that seem perfectly ordinary. He in-

cluded an illustration of Wright's Ward Willits House (1901) and a restricted view of a terrace at Taliesin in Spring Green. This was 1926
and Wright had produced a substantial oeuvre, but he just barely
made it into this very broad survey. Like Mumford, Hamlin would re-
vise his opinions later.[7] But since Mumford's list was highly restricted
and Hamlin's was so universal, mention in the first book was much
more significant than mention in the second.

In 1927 another full survey of United States architectural history was published. Thomas E. Tallmadge was a practicing architect
in Chicago. He had begun his career in 1898 in the office of D. H.
Burnham & Company, five years after the World's Columbian Exposition had shown that Burnham turned from the earlier severity to historical ornamentation. In 1908 Tallmadge wrote an influential article
on the architecture of Chicago that was used as source material by
many others (though not by Mumford).[8] His *Story of Architecture in
America* (1927) was the first to mention Jenney and he discussed
nearly all of the Chicago commercial buildings that henceforth would
be included in surveys. He included Burnham & Root's Tacoma Building, which he called "one of the architectural milestones of the
world."[9] In his view, this was the first skeletal iron building, not Jenney and Mundie's Home Insurance Building, which had two masonry
party-walls.

Like Mumford, Tallmadge bounced very lightly over American
architects before Richardson and contributed no further new heroes
from this early period. He had lavish praise for seven men—Richardson, Root, Sullivan, Wright, McKim, Cram, and Goodhue—and for
two specific buildings—Cass Gilbert's Woolworth Building (1911–
1913) in New York and Eliel Saarinen's Chicago Tribune Building
competition entry of 1922. Thus he joined the ranks of historians who
elevated a few to fame, and, in spite of the mushy quality of his
scholarship and his pleasure in Beaux-Arts buildings of the 1895–1915
period, his book was acknowledged in the bibliographies or introductions of many of the more potent fame makers because he also contributed information on the sequence of heroes that they themselves
wished to establish.

Still another survey was published at that time, again by an
author who was too tolerant to be a successful fame maker. Fiske
Kimball was a major scholar of the federal period and had written his
doctoral dissertation on Jefferson as an architect, as well as many articles on his work and that of his associates. His world history and the
book on colonial and federal architecture in America have been cited.
Kimball knew of some of the avant-garde publications of Europe and
acknowledged Jacques Greber's *L'Architecture aux Etats-Unis: Preuve*

de la force d'expansion du genie français (1920) and Eric Mendelsohn's *Amerika* (1926) in his introduction. Perhaps because he was
aware of this international acclaim, he was the first American writer
to include a great deal of material on Sullivan, and he was also interested in those other Chicago architects who had attracted European
attention: Jenney, Holabird & Roche, Burnham & Root, and Wright. He
found Albert Kahn, Stanford White, and Bertram Goodhue equally
worthy of attention. Like Mumford, he depended on Van Rensselaer
and Montgomery Schuyler and their critical writings for his material
on the latter part of the nineteenth century. Again, like Mumford, he
did not name many people in his chapter on contemporary architecture. Kimball's book, *American Architecture,* was published in 1928.

Kimball was the first to raise Joseph Wells to hero status for his
contribution to McKim, Mead & White's Villard Houses. (Wells was
even mentioned in Kimball and Edgell's 1918 world history.) But, except for several federal period architects he favored, he was content to
restrict himself to those names previously introduced by Mumford,
Hamlin, and Tallmadge. One senses tracking, a heavy reliance on the
previous writers, and an expanded interest in the associates and employers of specific architects. He was in agreement with Mumford,
Tallmadge, Greber, and Mendelsohn as to who were the significant
creators of American architecture and he gave his attention to the employers of those heroes. For example, in the 1920s, Frank Furness'
work was universally considered to represent the extreme of bad
taste. Kimball said, "There were not lacking men who dared to laugh
at 'consistency of style' and to combine elements from many styles
to create a hybrid, personal means of expression. Frank Furness of
Philadelphia—in spite of his Academy—was one of these, whose buildings now thought of more as aberrations, had the power to fire the
youthful enthusiasm of a later apostle of individuality, Louis Sullivan."[10] Kimball lived in Philadelphia at that time and knew Furness'
work firsthand, but one wonders if he would have mentioned him if
Sullivan had not been in his office.

Mumford, Tallmadge, and Kimball were all looking for what
Tallmadge called "the pivotal buildings [which] alone are described
in detail, and only those few greatest personalities who, like mountain
peaks, elevate themselves above the foot hills. These men are the 'heroes' of architects, and their names will live long after earthly works
have perished."[11] These two sentences express the essence of historians' fame making.

In 1929 Henry-Russell Hitchcock fused American architectural
history with European avant-garde work. He acknowledged Kimball,
Edgell,[12] and Tallmadge in his bibliography, and his basic philosophy

was akin to that of Mumford. In order to establish forerunners (in the German art-historical tradition) Hitchcock dipped back into American history to the mid-eighteenth century to begin his book *Modern Architecture: Romanticism and Reintegration.* So, in spite of its title, this book qualified as a survey that could be used to compile the Index of Fame. However, he rushed through the first hundred years of American history, gave Latrobe one paragraph, and called Bulfinch, of all things, "a precursor of the New Tradition."[13] This was also the way he wanted to interpret Richardson. In other words, all good architecture formed a chain of links to the Modern. Hitchcock had not yet fully accepted Sullivan, nor could he appreciate work by Wright that demonstrated no kinship to European Modernism.

He tossed out everything after about 1830 as disastrous Victorian Gothic (except for Richardson's buildings and work in Chicago). Like Kimball, he included Furness because Sullivan had worked for him. "Furness was," he said, "an extraordinary architect of the mid-century whose buildings in their all but complete originality and independence illustrate how generally unfitted the earlier generation in America, devoid of sound tradition, and without any wide knowledge of the architecture of the past, was for stylistic experimentation. All the same, in his youth there was perhaps no better office in America in which Louis Sullivan might gain courage to believe that anything was possible to the architect who willed it."[14] Hitchcock's comment about courage and Kimball's about Furness' "power to fire the youthful enthusiasm" of Sullivan should be noted. Courage and enthusiasm have much to do with the transmission of genius, or, if you prefer, the quality that attracts the historians who are looking for "mountain peaks."

Hitchcock paid but passing attention to the Beaux-Arts period and had only faint praise for McKim, Mead & White's Boston Public Library. He was quite specific about his dislike for what, much later, became labeled Art Deco—which at that time had not yet been successfully sorted out from Modern as a distinct style by other writers. (Hitchcock and the Museum of Modern Art did that cleansing.) Of the work of Cass Gilbert, Carrère & Hastings, James Gamble Rogers, and Arthur Loomis Harmon, Hitchcock said, "One or another sort of 'architectural' coating to the skyscrapers has only succeeded in obscuring the unconscious aesthetic achievements of their engineers. The more studied the shape of the mass, the more skillfully adjusted the ornamentation by the architects, the more surely is the integrity and the scale of the engineering lost."[15] But he introduced the name of Neutra into many subsequent architectural history texts and also established Lescaze and Schindler as worth notice, though to a lesser degree. He had warmer praise for Lawrence Kocher than for Schindler at that time.

Like Mumford, Hitchcock had something to sell. Still in his twenties, he would mature into a scholar rather than a propagandist and would become the dominant architectural historian in America, perfectly willing to look at the architecture he had once despised with a fresh appraisal. But those architects who were totally committed to the belief that their personal version of architecture could cure the ills of society needed historians like Hitchcock, Mumford, Pevsner, and Giedion. While the messianic tone of the surveys helped, it was the descriptions and illustrations of specific buildings and the featuring of selected architects that brought about the eventual acceptance of Modern architecture. The carefully selected photographs used as illustrations were artistically composed by photographers who were part of the same Modern movement and were of immense importance in this process. Hitchcock was an early master of this technique.

A detailed analysis of writings by Pevsner and Giedion has become a new intellectual discipline, and it would be presumptuous to go into much detail here. However, these two architectural historians had such dramatic impact on the architectural profession in terms of the creation of its heroes (and, eventually, even its antiheroes as the mood swung to boredom with Modern) that they must be mentioned. Like Hitchcock, both men were interested in and wrote critically about other periods in architectural history, but their major impact was in their interpretations of nineteenth- and twentieth-century European and American architectural history.

Giedion was the older of the two, but Pevsner was the first to have a book published in English. Nikolaus Pevsner was born in Leipzig in 1902 and therefore was just one year older than Hitchcock. He attended universities in Leipzig, Munich, Berlin, and Frankfurt and in 1924 wrote his dissertation on sixteenth-century Italian architecture. By 1930 he was lecturing on Modern architecture at the University of Göttingen and had become familiar with the work of Gropius and the Bauhaus, then located in Berlin under Mies' direction. In a series of lectures on nineteenth- and twentieth-century architecture, Pevsner developed his argument that Modern architecture would evolve rationally out of the needs of society—that he was not championing an option, but a morally unquestionable inevitability for the betterment of mankind.

Pevsner left for England in 1934, in response to Hitler's rise in Germany, and carried with him the preconditioning of Muthesius' admiration for the mid-nineteenth century Arts and Crafts Movement founder, William Morris, whom he accepted as progenitor of Germany's Peter Behrens. Since Gropius and Le Corbusier (and Mies, though it would be a while before Pevsner would give him equal rank) carried on this lineage in their own work, Pevsner chose to title his 1936 book *Pioneers of the Modern Movement from William Morris to Walter Gropius.* He acknowledged Tallmadge but did not mention Mumford. He was "grateful" to have a copy of the catalog of the MOMA exhibition of 1932 and praised Giedion's "excellent" *Bauen in Frankreich.* In his introductory chapter he discussed Muthesius, confirming the fact that he had fully conflated Muthesius' iron-span and Arts and Crafts "great monuments" with a Morris-to-Gropius genealogy. Like earlier Germans he also reached across the Atlantic to include Richardson as a forerunner. He knew Richardson principally as the architect of the "severe," "simple," "famous and significant Marshall Field Building in Chicago" and of fat and relatively plain shingled New England houses, although they were not illustrated.[16]

Louis Sullivan and John Wellborn Root were described as young leaders by Pevsner, followers of Richardson. Only one photograph was included, and it is no surprise that it was the Monadnock Building (1891–1893) by Burnham & Root—not, in fact, a steel-framed skyscraper but an unusually severe building of load-bearing masonry. By now most architectural students know that the building as first designed by Root was ornamented and that the client demanded that the decoration be stripped off. (Pevsner would have blanched at some of Root's other buildings.)

Wright was also woven into this European sequence, and justifiably so. But with Pevsner this interwoven chain of architects—English Arts and Crafts designers, the European engineers who worked with iron and glass in large-span systems, four or five Americans, and the twentieth-century Germans and Le Corbusier—became a finished system. Others were added in later books and the emphasis shifted, but this was the backbone to be fleshed out. An international set of heroes was firmly established in 1936.

Even Pevsner's title was hero-focused. William Morris happened to be vocally anti-elite and convinced that art would come from the little man, the concerned anonymous, Neo-Medieval craftsman. Walter Gropius always praised the concept of team design. But individual designers were so important to Pevsner that he chose to include portraits of Morris and Gropius as his frontispiece instead of their designs and made the statement that "the opening of the firm of Morris, Marshall & Faulkner marks the beginning of a new era in Western Art."[17] (That would mean that the new era began in 1861.)

The book was revised and rewritten and republished more than once; because Pevsner was so unquestionably a fame maker, one edition seemed necessary in compiling the Index of Fame. But because he limited his featured Americans so severely, a different book by the same author was used—one that had a bit more breadth, albeit still one of the most restricted of all the surveys indexed. Pevsner's first *Outline of European Architecture* to have an American chapter was published in 1948, but it was still very restrictive. In his expanded jubilee edition of 1966 twenty-four American architects represented a two-hundred-year period. The *Outline* has been a popular text for architectural history survey courses.

Mumford, Hamlin, Hitchcock, Pevsner, and Giedion—not one of these authors stopped with one major book. Mumford's *Brown Decades* expanded what he had begun seven years earlier and concentrated on a narrower slice of history. He introduced a few new stars and expanded and intensified his treatment of Olmsted, Sullivan, Wright, Richardson, Root, and Schuyler, and though he did not, in fact, have much to say about them, he apologized for having omitted Maybeck, Greene & Greene, and Gill from *Sticks and Stones*—they had become known to him through issues of Gustav Stickley's the *Craftsman* (and Sheldon Cheney had praised Maybeck in *The New World Architecture* in 1930).

Sigfried Giedion's *Space, Time and Architecture* was first published in 1941. As Bonta points out, Giedion named many architects but, like Pevsner, he devoted full attention to remarkably few of them. As secretary of CIAM from its inception until this book was written, he was aware of the American members of that organization, like Neutra and Harris, as well as its European supporters. Unlike Pevsner, who believed that Modern architecture began with the founding of Morris' firm to produce wallpapers, carpets, fabrics, furniture, and the like, Giedion saw the beginning of Modern architecture in the Baroque period's new spatial concepts. Like Pevsner, he agreed with Muthesius that the nineteenth-century engineers and Chicago buildings were essential links to Modern architecture. But he was fascinated by the American cast-iron fronts that preceded the skyscraper and was the first to discuss James Bogardus, strictly an inventor and businessman, not an architect, who was involved with the possibilities of iron as a structural material. Bogardus was responsible for the Laing Stores (1848), his own factory, and the Harper & Brothers Printing Plant (1854) in New York. After Giedion showed an interest in Bogardus' work, others began looking seriously at this sort of architecture. He also showed considerable interest in the Chicago area, and Wright's resurgence in the 1930s made Giedion look at the work of several of

Wright's contemporaries, like Schmidt, Garden & Martin, George Elmslie, George Maher, Walter B. Griffin, and William Purcell—though he dropped references to nearly all of them in his revised and expanded edition of 1966. His was the first comprehensive survey to discuss Gill fully, and, surprisingly enough, he also dropped Gill in the later book. Other than these changes, Giedion stuck very precisely to the roster of names that Mumford and Hitchcock deemed significant.

Space, Time and Architecture was so handsome, so dramatically illustrated, and written with such persuasion, even religious conviction, that most readers were converted to his point of view. In the next ten years the English-speaking architectural world formed a coherent body of Giedion followers, and his book surely accelerated the demise of the Ecole des Beaux-Arts methods as the Bauhaus became the prototype. The great masters of the Modern era were fully established. Although many subtleties were overlooked, each author either wanted or felt obliged to consider the same group of famous architects. Thus Sullivan might be seen as one thing by Giedion and another by Pevsner, and be seen in still a different light by other authors like Behrendt or Zevi,[18] but Sullivan would always be discussed.

The Museum of Modern Art had also had its impact. Even Talbot Hamlin, who still thoroughly disliked what was called the International Style in the mid-1930s, had come around when he wrote his world history survey, *Architecture through the Ages* (1940). After World War II propagandistic architectural history lost its cutting edge as more and more architects, and clients as well, accepted Modern architecture (that is, until the premise shifted in the 1960s). However, propaganda was still effective—even when it continued to support the heroes of Giedion and others—when the author could fatten his survey with new insights.

James Marston Fitch was a follower of the Muthesian set and an admirer of both Gropius and Mumford. His *American Building: The Forces That Shaped It* (1948) continued to feature many of the same architects. He even interjected the Crystal Palace and Eiffel Tower into this survey of American architecture from 1620 and 1948. But he poked needles at what had become bloated adulation of particular buildings and architects. In considering the great monuments established by previous survey writers, he enlarged his survey into two volumes published in 1966 and 1971, the first a chronological history, the second a study of environmental and behavioral factors. He had fresh insights into unsolved problems of livability, environmental suitability, and energy use. He introduced few new names until he got to his own contemporaries but he had little luck in interesting future writers in their work. Fitch's roster remained surprisingly rigid for earlier architects. He even dropped his own candidates named in the 1948 book when he wrote the larger version eighteen years later; Bruce Goff, Bertrand Goldberg, Carl Koch, Ernest Kump, Hugh Stubbins, Konrad Wachsmann, and Antonin Raymond no longer seemed so important to him. But in one or the other of the versions, he illustrated or mentioned work by quite a number of other contemporaries whom other writers in the future did not consider important: O'Neil Ford, Robert Anshen, Paul Nelson, John Early, Herbert Stevens, and James Workman, to name a few (and strangely enough, most of these men were loners). He also featured work by a number of the younger designers then being promoted by the Museum of Modern Art, such architects as Alden Dow, Gardner Dailey, and Pietro Belluschi. However, as a fame maker, Fitch had only partial success.

Just as there had been a spate of books in the late 1920s, so there were a number of new histories in the late 1940s. No one could resist a last chapter that selected work then current, and no historian can appraise the present with even that modicum of objectivity given to the past. Libraries were beginning to fill with biographies, good regional studies, and surveys limited to one style, one building type, or one topic. The *Journal of the Society of Architectural Historians* had become a high-quality and scholarly source of new information. The challenge for a descriptive and objective survey lay in an overabundance of data to be wrestled into a readable summary; yet, as the Index of Fame shows, the same buildings and the same architects continued to dominate these newer surveys.

In 1947 Wayne Andrews wrote a social history of American architecture that introduced a great deal of information about clients and about the careers of their architects. In the profession the image of the client—in part derived from fame makers, in part from the attitude of the architects themselves—is that of a cipher with no role in design judgments—that is, unless the architect does not like the result. Andrews was the first historian to fully consider this relationship. *Architecture, Ambition and Americans* (1947) also looked afield from the Mumford-Giedion selections and included work by several of the architects mentioned by Hamlin in the 1920s. Among these were a few more loners, all of whom designed lavish mansions for the type of wealthy client that most interested Andrews. He was also the first writer to include several of the early practitioners: Solomon Willard, John Notman, Samuel Sloan, and the four architects who made up a subset of connections in Rhode Island: John Holden Greene, Russell Warren, James Bucklin, and Thomas Tefft.

But there was a change in degree in the postwar historians' magnification of heroes. Hitchcock, former fame maker, turned to a much more inclusive view of history in his scholarly survey *Architecture: Nineteenth and Twentieth Centuries* in 1958. His view of these two centuries was broader and less biased than it had been in 1929. He considered hundreds of designs in some depth and with considerable documentation. He included nearly every architect in America that any previous author had mentioned. It was encyclopedic and profited from the growing numbers of regional studies (one of which was his own, on Rhode Island architecture) and surveys of somewhat limited nature, like Carl Condit's on skyscrapers and Chicago and Hamlin's on Greek Revival buildings. Yet surprisingly few new names were introduced, except those youngest architects mentioned. Designers like Philip Johnson entered the scene.

Because it related to Sullivan, the Jayne Building (1849) in Philadelphia, designed by the loner William L. Johnston, was discussed. He also included three loners who had received a great deal of laudatory critical comment in Vincent Scully's *The Shingle Style*, published in 1955 (with counsel from Hitchcock). William Ralph Emerson had been included in Hamlin's big 1926 volume and also by Andrews, though Andrews dropped him in later revisions. Wilson Eyre had also been mentioned in the 1920s, but Dudley Newton made his first appearance in a textbook. (Thus every one of the loners in the Index of Fame had been mentioned by 1958.)

Hitchcock was tracked almost architect by architect when John Burchard and Albert Bush-Brown wrote their AIA-sponsored survey three years later. *The Architecture of America: A Social and Cultural History* added a lot of names gleaned from the archives of the AIA, but, by trying to report something about hundreds of designers, edged perilously close to simply providing lists of names and buildings. But there was valuable information on periods that were ignored by the supporters of the International Style, such as the extensive material on the Depression years, which is thoroughly documented and discussed. Burchard and Bush-Brown may have been uncomfortable about their selections in the last chapters since they had to exclude many AIA members for want of space, but they effected little change in the list of the famous, for the most part simply reinforcing the fame of those whom other authors had promoted.

Alan Gowans' *Images of American Living: Four Centuries of Architecture and Furniture as Cultural Expression* (1964) is weighted in favor of early American architecture. It is likely that Gowans wanted to continue with the same universal inclusiveness but made the later chapters shorter. But for all of its apparent breadth, the index of the

book reveals that Gowans stuck to the same set of designs and designers that had become accredited by others.

The torch passed from Giedion, Pevsner, and Hitchcock to Vincent Scully as fame maker par excellence. If Hitchcock became the
dean of American architectural history, Scully became the star per-
former.[19] (It is traditionally rumored that divinity students and law
students at Yale are required to take his history of architecture course
in order to enhance their own skills at oral persuasion.) Scully com-
bines his command of poetic English and architectural history with a
dramatic delivery. He also writes fluently. In 1942 Scully's mentor
at Yale, Carroll L. V. Meeks, called for "a new kind of architectural
history, frankly subjective, an analytic system based on scholarship
and brought to life in creative imagination."[20] Giedion and Pevsner
had been successful writers of this type, but they would be almost
outclassed by Meeks' own student. Professors who graduated from
Scully's courses often contribute to what Peter Collins once termed
the "Pseudoscullyfication" of architectural history: in trying to imitate
the master they present an overwrought and distressingly biased view
of history, albeit a dramatic appreciation of architecture as façades
(paintings) and form (sculpture). This kind of impassioned view of architecture is now out of style, yet ornate verbal interpretation con-
tinues to be effective in promotional works on architecture. (Charles
Jencks, currently busy as an architectural historian, gives the impression in public that he aches to be Scully's and Giedion's successor.[21]
His version is the rather brittle and breezy journalistic speech developed by Tom Wolfe, but the effect is similar.)

Vincent Scully's brief and poetic *Modern Architecture* (1961) was
the type of textbook that was handy for introductory courses. Handsomely and profusely illustrated, it gave the student an inexpensive
and very selective overview of architectural history, a skimming off
the top of Giedion and Pevsner. Scully admitted twenty-one American
architects from about 1750 onward into his survey of architecture. He
included the same number of architects but covered a longer period than Pevsner did in *Pioneers of the Modern Movement.* Three of
Scully's twenty-one were principally Shingle Style architects. Edward
Durell Stone and Minoru Yamasaki were presented as bad examples;
their work was too fussy for Scully's taste. But from Jefferson through
Gropius and Neutra and Mies, the others were the standard heroes.
However, this first edition of *Modern Architecture* gave the same num-
ber of pages to the newcomer Louis I. Kahn as it did to the old-timer
Walter Gropius.

By 1974 Scully was quite apologetic about his failure to antici-
pate the great cultural changes that occurred during the 1960s and he

added a third more pages to bring his book up-to-date. He also had become a revisionist. Without altering his first two chapters, he dipped back into European history and picked up formerly uncelebrated heroes. He also added a few architects who, like Kahn, had become his colleagues at Yale—Robert Venturi, Charles W. Moore, and others—and he expanded the material on Kahn himself. Since their work is still relatively recent, it is difficult to know how much effect Scully will have on their subsequent fame. He certainly did not hinder their rise to prominence.

Not content to rewrite *Modern Architecture,* Scully also rewrote *The Shingle Style* as *The Shingle Style Today or the Historian's Revenge* (1974). This book united the work of Scully's young favorites in a reprise of the style that Scully had named: Robert Venturi, Charles W. Moore, Robert A. M. Stern, Jacquelin Robertson, Charles Gwathmey, Romaldo Giurgola, and others—all students or colleagues—became Shingle Style descendants.

In compiling the Index of Fame, Scully's *American Architecture and Urbanism* (1969) was used since it was his broadest survey of the two-hundred-year period in question. It was abundantly illustrated, available in paperback, and thus used often in survey courses. Like the rest of the later surveys indexed, there were major changes in the amount of attention given to the famous architects previously selected by other historians. Among the most recent books tabulated into the Index of Fame were Leland Roth's *A Concise History of American Architecture* (1979) and Marcus Whiffen and Frederick Koeper's *American Architecture 1607 to 1976* (1981). Roth, like Giedion and Benevolo, had a bit more on city planning than do most surveys, and Whiffen and Koeper manage to discuss almost everyone mentioned by other previous survey writers. Spiro Kostof's *A History of Architecture* (1985) and the expanded edition of Sir Banister Fletcher's *A History of Architecture* (1987), edited by John Musgrove, complete the surveys with indexes that make up this definition of fame.

Finally, the four-volume *Macmillan Encyclopedia of Architects* was published late in 1982. It would seem to be the last word in determining degrees of fame. Yet, even with hundreds of Americans included, it also was selective, and there are architects in the Index of Fame who were not given even minimum entries in this encyclopedia. That bias persists is clear when the contributions on Texas architects were limited to fifty- or one-hundred-word maximums, yet the Newsom brothers of California, whose work was much like that of Galveston's Nicholas Clayton, were awarded nine columns and four photographs. Nevertheless, the upper ranks in the Index of Fame were also the architects considered most important by the advisors and editors of the Macmillan venture. The last column in the Index of Fame indicates the approximate number of full columns of text awarded to each architect and the number of illustrations allotted (though these vary considerably in size).

As soon as any design or building is selected for inclusion in a textbook or an architect is allotted a biography of so many words in an encyclopedia—or the opposite occurs and that work or person is deemed of too little significance to take up space—a positive or negative value has been established. What is selected becomes more important than what was not chosen. No writer or editor can erase these subjectively based responses, although some will try harder than others to do so. Truly biased authors, like Sullivan and Wright when they wrote, or the most powerful of the historians, conveyed such quasi-religious conviction about Modern architecture that what they selected as morally justified and unquestionably correct—at least by the time when readers were ready to receive these ideas in the 1940s and 1950s—gave us an established roster of famous designers. Tastes have changed and certain architects in Europe and America are presently emerging as current stars and role models, and even older architects, like Philip Johnson, have turned with the tide. They have their own set of fame makers, historians and writer-architects, like Charles Jencks, Robert Stern, and Kenneth Frampton. Their technique does not differ from that used earlier—only their style.

Apart from the apprenticeship/colleague connection, it seems that the historian connection is the most influential mechanism of fame. But the processes are very different. From a colleague one gains inspiration, confidence, insight—what I call design power—during a pivotal point in the other's career. From historians one gets validation that pivotal buildings exist. A curiosity of the mechanics of fame is that a pivotal building is necessary for subsequent pivotal buildings. Architect C becomes famous in large part for famous building D because he or she once worked with architect A on a famous building B.

SEVENTEEN

Afterword on the Fame-Making System

The enormous popular appeal of the bestseller *The Fountainhead* in the late 1940s signaled the widespread acceptance of the idea that certain architects are heroic geniuses, great masters who can reshape the world and know, instinctively, what is best for mankind. The Museum of Modern Art and writers like Mumford, Giedion, and Pevsner reinforced this idea and the names of Wright, Sullivan, and Gropius became sacred. What was known as Modern architecture was fully accepted by both the profession and the public at large.[1]

By the late 1950s, however, disenchantment had begun to set in. A restlessness was becoming apparent in stylistic experiments by men like Eero Saarinen, Paul Rudolph, and Louis Kahn, who were being labeled by new fame makers as the stars of a second generation. The earlier vision of a new and improved society through a new sort of architecture became clouded, and the great heroes of the recent past began to seem less wonderful even as new fame was being generated.

The most startling warning that attitudes were changing was the publication of Bernard Rudofsky's *Architecture without Architects* (1964) by the fame-making Museum of Modern Art. This was a dramatic catalog of sensuous and glamorized photographs of primitive and indigenous buildings in remote regions of the world where long tradition and common sense had solved problems of harsh climates. Passed from hand to hand in the architectural schools, the catalog created small shock waves. Two years later the museum published Venturi's first powerful outcry against the Modern movement as a style. *Complexity and Contradiction in Architecture* (1966) provided the justification for all sorts of whimsical, overt, and brutal stylistic mannerisms. With almost a complete aboutface, the museum again was setting the pace for the profession. The two books spurred on

growing conflict between a de facto star system and antistar sentiment. The assumptions of Wright, Gropius, Le Corbusier, and others,
including the most effective historians, that certain architects knew
how to supply all of society's physical needs seemed suspect. The
change in attitudes was dramatized when Peter Blake, former fame
maker and author of *The Master Builders: Le Corbusier, Mies van der
Rohe, Frank Lloyd Wright* (1960), revised his position in the vitriolic
Form Follows Fiasco: Why Modern Architecture Hasn't Worked (1977).

In fact, the role of the architect had been under attack for quite
some time before that. By the early 1960s Jane Jacobs (former MOMA
employee) and Kevin Lynch were writing about the design of cities
from the point of view of the everyday activities of the population
rather than the visionary, formalist bent of urban renewal advocates
who were still under the sway of the polemics of the Modern movement. A whole series of books had been published that put the users
of buildings into the forefront rather than architects or their styles: *A
Place to Live: The Crisis of the Cities* (1967); *Personal Space: The Behavioral Basis of Design* (1969); *With Man in Mind: An Interdisciplin-
ary Prospectus for Environmental Design* (1970); *Design with Nature*
(1972); *Architecture versus Housing* (1971); *Architecture in a Crowded
World* (1972); *People and Buildings* (1972); and many others with
similar titles. The mood was by no means restricted to America. In
France Philippe Boudon focused on one specific project and thoroughly studied the contrasts between the architect's intentions and
the users' responses in *Lived-In Architecture: Le Corbusier's Pessac Revisited* (1969 in French, 1972 in English). The 1970s were angry years
and Herbert Muchamp's musing prose-poem *File under Architecture*
(1974) was published with a cover that looked like a grocery sack
pasted on a piece of cardboard.

With this growing, often peevish call for a herofree architecture,
architects found their interests split between a continuing desire to
create memorable or spectacular buildings and a concern with context and content. The phrase "a sense of place" had passed into the
koine, and urban and suburban areas made up of many similar, semi-
anonymous, ordinary old buildings had begun to attract considerable
sentiment. The concepts of neighborhood identity and historic preservation had become popular and valued above the international and
new. The consequence of these attitudes might be a new system for
achieving fame. But, for the moment, the older mechanics prevail.
Again, the Museum of Modern Art heralded a return to architecture
as art, when it presented the work of the architects of the Ecole des
Beaux-Arts—anathema to the hero makers of the previous period—
but indicating another professional mood shift to be followed by the

ultimate of architecture as art with an attempt to promote the "Deconstructivists" as leaders for the profession.

Thus, though interest in unheroic architecture may again surface (and there are signs that currently there is a bit of disenchantment with fancy, star architecture), my first conclusion from the study is that any truly objective view of architectural history and its future will have to include the concept of talented individuals and pivotal buildings as well as vernacular patterns. The word "architect" is sometimes used as a substitute for "creator," and it is impossible to conceive of a state of affairs so stagnant that there would be no fresh approach taken by an innovator. For better or worse, it is in the nature of the profession to seek and celebrate its strongest designers.

A second conclusion is that the publication of work by regionally significant architects from the past might add a star or two to the roster of fame in the future, but the names of famous architects from the past will continue to be noted. The way the Index of Fame will expand is through addition of new talent, for we enjoy heroes and are delighted to discover new ideas and solutions, such as Maya Ying Lin, who won the $20,000 prize for the design of the Viet Nam Memorial in Washington while still a student at Yale. Like it or not, it will be the aesthetic appearance (especially of the exterior) of their contributions that will determine future architects' fame. Though attitudes appear to have changed, there is no obvious change in the system.

We cannot predict fame by a simple formula: if one of the many energetic and self-possessed young men or women of talent who hope to become a major architect works for an architect in practice who is just at the point of receiving a great deal of laudatory attention, the younger designer will not necessarily be rewarded with fame. However, it is the rare person who achieved that goal without following the formula.

In order to be more accurate, the formula would require more factors in the equation representing family background and self-promotional activities. And the formula still could not predict absolutely which young architect would become the exceedingly strong designer who would end up in a history textbook.

The prevalence of the connection in the offices where training takes place in the careers of those designers who become famous cannot be coincidental. At that specific moment when the senior architect grows in boldness, if the younger member is not in awe of the emerging master and can imagine himself or herself in the same role, a generative spark passes from the master to the apprentice. The apprentice gains in self-assurance and produces stronger work. Rarely does a similar spark pass when the younger person joins a firm after it has become undeniably famous. The exceptions come only if there has been a period of considerable decline in attention and a new burst of energy paralleling the first attention-getting strengths.

A corollary to this relationship is that famous architects respond with surer designs *after* they receive their first major attention in the press. It is a gross oversimplification, but nevertheless there is truth in the proposition that fame rests squarely on the achievement of self-confidence and publicity tends to heighten one's self-esteem and courage. The kind of design that attracts attention is simply stronger design than most.

Underlying my concern to document the mechanics that created architecture's role models is the conviction that a very select set of authors have wielded enormous power in selecting who and what would be famous, and in so doing have actually shaped the direction taken by the profession. It is their concentration on designs that have stunning *visual* impact when photographed that I see as warping the reality of architecture. Fame has been built on one aspect—appearance. All too often these were extremely expensive commissions, luxury homes like Falling Water built in the depths of the Depression, or commercial buildings like the Woolworth, Seagram, and AT&T buildings where the clients opened their wallets wide. They are governmental, civic, and campus buildings with comparatively high budgets. The day-to-day commissions of the profession are not these jewels, and many with the potential for genius do not have clients who can provide funding for a building that has the flash to attract the interest of fame makers.

Beauty, novelty, and excitement are the joyous part of design. They can be achieved with gentleness and tenderness and provide great pleasure and contentment to users and yet not be photogenic. That several of the photogenic "great monuments" featured in history surveys are patently unsympathetic to their users' needs and that others have not worn well is forgotten because they remain newly born through the photographs made when they were first finished. Throughout all time the basis for truly fine architecture has been threefold—the Vitruvian triad of form, function, and structure. Beauty gives pleasure, but of equal value are soundness, usefulness, and comfort. The past decade added a fourth requirement—economy, both financial and fuel economy.

If a high school student were to ask how to manipulate a career in order to become a name in future histories, right or wrong, the following steps would seem recommended. First, get an undergraduate degree in liberal arts at a school where your classmates are likely to become future clients. Be a joiner; make friends with those who look to be successful someday. Take courses in journalism and feature article writing. Second, upon graduation from architectural school, fully believe that there is much yet to learn and that your designs and taste will change. Search the most recent professional journals for an architect or firm that is just receiving its first major publicity (or one experiencing a fresh burst of attention after a long dormant period). Third, do not stay very long in that office. Expect that for a while your work may evolve from the style of your employer, but in time will change into something uniquely your own. Fourth, promote yourself actively in exhibitions, articles, and theoretical tracts. Fifth, use whatever family connections you can and/or marry wealth.

I am not happy with these conclusions. I was not comfortable with the implications of my hypothesis at the beginning of this research, but I agree with Charles W. Moore, who began his doctoral dissertation by saying, "Dissatisfaction is the provocation for every thesis—dissatisfaction, and the hope that the discovery, organization, and possibly creation of ideas might do something to improve the situation."[2] So I end with a different series of questions from those with which I began. Is the system that created our boldest architects fixed? Are the mechanics of fame so rigid that they will continue to preselect nearly all of those architects who will be the leaders of the profession? Does it exclude many with potential?

Notes

1. A Network of Connections

1. "Apprenticeship" and "apprenticeship period" are not used in this study in the formal meaning that, in history, signified that a young man or, more often, his parents paid an employer to train him. It happens this was the system used by Wright at Taliesin in the 1930s and some of the earlier apprenticeships discussed in this book were of that sort. However, I use the term more casually for that two- or three-year period of work in a licensed architect's office that is required before one is permitted to take the licensing examination oneself. Because the position of employees is only rarely made clear, the term is sometimes used for any employment before an individual either sets up his or her own practice or becomes a partner in the firm.

2. The Time as Well as the Place

1. Stanford Anderson, "Behrens, Peter," *Macmillan Encyclopedia of Architects* (Adolf Placzek, editor-in-chief), v. 1, p. 165.
2. Jacques Barzun, "The Architect and the Aspirations of His Day," in *Four Great Makers of Modern Architecture: The Verbatim Record of a Symposium Held at the School of Architecture, Columbia University, March–May, 1961,* ed. Adolf Placzek, p. 13.
3. Thomas E. Tallmadge, *The Story of Architecture in America,* p. 6.
4. George Kubler, *The Shape of Time: Remarks on the History of Things,* p. 7.

4. Louis Sullivan

1. Louis H. Sullivan, *The Autobiography of an Idea,* p. 185.
2. Ibid., p. 33.
3. Ibid., p. 190.
4. Robert Twombly, in his biographies of Sullivan and of Wright, seems to be the most reliable source for specific dates. These do differ markedly from those given in the men's autobiographies.
5. Sullivan, *Autobiography,* pp. 193–194.
6. Theodore Turak, "The Ecole Centrale and Modern Architec-

ture: The Education of William Le Baron Jenney," *Journal of the Society of Architectural Historians* 29/1 (1970): 40–47.

7. John Jacobus, "Eiffel, Gustave," *Macmillan Encyclopedia of Architects,* v. 2, p. 18.

8. Sullivan, *Autobiography,* p. 204.

9. Jenney had other employees that, though less famous, have been mentioned in architectural history, among them Adolph Cudell, of whom Sullivan said "with some disillusionment" in his autobiography (p. 202) that he, not Jenney, had designed the Portland Block. Cudell was German-born. In partnership with A. Blumenthal, he later designed the Cyrus McCormick townhouses in Chicago. James Gamble Rogers [A12] later designed the Harkness Quadrangle at Yale (1917). He worked for Jenney late, but at an important time, 1889–1893, when the second Leiter Building was Jenney's commission. His younger brother, John Rogers, worked for both Jenney and Silsbee. Irving K. Pond of Pond & Pond [A3] worked for Jenney and also for Solon S. Beman [A5] before establishing his own firm with his brother Allen. Howard Van Doren Shaw [A4], an AIA Gold Medal winner, worked for Jenney late, 1893–1895. William B. Mundie was hired by Jenney in 1884 and became his partner in 1891.

10. William H. Jordy, *American Buildings and Their Architects: Progressive and Academic Ideals at the Turn of the Twentieth Century,* v. 3, p. 85.

11. Sullivan, *Autobiography,* pp. 193–194.

12. Robert Twombly, in *Louis Sullivan: His Life and Work,* p. 96, believes that Sullivan did not join Adler until late 1881 or early 1882. Paul Sprague, in a review of this book, disagrees and accepts the earlier date (*Journal of the Society of Architectural Historians* 44/4 [1985]: 425).

13. Augustus Bauer was educated at the technical school in Darmstadt and thus had a more formal training than most American architects at that time. We know that he served an apprenticeship in Germany, but, unfortunately, we do not know with whom. He immigrated to America at the age of twenty-three and upon his arrival was hired by Carstensen & Gildemeister [A4], who were working on the New York Crystal Palace, 1852–1853 (won in a competition that included an entry by Joseph Paxton). Carstensen had, earlier, designed the Tivoli Gardens in Copenhagen. Bauer next found employment with John B. Snook, known for the A. T. Stewart Store, 1845–1846. Since it had been completed several years earlier, and it would be more than a decade before Snook's other major designs were done (while John Wellborn Root was an employee), Bauer would have missed any show of power on Snook's part. Bauer moved to Chicago in 1853 and until 1866 was in partnership with Asher Carter, a future employer of Root and Burnham.

14. Rochelle S. Elstein, "The Architecture of Dankmar Adler," *Journal of the Society of Architectural Historians,* 26/4 (1967): 242.

15. Paul E. Sprague, "Sullivan, Louis H.," *Macmillan Encyclopedia of Architects,* v. 4, p. 154.

16. Esther McCoy, "Gill, Irving," *Macmillan Encyclopedia of Architects,* v. 2, p. 204.

5. Frank Lloyd Wright

1. Irving Gill [A13] and George Elmslie [A7] were in the office. George Maher [A7] worked first for Bauer and then for Silsbee. He left in 1888 and eventually won praise as one of the Prairie School architects.

2. Frank Lloyd Wright, *An Autobiography,* p. 70.

3. Ibid., p. 71.

4. Willard Connely, *Louis Sullivan as He Lived: The Shaping of American Architecture,* p. 112.

5. Wright, *An Autobiography,* p. 101.

6. Ibid., p. 71.

7. Ibid., p. 99.

8. Connely, *Louis Sullivan,* p. 128.

9. Frank Lloyd Wright, *A Testament,* pp. 15, 24, 26.

10. Wright, *An Autobiography,* p. 237.

11. James Marston Fitch in conversation with the author, 1979.

12. See Donald Hoffmann, *Frank Lloyd Wright's Falling Water: The House and Its History.*

13. Many of the names of the following early employees were mentioned (pp. 70, 82–85) in H. Allen Brooks, *The Prairie School: Frank Lloyd Wright and His Midwest Contemporaries,* and in a 1908 list from Wright himself, cited by Grant Manson in *Frank Lloyd Wright to 1910,* p. 217. A few of the names were found in casual asides in other books.

William Drummond [B4] had also worked for Silsbee. He was employed by Richard E. Schmidt from 1901 to 1903 and for Burnham from 1903 to 1905. In 1905 he returned to Wright's office and did the working drawings for the Larkin Building in Buffalo, the Cheney House, and the Isabel Roberts House in the Chicago area (Brooks, *Prairie School,* p. 80). Isabel Roberts managed the office but also seems to have done some drafting. Drummond was one of the employees left to finish off Wright's commissions without compensation for their work in 1909. In 1910 he set up his own practice with an ex-Sullivan employee, Louis Grunzel.

Hugh Mackie Gordon Garden [A3] was a freelance architect and worked for a number of Chicago firms as well as for Wright. By 1906 he was a partner in Richard E. Schmidt, Garden & Martin [A6]. Schmidt was in practice before Wright was, but did occasional drawings for Wright. (The most famous employee of Schmidt, Garden & Martin would be George Fred Keck.)

In the early period the following people also worked for Wright: Ernest Albert, a renderer; Cecil Barnes, from Texas, in the office in 1902; Edwin Barglebaugh, about 1908; Emile Brodelle, a renderer in 1914, killed in the Taliesin murders; Cecil Corwin, Wright's good friend and co-worker in Silsbee's office; Robert Harden in 1908; Ana Hicks in the 1890s; Burch Burdett Long; Harry F. Robinson, in the office 1906–1909 and 1910–1916. Francis C. Sullivan was in the office about 1907 and again in 1911, but returned to Canada to practice. Charles E. White was there with Wright, in 1907; George Wills, from Texas, in the early 1900s. Andrew Willatsen, from Denmark, came in 1901 but moved to Spokane, Washington, in 1907. Taylor Wooley was hired in about 1908 and worked on the Wasmuth drawings in Italy with Wright in 1910. William Wells was in the office from 1904 to 1914 before he eventually joined in partnership with the much younger designer Vernon De Mars [C3], in Washington. John S. Van Bergen first worked for Griffin but was in Wright's office in 1909. In 1910 he was employed by Drummond and then set up his own practice in 1912. Arthur McArthur was hired in 1908 and was still with Wright as a "pupil" when Neutra visited in 1924. Neutra remembered McArthur as "unhappily resentful" with no work and no projects (Neutra, *Life and Shape,* p. 185).

William Wesley Peters was the first of the Taliesin Fellows in 1932 and was present during the Falling Water and Johnson Wax designs.

Peters stayed on and eventually inherited the leadership of Taliesin. (He is not given an entry in the Macmillan encyclopedia.) Other Fellows, though by no means all, were Raja Aederi, John Armantites, Bob Beharka, Fritz Benedict, Curtis Besinger, Robert F. Bishop, Cornelia Brierly, Donald Brown, Thomas Casey, David Dodge, Abrom Dombar, Blaine Drake, Herbert Fritz, Robert Goodall, John de Koven Hill, John Howe, Mark Hyman, Henry Klumb, Fred Lanhorst, John Lautner, Yen Liang, Kenneth Lockhart, Eugene Masselink, Bryon (Bob) Mosher, Steven Oyakawa, James Pfefferkorn, Ling Po, Manuel Sandoval, Edgar Tafel, Robert Warn, and Alan Wool.

14. Brooks, *Prairie School,* p. 80.

15. The large firm of Perkins & Will [C5] was founded by Perkins' son, Lawrence Perkins, in partnership with Philip Will (who had worked for Shreve, Lamb & Harmon [B10] on the Empire State Building). Gunnar Birkerts and Robert A. M. Stern were among their most famous employees.

16. Von Holst had studied at the University of Chicago and MIT and then served his apprenticeship in the Chicago office of Shepley, Rutan & Coolidge.

17. Barry Byrne, "Frank Lloyd Wright and His Atelier," *Journal of the Society of Architectural Historians* 39/6 (June 1963): 120.

18. David Gebhard and Harriette Von Breton, *Lloyd Wright, Architect: An Exhibition, November 22 to December 22, 1971,* pp. 18–19.

19. Antonin Raymond, *Antonin Raymond, an Autobiography,* pp. 26–32.

20. Ibid., p. 49.

21. Ibid., p. 53.

22. Hiroshi Yamaguchi, "Raymond, Antonin," *Macmillan Encyclopedia of Architects,* v. 3, p. 535.

23. A turn of interest to Art Nouveau and the related Viennese Secession movement has given Wagner's dressier early work great appeal today, but Giedion and Scully featured the Postal Savings Bank in their influential major surveys as seminal.

24. Thomas S. Hines, *Richard Neutra and the Search for Modern Architecture: A Biography and History,* p. 18.

25. David Gebhard, *Schindler,* p. 18.

26. Ibid.

27. Ibid., p. 49.

28. Ibid., p. 45.

29. Neutra, *Life and Shape,* p. 154.

30. Ibid., p. 160.

31. While he was with Neutra, Harris worked on the city planning scheme "Rush City Reformed" and CIAM projects. Gregory Ain worked for Neutra from 1931 to 1935. Raphael Soriano [C3] entered Neutra's office in 1934. Craig Ellwood worked for him at a later period, as a contractor, before he became an architect. Robert Alexander was Neutra's partner from 1949 to 1958.

32. Edgar Tafel, *Apprentice to Genius,* pp. 20, 23, 25, 10, 42.

33. Alison Sky and Michelle Stone, *Unbuilt America: Forgotten Architecture in the United States from Thomas Jefferson to the Space Age,* p. 321.

34. There were numerous students and apprentices during Wright's later career. Men like Fay Jones and John Lautner are receiving attention from the fame makers by now and gaining national standing. Others of more than regional interest may be "discovered" in the future.

6. Henry Hobson Richardson

1. Henry-Russell Hitchcock, *The Architecture of H. H. Richardson and His Times,* pp. 25–40.

2. Mariana Griswold Van Rensselaer, *Henry Hobson Richardson and His Works* (now in a Dover reprint, 1969), p. 13.

3. Ibid., p. 14.

4. Ibid., p. 15. Also see Richard Chafee, "Richardson's Record at the Ecole des Beaux-Arts," *Journal of the Society of Architectural Historians* 36/3 (1977): 175–188.

5. Littel's employee at the time Richardson was sharing his office was Charles Coolidge Haight, who became a much more important architect than Littel. Haight had graduated from Columbia in 1861 and then served in the Union Army. He began his apprenticeship to Littel about 1865 and opened his own office in 1867. By 1899 he had produced enough important collegiate buildings at Columbia and Yale to be featured by the critic Montgomery Schuyler. Two of Haight's employees were H. Van Buren Magonigle and Alfred Morton Githens, both of whom appear in the employee rosters of other more famous architects.

6. Gambrill studied in the office of George Snell in Boston before he entered Hunt's atelier.

7. Winston Weisman, "Post, George Brown," *Macmillan Encyclopedia of Architects,* v. 3, p. 462. Post's employees are discussed in the chapter on the Renwick line.

8. Dennis Steadman Francis (ed.), *Architects in Practice: New York City 1840–1900.*

9. At fifteen Olmsted served a three-year apprenticeship to a civil engineer. He attended Yale briefly. After a trip to China his interest turned to farming and he developed the farm he owned on Staten Island into a showplace. It was this talent that eventually inspired one of the commissioners of the proposed Central Park to invite Olmsted to enter the competition for its design. Olmsted had met Andrew Jackson Downing in 1845 in Albany and, although it was largely through Downing's influence that Central Park was conceived and Downing had published some of Olmsted's writings, Olmsted never actually worked for Downing. However, he joined with Downing's former partner, Calvert Vaux, for the 1857 competition and their partnership was valuable to Olmsted while he mastered the field of landscape architecture. See Charles C. McLaughlin (editor), *The Papers of Frederick Law Olmsted,* and McLaughlin's entry in the *Macmillan Encyclopedia of Architects,* v. 3, pp. 319–323. Olmsted became the dominating figure in American park and campus planning. John C. Olmsted, his nephew and stepson, and Frederick Law Olmsted, Jr., his son, eventually inherited his very major practice. Olmsted, Jr., has been cited as an employer of Lloyd Wright and was a close friend of Irving Gill. Henry Sargent Codman [A3] was the senior Olmsted's brilliant young assistant on the planning and landscaping for the World's Columbian Exposition of 1893.

10. Wight's training had begun in the office of Thomas R. Jackson, an English immigrant who had worked for Upjohn. The other competitors for the National Academy were named by Sarah Bradford Landau in *Edward T. and William A. Potter: American Victorian Architects,* p. 122.

11. Henry Ogden Avery, the son of a noted art collector, worked for Sturgis in the 1870s, attended the Ecole, and then worked for Hunt from

1879 to 1882. Avery set up practice in 1883 but died seven years later. His name survived in the Avery Memorial Library at Columbia.

   12. Hitchcock, *Richardson,* p. 177.

   13. Ibid., p. 173.

   14. James O'Gorman, *Selected Drawings of H. H. Richardson and His Office,* p. 19, citing W. A. Langston, "The Method of H. H. Richardson," *Architect and Contract Reporter* 63 (March 9, 1900): 156–158.

   15. Hitchcock and O'Gorman were the sources for a number of the following names. I have added others who claimed to have been in Richardson's office in the biographies in Withey and Withey, *Biographical Dictionary of American Architects (Deceased).* But none of these architects, however successful financially and with contemporaries, achieved the fame of McKim and White. William Martin Aiken was in the office about 1879–1885. He became supervising architect of the U.S. Treasury, 1895–1897. Frank E. Alden was there in 1885. He joined in partnership with another ex-employee, Alexander Wadsworth Longfellow, and a McKim, Mead & White graduate, Alfred B. Harlow. Alden & Harlow was established in Pittsburgh after work on Richardson's courthouse there. Longfellow and his brother R. K. Longfellow established a Boston practice in 1895. Robert D. Andrews formed Andrews, Jones, Boscoe & Whitmore in Boston, but had first been in partnership with Herbert Jacques, who had been in Richardson's office in 1882. William Welles Bosworth [A5] also worked for Shepley, Rutan & Coolidge, for Olmsted, and for Carrère & Hastings. He became the architect of the Administration Building at MIT (1912–1915) and the AT&T building in New York (1924). Glenn Brown, an important Washington, D.C., architect, was with Richardson from 1875 to 1880. Herbert C. Burdett died soon after establishing a practice in Buffalo. J. Edwin Carpenter won a Gold Medal for 907 Fifth Avenue in New York (1916). Theodore Minot Clark, Richardson's superintendent on Trinity Church, became an MIT professor and, later, the editor of *American Architect and Building News,* 1889–1909. Frank Irving Cooper became a school designer. Edward F. Ely went to Providence, Rhode Island. Alfred O. Elzner also worked for McKim, Mead & White. He joined in partnership with Edward C. Cabot and Samuel Mead in Boston. David Hale died in 1896 while still in the firm of Shepley, Rutan & Coolidge. Frank A. Kendall joined with his brother Frederick to practice in Boston. W. W. Kent was listed by O'Gorman and is unknown—unless this was a misreading of a handwritten ledger and the name should be William Mitchel Kent, an important designer for McKim, Mead & White and a partner in that firm after 1906. Edward F. Maher also worked for Fehmer & Page in Boston. T. Henry Randall was also employed by McKim, Mead & White before he opened his own office in 1890. Frederick A. Russell was Richardson's supervisor for the Allegheny County Courthouse (1884–1888) and joined Frank Rutan, Charles Rutan's brother, in partnership in Pittsburgh. Richard Gustave Schmid became a Chicago architect. Rudolf Vogel was in the office early. He returned to Germany and was responsible for some of Richardson's publicity there (and Wright's as well) with the publication of *Das amerikanische Haus* in Berlin in 1910 (see Arnold Lewis, *Journal of the Society of Architectural Historians* 31/4 [1972]: 276). The following seem to have left no other record than their names: Francis Bacon, E. R. Benton, G. L. Billings, G. F. Bosworth, John Burrows, E. A. Cameron, C. J. Coffin, C. F. Crosby, Otto Grunner, H. G. King, W. A. Langston, L. B. Riley, James D. Rogers, Jr., and F. M. Wakefield.

   16. Both were MIT graduates. Christopher Grant La Farge [A3], the

son of Richardson's associate, won his most important commission very early, in 1886, in partnership with George Heins. This was the first design for St. John the Divine, although the project was reassigned in 1911 to Cram & Goodhue. Heins & La Farge also did St. Matthews Church in Washington, D.C. (1893). By 1910 La Farge had joined in partnership with Benjamin Wistar Morris [A3], a graduate of the office of Carrère & Hastings.

17. The firm went through the following permutations: Shepley, Rutan & Coolidge (1888–1915); Coolidge, Shepley, Bulfinch & Abbott (1924–1952); Shepley, Bulfinch, Richardson & Abbott (1952–). Coolidge opened a Chicago office in 1892 for which many of Wright's colleagues and employees worked at the onset.

18. Information on the Boston years of the Greene brothers was taken from Randall L. Makinson, *Greene and Greene: Architecture as a Fine Art.*

19. Joan Draper, "The Ecole des Beaux-Arts and the Architecture Profession in the United States: The Case of John Galen Howard," in *The Architect: Chapters in the History of the Profession,* ed. Spiro Kostof.

20. He is known to have been a Peabody & Stearns employee, perhaps in about 1886, to have worked for Henry Ives Cobb [A6] from 1891 to 1895, and for Willis Polk [A14] about 1902.

21. Frost was a Peabody & Stearns graduate and was a partner of the talented Henry Ives Cobb from 1882 to 1889. Frost was the designer of the Potter Palmer House in Chicago. At some point, Granger was in partnership with William D. Hewitt, the younger brother of Furness' partner George Hewitt. He was also a partner, briefly, with Merrill (of SOM), who had worked for Lowe & Bollenbacher in Chicago from 1921 to 1926. When Lowe retired, Merrill and Granger joined in partnership with John C. Bollenbacher.

7. McKim, Mead & White

1. Babb [A4], although only twenty-five to Mead's twenty-two, was a veteran of nine years' experience. Thomas R. Jackson hired Babb as an apprentice in 1859 just as Peter B. Wight left Jackson's employment for his first trip to Chicago. Babb also left soon and practiced as Babb & Foster briefly, but joined Sturgis as senior draftsman in 1868. In 1877 he joined in partnership with Walter Cook—a man trained at Harvard, Munich, and the Ecole. Daniel Willard joined them in 1883. Among the works of Babb, Cook & Willard is the Carnegie Mansion (1899) in New York, which is now the Cooper-Hewitt Museum.

2. Charles C. Baldwin, *Stanford White,* pp. 111–112.

3. Ibid., p. 116.

4. Leland M. Roth, *The Architecture of McKim, Mead & White 1870–1920: A Building List,* p. xxx.

5. Ibid.

6. Baldwin, *White,* pp. 262–263.

7. See note 33 below for some of the more interesting employees not mentioned in the text.

8. Baldwin, *White,* p. 358.

9. Henry-Russell Hitchcock and William Seale, *Temples of Democracy: The State Capitols of the United States of America,* p. 216.

10. Robert Allen Jones, "Cass Gilbert, Midwestern Architect in New York," p. 14.

11. Taylor practiced in Philadelphia in 1892–1895 and then be-

came senior draftsman in the Treasury Department for two years before he assumed command. While supervising architect he was instrumental in bowing to the wishes of the AIA and opened up commissions to its members and others.

12. Donn Barber worked for Gilbert, probably at about this time. He had a Ph.D. before he began studying architecture. He also worked for Carrère & Hastings and for Lord & Hewlett. Barber designed the Chattanooga Station (1907).

13. Carol Willis, "Corbett, Harvey Wiley," *Macmillan Encyclopedia of Architects,* v. 1, p. 451.

14. Alfred Dwight Foster Hamlin, with McKim, Mead & White from 1881 to 1883, was a graduate of Amherst, MIT, and the Ecole. In 1883 he was appointed assistant to William Ware in the new architectural school at Columbia. His son, Talbot Hamlin, was even more successful in the same role. Royal Cortissoz, another McKim, Mead & White employee, became a major early twentieth-century critic and writer.

15. Kenneth H. Cardwell, *Bernard Maybeck: Artisan, Architect, Artist,* p. 16.

16. Arthur Page Brown worked for McKim, Mead & White from 1882 to 1884, when he left for a year in Europe. Brown opened an office in New York in 1885, but four years later set up practice in San Francisco. Brown's son, A. Page Brown, Jr., was just twenty-two when his father died, but took over the practice and designed such San Francisco monuments as the Coit Tower (1933), the City Hall (1912–1915), and the Opera House (1922–1932).

17. Morgan worked briefly for John Galen Howard just as he also was making his bid for fame.

18. Philip D. Will was an employee from 1930 to 1932. In 1935 Will joined in partnership with Lawrence Bradford Perkins. Perkins & Will proved to be very successful (see chapter 5, note 15). Later on Richmond Shreve teamed with William Lescaze for the Williamsburg Houses (1937) in Brooklyn; Minoru Yamasaki, the architect of the World Trade Center in New York, was his employee at that time (see note 30).

19. Delano served as a professor at Columbia from 1903 to 1910 and, later, Aldrich was also on the faculty before he became director of the American Academy in Rome from 1935 to 1940. Philip Goodwin, to be mentioned below as Stone's partner on the Museum of Modern Art, was in the office from 1914 to 1916. Other employees were F. Burrall Hoffman [A4], the architect of Viscaya on Biscayne Bay near Miami; Richard Henry Dana, a residential architect of some merit; Everett V. Meeks, who became dean at Yale; Jacques B. Benedict, with the firm from 1906 to 1909, became a Denver architect; H. Craig Severance was William Van Alen's [B4] partner on the Chrysler Building (1928–1930). Benjamin Wistar Morris [A3], the architect of the once celebrated Cunard Building (1921) in New York and the first major designer of Rockefeller Center, was in the firm early, about 1895. Whitney Warren [A10] was also there at that time and won his first major commission, the Newport Yacht Club, in 1894. In 1896 he formed a partnership with Charles D. Wetmore and they were the architects of the Broadmore Hotel (1915) in Colorado Springs and the more significant Grand Central Station (1903–1913) in New York City (with Charles A. Reed and Allen H. Stem).

20. Catherine Bauer, the city planner and writer, was Wurster's wife. In 1943 he won a fellowship to Harvard that put him in close contact with Gropius and Breuer in their early years in America. In 1945

Wurster formed a partnership with Theodore Bernardi and Donn Emmons. John Funk was his employee from 1936 to 1938.

21. For a number of years before World War II Albert Kahn was one of America's few internationally known architects and was featured in books and exhibitions that propagated "modern" styling. Thus the connection between Bacon and Kahn, who began his climb to fame with factories, was assuredly not one of stylistic influence. Kahn was born in Germany and came to America with his parents in 1880. He was the eldest son of a rabbi and was apprenticed to a Detroit architect, John Scott. At nineteen he was hired by the very capable George DeWitt Mason [A5] and while in his office won a traveling scholarship sponsored by *American Architect.* He returned to become chief designer for Mason & Rice and then joined in partnership with the young Alexander Trowbridge and George W. Nettleson. Shortly thereafter Trowbridge left to attend Cornell and later was in partnership with Frederick Lee Ackerman [A4].

Between 1903 and 1910 Kahn worked on a factory for Packard. Finished a year before Gropius' Faguswerks, his utterly simple solution was noted as an example of the avant-garde aesthetic. Kahn's most interesting employee at that time, Fouilhoux, is discussed below.

22. Albert E. Doyle was an early employee of Bacon. In turn, Doyle's Portland, Oregon, office attracted the Italian-trained Pietro Belluschi in 1925. Doyle also employed another competent architect, John Yeon.

23. Gmelin's name is probably unfamiliar outside of Manhattan. His New York Times Building is now only a memory. In the 1920s Gmelin & Voorhees' Barclay-Vesey Building (1923–1926) was one of the first skyscrapers to show the stylistic influence of Eliel Saarinen's second place entry for the 1922 *Chicago Tribune* competition. Gmelin was born and educated in Germany and came to the United States at the age of twenty-seven as a skilled draftsman. His obituary in the *New York Herald Tribune* (11/21/37) stated that he had been imported by the *Bridge Builder's Magazine* and that McKim was so impressed by his ability that he was hired to do the presentation drawings of the Boston Public Library. Gmelin next worked for Babb, Cook & Willard. In 1921, the year Cyrus Eidlitz died, he joined in partnership with Andrew McKenzie, who had been Eidlitz' partner. With Stephen Voorhees, this firm wove together the Upjohn-Eidlitz and McKim, Mead & White lineage into one firm. Ralph Walker, hired in 1919, became a partner and in the late 1920s was heralded as "the architect of the century." Eventually Walker inherited the practice and the successor firm today is Haines Lundberg Waehler.

24. Among their designs were Seely Hall at Smith College (1900), the Fifth Avenue Hospital in New York, and the Providence Savings Bank in Baltimore.

25. Price would be a loner except for Pope's presence and colleague connections. When Price's father died, he left Princeton and apprenticed himself to Niernsee & Nielson in Baltimore. Claude Bragdon [A7] was an employee of Bruce Price in 1889.

26. Two of his employees from 1922 to 1937, Otto R. Eggers and Daniel Paul Higgins, joined to form one of the largest U.S. firms, now named the Eggers Group.

27. Henry Hofmeister of Reinhard & Hofmeister [B6] was with Warren & Wetmore [A10] for seventeen years. L. Andrew Reinhard, his partner from 1928 on, had worked for the same firm after starting as an

office boy for Benjamin Wistar Morris [A3]. Morris Lapidus had also been a Warren & Wetmore employee and worked for Harrison as well.

28. Frederick Kiesler [B8] had been a student of Adolf Loos in Vienna and a close friend of Franz Kafka. In the United States by 1926, he found mentors in Corbett and the Theater Guild, and later in the Film Guild of MOMA. He claimed to have worked for Corbett from 1936 to 1942. Raymond Abraham was his own protégé.

29. Harrison's employee Robert Allan Jacobs worked for him from 1935 to 1938, but he had earlier been employed by Le Corbusier in 1934. He became the partner of Ely Jacques Kahn [B4] from 1940 to 1966. Except for this connection with Jacobs, Ely Jacques Kahn was a loner.

30. Minoru Yamasaki [C9] started with Githens & Keally at the time that Keally was working on the Oregon State Capitol (1938–1941). Alfred Morton Githens had worked for McKim, Mead & White, Cope & Stewardson, and Gilbert. Francis Keally had also worked for Gilbert from 1919 to 1928. Yamasaki then worked for Shreve well after the event of the Empire State Building but at the time Shreve was partnered by William Lescaze [B13]. In 1943 Yamasaki was employed by Harrison & Abramovitz [B16] and then spent one year with Raymond Loewy. In 1945 he was chief designer for the very large firm of Smith, Hinchman & Grylls in Detroit. Yamasaki formed his own office in 1949 with G. F. Hellmuth and William Leinweber. At that time Gunnar Birkerts was his employee.

31. Carl Koch [C3] entered a competition with Stone in 1938 while MOMA was under construction. He had worked for six months in Sweden for Sven Markelius. He was a prize winner in the 1950s. The 1972 Lewis Wharf Rehabilitation project in Boston was done by his firm.

32. Philip Goodwin [B7] worked for McKim, Mead & White from 1914 to 1916.

33. McKim, Mead & White employees who established regional reputations but are not mentioned in the text include the following. Will S. Aldrich was hired in 1903. He also worked for Peabody & Stearns before setting up practice in 1910. Louis Ayres was with McKim, Mead & White in 1897–1900 and then worked for York & Sawyer, becoming a partner in 1910. Ayers designed the library at Rutgers (1908) and the firm received an AIA medal for its Guaranty Trust Building (1911). Walter Bliss was hired in 1897 and the following year joined in partnership with William B. Faville, employed in 1895. The St. Francis Hotel in San Francisco and the Oakland Hotel are by their firm. William A. Boring had opened a practice in California before he worked for McKim, Mead & White. His future partner, Edward Tilton, was also on their staff. James Bright was associated with Henry Bacon in 1897–1902. Harold Bush-Brown worked for McKim, Mead & White but reported that he never saw Mead and that neither McKim nor White was alive at the time. He moved to the office of Cram & Ferguson in 1915, well after Cram's initial success. Bush-Brown was active in the HABS survey in the 1930s and became dean at Georgia Tech after 1948.

Edward Pearce Casey, the man who took over the design of the Library of Congress, had been a McKim, Mead & White employee. William Chamberlain and William Whidden were in the firm early. Whidden, once an employer of Charles Greene, accompanied McKim to Oregon for the Villard commission of the Hotel Portland (Baldwin, *White*, p. 156). He and Ion Lewis, another graduate, joined in partnership there. Arthur G. Everett became a partner of Edward Clarke Cabot and Samuel Mead for dormitories for Harvard. Lindley M. Franklin moved over to York & Sawyer in 1898 and became a partner in 1910. Goldwin Goldsmith first went into partnership with Von Vleck in New York and then founded the architectural schools at Kansas and Texas. Carl F. Gould also worked for George B. Post. He became a principal in Bebb & Gould in Seattle. Alfred B. Harlow also worked for Cabot & Chandler. Henry Hornbostel did freelance work for McKim, Mead & White. He graduated at the head of his class at Columbia in 1891, worked for Palmer & Wood for two years, then attended the Ecole and worked in France. George Carnegie Palmer employed Hornbostel and William Palmer and then became Hornbostel's partner. Hornbostel taught at Columbia from 1903 to 1907 and founded the school of architecture at Carnegie Tech. His best-known employees were Raymond Hood and Henry Hofmeister.

Harrie T. Lindeberg was with McKim, Mead & White in 1900–1906. He eventually had such prestigious clients as the Armours and Pillsburys. A handsome book has been published on the work of his employee John Staub. George R. Mann was a McKim, Mead & White employee who later worked on the Arkansas State Capitol (1900–1917) with Gilbert. Lorimer Rich worked for Charles A. Platt in 1919–1921 and McKim, Mead & White in 1922–1928 when it was in the hands of the inheriting partners. He was the architect of the Tomb of the Unknown Soldier in Arlington, Virginia. After 1945 his partner was Robbins Conn.

Egerton Swartwout was with McKim, Mead & White in 1891–1901. In 1904 he designed the Connecticut Savings Bank in New Haven and from 1912 to 1916 worked on the Mississippi State Capitol. Edmund Wheelwright was with McKim, Mead & White very early and also worked for Peabody & Stearns. Parkman B. Haven was his partner and they were later joined by Edward A. Hoyt. Charles Maginnis [A5] of Maginnis & Walsh was an employee.

8. *Latrobe and His Descendants*

1. Samuel Wilson, Jr., "Latrobe, Benjamin," *Macmillan Encyclopedia of Architects,* v. 2, p. 611.

2. Edward C. Carter II et al. (eds.), *The Journals of Benjamin Henry Latrobe,* Series I, v. 3, p. 48 n. 24.

3. David Watkin, *The Life and Work of C. R. Cockerell,* p. 3.

4. John Soane, the son of a builder, worked for George Dance the Younger from the age of fifteen to seventeen and then spent seven years in the office of Henry Holland while attending lectures at the Royal Academy. He eventually won a traveling scholarship in 1778. His wife, incidentally, was the niece of George Wyatt.

5. Wilson, "Latrobe," p. 613.

6. Paul F. Norton, *Latrobe, Jefferson and the National Capitol,* p. 8.

7. Ibid., p. 6.

8. Hoban was Irish born and trained. In 1790 he had advertised himself as a teacher of architecture and carpentry in Charleston (Alan Gowans, *Images of American Living,* p. 235). It is possible that Mills had been his pupil.

9. Jefferson himself became involved in the final design of the building (Egon Verheyen, "James Hoban's Plan for the White House," Society of Architectural Historians Annual Meeting abstract, 1979).

10. After 1814 Hoban was in charge of rebuilding a number of gov-

ernment buildings in Washington and he designed the first state and war office in 1818. Etienne Hallet was his assistant on the Capitol.

11. One of Mills' assignments while he worked for Latrobe was a fireproof addition to the existing U.S. Treasury Building.

12. George Hadfield worked for Latrobe for a short while as an assistant at the Capitol (Carter, *Journals,* v. 3, p. 72). Hadfield had an even more impressive background than did Latrobe, with training by James Wyatt and as the first winner of the Royal Academy's Traveling Fellowship to Rome (1790–1794). Both Jefferson and Trumbull were his sponsors. Hadfield designed a number of impressive government buildings in Washington as well as the expansion of the Curtis-Lee mansion (1820) in Arlington, Virginia.

13. Other employees were Frederick Graff, Adam Traquair, a Monsieur Breillat, and Louis de Mun, a draftsman who stayed with him briefly before leaving the United States. In Washington John Lenthall was his chief assistant, but was killed in a building accident. Latrobe had one partner who was a fine designer in his own right, Maximilian Godefroy. Writers have speculated about his background with at least the consensus that he had a good education that included some training in engineering in France. He was in Baltimore for fourteen years.

14. Shryock's father, a prosperous Kentucky builder, had sent him to Philadelphia in 1822 to learn from Strickland. By 1825 the younger Shryock had the commission for the Kentucky State Capitol in Frankfort, soon followed by his appointment as the architect for Morrison College in Lexington (1833).

15. Agnes Addison Gilchrist, *William Strickland, Architect and Engineer,* p. 22.

16. David Gebhard and Deborah Nevins (eds.), *200 Years of American Architectural Drawings,* p. 122.

17. His only employee of note between 1830 and 1851 worked for him in the early period, in 1836. Napoleon LeBrun is not well known today, but in the 1880s he was considered a leader by his professional colleagues. His sons, Michael and Pierre LeBrun, carried the firm's name into the twentieth century.

18. Edward Clark was Walter's chief assistant for the Capitol.

19. Paul R. Baker, *Richard Morris Hunt,* pp. 87–91.

20. Henry Van Brunt, "Richard Morris Hunt 1828–1895," *Journal of the American Institute of Architects* 8/4 (October 1947): 182.

21. Other men who worked for Hunt over the years included not only Edmund Quincy, who became a painter, and E. L. Hyde, who entered the clergy (Baker, *Hunt,* p. 102), but Hollard C. Anthony, Maurice Fornachon, Warrington G. Lawrence, E. D. Lindsey, E. L. Marsh, E. L. Masqueray, Alexander F. Oakey, E. E. Raht, William Schickel, Sidney V. Stratton, and Frank E. Wallis (Baker, *Hunt,* pp. 493–494 n. 6). Joseph Wells, discussed for his part in the design of the Villard Houses, worked for Hunt before he established his own practice in 1881. Henry Ogden Avery worked for Russell Sturgis first and was in Hunt's office from 1879 to 1883. Richard Howland Hunt and Joseph Howland Hunt continued their father's practice.

22. Gilman had studied abroad. He was associated with several Boston and New York architects who were important in the nineteenth century, first with Edward C. Cabot through 1857, then in 1859 as sole designer of the Arlington Street Church in Boston. From 1861 to 1867 he was in partnership with Gridley James Fox Bryant, the winner of the Boston City Hall competition. Kendall, like Hunt, had attended the Ecole.

He had worked for Bryant and was also the son of the assistant supervising architect of the U.S. Treasury Department. Harvey Ellis was an employee in 1875.

23. Post's practice was eventually inherited by his sons, William Stone Post and James Otis Post, in 1905. Post's grandsons succeeded to the helm in time. Among Post's employees, none of whom reached the first ranks of fame, were Edward H. Bennett [A6], who became one of Burnham's major lieutenants, Samuel B. Parkman Trowbridge, and his partner Goodhue Livingston. Trowbridge designed the St. Regis Hotel (1904) and B. Altman's (1906) in New York. Burnham Hoyt also worked for Goodhue, for Peabody & Stearns, and for Pelton, Allen & Collens. He taught at NYU for four years before he moved to Denver in 1936. Arnold Brunner became the architect of Barnard Hall at Barnard College (1917). Stockton B. Colt, Robert H. Robertson, and T. Markoe Robertson of Sloan & Robertson all began in Post's office.

24. Cabot was privately educated and launched his career by winning a competition for the Boston Athenaeum while he was working for George Minot Dexter.

25. C. Ford Peatross, "Smithmeyer and Pelz," *Macmillan Encyclopedia of Architects*, v. 4, p. 91.

26. Two of Lienau's other employees were commercially successful, though, like Lienau, they were not featured by architectural historians. Henry Hardenbergh, the architect of the Dakota Apartments (1884), the Hotel Astoria (1894–1898), and the Plaza Hotel (1907) in New York, was in Lienau's office from 1863 to 1870. Paul Pelz, born in Prussia, was with Lienau from 1859 to 1864 and then worked for Henry Fernbach. In 1873 Pelz won the commission for the Library of Congress in partnership with John L. Smithmeyer. The library was eventually built by others, but Smithmeyer is known for the main building at Georgetown University.

27. Wheaton Holden provided a list with most of the following names in "The Peabody Touch: Peabody & Stearns of Boston, 1870–1917," *Journal of the Society of Architectural Historians* 32/2 (May 1973): 131. There are so many who achieved enough status to have been given entries in Withey and Withey's *Dictionary of American Architects (Deceased)* and the encyclopedic survey of American architectural history written by Burchard and Bush-Brown that I have listed them here in alphabetical order.

Will S. Aldrich, a Rotch scholar, was noted as a McKim, Mead & White employee, but also worked for Peabody & Stearns. Robert Peabody Bellows became the partner of William T. Aldrich from 1911 to 1923 when both began independent careers. Aldrich had worked for Carrère & Hastings in 1910. Bellows became a professor at the University of Illinois in 1920. Clarence H. Blackall, another Rotch scholar, was the designer of the Copley Plaza Hotel in Boston. His partners were James F. Clapp and Charles A. Whittemore. Blackall was an organizer of the Boston Architectural Club and a founder of the Architectural League of New York. Dwight Blaney became an artist. Warren R. Briggs became a Bridgeport, Connecticut, architect. J. Cleveland Cady and his son, John Cady, worked for Peabody & Stearns, but the senior Cady had also worked for Town & Davis before he founded the firm of Cady, Berg & See [A4]. On his first independent commission, the Brooklyn Academy of Design, he was in partnership with Henry M. Congdon. The Metropolitan Opera House (1883), the Museum of Natural History (1900), and fifteen buildings at Yale were designed in partnership with Charles I.

Berg and Milton See. Bradford Lee Gilbert [A4], Cady's employee, designed the first "Chicago construction" in New York in 1888–1889, the Tower Building.

Henry Ives Cobb began with Peabody & Stearns. His partner Charles Sumner Frost was also a Peabody & Stearns graduate. They have been mentioned in previous notes as employers of Purcell and Frost as a partner of Granger. Albert W. Cobb worked for Peabody & Stearns and for William Ralph Emerson [A9] and for Shepley, Rutan & Coolidge [A8] before he joined in partnership with John Calvin Stevens [A7], an ex-McKim, Mead & White employee. Francis W. Chandler joined in partnership with the much older Edward Cabot before he became a professor at MIT, 1888–1925. His most important commission was done with Cabot, the Johns Hopkins Hospital (1889) in Baltimore, though in that case the client, Dr. J. S. Billings, influenced the successful outcome.

Theophilus P. Chandler was almost the only link of Boston or New York firms to the Philadelphia architects, with the exception of Frank Furness, of course. Chandler professionally sired many of the locally prominent Philadelphia designers. Charles C. Collens, architect of the Vassar and Williams libraries, and, with Frederick R. Allen and Henry C. Pelton and Burnham Hoyt, a designer of Riverside Church (1929) in New York, began at Peabody & Stearns. George Porter Fernald became a landscape painter. Edwin J. Lewis, Jr., designed the Second Unitarian Church in Boston. Ion Lewis also worked for McKim, Mead & White before becoming a Portland architect. Arthur Little [A6] designed in the Shingle Style in the Boston area and was one of the first promoters of early American architecture and its restoration. From 1889 to 1925 he was in partnership with Herbert W. C. Browne. Benjamin Wistar Morris [A3] was mentioned as a Carrère & Hastings employee but he also worked for Peabody & Stearns. George F. Newton became the architect of the First Congregational Church in Wellesley. Hubert G. Ripley was Charles Atwood's chief draftsman but returned to Peabody & Stearns until 1928.

The three Schweinfurths, Albert, Julius, and Henry, all worked for Peabody & Stearns. Albert moved to the office of Arthur Page Brown from 1892 to 1894 but had only a few years of independent practice before his death. (A fourth Schweinfurth, Charles Frederick, did not work for Peabody & Stearns. He was the designer of buildings for Western Reserve and Wellesley colleges.) Timothy F. Walsh worked for Peabody & Stearns from 1887 to 1897 and became a partner of the Irishman Charles Maginnis, who had worked for a former Peabody & Stearns employee, Edmund Wheelwright, upon his arrival in America. Maginnis & Walsh [A5] specialized in churches and the firm's most famous employee was Louis Skidmore.

Joseph M. Wells [A3] was one of the earliest employees on the staff of Peabody & Stearns and was discussed in connection with the Villard Houses of McKim, Mead & White. Holden also named the following in his list: W. C. Appleton, William E. Barry, Walter Campbell, Pierce Furker, Edward T. Graham, Davis Gregg, Llewellyn Herford, Joseph D. Leland, Colbert A. McClure, Albert H. Spahr, and J. F. Spalding.

28. Hubert Howe Bancroft, *The Book of the Fair: Volume 1*, p. 65.

9. The Bulfinch and Renwick Lines

1. Harold Kirker and James Kirker, *Bulfinch's Boston 1787–1817*, is a good source for Bulfinch's early career.

2. Ibid., p. 44.

3. Fiske Kimball, "McIntire, Samuel," *Encyclopaedia Britannica* (1968), v. 12, p. 520.

4. Ibid.

5. Kirker, *Bulfinch's,* p. 52.

6. Jack Quinan, "Asher Benjamin's Use of a Neo-Classical Spatial Innovation," Society of Architectural Historians Annual Meeting, abstract, 1978.

7. Elias Carter [A3] was employed by Benjamin later, before he settled in Worcester, Massachusetts, in 1828.

8. Town's employee in New Haven, Henry Austin [A8], stayed in that city and opened a successful practice in 1841. Richard Lathers and Thomas Carmichael were Town's "pupils."

9. Robert Cary Long, Jr. [A4], the son of the designer of the Peale Museum in Baltimore, worked for Thompson while this building was under construction. He returned to practice in Baltimore. James K. Wilson of Ohio was a Thompson employee much later. Wilson also worked for Renwick before he established his own firm and designed the Isaac M. Wise Temple (1866) in Cincinnati. Wilson was at one time in partnership with William Walter, the son of the architect Henry Walter—who until recently was credited with much of the design of the Ohio State Capitol (see Hitchcock and Seale, *Temples of Democracy*).

10. John Trumbull was a patriot, author, painter, architect, and aide to Washington during the Revolutionary War. It is said that when he visited Jefferson in Paris, Jefferson agreed with Trumbull's friend, mentor, and teacher, Benjamin West, that Trumbull should concentrate on painting historical scenes from American history rather than practice architecture, though Trumbull did design a few buildings. It is not certain that Davis actually studied under Trumbull. They were friends.

11. Wayne Andrews, *Architecture, Ambition and Americans,* p. 105.

12. Martin Thompson may have worked for Brady much earlier.

13. Dakin and his brother Charles were trained by their guardian, a carpenter.

14. Charles Dakin died at the age of twenty-eight, James at forty-six, but, with Gallier, they created many of the major buildings of the period in the South. Henry Howard [A4], the designer of several impressive mansions, and, like Gallier, Irish born, was Dakin's employee in 1845.

15. Some books indicate that Downing met Olmsted through Davis and that Olmsted was actually working for Davis. In fact, Olmsted hired Davis in 1845 to draw plans for a house and met Downing on his own that same year. However, Downing was utterly charmed by Olmsted and became his patron and mentor. Downing needed an architect as partner and visited England and talked Calvert Vaux [A11] into joining him. Vaux had been trained by Lewis N. Cottingham. Downing was killed a year later and Vaux joined with another Downing import, Frederick Withers, who had been an employee of the well-known English architect Thomas Henry Wyatt. Their partnership lasted from 1852 to 1854 then resumed from 1863 to 1876, with Olmsted and Vaux as partners from 1858 to 1863 and 1865 to 1886. Still another Englishman tied in with the associates. Jacob Wray Mould [A4] was employed by Vaux in 1867 and designed the Tavern on the Green in Central Park. He was the designer of All Soul's Church (1853–1855) in New York and his English background was said to be as an assistant to Owen Jones in the color schemes for the Crystal

Palace in 1851 (David Van Zanten, *Journal of the Society of Architectural Historians* 28/1, 41).

16. Jacob Landy, *The Architecture of Minard Lafever,* p. 22. Both Josiah Brady and John Trumbull were Lafever's friends. They were probably not his teachers or employers.

17. Ibid., p. 13.

18. Talbot F. Hamlin, *Greek Revival Architecture in America,* p. 146.

19. Lafever's partners were Lewis M. Lindsley in 1829, Gallier in 1832–1834, Charles L. Bell in 1835, and Benjamin F. Smith in 1848–1850 (Jacob Landy, "Lafever, Minard," *Macmillan Encyclopedia of Architects,* v. 2, p. 146).

20. Gebhard and Nevins, *Architectural Drawings,* p. 76.

21. William H. Pierson, Jr., *American Buildings and Their Architects: The Colonial and Neo-Classical Styles,* p. 419.

22. Osmond Overby, "Young, Ammi B.," *Macmillan Encyclopedia of Architects,* v. 1, p. 315.

23. Robert Mills did not have the same title when he supervised the federal buildings from 1836 to 1842.

24. Robert B. MacKay, "Bryant, Gridley James Fox," *Macmillan Encyclopedia of Architects,* v. 1, p. 315.

25. Bryant employed John Hubbard Sturgis [A4] in the 1850s and made him his partner in the early 1870s when the Museum of Fine Arts was Sturgis' best known work. Sturgis also worked in partnership with Charles Brigham, a former employee of Bryant & Gilman. Bryant's partner from 1859 to 1866, Arthur Gilman, Jr., is often given much of the credit for the building. Bryant's employees at that time included Robert Peabody, before he worked for Ware & Van Brunt, Charles A. Cummings, and Willard T. Sears. Cummings & Sears [A5] was formed in 1867 and by 1871 had the commission for the New Old South Church in Boston. Sears, on his own after 1890, was the designer of Fenway Court.

26. However, no employee of note came out of his office in the 1829–1834 period when this was most likely to occur. Years later, in 1857, Rogers, in partnership with his son, Solomon Willard Rogers, hired one of his former pupils, Alfred B. Mullett [A7]. Mullett became a partner for one year and then followed Rogers to Washington as an employee. In 1863 Rogers replaced Ammi B. Young as supervising architect of the U.S. Treasury Department. Mullett was next, from 1866 to 1874. He designed the State, War and Navy Building (now the Executive Office Building, 1871–1889), and other major federal buildings.

27. Upjohn's employees and partners include his son, Richard Mitchell Upjohn, who became his partner in 1851 and assumed control of the office in 1872. Charles Babcock was Upjohn's son-in-law and worked for him from 1853 to 1858. Babcock became a professor at Cornell from 1871 to 1897 and then was ordained to the ministry. Edward Tuckerman Potter [A6], son and brother of Episcopal bishops, also worked for Upjohn before he set up his own office in 1855 with John W. Roberts. After practice alone he asked Alfred H. Thorp, Jr., to join him in partnership in 1873. His brother William Appleton Potter began in this office in 1869 after two years of travel in Europe. William was in partnership, at different times, with James Brown Lord and Robert Robertson. He served a term as supervising architect of the U.S. Treasury Department. Both brothers were successful designers of collegiate and religious buildings. Edward Potter was the architect of the Mark Twain House (1873–1874) in Hartford, Connecticut. Charles W. Clinton was employed by Upjohn from about 1853 to 1857 and was also Upjohn's

son-in-law. Clinton also worked for his great-uncle, James Renwick, Jr. Anthony B. McDonald, Jr., joined him in partnership in 1864 and Clinton sometimes worked in association with Edward Potter. William Hamilton Russell, another Renwick great-nephew, also worked for Upjohn and was Renwick's partner from 1878 to 1894 when he and Clinton joined in practice. Their employees included DeWitt Clinton, Charles K. Clinton, and the future architect of the Chrysler Building, William Van Alen [B4]. Thomas R. Jackson, Wight's employer, Henry W. Cleveland, and Alphaeus C. Moore were other Upjohn employees.

Upjohn's grandson and great-grandson eventually inherited the practice and Hobart B. Upjohn and Evarard M. Upjohn became members of a true dynasty. Solon Spencer Beman [A5] was with the Upjohns for eight years, 1868–1876, long after the father had made his first step to fame but at the time when the son was working on the Connecticut State Capitol. In 1879, through the auspices of a colleague, Beman was commissioned to design the company town of Pullman, Illinois. His work could be extremely fine but was uneven. Beman's practice flourished and he was the designer of such major buildings as the Studebaker Building (1895) and Grand Central Station (1889–1890) in Chicago.

28. Selma Rattner, "Renwick, James," *Macmillan Encyclopedia of Architects,* v. 3, p. 541.

29. Before 1859 Renwick worked without partners, but his practice grew too large to handle alone. Joseph Sands, Richard T. Auchmuty, William Hamilton Russell, and James L. Aspinwall were partners at various times.

30. Roth came to the United States as a Czechoslovakian orphan at the age of thirteen and had worked in offices in Bloomington and Kansas City.

31. Burnham's sons, Daniel and Hubert, were in the firm by 1912. Pierce Anderson joined the office in 1900. Edward Probst was hired in 1893. Howard J. White joined Burnham in 1898. Graham, Anderson, Probst & White [A6] became a successor firm. Other employees included George R. Dean, Henry Codman, William Drummond, Allen Pond, Clinton J. Warren, three of the five Starrett brothers, and Thomas Eddy Tallmadge.

32. Carl W. Condit, *The Chicago School of Architecture: A History of Commercial Building in the Chicago Area 1875–1925,* p. 58.

33. Burnham & Root became D. H. Burnham & Company in 1891; Graham, Burnham & Co. in 1912; Graham, Anderson, Probst & White in 1917; and later Naess & Murphy; then C. F. Murphy; then Murphy Jahn. In addition, Burnham's sons created Burnham Brothers Inc. in 1928; changed to Burnham Bros. & Hammond in 1933; then Burnham & Hamond. Edward Bennett, Hubert Burnham, and John Holabird joined together on the Travel and Transportation Building (1933). Root's son, John Wellborn Root, Jr., joined John Augustus Holabird in Holabird & Root.

34. Rotch, however, served his own apprenticeship in France under the famous Viollet-le-Duc (late in his employer's career). Tilden was trained by Ware & Van Brunt. Rotch & Tilden designed the art museum at Wellesley College. H. Van Buren Magonigle worked for them as well as for several better-known architects.

35. Gebhard and Nevins, *Architectural Drawings,* p. 157.

36. Richard Oliver, "Goodhue, Bertram Grosvenor," *Macmillan Encyclopedia of Architects,* v. 2, p. 230.

37. Clarence Stein trained as an architect at Columbia and at the

Ecole. He worked for Goodhue on the design of St. Bartholomew's Church (1914–1918) in New York and on the overall plan of Goodhue's San Diego exposition of 1915—two of Goodhue's more important commissions. Stein became a major urban planner.

38. Carl W. Condit, *Chicago, 1910–1929: Building Planning and Urban Technology,* pp. 108–112.

39. Robert A. M. Stern and Thomas P. Catalano, *Raymond Hood,* p. 7.

40. Joseph Urban [A4] was an associate of Hood's in the early stages of Rockefeller Center. Urban was trained in Vienna and his designs include the Ziegfeld Theater (1926–1927) and the New School of Social Research (1930) in New York.

41. Raymond Hood and Paul Cret were the first consultants. Corbett, Walker, and Arthur Brown, Jr., were added. The first meeting was in May 1928. The program was adopted in the summer of 1929. E. H. Bennett, Hubert Burnham, and John Holabird were put on the commission (Carl W. Condit, *Chicago, 1930–1970: Building, Planning and Urban Technology,* pp. 6–7). Harris Armstrong worked for Hood at that time.

42. Alfred Bendiner, "Wild Gold Medal Winners I Have Known," *Journal of the American Institute of Architects,* May 1957, 24–25.

43. Maginnis was certainly highly respected among his colleagues. He not only served as a president of the AIA, but won the Gold Medal in 1948. Skidmore won it nine years later.

44. Owings had worked for York & Sawyer and then joined briefly in partnership with Henry B. Crosby of New Jersey.

10. The European Immigrant Masters in the Twentieth Century

1. Adolf Meyer had also been in Behrens' office in 1908. In 1909 he worked for Bruno Paul, Mies' first significant employer. Meyer and Gropius were partners from 1911 to about 1925. Gropius had first worked for Solf & Wichards in Berlin. In 1904 he left to study at the technical schools in Berlin and Hamburg.

2. Mies was the son of a master stonemason and began his architectural training in a firm in Aachen that mass-produced stucco architectural ornaments for traditional façades. He went to Berlin in 1905 and was first employed by Bruno Paul, an architect whose subsequent reputation was based mainly on his furniture and interior design.

3. Perhaps a German scholar could look for outstanding European architects who intersected with Gropius at the time of the Faguswerk and in 1925. According to this theory, it is quite likely that there were some major connections at these two times. It would also be interesting to know who might have worked for Mies in 1929 and 1930.

4. Breuer had begun to move in 1932 when he found work with A. & E. Roth, designing an apartment block in Switzerland for Sigfried Giedion (Peter Blake, *Marcel Breuer,* p. 49).

5. Keck was a creative designer who began to practice in 1926 after employment by D. H. Burnham & Co. and Schmidt, Garden & Erickson. Somehow Keck's work did not attract the most potent fame makers of the 1930s or later. This is surprising since his demonstration houses at the Chicago Fairs were as interesting as anything being done at that time by Gropius, Breuer, Mies, or Wright. Some of the other architects who worked for Keck at various times include Stanley Tigerman, Ralph Rapson, Leland Atwood, Robert B. Tague, and Buford

Pickens, as noted by Kihlstedt, *Macmillan Encyclopedia of Architects,* v. 2, p. 555.

6. Landis Gores, one of Johnson's classmates, became his partner from 1945 to 1951, crucial years in terms of Johnson's first designs. On his own in 1954, Gores won first prize in an international competition in São Paulo, Brazil. With this sort of beginning it is surprising that his name is not more familiar today; however, he was stricken by polio and had to reduce his practice. Howard Barnstone also worked for Johnson in the early 1950s. Richard Foster was with Johnson from 1950 to 1964.

7. "Wills was a popular Eclectic of the 1930s and 1940s, specializing in houses, who retained a mastery of proportion and detail; among other styles in his repertoire was a mild form of the International Style" (Walter C. Kidney, *The Architecture of Choice: Eclecticism in America, 1880–1930,* # 148).

8. Norman Bel Geddes was a designer, not an architect. Although he built his considerable reputation through innovative theater design, his most famous work in the public estimate was the Futurama, the GM panorama at the New York World's Fair, 1939–1940. His employee at that time was Victor Gruen, who had been trained in the same academy and school that Neutra and Schindler attended. He was a student of Behrens and knew Loos, but several years after they had emerged as famous. Gruen worked for Melcher & Steiner for nine years. He entered Bel Geddes' office in 1938. Later, in a highly successful firm, Gruen's employees included Victor Lundy, Cesar Pelli, and Frank Gehry, all with ties to other architects as well.

9. Millard not only worked for Noyes, but was an employee of Paul Schweikher. Peter Millard eventually set up practice with Earl Carlin, who had also worked for Schweikher and for Louis Kahn at the time of Kahn's emergence in the 1950s.

10. Others who achieved some prominence include John Carl Warneke. Reginald R. Isaacs listed the following as prominent architects and planners who were students (not employees) of Breuer: Charles Burchard, Arthur Davis, Frederick Day, Emilio Duhart, Louis Fry, John Harkness, Samuel Hurst, Ernest J. Kump, John Parkin, and Harry Seidler (Reginald Isaacs, "Breuer, Marcel," *Macmillan Encyclopedia of Architects,* v. 1, p. 286).

11. Hejduk was also employed by the famous Italian engineer Pier Luigi Nervi while on a Fulbright Grant to Rome. He also worked for the less famous firm of Fellheimer & Wagner.

12. Tigerman also worked for Harry Weese, for SOM, and for George Fred Keck, whom he most admired.

13. Gropius went into a teamwork practice, The Architects' Collaborative (TAC) in 1945, although it would be Gropius' name that would continue to dominate. Sarah Harkness, John Harkness, Jean Fletcher, Norman Fletcher, Louis McMillan, and Benjamin Thompson were the original TAC partners with Gropius. Several went on to establish individual reputations when they opened firms in their own names.

14. Jordy, *American Buildings,* v. 4, p. 165.

15. Eisenman also had degrees from Cornell and Columbia and a Ph.D. from Cambridge. He worked for TAC and for Percival Goodman soon after Goodman completed his influential book *Communitas* (1960).

16. Adolf K. Placzek (ed.), *Four Great Makers of Modern Architecture,* p. 246.

17. Ibid., p. 93.

18. Ibid., p. 111 (although Mies did do some writing in the 1920s).

19. Ibid., p. 111.

20. Ibid., p. 105.

21. Kallmann, though born in Germany, was a graduate of the AA in London and was trained in English offices. He came to the United States in 1948 and worked for various firms. McKinnell arrived from England to graduate from Columbia in 1959, where he was one of Kallmann's students.

22. Ludwig Glaeser, "Mies van der Rohe, Ludwig," *Macmillan Encyclopedia of Architects*, v. 3, p. 194.

23. John Jacobus, Jr., "Saarinen, Eliel," in Gerd Hatje (ed.), *Encyclopedia of Modern Architecture*, p. 250.

24. James Dinwiddie has faded from prominence, though he was at one time a favorite of the professional press. He was a student in this earlier period and later, in 1946, before he began to generate interest, was briefly in partnership with Eric Mendelsohn.

25. Maeve Slavin, "Aesthetic Revolutionary," *Working Woman*, January 1984, 74–78.

26. Geoffry Holroyd, "Charles Eames and Eliel Saarinen," *Royal Institute of Architects Journal* 86 (January 1979): 29.

27. Ibid.

28. Esther McCoy, "Charles Eames Obituary," *Journal of the American Institute of Architects* 67 (October 1978): 108.

29. Obata, Hellmuth, and Kassabaum had all been students at Washington University, St. Louis. George Hellmuth was in partnership with Minoru Yamasaki from 1949 to 1955, with William Lienweber as the third partner. This was Yamasaki's takeoff point. Hellmuth left in 1955. The firm today is very large and important. Among its designs is the Air and Space Museum for the Smithsonian in Washington, D.C.

11. Louis Kahn

1. William D. Hewitt, the younger brother of Frank Furness' partner, joined Percy Ash in 1917, but Ash also served as a professor at George Washington University and at the University of Michigan between 1918 and 1924. Ash had been a Fellow at the American Academy in Rome, an honor Kahn would also have.

2. Alexandra Tyng, *Beginnings: Louis I. Kahn's Philosophy of Architecture*, p. 8.

3. Born in France, Cret was apprenticed to his uncle and studied at the Ecole des Beaux-Arts in his native city of Lyons and then in Paris, where he was a prize winner. In 1903 Cret was invited to teach at the University of Pennsylvania, a position he held until his retirement in 1937, assuring the school of Beaux-Arts approach to architectural education. At the same time he carried on an active practice. He won seven of the many competitions he entered.

4. Chandler was certainly not a nationally famous architect, though, except for Furness, he was the only one of these Philadelphia architects to have an East Coast apprenticeship; he had worked for Ware & Van Brunt.

5. Robert A. M. Stern, *George Howe: Toward a Modern American Architecture*, p. 87.

6. In 1928 Karl Moser was the first president of CIAM, that professional fraternity of men who would almost all become famous modern architects.

7. Stern, in *George Howe,* gives different information on Lescaze in the 1920s—that he arrived in 1923, ahead of Moser, and worked only six months in Cleveland.

8. Lescaze and Howe finally broke off their relationship, which had never been close since Lescaze had continued to maintain his office in New York while Howe stayed in Philadelphia. Richmond Shreve became Lescaze's partner just after he finished the Empire State Building. Their Williamsburg Housing Project (1934) in Brooklyn was another MOMA favorite. In 1939 Lescaze was awarded a Silver Medal by the AIA for his Swiss Pavilion at the New York World's Fair. Albert Frey worked for Le Corbusier in 1928–1929 and then for Lescaze in 1931–1933 while the PSFS was going up. Frey was featured by MOMA for work done in partnership with Lawrence Kocher, the editor of *Architectural Record.* His later firms were Clark & Frey (1943–1956), Frey & Chambers (1957–1966), and then simply Albert Frey. His firm designed the Social Science and Humanities Building at the University of California at Riverside (1953) and, with his background, it is a surprise that he did not become more famous.

9. Joseph Esherick [C7] was a student under Cret and worked for Howe briefly in the late 1930s. He also worked for Clauss & Daub before moving to California where he was employed by Walter Steilberg, Julia Morgan's former chief draftsman. Esherick then worked for Gardner Dailey [B5] and established his own office in 1946. He joined the faculty of the University of California in 1952 and eight years later was one of the designers of Wurster Hall. The Cannery (1968) in San Francisco was designed in his office. Others who worked for Howe include Louis McAlister, Earl W. Bolton, and Daub.

10. Richard Pommer, "The Architecture of Urban Housing in the United States during the Early 1930s," *Journal of the Society of Architectural Historians* 37/4 (1978): 244.

11. Stern, *George Howe,* p. 195.

12. Pommer, "Architecture," p. 237.

13. Stern, *George Howe,* p. 199.

14. Peter Blake, better known as an author and dean than as a designer, worked for Kahn & Stonorov in the early 1940s before he joined the staff of MOMA. German-born, he was educated in England and had served his apprenticeship to Serge Chermayeff. Anne Tyng, with them by 1945, is credited by her daughter as being responsible for building Kahn's self-esteem at that time (Tyng, *Beginnings,* p. 21).

15. Fuller is discussed in the chapter on loners.

16. Robert A. M. Stern, "History: Yale 1950–1965," *Oppositions* 4 (October 1974): 40–41.

17. Auguste Komendant, *18 Years with Architect Louis I. Kahn,* p. 172.

18. Moore had his first professional degree from the University of Michigan. By the time he went to Princeton he had worked for Mario Corbett, Joseph Allen Stein, and Clark & Buettler in San Francisco, had been an assistant professor at Utah, and had served in the army in Korea. Mario Corbett worked for Reginald Johnson and for Myron Hunt before setting up practice in the mid-1930s.

19. Schweikher had been an associate of George Fred Keck in the 1930s and also worked with Hamilton Beatty, a Le Corbusier apprentice. Ralph Rapson was also an employee of Schweikher as well as of Vernon De Mars and George Fred Keck.

20. This opinion came initially from Professor Robert Walker, who knew Kahn before and after his rise to fame. It was reinforced by Anatole Senkevich, who tells a story about Kahn's posturing when he accompanied a group of students to Moscow. Komendant seems to confirm this, and one of Kahn's employees, Leslie Gallery, has explained that Kahn could never admit to finishing a concept and would continue making changes in a private room while the staff proceeded independently with the actual design.

12. The Loners

1. Thornton might possibly be considered to have been an associate of Jefferson's. In 1802 the president appointed Thornton head of the patent office, a position he held until his death. Thornton is credited with influencing the design of Pavilion 7 at the University of Virginia.

2. See David de Penanrun, Roux, et Delaire, *Les Architectes élèves de L'Ecole des Beaux-Arts.*

3. Douglas R. Kent, "Hooker, Philip," *Macmillan Encyclopedia of Architects,* v. 2, p. 417.

4. Hatfield was the first treasurer of the AIA. He is credited with the design of the Seaman's Savings Bank on Wall Street and the Westchester County Courthouse. Three loners were mentioned in four or five of the histories. However, there is "considerable question as to the merit" of David Hoadley [A5], a "victim of excessive local adulation in the 1920s and 1930s." As noted in the chapter on fame makers, local bias can skew the lists (Elizabeth Mills Brown, "Hoadley, David," *Macmillan Encyclopedia of Architects,* v. 2, p. 396).

5. John Mills Van Osdel [A5] is mentioned because he was the earliest professional architect in Chicago, though his work is not discussed because many of his buildings were destroyed in the fire. William Ittner [A4] was praised for his "modernized and eclectic Jacobean schools" in St. Louis by Hitchcock et al., *Modern Architects.*

6. From the time of Strickland, Walter, and Haviland onward there was a good deal of inbreeding in terms of the architectural profession in Philadelphia with men like John Notman and Samuel Sloan forming links. Philadelphia architects have their own web of connections. After the Civil War they would go to the Ecole and return to work in local firms, or if, like Kahn, they were unable to study abroad, they stayed in the Philadelphia area. Chandler, mentioned in the text, was an exception when he worked for Ware & Van Brunt. In Philadelphia he employed Walter Cope and John Stewardson, who also worked for Furness. Cope & Stewardson did a number of campus buildings in the area. When Stewardson died, the practice passed into the hands of his younger brother, Emlyn. Cope then joined with Frank Miles Day and Wilson Eyre. Cope died at the age of forty-two and a former employee, George Bispham Page, succeeded to that practice. Day formed a partnership with his brother H. Kent Day.

Charles Zeller Kauder began in Chandler's office and then worked for Cope and for Horace Trumbauer. Klauder joined Frank and Kent Day in partnership in 1910 but after 1918 was in independent practice. He designed the Cathedral of Learning in Pittsburgh (1928). Trumbauer had worked for George and William Hewitt when he was sixteen. He opened his own office in 1892. His chief designer, Julian F. Abele, was a University of Pennsylvania graduate and one of the few black architects to have his work mentioned by major architectural historians. Among their buildings were Widener Memorial Library at Harvard, several buildings at Duke, and the Philadelphia Museum of Art done in association with Zantzinger, Borie & Medary. Though Milton Medary is virtually unknown nationally today, he was an AIA Gold Medal winner and the designer of the Bok Carillon Tower, Mountain Lake, Florida (1929).

There was a similar subset in Rhode Island. John Holden Greene [A6] worked on Caleb Ormsbee's First Congregational Church. By 1806 he was in practice and James C. Bucklin [A7] was one of Greene's apprentices. In 1822 Bucklin was in partnership with William Tallman and in 1828 his partner on the Providence Arcade was Russell Warren [A8]. Warren worked in association with Town & Davis in the early period of that firm's existence and thus this whole group could have been drawn onto the Bulfinch chart. Tallman & Bucklin were the employers of Thomas Tefft [A6], whose most important work was the train station in Providence.

7. See George B. Tatum, "Johnston, William L.," *Macmillan Encyclopedia of Architects,* v. 2, p. 503.

8. McArthur was born in Scotland and trained by his uncle in Philadelphia. Although he studied under T. U. Walter, he is not recorded as having worked for Walter.

9. Vincent Scully, *The Shingle Style and the Stick Style,* p. liv and n. 93.

10. Buffington was born in Michigan, the son of an engineer. He served his apprenticeship to George M. Anderson and Samuel Hannaford in Cincinnati.

11. Fuller attended Harvard in 1913–1914 and received some training at Annapolis while in the navy during World War I.

12. In 1956 Goff had an office in Wright's Price Tower in Bartlesville, Oklahoma. See David G. DeLong, "Goff, Bruce," *Macmillan Encyclopedia of Architects,* v. 2, pp. 221–224. In a lecture he gave on his work, at the University of Texas in the fall of 1979, Goff stated that he never worked for Wright.

13. Connections: Family, Friends, Schools

1. William H. Pierson, Jr., *American Buildings and Their Architects: I,* p. 240.

2. Alan Gowans, *Images of American Living: Four Centuries of Architecture and Furniture as Cultural Expression,* p. 261.

3. See Hanna H. Lerski, *William Jay: Itinerant English Architect 1792–1837.*

4. Pierson, *American Buildings,* v. 1, p. 373.

5. Hitchcock, *Richardson,* p. 3.

6. Ibid., p. 53.

7. Mardges Baker, "Flagg, Ernest," *Macmillan Encyclopedia of Architects,* v. 2, p. 88.

8. Antoinette Downing, "Greene, Charles and Greene, Henry," *Macmillan Encyclopedia of Architects,* v. 2, p. 239.

9. John McHale, *R. Buckminster Fuller,* p. 43, n. 3.

10. "Hewlett, James Monroe," Withey and Withey, *Biographical Dictionary.*

11. O'Gorman, *Furness,* p. 18.

12. Robert Allen Jones, "Cass Gilbert, Midwestern Architect in New York," p. 3.

13. Price's daughter married George B. Post's son and became well known as Emily Post.

14. Paul Heyer, *Architects on Architecture: New Directions in America*, p. 173.

15. Brooks, *The Prairie School*, p. 173.

16. Not only did Johnson's father help in the funding of the 1932 MOMA exhibition—he backed Richard Neutra in the design of an experimental automobile, at his son's urging.

17. Manson, *Frank Lloyd Wright*, p. 48.

18. Carol Herselle Krinsky, *Rockefeller Center*, p. 103.

19. Baker, *Hunt*, p. 2.

20. Ibid., p. 36.

21. Ibid., p. 63.

22. Ibid., p. 68.

23. Ibid., p. 78.

24. Ibid., p. 124.

25. Ibid., p. 128.

26. Esther McCoy, *Five California Architects*, p. 2.

27. Robert A. M. Stern, *George Howe, Toward a Modern American Architecture*, p. 87.

14. Self-promotion and Publicity

1. Baker, *Hunt*, p. 148. Hunt also entered a number of competitions, among them the competition for the National Academy of Art won by Peter B. Wight in 1862. (Eidlitz, Mould, and Van Brunt also submitted entries.)

2. See Robert Twombly, *Frank Lloyd Wright*, p. 27 and following pages.

3. Brooks, *Prairie School*, pp. xii–xiii.

4. Ibid., p. 172.

5. Ibid., p. 171.

6. Jacob Landy, *Lafever*, p. 22, and Sir John Summerson, *Heavenly Mansions and Other Essays on Architecture*, p. 52.

7. R. F. Jordan, "Walter Gropius," in *Who's Who in Architecture from 1400 to the Present*, ed. J. M. Richards with Adolf Placzek, p. 124.

8. Reyner Banham, *Age of the Masters*, p. 3.

9. Reyner Banham, *Theory and Design in the First Machine Age*, p. 285. Marcel Breuer also benefited from the promotional efforts of the Bauhaus, which featured his furniture designs in the 1920s.

10. Sigfried Giedion, *Space, Time and Architecture*, p. 124.

11. William Jordy, "Mies van der Rohe," in *Encyclopedia of Modern Architecture*, ed. Gerd Hatje, p. 192.

12. See Juan Pablo Bonta, *An Anatomy of Architectural Interpretation: A Semiotic Review of the Criticism of Mies van der Rohe's Barcelona Pavilion*.

13. Henry-Russell Hitchcock, *Architecture, Nineteenth and Twentieth Centuries*, 363, n.1.

14. Conrad Jamison, "Modern Architecture as an Ideology," *Via IV*, 1980, 20–21.

15. Much of the information on works by American architects published in the nineteenth century was taken from Henry-Russell Hitchcock, *American Architectural Books*.

16. It is of note that Elmes' first book had been on the subject of prisons (1816).

17. In 1887 Bruce Price published one of his first commissions. His employee, Claude Bragdon, became an important writer on architecture.

18. There were two Paul Frankls, both born in Austria in the 1880s. One became a major historian and the other an architect and writer in New York.

19. Howells was also the father of John Mead Howells, who first practiced with I. N. P. Stokes from 1897 to 1917 before he became the senior partner in Howells & Hood at the time they won the *Chicago Tribune* competition.

20. William H. Jordy and Ralph Coe (eds.), *American Architecture and Other Writings by Montgomery Schuyler*, p. 7, n.7.

21. Jordy, *American Buildings*, v. 3, p. 318, nn. ix–x.

22. Hitchcock, *Richardson*, pp. 126 and 152.

23. Jordy and Coe, *American Architecture*, p. 2.

24. Several of the writers were members of the establishment traced in the first part of this book. Charles Babcock (Upjohn's son-in-law), Charles Cummings (Bryant's apprentice), Arthur Rotch (Cram's employer), Henry Van Brunt and William Ware (Hunt's students), and Mrs. Schuyler Van Rensselaer (Richardson's biographer) all contributed to the journal in 1882.

25. James F. O'Gorman, *Furness*, p. 69.

26. Russell Sturgis quoted in Nikolaus Pevsner, *Pioneers of Modern Design from William Morris to Walter Gropius*, pp. 28–29.

27. Jordy and Coe, *American Architecture*, p. 2.

28. Edward D. Stone, *The Evolution of an Architect*, p. 2.

29. Huxtable also changed and was one of the first to develop a strong interest in preservation of older buildings. Blake did a real turn-about by first writing *The Master Builders* on Wright, Le Corbusier, and Mies in 1960 and then, in 1977, the bitterly antihero *Form Follows Fiasco: Why Modern Architecture Hasn't Worked*.

30. Stern, *George Howe*, p. 24.

31. Ibid., p. 134.

32. Ibid., p. 137.

33. Ibid., p. 140.

34. Ibid.

35. Ibid., p. 156.

36. Ibid., p. 221.

15. Other, Weaker Patterns

1. Even Jefferson seems to have entered the competition for the president's house, although it is puzzling to reflect on how he would have managed if he had won with his entry (inspired almost line for line by an illustration of the work of Palladio).

2. Latrobe also lost several competitions, including the New York City Hall won by Mangin & McComb.

3. Strickland believed that he won in part because of personal contact with some of the jurors (Gilchrist, *William Strickland*, p. 4).

4. Haviland, Town & Davis and Isaiah Rogers also entered that competition.

5. Gridley James Fox Bryant made his reputation with the Boston City Hall (1865); Napoleon LeBrun won both of his major works in competition, the Roman Catholic Cathedral (1846–1865) and the Academy of

Music (1855) in Philadelphia. He was only twenty-four when he was given the cathedral and had to be teamed with the more experienced John Notman for its execution. The year that Frank Miles Day returned from his apprenticeship in London, he won the competition for the Philadelphia Art Club (1887). Whitney Warren began his practice with the competition for the Newport Yacht Club (1899).

6. According to Hitchcock and Seale, *Temples of Democracy*, p. 160, the following architects entered the Connecticut capitol competition: R. M. Upjohn, George B. Post, Charles B. Atwood, Peabody & Stearns, G. J. F. Bryant, and H. H. Richardson, among others.

7. Ibid., p. 216.

8. See Mark L. Peisch, *The Chicago School of Architecture: Early Followers of Sullivan and Wright*, and Henry-Russell Hitchcock, "The Evolution of Wright, Mies and Le Corbusier," *Perspecta* 1 (1955): 15.

9. Richard Pommer, "The Architecture of Urban Housing in the United States during the Early 1930s," *Journal of the Society of Architectural Historians* 37/4 (1978): 237.

10. See L. Valentine and A. Valentine, *The American Academy in Rome 1894–1969*, pp. 210–211.

11. Interview with Michael Graves, 1977. Kahn's experience in Rome was as enriching as Venturi's. He found himself in the massive geometries of raw brick and concrete ruins of the ancient civilization and finally was able to integrate his Beaux-Arts training and modern architecture. Charles Moore's stay in Rome, though not as an official Fellow, was also a significant event in his career.

12. On the Rotch scholars, see William Graves Perry, *The Rotch Travelling Scholarship: A Review of Its History 1883–1963*, and *The Rotch Travelling Scholarship*, p. 81.

13. The other three were Charles F. Reichardt, said to have been a pupil of the famous Schinkel, a man named Schmidt, and Thomas Thomas, who was later joined in practice in New York by his sons, who came from England to join him.

14. Turpin Bannister (ed.), *The Architect at Mid-Century*, p. 72.

15. The founders were Upjohn, Hunt, Charles Babcock, Leopold Eidlitz, Jacob Mould, Joseph C. Wells, Calvert Vaux, Frederick Withers, Frederick Diaper, John Notman, T. U. Walter, Alexander J. Davis, and R. G. Hatfield. Wells faded into obscurity. (He was not the Joseph Wells of the Villard Houses.) Diaper had studied with the major English designer Robert Smirke and was a member of the RIBA before coming to America in 1839. His work was confined largely to the New York area. Hatfield is mentioned in textbooks for cast-iron fronts.

16. Ian McCallum, *Architecture U.S.A.*, p. 108.

17. Wölfflin, in turn, was the pupil of Jakob Burkhardt and succeeded him at the University of Basle (Banham, *Theory and Design*, p. 205).

18. Reyner Banham, "CIAM," in *Encyclopedia of Modern Architecture*, p. 72.

19. Sigfried Giedion, *Space, Time and Architecture*, p. 697.

20. Banham, "CIAM," p. 72.

21. 1928, 1929, 1930, 1933, 1937, 1947, 1949, 1951, 1956, 1959 (ibid.).

22. Banham, *Theory and Design*, pp. 79–80.

23. Much of the following information is from Russell Lynes, *Good Old Modern*, and from the special issue of *Art News* on MOMA, 78/8 (October 1979).

24. Henry-Russell Hitchcock, "Modern Architecture—A Memoir," *Journal of the Society of Architectural Historians* 27/4 (1968): 227–233.

25. Lynes, *Good Old Modern*, p. 137.

26. Ibid., p. 136.

27. Ibid., p. 13.

28. A few Americans were mentioned in the introduction, but not in a flattering way.

29. Hitchcock et al., *Modern Architects*, p. 171.

30. Monroe Bowman was born in Chicago in 1901, attended the Armour Institute, and worked for his father, who was a builder. From 1924 to 1928 he "worked for various Illinois architects, including Holabird & Root" (ibid., p. 173). Irving Bowman was five years younger and also attended Armour. They were partners from 1929 to 1936. In 1976 Monroe Bowman was "still in practice in Chicago." He is the architect of 4180 Marine Drive. Irving Bowman practiced in Charleston, West Virginia (Stuart E. Cohen, *Chicago Architects*, p. 21).

31. Peter Blake in *Art News* 78/8, 101.

16. The Historians as Fame Makers

1. The surveys mentioned in this chapter that were used to compile the Index of Fame are listed in chapter 3.

2. The following were included in the text: Attwood [*sic*], Blodget, Bulfinch, Burnham, Carrère & Hastings, Cram, Ellis, Gilbert, Godefroi [*sic*], Goodhue, Hallet, Haviland, Hunt, Jefferson, Latrobe, Renwick, Richardson, Rogers, Root, Strickland, Sullivan, Thornton, Upjohn, Walter, Wells, Wright, and the prerevolutionary designer Peter Harrison.

3. Matthew Nowicki had his professional training in Warsaw and at the Chicago Art Institute. He was cultural attaché for Poland and he represented Poland in the design of the UN building. His State Fair arena in Raleigh, North Carolina (1952–1953), was constructed after his death.

4. Bonta, *Architecture and Its Interpretation*, p. 177.

5. Hamlin, *The American Spirit in Architecture*, p. 177.

6. Ibid., p. 233.

7. Both Mumford and Hamlin would be involved with the Museum of Modern Art at a later date.

8. For *Brown Decades* Mumford's acknowledgments included *Skyscrapers and the Men Who Built Them* (1929) by William Starret (which claimed that Jenney & Mundie's Home Insurance Building was the first true skyscraper). The earlier *Sticks and Stones* was not indexed, but several careful readings indicate that Jenney's name was not mentioned in 1924.

9. Tallmadge, *Story of Architecture in America*, p. 179.

10. Fiske Kimball, *American Architecture*, p. 125.

11. Tallmadge, *Story of Architecture in America*, p. 6.

12. George Edgell's *The American Architecture of Today* was published in 1928. It did not attempt to cover nineteenth-century architecture and therefore was not used in the compilation of the Index of Fame.

13. Henry-Russell Hitchcock, *Modern Architecture: Romanticism and Reintegration*, p. 25.

14. Ibid., p. 29.

15. Ibid., p. 104.

16. Nikolaus Pevsner, *Pioneers of the Modern Movement from William Morris to Walter Gropius*, acknowledgments and pp. 10, 219.

17. Ibid., p. 10.

18. Walter Behrendt and Bruno Zevi wrote influential surveys. However, their indexes show very similar selection to those of Giedion and Pevsner, even though the amount and quality of attention they devoted to the various individuals often differed. Zevi's list of promising American contemporary architects was copied in its entirety (with appropriate credit) into Benevolo's survey and thus is incorporated in the Index of Fame.

19. For a profile of Scully, see James Stevenson, "What Seas What Shores," *New Yorker,* February 18, 1980.

20. Carroll L. V. Meeks, "The New History of Architecture," *Journal of the Society of Architectural Historians* 2/1–2 (1942): 3.

21. Charles Jencks, in an interview, considered Giedion his teacher-mentor, but he also studied under Reyner Banham while on a Fulbright grant to England. Robert Stern is a practicing architect but also an architectural historian of merit. He was a graduate student under Scully, Kahn, and Venturi.

17. Afterword on the Fame-Making System

1. Public acceptance of modern styling for houses and some churches came later, if at all.

2. Charles W. Moore, "Water and Architecture" (Ph.D. dissertation, Princeton University, 1957), p. iv.

Bibliography

Much of my original research had been undertaken before the publication of the *Macmillan Encyclopedia of Architects* (4 vols.; Adolf Placzek, editor-in-chief; New York: Free Press, 1982). As the notes indicate, I accepted the entries in this encyclopedia as probably having the most accurate biographical information. In addition, I read every article on American architects published in the *Journal of the Society of Architectural Historians;* a number are cited in the notes. Articles in *American Architect and Building News, Architectural Record, Architectural Forum, Journal of the American Institute of Architects*, and *Progressive Architecture* were also useful. Various editions of *Who's Who in America* were also used.

Alexander, Robert L. *The Architecture of Maximilian Godefroy.* Baltimore: Johns Hopkins University Press, 1974.

Allsopp, Bruce. *The Study of Architectural History.* New York: Praeger, 1970.

Andrews, Wayne. *Architecture, Ambition and Americans: A Social History of American Architecture.* London: Collier-Macmillan, 1947; rev. ed. New York: Free Press, 1978.

Architectural League of New York. *Five Architects: Eisenman, Graves, Gwathmey, Hejduk, Meier.* New York: Wittenborn, 1972.

Attoe, Wayne. *Architecture and Critical Imagination: A Study of the Methods of Criticism and Its Effect on the Design Process.* New York: Wiley, 1978.

The Avery Index to Architectural Periodicals. 2nd ed., revised and enlarged. Boston: G. K. Hall, 1973.

The Avery Obituary Index of Architects and Artists. Boston: G. K. Hall, 1963 (and clippings in the Avery Library, Columbia University, New York).

Baker, Paul R. *Richard Morris Hunt.* Cambridge, Mass.: MIT Press, 1980.

Baldwin, Charles C. *Stanford White.* 1931. Reprint. New York: Da Capo, 1976.

Bancroft, Hubert Howe. *The Book of the Fair: Volume 1.* New York: Bounty, 1894.

Banham, Reyner. *Age of the Masters.* New York: Harper & Row, 1962.

———. *Theory and Design in the First Machine Age.* New York: Praeger, 1960.

Bannister, Turpin, ed. *The Architect at Mid-Century.* New York: Reinhold, 1954.

Bayer, Herbert. *Bauhaus: 1919–1929.* New York: Museum of Modern Art, 1938.

Behrendt, Walter Curt. *Modern Building: Its Nature, Problems, and Forms.* New York: Harcourt, 1937.

Benevolo, Leonardo. *History of Modern Architecture.* 1961. 2 vols. Translated by H. J. Landry. Cambridge, Mass.; MIT Press, 1966, 1971.

Blake, Peter. *Form Follows Fiasco: Why Modern Architecture Hasn't Worked.* Boston: Little, Brown, 1977.

———. *Marcel Breuer.* New York: Museum of Modern Art, 1949.

———. *The Master Builders: Le Corbusier, Mies van der Rohe, Frank Lloyd Wright.* New York: Knopf, 1960.

Bonta, Juan Pablo. *An Anatomy of Architectural Interpretation: A Semiotic Review of the Criticism of Mies van der Rohe's Barcelona Pavilion.* Barcelona: Gustavo Gill, 1975.

———. *Architecture and Its Interpretation: A Study of Expressive Systems in Architecture.* New York: Rizzoli, 1979.

Boudon, Philippe. *Lived-in Architecture: Le Corbusier's Pessac Revisited.* Cambridge, Mass.: MIT Press, 1972.

Braudy, Leo. *The Frenzy of Renown: Fame and Its History.* New York: Oxford University Press, 1986.

Brooks, H. Allen. *The Prairie School: Frank Lloyd Wright and His Midwest Contemporaries.* Toronto: University of Toronto Press, 1972.

———. *Prairie School Architecture: Studies from "The Western Architect."* Toronto: University of Toronto Press, 1975.

Brown, Glenn. *History of the United States Capitol.* 1903. Reprint. 2 vols. New York: Da Capo, 1970.

Burchard, John Ely, and Albert Bush-Brown. *The Architecture of America: A Social and Cultural History.* Boston: Little, Brown, 1961, 1966.

Bush-Brown, Albert. *Louis Sullivan.* New York: Braziller, 1960.

Caemmerer, H. Paul. *The Life of Pierre Charles L'Enfant, Planner of the City Beautiful, the City of Washington.* Washington, D.C.: National Republic, 1950.

Cardwell, Kenneth H. *Bernard Maybeck: Artisan, Architect, Artist.* Salt Lake City: Peregrine Smith, 1983.

Carter, Edward C., II, John C. Van Horne, and Lee W. Formwalt, eds. *The Journals of Benjamin Henry Latrobe, 1799–1820: From Philadelphia to New Orleans.* New Haven: Yale University Press, 1980.

Caudill, William W. *Architecture by Team.* New York: Van Nostrand, 1971.

Cheney, Sheldon. *The New World Architecture.* London: Longmans Green, 1930.

Christ-Janer, Albert. *Eliel Saarinen.* Chicago: University of Chicago Press, [1948].

Cohen, Stuart E. *Chicago Architects.* Chicago: Swallow, 1976.

Collins, George R. *Visionary Drawings of Architecture and Planning: 20th Century through the 1960s.* Cambridge, Mass.: MIT Press, 1979.

Condit, Carl W. *American Building: Materials and Techniques from the First Colonial Settlements to the Present.* Chicago: University of Chicago Press, 1968.

———. *American Building Art: The Nineteenth Century.* New York: Oxford University Press, 1960.

———. *Chicago, 1910–1929: Building, Planning and Urban Technology.* Chicago: University of Chicago Press, 1973.

————. *Chicago, 1930–1970: Building, Planning and Urban Technology.* Chicago: University of Chicago Press, 1974.

————. *The Chicago School of Architecture: A History of Commercial and Public Building in the Chicago Area, 1875–1925.* Chicago: University of Chicago Press, 1964.

————. *The Rise of the Skyscraper.* Chicago: University of Chicago Press, 1952.

Connely, Willard. *Louis Sullivan as He Lived: The Shaping of American Architecture.* New York: Horizon, 1960.

Cook, John W., and Heinrich Klotz. *Conversations with Architects.* New York: Praeger, 1973.

Cortissoz, Royal. *The Architecture of John Russell Pope.* New York: Helburn, 1924.

————. *Monograph on the Work of Charles A. Platt.* New York: Architectural Books, 1913.

Cram, Ralph Adams. *My Life in Architecture.* Boston: Little, Brown, 1936.

Danz, Ernest. *The Architecture of Skidmore, Owings and Merrill, 1950–1962.* London: Architectural Press, 1963.

David de Penanrun, Roux, et Delaire [no first names given]. *Les Architectes élèves de l'Ecole des Beaux-Arts.* Paris: Chaix, 1895.

Davidson, Marshall B. *The American Heritage History of Notable American Houses.* New York: American Heritage, 1971.

Delong, David G. *The Architecture of Bruce Goff: Buildings and Projects, 1916–1974.* New York: Garland, 1977.

Detroit Institute of Arts. *The Legacy of Albert Kahn.* Detroit: Detroit Institute of Arts, 1970.

Dictionary of American Biography. New York: Scribner, 1931.

Downing, Antoinette F., and Vincent Scully. *The Architectural Heritage of Newport, Rhode Island, 1640–1915.* Cambridge, Mass.: Harvard University Press, 1952.

Drexler, Arthur. *Ludwig Mies van der Rohe.* New York: Braziller, 1960.

————. *Transformations in Modern Architecture.* New York: Museum of Modern Art, 1979.

Eaton, Leonard. *Two Chicago Architects and Their Clients: Frank Lloyd Wright and Howard Van Doren Shaw.* Cambridge, Mass.: MIT Press, 1969.

Edgell, George H. *The American Architecture of Today.* New York: Scribners, 1928.

Emanuel, Muriel, ed. *Contemporary Architects.* New York: St. Martin's, 1980.

Encyclopaedia Britannica. Chicago: Benton, 1968.

Encyclopedia of World Art. New York: McGraw-Hill, 1959.

Fein, Albert. *Frederick Law Olmsted and the American Environmental Tradition.* New York: Braziller, 1972.

Fitch, James Marston. *American Architecture and the Esthetics of Plenty.* New York: Columbia University Press, 1961.

————. *American Building: The Environmental Forces That Shaped It.* Boston: Houghton Mifflin, 1966.

————. *American Building: The Forces That Shaped It.* Boston: Houghton Mifflin, 1948.

————. *American Building: The Historical Forces That Shaped It.* Boston: Houghton Mifflin, 1966.

————. *Walter Gropius.* New York: Braziller, 1960.

Fletcher, Banister. *A History of Architecture on the Comparative Method.* 17th ed. New York: Scribners, 1961. [See also John Musgrove.]

Francis, Dennis Steadman, ed. *Architects in Practice: New York City, 1840–1900.* New York: Committee for the Preservation of Architectural Records, 1980.

Frankl, Paul T. *New Dimensions.* New York: Payson & Clarke, 1928.

Frary, I. T. *Thomas Jefferson Architect and Builder.* Richmond: Garrett and Massie, 1931.

Gallagher, Helen M. Pierce. *Robert Mills, Architect of the Washington Monument, 1781–1855.* New York: Columbia University Press, 1935.

Gallier, James. *Autobiography of James Gallier, Architect.* 1864. Reprint. New York: Da Capo, 1973.

Gardner, Helen. *Gardner's Art through the Ages.* 7th ed., revised by Horst de la Croix and Richard G. Tansey. New York: Harcourt Brace Jovanovich, 1980.

Gayle, Margot, and Edmund V. Gillon. *Cast Iron Architecture in New York: A Photographic Survey.* New York: Dover, 1974.

Gebhard, David. *Schindler.* New York: Viking, 1972.

———. *The Work of Elmslie and Purcell: Architects.* Park Forest, Ill.: Prairie School Press, 1965.

Gebhard, David, and Deborah Nevins, eds. *200 Years of American Architectural Drawings.* New York: Watson Guptill, 1977.

Gebhard, David, and Harriette Von Breton. *Lloyd Wright, Architect: An Exhibition. November 22–December 22, 1971.* Santa Barbara: Santa Barbara Museum, 1971.

Giedion, Sigfried. *A Decade of New Architecture.* Zurich: Girsberger, 1951.

———. *Space, Time and Architecture: The Growth of a New Tradition.* Cambridge, Mass.: Harvard University Press, 1941, 1967, 1974.

Gilchrist, Agnes Addison. *William Strickland, Architect and Engineer.* Philadelphia: University of Pennsylvania Press, 1950.

Gill, Brendan. *Many Masks: A Life of Frank Lloyd Wright.* New York: Putnam's, 1987.

Giurgola, Romaldo, and Jaimini Mehta. *Louis I. Kahn.* Boulder, Colo.: Westview, 1975.

Gowans, Alan. *Images of American Living: Four Centuries of Architecture and Furniture as Cultural Expression.* New York: Lippincott, 1964.

Granger, Alfred Hoyt. *Charles Follen McKim.* Boston: Houghton Mifflin, 1913.

Gray, David. *Thomas Hastings, Architect.* Boston: Houghton Mifflin, 1933.

Greene, John F. *American Architect's Directory.* 3rd ed. New York: Bowker, 1970.

Gropius, Walter. *The New Architecture and the Bauhaus.* Translated by P. Morton Shand. Cambridge, Mass.: MIT Press, 1936.

Gubitosi, C., and A. Izzo. *Pietro Belluschi: Buildings and Plans, 1932–1973.* Rome: Officina Edizioni, 1974.

Guinness, Desmond, and Julius T. Sadler, Jr. *Mr. Jefferson Architect.* New York: Viking, 1973.

Gutheim, Frederick. *1857–1957: One Hundred Years of Architecture in America: Celebrating the Centennial of the American Institute of Architects.* New York: Reinhold, 1957.

Hamlin, Talbot F. *The American Spirit in Architecture.* The Pageant of America Series. New Haven: Yale University Press, 1926.

———. *Architecture through the Ages.* New York: Putnam's, 1940, 1953.

————. *Benjamin Henry Latrobe.* New York: Oxford University Press, 1955.

————. *Forms and Functions in 20th Century Architecture.* 4 vols. New York: Columbia University Press, 1952.

————. *Greek Revival Architecture in America.* London: Oxford University Press, 1944.

Hammett, Ralph Warner. *Architecture in the United States: A Survey of Architectural Styles since 1776.* New York: Wiley, 1976.

Hatje, Gerd, ed. *Encyclopedia of Modern Architecture.* New York: Abrams, 1964.

Heyer, Paul. *Architects on Architecture: New Directions in America.* New York: Walker, 1966.

Hines, Thomas S. *Burnham of Chicago, Architect and Planner.* 2nd ed. Chicago: University of Chicago Press, 1979.

————. *Richard Neutra and the Search for Modern Architecture: A Biography and History.* New York: Oxford University Press, 1982.

Hitchcock, Henry-Russell. *American Architectural Books.* Minneapolis: University of Minnesota Press, 1962.

————. *Architecture: Nineteenth and Twentieth Centuries.* Baltimore: Penguin, 1958.

————. *The Architecture of H. H. Richardson and His Times.* Cambridge, Mass.: MIT Press, 1966.

————. *In the Nature of Materials: The Buildings of Frank Lloyd Wright 1887–1941.* New York: Duell, Sloan & Pearce, 1942.

————. *Modern Architecture: Romanticism and Reintegration.* 1929. Reprint. New York: Hacker Art Books, 1970.

Hitchcock, Henry-Russell, Alfred H. Barr, Jr., Philip Johnson, and Lewis Mumford. *Modern Architects.* New York: W. W. Norton, 1932.

Hitchcock, Henry-Russell, and Arthur Drexler, eds. *Built in USA: Post-War Architecture.* New York: Simon & Schuster, 1952.

Hitchcock, Henry-Russell, and Philip Johnson. *The International Style.* New York: W. W. Norton, 1932.

Hitchcock, Henry-Russell, and William Seale. *Temples of Democracy: The State Capitols of the United States of America.* New York: Harcourt, 1976.

Hoffmann, Donald. *The Architecture of John Wellborn Root: A Study of His Life and Work.* Park Forest, Ill.: Prairie School Press, 1966.

————. *Frank Lloyd Wright's Falling Water: The House and Its History.* New York: Dover, 1978.

Howland, Richard H., and Eleanor Spenser. *The Architecture of Baltimore.* Baltimore: Johns Hopkins University Press, 1953.

Huxtable, Ada Louise. *Classic New York.* Garden City, N.Y.: Doubleday, 1964.

Jacobus, John M., Jr. *Philip Johnson.* New York: Braziller, 1962.

Jackson, Huson. *New York Architecture, 1650–1952.* New York: Reinhold, [1952].

Jackson, Joseph. *Development of American Architecture 1783–1830.* Philadelphia: David McKay, 1926.

————. *Early Philadelphia Architects and Engineers.* Philadelphia: privately printed, 1923.

Jacob, Eva. *New Architecture in New England.* Lincoln, Mass.: DeCordova Museum, 1974.

Jacobs, Jane. *The Death and Life of Great American Cities.* New York: Random House, 1961.

Jacobus, John M., Jr. *Twentieth-Century Architecture: The Middle Years: 1940–65.* New York: Praeger, 1966.

Janson, H. W. *History of Art.* Englewood Cliffs, N.J.: Prentice-Hall, 1964.

Jencks, Charles. *Modern Movements in Architecture.* Garden City, N.Y.: Doubleday, 1973.

Jenkins, Frank. *Architect and Patron: A Survey of Professional Relations and Practice in England from the Sixteenth Century to the Present Day.* London: Oxford University Press, 1931.

Jöedicke, Jurgen. *Architecture since 1945.* New York: Praeger, 1969.

———. *A History of Modern Architecture.* New York: Praeger, 1959.

Johnson, Philip. *Ludwig Mies van der Rohe.* New York: Museum of Modern Art, 1947.

Jones, Robert Allen. "Cass Gilbert, Midwestern Architect in New York." Ph.D. dissertation, Case Western Reserve University, 1976.

Jordy, William H. *American Buildings and Their Architects: Progressive and Academic Ideals at the Turn of the Twentieth Century,* Vol. 3. Garden City, N.Y.: Anchor, 1972.

———. *American Buildings and Their Architects: The Impact of European Modernism in the Mid-Twentieth Century,* Vol. 4. Garden City, N.Y.: Anchor, 1972.

Jordy, William H., and Ralph Coe, eds. *American Architecture and Other Writings by Montgomery Schuyler.* Cambridge, Mass.: Harvard University Press, 1961.

Kaufman, Edgar, Jr., ed. *The Rise of an American Architecture.* New York: Praeger, 1970.

Kidney, Walter C. *The Architecture of Choice: Eclecticism in America, 1880–1930.* New York: Braziller, 1974.

Kilham, Walter H. *Boston after Bulfinch: An Account of Its Architecture, 1800–1900.* Cambridge, Mass.: Harvard University Press, 1946.

Kilham, Walter H., Jr. *Raymond Hood, Architect: Form through Function in the American Skyscraper.* New York: Architectural Book Publishing Company, 1973.

Kimball, Fiske. *American Architecture.* New York: Bobbs-Merrill, 1928.

———. *Domestic Architecture of the American Colonies and the Early Republic.* New York: Scribners, 1922.

———. *Thomas Jefferson, Architect.* Boston: private printing, 1916.

Kimball, Fiske, and George H. Edgell. *A History of Architecture.* 1918. New York: Harper, 1946.

Kirker, Harold. *The Architecture of Charles Bulfinch.* Cambridge, Mass.: Harvard University Press, 1969.

Kirker, Harold, and James Kirker. *Bulfinch's Boston 1787–1817.* New York: Oxford, 1964.

Komendant, Auguste. *18 Years with Architect Louis I. Kahn.* Englewood Cliffs, N.J.: Aloray, 1975.

Kostof, Spiro, ed. *The Architect: Chapters in the History of the Profession.* New York: Oxford University Press, 1976.

———. *A History of Architecture: Settings and Rituals.* New York: Oxford University Press, 1985.

Kowsky, Francis R. *The Architecture of Frederick Clarke Withers and the Progress of the Gothic Revival in America after 1850.* Middleton, Conn.: Wesleyan University Press, 1980.

Krinsky, Carol Herselle. *Rockefeller Center.* New York: Oxford University Press, 1978.

Kubler, George. *The Shape of Time: Remarks on the History of Things.* New Haven: Yale University Press, 1970.

Kuhn, Thomas. *The Structure of Scientific Revolutions.* Chicago: University of Chicago Press, 1962.

Kultermann, Udo. *Architecture of Today: A Survey of New Building throughout the World.* New York: Universe Books, 1969.

Landau, Sarah Bradford. *Edward T. and William A. Potter: American Victorian Architects.* New York: Garland, 1979.

Landy, Jacob. *The Architecture of Minard Lafever.* New York: Columbia University Press, 1970.

Larkin, Oliver. *Art and Life in America.* New York: Rinehart, 1949.

Lerski, Hanna H. *William Jay: Itinerant English Architect 1792–1837.* Lanham, Md.: University Press of America, 1983.

Lieberman, Herbert, ed. *Award Winning Architecture/USA.* Philadelphia Artists/USA, 1973.

Lynes, Russell. *Good Old Modern: An Intimate Portrait of the Museum of Modern Art.* New York: Atheneum, 1973.

McCallum, Ian. *Architecture U.S.A.* New York: Phaedon, 1959.

McCoy, Esther. *Five California Architects.* New York: Reinhold, 1960.

———. *Richard Neutra.* New York: Braziller, 1960.

McHale, John. *R. Buckminster Fuller.* New York: Braziller, 1962.

McLaughlin, Charles C., ed. *The Papers of Frederick Law Olmsted.* Baltimore: Johns Hopkins University Press, 1977–.

Major, Howard. *The Domestic Architecture of the Early American Republic: The Greek Revival.* Philadelphia: Lippincott, 1926.

Makinson, Randall L. *Greene and Greene: Architecture as a Fine Art.* Salt Lake City: Peregrine Smith, 1977.

Manson, Grant. *Frank Lloyd Wright to 1910.* New York: Reinhold, 1958.

Menocal, Narciso G. *Keck and Keck—Architects.* Madison: Elvehjem Museum of Art, 1980.

Millon, Henry A., ed. *Key Monuments of the History of Architecture.* Englewood Cliffs, N.J.: Prentice-Hall, 1964.

Mock, Elizabeth. *Built in USA—Since 1932.* New York: Museum of Modern Art, 1945.

Monroe, Harriet. *John Wellborn Root: A Study of His Life and Work.* Reprint. Park Forest, Ill.: Prairie School Press, 1966.

Moore, Charles. *The Life and Times of Charles Follen McKim.* 1929. Reprint. New York: Da Capo, 1969.

Moore, Charles W. "Water and Architecture." Ph.D. dissertation, Princeton University, 1957.

Morrison, Hugh. *Early American Architecture from the First Colonial Settlements to the National Period.* New York: Oxford University Press, 1952.

———. *Louis Sullivan: Prophet of American Architecture.* 1935. Reprint. Westport, Conn.: Greenwood, 1971.

Mujica, Francisco. *History of the Skyscraper.* Paris: Archaeology and Architecture Press, 1929.

Mumford, Lewis. *The Brown Decades: A Study of the Arts in America
     1865–1895.* New York: Harcourt Brace, 1931.
———, ed. *Roots of Contemporary American Architecture.* 1952. Reprint.
     New York: Dover, 1972.
———. *Sticks and Stones: A Study of American Architecture and Civiliza-
     tion.* New York: Boni and Liveright, 1924.
———. *The Story of Utopias.* New York: Boni and Liveright, 1922.
Muschamp, Herbert. *File under Architecture.* Cambridge, Mass.: MIT
     Press, 1974.
Musgrove, John, ed. *Sir Banister Fletcher's A History of Architecture.* 19th
     ed. London: Butterworths, 1987.
Neutra, Richard. *Life and Shape.* New York: Appleton-Century-Crofts,
     1962.
Nevins, Deborah, and Robert A. M. Stern. *The Architect's Eye: American
     Architectural Drawing from 1799–1978.* New York: Pantheon, 1979.
Newcomb, Rexford. *Architecture of the Old Northwest Territory.* Chicago:
     University of Chicago Press, 1940.
Newton, Roger Hale. *Town and Davis, Architects: Pioneers in American
     Revivalist Architecture 1812–1870.* New York: Columbia University
     Press, 1942.
North, Arthur T. *Ely Jacques Kahn.* New York: McGraw-Hill, 1937.
———. *Ralph Adams Cram.* New York: McGraw-Hill, 1937.
———. *Raymond Hood.* New York: McGraw-Hill, 1937.
Norton, Paul F. *Latrobe, Jefferson and the National Capitol.* New York:
     Garland, 1977.
Ochsner, Jeffrey Karl. *H. H. Richardson: Complete Architectural Works.*
     Cambridge, Mass.: MIT Press, 1984.
O'Gorman, James F. *The Architecture of Frank Furness.* Philadelphia:
     Philadelphia Museum of Art, 1973.
———. *Selected Drawings: H. H. Richardson and His Office.* Boston: Har-
     vard College Library, 1974.
Oliver, Richard. *Bertram Grosvenor Goodhue.* New York: Architectural
     History Foundation, 1982.
Olmsted, Roger R., and T. H. Watkins. *Here Today: San Francisco's Archi-
     tectural Heritage.* San Francisco: Chronicle Books, 1969.
Peisch, Mark L. *The Chicago School of Architecture: Early Followers of
     Sullivan and Wright.* New York: Random House, 1964.
Perry, William Graves. *The Rotch Travelling Scholarship: A Review of Its
     History 1883–1963.* [Boston?]: privately printed, 1963.
Pevsner, Nikolaus. *An Outline of European Architecture.* London: John
     Murray, 1948; Baltimore: Penguin, 1960, 1968.
———. *Pioneers of Modern Design from William Morris to Walter Gro-
     pius.* 2nd ed. revised. Middlesex: Penguin, 1960.
———. *Pioneers of the Modern Movement from William Morris to Walter
     Gropius.* London: Faber, 1936.
———. *Some Architectural Writers of the Nineteenth Century.* Oxford:
     Clarendon, 1972.
———. *The Sources of Modern Architecture and Design.* New York:
     Praeger, 1968.
Pierson, William H., Jr. *American Buildings and Their Architects: The Co-
     lonial and Neo-Classical Styles,* Vol. 1. Garden City, N.Y.: Anchor,
     1970.
———. *American Buildings and Their Architects: Technology and the Pic-
     turesque: The Corporate and the Early Gothic Styles,* Vol. 2A. Gar-
     den City, N.Y.: Anchor, 1978.

Place, Charles A. *Charles Bulfinch: Architect and Citizen.* 1925. Reprint. New York: Da Capo, 1968.

Placzek, Adolf K., ed. *Four Great Makers of Modern Architecture: The Verbatim Record of a Symposium Held at the School of Architecture, Columbia University, March–May, 1961.* New York: Da Capo Press, 1970.

Prak, Niels L. *Architects: The Noted and the Ignored.* New York: Wiley, 1984.

Randall, Frank A. *A History of the Development of Building Construction in Chicago.* Urbana: University of Illinois Press, 1949.

Raymond, Antonin. *Antonin Raymond, an Autobiography.* Rutland, Vt.: Charles E. Tuttle, 1973.

Richards, J. M., with Adolf Placzek, eds. *Who's Who in Architecture from 1400 to the Present.* New York: Holt, Rinehart & Winston, 1977.

Robinson, Cervin, and Rosemarie Haag Bletter. *Skyscraper Style: Art Deco New York.* New York: Oxford University Press, 1975.

The Rotch Travelling Scholarship. Boston: Rotch Travelling Scholarship, 1980.

Roth, Leland M. *The Architecture of McKim, Mead & White 1870–1920: A Building List.* New York: Garland, 1978.

———. *A Concise History of American Architecture.* New York: Harper and Row, 1979.

Rudofsky, Bernard. *Architecture without Architects.* New York: Museum of Modern Art, 1964.

Saarinen, Aline, ed. *Eero Saarinen and His Work.* New Haven: Yale University Press, 1962.

Saint, Andrew. *The Image of the Architect.* New Haven: Yale University Press, 1983.

Scully, Arthur, Jr. *James Dakin, Architect: His Career in New York and the South.* Baton Rouge: Louisiana State University Press, 1973.

Scully, Vincent. *American Architecture and Urbanism.* New York: Praeger, 1969.

———. *Louis I. Kahn.* New York: Braziller, 1962.

———. *Modern Architecture: The Architecture of Democracy.* New York: Braziller, 1961; rev. ed. 1974.

———. *The Shingle Style: Architectural Theory and Design from Richardson to the Origins of Wright.* New Haven: Yale University Press, 1955.

———. *The Shingle Style and the Stick Style.* Rev. ed. New Haven: Yale University Press, 1974.

———. *The Shingle Style Today or The Historian's Revenge.* New York: Braziller, 1974.

Sert, Josep Lluis. *Can Our Cities Survive?.* Cambridge, Mass.: Harvard University Press, 1942.

Sky, Alison, and Michelle Stone. *Unbuilt America: Forgotten Architecture in the United States from Thomas Jefferson to the Space Age.* New York: McGraw-Hill, 1976.

Spade, Rupert. *Paul Rudolph.* New York: Simon & Schuster, 1971.

Spaeth, David. *Ludwig Mies van der Rohe: An Annotated Bibliography and Chronology.* New York: Garland, 1979.

Stern, Robert A. M. *40 under 40: An Exhibition of Young Talent in Architecture.* New York: Architectural League, 1966.

———. *George Howe: Toward a Modern American Architecture.* New Haven: Yale University Press, 1975.

————. *New Directions in American Architecture.* New York: Braziller, 1969; revised and enlarged, 1977.

Stern, Robert A. M., and Thomas P. Catalano. *Raymond Hood.* New York: Rizzoli, 1982.

Stone, Edward D. *The Evolution of an Architect.* New York: Horizon, 1962.

Stonorov, Oskar, and W. Boesiger. *Le Corbusier und Pierre Jeanneret.* Zurich: Girsberger and Artemis, 1930.

Sullivan, Louis H. *The Autobiography of an Idea.* 1924. Reprint. New York: Dover, 1956.

Summerson, John. *Heavenly Mansions and Other Essays on Architecture.* New York: Norton, 1963.

Tafel, Edgar. *Apprentice to Genius.* New York: McGraw-Hill, 1979.

Tallmadge, Thomas E. *Architecture in Old Chicago.* Chicago: University of Chicago Press, 1941.

————. *The Story of Architecture in America.* New York: Norton, 1927.

Tatum, George B. *Penn's Great Town: 250 Years of Philadelphia Architecture.* Philadelphia: University of Pennsylvania Press, 1961.

Taut, Bruno. *Modern Architecture.* London: Studio, 1929.

Torre, Susana, ed. *Women in American Architecture: A Historic and Contemporary Perspective.* New York: Whitney Library of Design, 1977.

Twombly, Robert C. *Frank Lloyd Wright: An Interpretive Biography.* New York: Harper and Row, 1973.

————. *Louis Sullivan: His Life and Work.* Chicago: University of Chicago Press, 1987.

Tyng, Alexandra. *Beginnings: Louis I. Kahn's Philosophy of Architecture.* New York: Wiley, 1985.

Upjohn, Everard M. *Richard Upjohn, Architect and Churchman.* New York: Columbia University Press, 1939.

Valentine, L., and A. Valentine. *The American Academy in Rome 1894–1969.* [No city given]: privately printed, 1973.

Van Rensselaer, Mariana Griswold. *Henry Hobson Richardson and His Works.* 1888. Reprint. New York: Dover, 1969.

Venturi, Robert. *Complexity and Contradiction in Architecture.* New York: Museum of Modern Art, 1966.

Von Eckardt, Wolf. *Eric Mendelsohn.* New York: Braziller, 1960.

Watkin, David. *The Life and Work of C. R. Cockerell.* London: Zwemmer, 1974.

————. *Morality and Architecture: The Development of a Theme in Architectural History and Theory from the Gothic Revival to the Modern Movement.* Oxford: Clarendon Press, 1977.

Whiffen, Marcus, and Frederick Koeper. *American Architecture 1607–1976.* Cambridge, Mass.: MIT Press, 1981.

White, Theo B. *Paul Philippe Cret: Architect and Teacher.* Philadelphia: Art Alliance, 1973.

————. *Philadelphia Architecture in the Nineteenth Century.* Philadelphia: Philadelphia Art Museum, 1953.

Withey, Henry F., and Elsie Rathburn Withey. *Biographical Dictionary of American Architects (Deceased).* Los Angeles: Hennessey & Ingalls, 1970.

Wright, Frank Lloyd. *An Autobiography.* New York: Longman, Green, 1932.

————. *A Testament.* New York: Bramhall, 1957.

Zevi, Bruno. *Frank Lloyd Wright.* Milan: Il Balcone, 1954.

Index of Architects